POLICING CONTINGENCIES

POLICING
CONTINGENCIES

Peter K. Manning

THE UNIVERSITY OF CHICAGO PRESS
CHICAGO AND LONDON

PETER K. MANNING is the Elmer V. H. and Eileen M. Brooks Chair in Policing at Northeastern University's College of Criminal Justice. He is the author or coauthor of a number of books, including *Police Work: The Social Organization of Policing* and *The Privatization of Policing: Two Views.*

The University of Chicago Press, Chicago 60637
The University of Chicago Press, Ltd., London
© 2003 by The University of Chicago
All rights reserved. Published 2003
Printed in the United States of America

12 11 10 09 08 07 06 05 04 03   1 2 3 4 5
ISBN: 0-226-50351-8 (cloth)
ISBN: 0-226- (paper)

Library of Congress Cataloging-in-Publication Data

Manning, Peter K.
    Policing contingencies / Peter K Manning.
        p. cm.
Includes bibliographical references and index.
    ISBN 0-226-50351-8 (cloth : alk. paper)
    1. Communication in police administration—Great Britain. 2. Communication in police administration—United States. 3. Police administration—Great Britain—Citizen participation. 4. Police administration—United States—Citizen participation. 5. Police and mass media—Great Britain. 6. Police and mass media—United States. 7. Police—Great Britain. 8. Police—United States. I. Title.

HV7936.C79 +
363.2—dc21

2002155304

CONTENTS

PREFACE AND ACKNOWLEDGMENTS

Policing is changing both in its societal role and in its internal dynamics, and I present here an assessment of the changes in policing in the last thirty years. While I was writing this book, my intent changed from a project designed to reassess and synthesize my previous work on policing, drawing together key themes and counterthemes, to a less grandiose scheme. In *Police Work* ([1977] 1997), I outlined the drama of control, citing anthropologists, sociologists, and literary critics, and argued for its relevance as a macro-level perspective on policing and social control. I did not include the role of the media, and focused on collective symbolism, emphasizing Durkheim's perspective; in the second edition, I reviewed changes in policing and dramaturgy. Subsequently, I wrote three additional books on policing, exploring variations on the theme of the role of information and ritual in policing.

In *Police Work*, I argued for the relevance of policing as a kind of sacred representation in a secularized society. In *Narcs' Game* (1980), I examined the extent to which proactive, police-initiated actions were information based. I found that because of organizational processes and agents' discretion information alone had a rather minimal effect. *Symbolic Communication* (1988) was based on the question of the extent to which the actions of the police were based on information, in this case "citizen demand." In each of these ethnographically based studies, I discovered that trust embedded information and converted "fact" into value-based conceptions and therefore was a condition making possible routinized work.

The present book, perhaps fortunately, is not the book I had planned. I first posed the question, Given the explosion of information, the media's influence, and periodic reform movements based on research, what accounts for the apparent but relatively modest changes in policing practice? While this book considers changes in Anglo-American policing in the last thirty years, it also suggests the failure of police reform.

I focus on stability and change in Anglo-American policing, using a dramaturgical perspective. I draw on some thirty years of fieldwork to support my analysis of changes in the environment of policing, especially the media, the mandate (the "impossible mandate" about which I first wrote in 1967 [the work now appears as chapters 4 and 5 of Manning 1997b]), and the symbolic or collective environment of policing and its internal features. These matters are modified in some fashion by what might be called a concern for connections between goals, objectives, and resources, or rationalizing policing, information technology, and the media's highly stylized and selective attention. Clearly, many subtle as well more dramatic changes, especially those noted above, have unfolded, back- and front stage, in policing. Regardless of their everyday effects on officers, which is not my interest here, these foreshadow the future of policing. My key concerns are how shifting levels of uncertainty and trust are affected by external and internal change. I use a dramaturgical framework. I consider change as the underlying process leading to reconsideration, or reflection upon the once taken for granted. Uncertainty is associated with decisions with unknown outcomes, usually stimulated by social change. Trust is a concept that refers to acceptance of forthcoming outcomes in situations—a multiform notion that changes in meaning when encounters change. I want to link aspects of organizational and environmental change, which makes outcomes uncertain, to the dramas they produce and to what they conceal. Uncertainty gives rise to emergent outcomes, unanticipated consequences, blurred boundaries, ambiguities, and differences, providing the fundamental social materials of drama. However, no drama can proceed absent trust among the players. Awareness of these contingencies does not drive policing directly, but the new level and kind of media and imagery that surround policing produce outcomes the police cannot anticipate fully as individuals or as an organization. They continue to struggle to legitimate themselves, sustain a mandate, and manage positive imagery where possible. The dramas of interest here are societal scenes that may be public and constitute big theater, media spectacles, and core dramas, rather than the situational dramas arising when officers cope with contingency, e.g., traffic stops, searches, arrests, raids, bookings, and detectives' investigative activities.

Policing as drama and the management of uncertainty perspective are a powerful means to articulate how the illusion of formal control is maintained and communicated in postindustrial societies. Rather than detailing the rather banal empirical questions that have driven criminological and criminal justice research in the last twenty years, I seek to theorize policing as a dramatic performance. This is not to claim that policing is exclusively about performance and communication, that the police are experts in creating and manipulating public opinion, or even, indeed, that they are effective in their self-publicizing efforts. The facts do not sustain this imputation. A police-as-drama perspective argues that organizations are structured selectively to process and shape information, not whether they do it effectively, whether they are equipped to do so using the most modern technology, or that the police see themselves in precisely this way. Further, it does not claim that police everywhere, behind our backs yet before our eyes, are sophisticated, proactive information-processing engines. The finances, aspirations, management, and budgets of local and state agencies put the lie to this claim, even if appearances do not. This book in one sense is a metaphoric exercise, as Goffman once wrote, pushing a metaphor to see how far it will go.

The combination of ethnography with dramaturgy facilitates examining these changes because much of what the public and scholars take to be real about policing is created by systematic representations, and re-representations, including official statistics, policy pronouncements by self-anointed reformers, and visuals produced by the media and the police. Often, public figures such as the police use very limited signs—official data—to characterize diffuse, complex operations. These are signs, or clusters of signs, as messages. I use semiotics, the science of signs, or how signs mean and frame analysis, to surface the context of viewing mediated messages issuing from organizations as well as actors. These mediated illusions are real in that they are central to shaping perceptions that are the bases for all forms of social control. Social control, like other social processes, begins with imagery and imagination. The police are primary in sustaining the social arrangements enjoyed by those with institutional authority to "give official imprint to versions of reality" (Goffman, 1983b: 17). Yet the constitution of these images is not entirely a result of individual actions and choices, but is a collage of choices, social constraints, and collective representations. Clearly, *organizational impression management,* rhetorical strategies in the form of accounts and official data, are systematically misleading when produced by and about policing as they are in all organizations. Image management and public relations have proliferated and become organizational requirements in the last thirty years; the present society is mediated, understood through stylized and edited imagery, beyond what any observer might once have predicted (Boulding, 1956; Gabler, 1998; Boorstein, 1987). In some sense, the types of natural events that the police deal with and create—corruption, scandal, extreme violence, incompetence, and conflict—have not changed as far as we are aware. The probability that the natural events with which police deal will become a public drama has increased.

I do not want to be spun away with images, nor to overemphasize the constraints of imagery; I seek to balance this aspect of the argument with grounded ideas and observations. If we keep a kind of binocular vision, focusing on the one hand on the police organization and its actions and on the other on the representations of policing, perhaps some instructive anomalies will surface.

As I edit this book, the horrific events of September 11, 2001, still resonate in our everyday lives. Given time and peace of mind, I might have written a different book had I started at this moment. The essential argument is valid, I think, although the scope and consequence of the newly central character of trust, its broad extension, and the ironies of control remain.

While this book is cast as a monograph, I nevertheless draw on *Police Work, Narcs' Game, Symbolic Communication,* and *Organizational Communication* (1992) as a grounding for my perspective. Issues of rationalization are addressed in my work with Brian Forst (Forst and Manning, 1999). Some materials appearing here, now much modified, have been published previously. Parts of chapters 3 and 4 appeared in *Sociological Quarterly* 37 (1996):101–18. Parts of chapter 4 are drawn from "Policing and Reflection," *Police Forum* 6, no. 4 (1996): 1–5; and "Media Loops," in *Media, Culture, and Crime,* edited by Frankie Bailey and Donna Hale (Belmont, Calif.: Wadsworth, 1996). I draw on my review of Lou Cannon's *Official Negligence* (1997), published as "Virtual Justice, Violence, and Ethics," *Journal of Criminal Justice Ethics* 19 (2000):44–54, in chapter 3. Portions of chapters 6 and 7 were presented as the opening address to the Canadian Police College–sponsored conference, "Police and Information Technology: Understanding, Sharing, and Succeeding" in May 1999 at Cornwall, Ontario. Versions of chapter 7 were presented to the Interdisciplinary Organizational Studies Seminar at University of Michigan in September 1991 and at a University Colloquium at Northern Michigan University in October 1991. Many of the arguments were initially outlined in the Seminar Series on Executive Issues, sponsored by the Law Enforcement Management Institute, Lubbock, Texas, July 17–19, 1991. A version of chapter 7 was published as "Technological Dramas and the Police," *Crim-*

inology 30 (1992):327–45. Some points on police use of cellular phones appeared in my "Information Technology in the Police Context: The 'Sailor' Phone," *Information Technology Review* 7 (1996):52–62; this paper was reprinted in John Van Maanen and Joanne Yates, eds., *Information Technology and Organizational Transformation* (Thousand Oaks, Calif.: Sage, 2001). Chapter 8 was presented in a different form at a conference on crime and social organization held in honor of Albert J. Reiss Jr. at Rutgers University, July 27–29, 1997. It appeared as "Authority, Loyalty, and Community Policing" in *Crime and Social Organization* (a festschrift volume for Albert J. Reiss Jr.), edited by David Weisburd and Erin Waring (New Brunswick: Transaction, 2002). I presented a rather briefer version of this focusing on the downfall of the police chief of Western ("Western" is the pseudonym of a city in which I did some fieldwork) at the American Bar Foundation in December 1998. Some of the complexities of trust and policing were presented to the Department of Sociology at Cleveland State University in February 1999. I discuss the methodological approach used here in appendix A, and outline the several sources of data on which the book is based in appendix B.

The research reported here has received support from many sources. Michigan State University granted me a sabbatical year, 1998–99. Merry Morash, Director of the School of Criminal Justice, was very supportive. For a fellowship, facilities, staff and financial help, I thank the American Bar Foundation and its Director, Bryant Garth. I was a visiting professor at York University, Toronto, in the Department of Sociology, during the winter semester, 1999. Des Ellis, Chair of Department, and the departmental staff were very helpful during my Toronto stay. I have been funded by several grants on technology and the self from the Defense Security Research Center. I thank Jim Riedel and Ted Sarbin for their help and encouragement in this connection. The Henry Fielding Centre for Crime and Risk Management at the University of Manchester, and its Director, Michael Chatterton, supported a portion of my research costs. The community policing research was funded by grants from the Community Oriented Policing Services Agency (COPS) to the Michigan State University School of Criminal Justice in 1996–98, and to the Western Police Department. Joe Schafer undertook fieldwork relevant to organizational transformation, and some data were gathered by Tracy O'Connell Varano. The "final" touches to the manuscript were carried out while I was a senior research scholar and later Brooks Professor of Criminal Justice at the College of Criminal Justice, Northeastern University, Boston. I am grateful for the support and good humor of Courtney Clifford, Shirley Davis, and Marilyn Kearney and the good advice and help of Marion Sullivan.

I am grateful to my friends and colleagues Betsy Cullum-Swan, Keith Hawkins, Mike Chatterton, John Van Maanen, and Rosanna Hertz for very helpful editorial suggestions and discussions. Elaine Yakura and David Altheide read chapters on media and television, and Jeff Farrell and Neil Websdale made perceptive and detailed remarks on the material on the media and the mediated society. Stephen Mastrofski read and commented on the Western materials. Albert J. "Jay" Meehan, my colleague and friend for many years, added much to the description of car and driver as basic technology. This chapter benefited from the fieldwork of Amanda Rigby and Jenny Young in Toronto and in the York Region Police in 1999. The careful readings of the drafts by Jennifer Balboni contributed beyond measure to whatever clarity now exists, although she is not at fault for matters taken to be errors remaining. For support and friendship through trying years, I thank warmly Laurie Beth, Sunshine, Robin259, Trish Murphy, Nigel Hadgkiss, Margaret Beare, Bridget Hutter, Maria Marcucelli, Mike and Brenda Chatterton, and Keith Hawkins.

Thank you: Vicky, Kerry, and Jim, Sean Peter and Shannon, Merry Kathleen and Kelley, and Jenny and Seth. I wish the next generation, especially my grandchildren, peace: Madeleine and Lilly Joseph; Samuel, Meredith, and Benjamin Patrick Riley; and Jackson West and Ian Peter Manning.

PART ONE
POLICING CONTINGENCIES

ONE

POLICING CONTINGENCIES

INTRODUCTION

Police are a very rich, almost natural material for drama, yet they are vulnerable, like all occupations that maintain a front- and backstage version of their work, to intrusions and the unexpected. Police order life and are ordered by it. How, on the one hand, can "police" be seen to count for (or appear to account for) something while, on the other hand, their performances, closely examined, are but thinly managed poses, rarely even concealing the abundant chaos of everyday life? They are more powerful and awesome versions of ourselves, after all. When shown in action, police are heroes, villains, fools, sometimes all at once, sometimes sequentially, and the credibility of their mandate is often stretched thin. I will argue that policing is a formally organized control agency with the potential for intervention in situations in which trust and mutual dependency have gone awry. Police work in order "to keep breakdowns of the interactional order within certain limits" (Goffman, 1983b: 6). Because agents of the state without review can construe such public matters and interventions they have undertaken, policing shadows the modern world, monitoring and shaping communication, and is both a private and public presence. Its actions in turn are selectively reproduced by mass media. And these images now elicit organized police response via "media offices" and public information personnel.

A DRAMATURGICAL ANALYTICAL PERSPECTIVE

Dramaturgy is best seen as a perspective, or way of seeing, using a theatrical metaphor to explore how the communication of messages to an audience conveys information and creates impressions that shape social interaction (Goffman, 1959, 1974, 1983b). Dramaturgy—based on the work of Erving Goffman, Kenneth Burke, Hugh D. Duncan, and Victor Turner—studies how symbols take on meaning in context. Although the dramaturgical perspective is traditionally associated with microinteractional analyses, this association is misleading, since during enactment, social role and social structure are realized. In this sense, dramaturgy is a second-order abstraction that does not base its findings on the perspective of the individual actor, but rather of the actor (of various social scales) in performance. It explicates both microdramas of control (or encounters), featuring apologies, repairs, and remedies of interactional slips, and macrodramas of control, where large entities—corporations, agencies, and even states—negotiate.[1] From a dramaturgy based on Goffman's face-to-face view, one can "translate" and generate an encompassing perspective that sees the links between contingencies, politics, and the media.

Dramaturgy emphasizes the importance of contingencies or unanticipated outcomes, managed performance of situated interactions, now richly mixed with images of such performances. Because it emphasizes the present, distrusts questions concerning "deeper meanings" and motivations, and elevates symbols and symbolization with loose connections to material reality, it both captures and reflects life in contemporary Anglo-American societies (see appendix A). Dramaturgy requires a notion of feedback and of audience, but the sources and consequences of reflexivity and feedback in complex and mediated societies are rather unclear. Its emphasis on voluntarism, on created extrinsic meanings (not inherent in the object), and on the interactions that yield interpretations attunes it to an age of relativism, pragmatism, and joint actions (Hall, 1972). It is sensitive to how patterns of communication selectively sustain definitions of situations and make it possible for actors to carry off a performance (Burke, 1989: 10). It implies an audience to which such performances are directed, who must frame messages, judge the credibility of the performance (its equivocality), and determine its communicative "core." It implies and depends on some notion of "information," a difference that makes a differ-

---

1. I consider other classic works in this near-tradition, cited in Manning, 1997b: chap. 2, as those by Edwin Lemert, Howard Becker, Clifford Geertz, Tom Burns, Edmund Leach, and Abner Cohen. The works of Gusfield (1981, 1986), Blumberg (1967), Garfinkel (1967), Cicourel (1969), and Feeley (1970) foreshadowed insights in the use of this perspective in criminology.

ence in context (Bateson, 1972), because information is the core of what is controlled, given, and given off in performances (Goffman, 1959: 7).

The core concern of dramaturgy is symbolic action, or, simply put, actions that represent something to somebody in a context. It is the representation process and what is represented that is critical, not the banal observation that human beings interpret their environment. Symbolic action is reflective and reflexive action—it incorporates reflection on the imagined reaction of others to one's own action. This process of reflection plays a role in the resultant behavior, and thus symbols provide a context for review of past and imagined future action. Social interaction is a communicative dance usually based on trust and reciprocity. This mutuality and duality constitute the "promissory, evidential character" (Goffman, 1983b: 3) of social life. Mutual obligations require sustaining the performance if not the person at risk. There are costs as well, for not attending to these obligations is dreadful. "Not to do so, one could hardly get on with the business at hand; one could hardly have any business at hand" (1983b: 6). But errors and delicts, betrayals and mistakes, deviance and crime unfold and are responded to and labeled, and this is one task of policing as political ordering.

The focus on the unanticipated and yet consequential is not an argument for unrelated action or mere behavioralism, or a sequence of barely connected actions. My concern, like that of Goffman, is with conduct—actions as assessed for their meaning. Each gesture, action, and presentation conveys interpretive possibilities, but not all consequences can be understood or predicted. Unanticipated consequences, positive and negative, also accompany deciding. In this way, the symbolization spiral arising in interactions, one symbol pointing to another and yet another, and so on and so on, without resolution, is noted but constrained by limits of time, energy, patience, and trust. The question is how, within what framework, to understand the spinning consequences of collective action.

Drama in various forms, along with business, war, and sport, is, it might be said, the dominant metaphor of our time, and well reflective of concerns for power, negotiation, merger, and acquisition in the political and business arena. At times, we consider ourselves as entertainers, players, and part of our own unfolding drama, but the metaphor of drama is not only about individual consciousness; it is about the structure of relations and the structure and dance of images. It "captures" our times, defines them, and perhaps reflects them, but we are also captured by the imagery of our times. In spite of contradictions and limited memory for facts, in time, in part because of the complexity of urban interactions, we develop sophisticated and semiformal secondary observation schemes that make our "raw observations" more understandable—we frame them and thus make them understandable in the short run. The social world is not simply seen, heard, or smelled, but it is interpreted.

The limits of dramaturgy and related perspectives have been debated, sometimes quite well, and it is important to see where the blurred edges lie (Reynolds, 1993; Young, 1990). Asserting that whenever people interact they must perform or act dramatically avoids the question of how such performances are stimulated, and where the boundaries of such compulsion lie. The assumed performance-oriented audience-related dynamic begs the question of the orientation of the perspective, whether individual or universal-"structural"—I assume it is structural and sociological and not rooted in the self or individual motivations. It is neither reductionistic nor based on the unit act notion, because the gesture, like the signifier, and the political act are "essentially incomplete" without a response from others. The dramaturgical metaphor can be exaggerated—not all requirements of social organization are ideational, nor is the actor fully aware of the contingencies of existence. Material constraints always exist and must somehow be taken into account. Not all drama is theatrical in a technical sense. The theatrical is a particular frame in society, and it requires suspension of disbelief, clear audience/actor distinctions, and a set of conventions about openings and closings of a performance, and it is scripted, planned, and designed for an effect. Everyday life may be played out to audiences, but it unfolds, or "couples itself" in a sense, and order without design results (Feldman, 1989). Because life is not scripted for anyone, the sense in which it is a theater is problematic and fleeting. Dramaturgy does eschew simple rationality based on precise referential language, emphasizes the expressive and performative aspects of language and symbols, and assumes that many realities exist, are marked or framed as contrasts against everyday life. In short, social reality is intersubjective and depends on interpretation, interactions, and communication of meanings. Dramaturgy presents a weak notion of structure and power, even though this is a controversial matter within interactionism. Dramas resonate with life as we know it and illuminate the darker side of choice and politics better than a vapid functionalism or policy-driven self-promotional programs.[2]

2. For admirable examples see Young, 1990; Reynolds, 1993; and Hall, 1972, 1987. Writers in the dramaturgical tradition who struggle to link politics and structural change (Hall [1987, 1972]; Maines [1977]; Lincoln [1991]; Wagner-Pacifici [1986, 1994]; Wagner-Pacifici and Schwartz [1991]) and to media effects in modern societies (Altheide and Snow [1991]; Altheide [1997]; Altheide and Michalowski [1999]; Denzin [1992]) have charted new and imaginative ground.

THE INFRASTRUCTURE OF MEANING

The abstract perspective of dramaturgy taken as a societal-level metaphor requires some logical and inferential infrastructure to connect social organization and meaning. Semiotics (Peirce, 1936–57), a technique that I use here, in particular is helpful in trying to discover what technology means in policing, how information is used, and the levels of abstraction that are associated with new forms of crime analysis and mapping. Semiotics, the science of how signs mean, or what makes lying possible, fits easily with dramaturgy (Manning and Cullum-Swan, 1992). Lying is important because to represent or symbolize leaves open the matter of interpretation and therefore of misrepresentation, intentional or not. Human beings perhaps essentially are misrepresenting beings, while they yearn for a basis for truth. Semiotics deals only with constituted difference, rather than "the real world." It is context-bound. It is also well suited to analyses of modern life (Eco, 1979, 1990a). The "semiotic of modern life," or its underlying order, is a code or set of codes that owes much to the theater and to existentialism (Vester, 1989). Since semiotics relies on an often unexplicated context, and this (appearing to be real) is the fundamental tool of modern politics and business, it is necessary to frame situations drawing on distinctive notions of reality and to mark them off from each other (Goffman, 1974). In many ways, framing is a process that relies on a semiotic of meaning. In the chapters on various framings of policing (4 and 5), on technology's meanings (8), and on trust and crime analysis (10), I use framing and semiotics to show how meanings are created and maintained and how they have changed in policing in the last thirty years.

Semiotics

In order to understand that semiotics relies on what is taken for granted, or how we read off the world as meaningful, it must be connected to social organization-structures of sentiment, norms, roles, and routines. Semiotics provides insights into the signs about signs that are social organization. A sign, something that represents or stands for something else in the mind of someone, is essentially incomplete without knowledge of a context that connects expression and content. A sign is composed in the first instance of an *expression,* such as a word, sound, or symbol, and a *content,* or something that is seen as completing the meaning of the expression. Signs are a function of difference and similarity in context. For example, a rose is conventionally an expression linked with romance as a content, and the American flag to courage. Each of these connections is social and arbitrary, so that many kinds of links exist between expression and content or signifier and signified. Semiotics adopts an observer's perspective. The connections made between expression and content and among signs are mental or "cultural." That which links the expression and the content, a nominal mental connection called "the interpretant," is brought to the signifying event by the observer. When the interpretant changes, signs change in their meaning. There is no reality lying under or behind a sign, no "real world" against which any sign can be checked. The interpretant of one sign is another sign, and that sign is validated, as it were by yet another sign, and so on without end. The question then, even in stable and "conservative" organizations, is how signs mean, and how they give stability in the face of uncertainty.

Semiotics depends upon a "primitive phenomenology," i.e., a meaningful connection between the expression and content that must be socially constructed. Typically, these connections are shared and collective and provide an important source of the ideas, rules, practices, codes, and recipe knowledge that is called "culture" (Culler, 1966; Barley, 1983). That which provides the social connection among the components of a sign or among a set of signs clustered as a text (or even assembled as discourse) is a code.

To some degree, the volatile and potentially unstable contextual nature of meaning is reduced by the shared knowledge, rules, and codes that are employed within a culture to make sense of fields of signs. More often, understandings are a matter of what Giddens (1984, 1990, 1991) terms "knowledgeability," or tacit and nonverbal meanings taken for granted and unrecognized even by participants. This is best discovered by fieldwork (Manning, 1989).

Frame Analysis

The argument here is that this knowledgeability can be explicated using Goffman's book *Frame Analysis* (1974), subtitled "an essay on the organization of experience." *Frame Analysis* is an attempt "to formalize our knowledge about the ways in which context structures our experiences of the world [showing that] context and meaning are interdependent" (Manning, 1992: 81). A frame is the book's fundamental organizing concept. It is a structure of knowledge, experience, values, and meanings that actors bring to an event. Perception is organized, Goffman claims, into primary social or natural frameworks (in natural frameworks, rules of physical causality govern interpretations). Humans attribute social meaning to events and seem to tolerate only briefly a state of social "meaninglessness." Actors look for cognitive cues that assure them that what is happening is genuine (Manning, 1992: 119). When proposing the strengths of frame analysis, Goffman assumes that from a first-order experience or *primary reality*, people carve out, identify, typify, abstract from, compare, and contrast ideas that they organize or frame as less complex but more meaningful and versions or a *secondary reality*. These frames organize what is happening, set aside cues that are seen as background to the salient frame, and distinguish among types of experiences.

Frame analysis provides a framework for considering the meanings of policing in a mass society because it is concerned with how the model of face-to-face reality, the "primary reality," is variously transformed not only in organizational actions, but also in mass communication. From the base of a primary reality, various "social worlds" (my term) can be signified and show "what's going on here" for participants. They *key* an event or "strip of activity" so that they can see how it is different from their primary world. A key is "a set of conventions by which a given activity, already meaningful in terms of some primary framework, is transformed into something patterned on this activity but seen by the participants to be something quite else" (Goffman, 1974: 43–44). Goffman intends that keying provide the linkage between experience and ordered perceptions, and keying is central in the argument of chapter 4 of this book. Contrasted with keys are *fabrications*, either benign or intended to deceive. Fabrications may be suspected and questioned as deceptive, and are therefore more vulnerable to disruption and countermeaning than are keys. Fabrications, the dynamic aspect of framing, are not my concern here.

Goffman identifies five keys: make-believe, contests, ceremonials, technical redoings, and regroundings, each of which produces kinds of experience. This list, three items of which will be illustrated in detail in chapter 4, ranges from the most abstracted and distant key—make-believe—to those that are more common and accessible, such as regroundings. The first key is make-believe, of which one type is "dramatic scripting" or "drama." Dramatic scripting lacks "playfulness." It is created and commercially sustained and guided by written texts. In make-believe, Vester (1989: 196) notes, "the code tends to refer to, or it alludes to other artificial and arbitrary codes, thereby establishing an intertextual system of reference." That is, dramas are set in a network of other dramatic works as resonating similarities. These arbitrary codes include rituals, plays, songs, shows, television dramas, books, poetry, and music. The intertextual references are to each other, not to "life" or primary reality, and can easily shade into the surreal or almost nonreferential social reality. Contests, the second kind of key, are more realistic (Goffman, 1974: 56). Ceremonials are the third type of key. Except in reference to funerals and parades, they are not my concern here. The fourth key, technical redoings, includes rehearsals, audio and video recordings, demonstrations, group psychotherapy, role-playing sessions, and experiments. These matters, as Vester observes (1989: 197), are versions of simulation, a "self-organizing process which generates structures of meaning." They are shown as changed. For example, a priest drinks at Mass; he joins Alcoholics Anonymous and is shown drinking. New motives are shown. Under the fifth and perhaps most realistic key, experiences done for one purpose are rekeyed to another, reflecting a new version of motive or intent. This key is regrounding, in which activities are seen as being done for "new" motives or at least something other than the original ones. Here, for the analysis of policing, I apply primarily the first, fourth, and fifth keys. Like Goffman, I recognize that once a frame is established, it can be reframed, and one frame can be embedded in another, but my analysis is limited to the preliminary framing with only suggestions of the potential reframing process.

WORKING CONCEPTS

The police inhabit a world that is not of their own making, even though they share the burdens of reordering it and sustaining an illusion of continuity and order. Working concepts will broadly implement change in policing in social context, and link uncertainty and drama.

Begin with the metaphor of the actor, recalling that this refers to a wide range of social objects, and the problem of uncertainty and contingency. I take "actor" to mean any socially constituted entity that has meaning and resembles the "acting unit" (Blumer, 1969). Actors act, interpret, and react within the constraints of structure—the density of interactions, the clarity of norms, the consistency of their being marked, and the sentiments attached to them. There is no knife-edged present without such history, but structure remains relative across situations. The broad contours of modern interactions induce superficial relations adapted to complex and unknown backgrounds, limited scope of knowledge, and little experience with the particular others encountered. While it is an empirical question, the degree to which biography, kin, and locality are unknown seems to be increasing. Style, or how one performs, and substance or social values and interests are disconnected (Ewan, 1988) in art, architecture, and social relations because deep knowledge is unavailable and performance and appearances are the most useful and salient clues to meaning. This means, in brief, that much of social life is based on glimpses, moments, in which social structure stands in the background rather than present. Yet the show must go on.

Contingency—the selective emphasis on some aspects of the performance rather than others in order to impress an audience—is the underlying source of performances called dramatic. Goffman presumes contingency, presumes the dramaturgical impulse in modern societies, as a
general feature. In this sense, the dramatic is intrinsic to all communicative processes. This implies that awareness and reflection, or reflexivity,
change the nature of the players' feelings and experiences as well as the
stability of social relations. Thus, while constraints of social interaction,
sentiments, and reflexivity remain problematic in mass society, an obligation to act is incumbent upon actors. In a complex, fact-ridden world in
which data abound and rapid decisions are required, a world in which
the assumption of any detailed knowability is dubious (Luhmann, 1998:
13–15), groups or acting units must act and decide, process information,
create distinctions and differences. The condition of deciding under uncertainty, a state in which anything that is not "impossible nor a necessity"
exists as a context for the deciding, is the *prevalent state of affairs in the modern world* (Luhmann, 1998: 45). Failure and modest success are always
present, given that expectations of success are assessed against the current
event. A flavor of contingency penetrates any process of deciding (Luhmann, 1998: 47–48); in fact, it may be inherent in deciding. Expectations,
plus the understanding of possible failure, make uncertain or contingent
situations risky. But they also accumulate and are laminated one on the
other over time, so that organizations internally are an odd collection of
stories, records, meetings, and positions that are inconsistent even as they
stage overt integrity and purpose. Policing is both a complex, unfolding
process-based idea and a firmly held conception of power, authority, and
revenge.

Trust has an important role among police. It is central to their function
and in their occupational culture. The police must assess others' trustworthiness, and their trust capacity, yet they are distrustful, cynical, and
watchful. Trust is a subtle matter in policing since the officer seeks control
and restricted outcomes, and must do this quickly although most interactions undertaken are with strangers with no history with the officer. In this
sense, policing is an exercise in assessing trust. Trust assessment requires
a degree of shrewdness in judging people—their affect, speech, nonlin-
guistic cues such as postures and gestures, biographies and past histories,
and present performances. Shrewdness and distrust or suspicion become
interwoven in practice, so perhaps suspicion is a police posture to the
world (Skolnick, 1966). Police are not trusting people, yet they must assess
trust, deal with interactions or cope with requests for help, fend off ag-
gressive and rude intrusions, cultivate compliance with requests, and main-

tain civility (Mastrofski, Snipes, and Parks, 2000; Mastrofski, Reisig, and McCloskey, 2002). At best, they are role models for civility. Once a decision about an intervention is made, trust is required if the officer is to carry out the necessary: fill out logbooks and official reports; interview witnesses and suspects in crime scenes; cooperate with other law enforcement agents—DEA, FBI, the state police, and others; and assess the veridicality and relevance of the evidence gathered. Is it possible to view all others as liars and take reports on their behavior as an officer of the court? The question more likely that police ask is, Given that everyone lies, is this person lying now?

If through negotiation a "working consensus" (Goffman, 1959: 10) emerges, and attributions of motives and intentions of others are read as clues to response and the validity of the impression, impressions are validated. Such modestly shared worlds, often laminated with multiple meanings, are produced and reproduced by acting out roles, protecting and displaying various organizational selves, and sustaining mutually useful fictions. Interaction is rarely explicitly rule guided, but has a poetic, momentary, aesthetic quality. Even within organizations and other authoritatively ordered structures, segments, cliques, cabals, and small groups provide counterpoint to an established order (Goffman, 1960; Burns, 1992). A working consensus in postindustrial society bows in the direction of structures, norms, rules, values, and sentiments that often remain opaque. Social differentiation and integration arise through concrete interactions leading to a division of labor while the collective consciousness is strengthened by symbolic representations that both reflect and express society (Durkheim 1961). It is the source and manipulation of these images that now confounds easy analysis. Concrete, embodied, and visible presence is the touchstone of preliterate and preindustrial societies; it activates self-control (Turner, 1976, 1978, 1990; Nadel, 1953) even as representations of the collective conscience are salient. Social reality in less differentiated societies was seen as grounded in a fundamental epistemological basis—personal experience. The grounding of interaction in personal experience, slowly shaped from preliterate societies and experience, meant that even in industrialized societies representations and copies were distinguished from the real (Benjamin, 1969).

When events are stripped of history and are presented and re-presented via mediated communication, sight as a sensory function is elevated in its importance. Sight, the visual, is a grounding for humans, much as smell is for other animals. We put great stock in what we say we see, as clichés will reveal—"let me see" (as a preface to action); "seeing is believing"; "a picture is worth a thousand words"; "every picture tells a story"; "I can see through that." On the other hand, we worry that we will lose sight—"he tried to pull the wool over my eyes"; "I am blind as a bat"; "I was blinded by love"; "it was hit or miss" (the sight of the objective was lost); and we have odd combinations such as "a clear mind" or "a foggy mind." Seeing and reflecting are joint activities that enable interaction, especially among strangers or near-strangers. Coming into copresence is a sighting and sighted experience. When interactions are based in affinal kin ties, a long history of interaction, and intertwined biographies, and where nonverbal and physical cues pin down meaning, trust is invisible. Sight and imagery confirm what is known by other means. The beginnings of social order arise in visible copresent interactions with known parties. In the opposite situation, when strangers interact, what you see may be what you get and the issue of trust immediately arises. Mass communications and differentiation now enable us to see people we do not know, know people we do not see, see without knowing, and know. We live in part within a mediated collective consciousness.

Emerging mediated societies, by elevating the visual, perhaps even above other modes of experience, dramatize the display of symbols and consumption as sources of horizontal differentiation (Jay, 1993; Ewan, 1988). Mass media provide both entertainment and information and willfully interdigitate real, lived experiences with purposively constructed realities. Passive consumption, in the sense of consuming images, especially mass-produced images, induces a distant and spectatorial attitude toward society (see chapter 10 below; see also Debord, 1990; Baudrillard, 1993). While cultural diversity and interests in empowerment and interpretation of the media create patterns of alternative meanings and resistance (Fiske, 1987), the overwhelming influence of the media comes in areas in which experience, biographical location, and history do not inform viewing.

These changes in social structure and relations have been wrought as a result of rapid, cheap digital communication, especially television, the Internet, satellite transmission, and personal communication devices of all kinds. These changes suggest a parallel and insidious decline in the value and quality of direct verbal and written communication and the elevation of the visual and imaginary to a central role in reality constitution. These all indicate the differential relevance of embedded social relations, time, and space (Harvey, 1989; Giddens, 1991). These are not politically unimportant trends. Lack of embeddedness (a local context of social relations enacted in a given setting with given persons at a specific time) increases the potential for governmental control and surveillance, the power of medialike interactions, and pseudomutuality (a false sense of intimacy and shared values). Stripping events of context or presenting them in ways that suggest an absence of context—a masterful capacity used and manipulated by television—changes the political and educational potential of events (Williams, 1992).

The pervasiveness of mass-produced imagery, especially in the movies, television, and videos and on the Internet, indicates the changing significance of the visual in social relations.[3] The role of the visual changes as societies differentiate and all forms of mass communications proliferate (Benjamin, 1969; Berman, 1982; Gabler, 1998). Perhaps as the capacity for rapid distant communication increases and its costs fall, the visual is a highly desirable means to expand one's experience and even one's network of acquaintances. Commercial interest in market share is easily complemented by desire for experience, whether vicarious, simulated, or immediate. Mass visual media produce a visual text that, when translated, shapes consciousness and action.

While all societies reflect upon themselves through collective symbolism and set moral boundaries, modern societies reflect, in part through mass communications and information technology, and then reflect upon their reflections. This reflective capacity is a distinguishing feature of postindustrial societies.[4] While this reflection is not all of a piece, and it affects groups, whether based on class, ethnicity, or gender, differentially, the net effect seems striking, and it has been escalating in the last twenty years. The intersubjectivity of what is framed remains problematic, but semiotics provides clues and directions when seeking ordering of meaning. Reflection is abundant: we see ourselves on screens now proliferating,

3. I hope to avoid the controversies implicit in terms like "postmodern," although I do use "postindustrial," because they obscure the continuities in thinking about mass societies over the last hundred years. These include ideas about imagery, politics, mass communications, and social relations, all of which are addressed in this book. For example, many ideas central to the analysis of modern politics are captured in phrases such as the "postmodern society" (Denzin, 1986), "postmodernism" (Jameson, 1992), "the society of the spectacle" (Debord, 1994), the "surveillance society" (Lyon, 1994), and the "simulated-surveillance society" (Bogard, 1996). These societies manifest superficial content of interaction, and diverse social control and integration; and the massification of experience, both its thin and elusive character and its homogenization, proceeds apace (Debord, 1990, 1994; Ortega y Gasset, 1932).

4. Many works on television and politics share the dramaturgical metaphor (Edelman, 1985; Kellner, 1990, 1992). Dramaturgy is closely associated with analyses of television in the rhetorical and Burkean traditions. The vast literature in communications considering the effects of TV on specific audiences draws also on the metaphor. My concern here is how the framing of television as real facilitates its potential political power, rather than its general dramaturgical effects. The role of media in policing is changed by the existence of a police media office or officer. The structure of police media information offices varies—some are very formal and well staffed, some are merely a designated officer to create an information tape and a press release; some departments have no media office. The frequency and quality of police interchanges with the media and between the media and their "sources" varies (Ericson, Baranek, and Chan, 1989). This channel for processing police news sustains the potential for differential response to natural events.

and it is abstract, a product of a consideration of the past and future meanings of our conduct and the responses of others. Memory is in part visual
history or replays of past scenes. Images, once produced and distributed,
are reflected, and this process is profoundly social. The concepts of "reflection" and "reflexivity" suggest a realizable substance or grounding; but
modern reflection seems notoriously elusive, resembling more a revolving
set of mirrors than a matter of perspectival representation. Perspective, or
standpoint, rather than reality representation, is the way into understanding images. Social mirrors and representational processes, that which
yields perspective, combine both subjective and objective factors.

TRUST IN SOCIAL LIFE

Although trust has been a longtime concern of social scientists, extending
at least from the time of the writings of Kierkegaard and Adam Smith, it
has been reduced to a social psychological property rather than a property
of social structures or of markets. Trust is that which is taken for granted
in advance about the risks of an encounter. Not only is trust an "individual"-level construct, but it bears on the collective mutual feelings of fate-
fulness extant in a society. The trust problem is made more profound for
the police as a result of technological developments since 1970, technology
that extends human senses, especially in terms of analytic ability and "prediction" of victimization and its links to crime prevention. I want to discuss the general properties of trust here and elaborate them with respect
to policing in chapter 9.

Trust, an a priori willingness to accept others' behaviors and speech at
face value, is the core of interpersonal relations, plays a major role in the
social integration of bureaucracies, and grounds social life. Granting that
trust is a matter of socialization and varies widely in individuals, it is also
a social necessity. It is usually present, but "invisible"; as soon as it appears,
or is noticed and attended to, it becomes problematic and has vanished.
Trust in written texts—of interviews, observations, or experiments—is
difficult to pin down because of the "transcription effect" (Bourdieu, 1998:
1), or the result of stripping interactional situations of their nonverbal and
intuitive aspects. We assess trust subtly and draw on interactional cues.
When interaction is decontextualized by removing, suppressing, playing
on and with that which grounds it, matters that orient us to each other,
such as gestures and postures, quasi verbals such as pragmatics, anaphora,
and deixis, honorifics, register, and personal history and mutual biography, trust surfaces (Garfinkel, 1967; Cicourel, 1966; Levinson, 1981). By
that I mean that it is difficult to imagine what is going on in the interaction

when it is "captured" only by words. Further, images can be reconfigured and reproduced out of context, so that screened imagery, a powerful source of information, is ambiguous and uncertain. Analogously, trust in the political system and in the legitimacy of institutions rests on a tacit trust and unexamined premises. Above all, trust inheres in a situation, not in a master trope, or macrosociological structure. One might say that if life is lived situationally, trust dances in and out of situations. Trust, as we shall see in chapter 9, is very fundamental in policing. Trust in many respects links the changes in policing, for it has a role in the changes in the com- municational context, the media in particular, the politics of policing, and changes in police roles. All create contingencies and raise the question of trust in new contexts for police.

THE DRAMA OF CONTROL

Dramaturgy implies control because performances must be validated (positively or negatively sanctioned) if they are to be sustained, and the obligation to interact and in some sense share social life remains a con- stant. A dramaturgical perspective asks how the social environment can be so scanned and constituted that governmental social control is understood as real, constraining, and lasting in spite of repeated evidence of its frailty. The police, as symbolized, play this role, notwithstanding their direct, ma- terial, and objective effects. Social control, the response to behavior de- fined as deviant, including overconformity to normative standards as well as "deviance" or underconformity to public norms, is closely linked to the authoritative or political process of ordering groups (Clark and Gibbs, 1965: 401). It should take into account the dualistic character of social con- trol organizations. They create subjective responses and are dependent upon them, shape and are shaped by social practices (Giddens, 1981: 27). They operate in fields composed of subjective and objective factors. The police, by habit and practice, reproduce notions and images of social con- trol characteristic of the police field strategically and tactically. A drama- turgical perspective on social control, with the police as the key player, is a perspective, or view, not a map of individual consciousness. Because ac- tions of agents of formal control, those vested with governmental autho- rity, are selective, invidious, differentially visible and consequential, they are chief players in, and often initiators of, communicative dramas, dramas of control. Law, in short, is governmental social control utilizing many strategies and purposes (Cohen, 1983; Black, 1976, 1980, 1983, 1996), each of which has both a performative or expressive facet and an instrumental facet—they convey direct effects on individual lives, and they represent or stand for something else. The police operate in an environment that includes differentially organized sources of communication and the different audiences they serve, and they claim the ability to control and modify this environment. They have massive impact, but this impact may not be what they claim. The consequences of policing are real and real in their imagined effects, but the social worlds in which these experiences reside differ. Thus, seizing any one measure or indicator from the family of indicators of policing's effects is misleading.

These processes of imagining and acting, anticipating, responding, rethinking, and reexpressing are real and truly constraining within organizations. Policing is at least in part a representation to which we look for the meaning of events. It is thus a translating device, a means to both amplify and reduce our sense of the fearful, the safe, the orderly, the risky, and the attractive. It frames the relationships between the immediate "business at hand," as Goffman terms it, and the mass-produced media images and collective representations that guide our reflections. Reflections in turn create the possibility of change, disruption, accommodations, and new forms of rationality or rationalities.

Policing is a special kind of controlling communication, even in democratic societies, that serves to mark moral boundaries. Operating as governmental social control and loosely coupled to the economy, law and local government, the police carry out moral, instrumental, and ritualistic functions. These functions are situated in contexts that vary in their dramaturgical and communicational potential. One of the most important of these is the nature and direction of organizational communication. Organizational communication is performative, the selective display of symbols, some of which are suppressed and concealed, others elevated and amplified in importance, often conventionalized, stylized, and formulaic, conveying messages to audiences. What is taken to be true about the work of control—keeping the peace, marking the thin blue line, controlling crime, "doing the job"—are clustered symbols that serve internally as shorthand codes for loyalty among officers. They are used externally as a gloss to identify for trustworthy and nontrustworthy citizens. While there are consequences of policing—arrests, beatings, tickets, arrest records, warrants served and stops, not to speak of systematic violence, both legitimate and illegitimate, directed primarily at the young, people of color, and other marginal populations—I focus here on the expressive and performative functions of police work. The precise features of the Anglo-American police organization, its definition and duties, are found in chapter 2.

Like the interactional situation that links person, role, and audience in an unfolding and emergent process, all formal, third-party interventions possess form and content and are grounded in communication. The naming and identification function of social control—the categorization and classification of the social world, and the labeling of people—is undertaken in the name of the state, and police authority reveals differentially their interests and brings to attention behaviors worthy of merit, condemnation, celebration, and stigmatization.

Policing in this sense is policing contingencies, some of them self-created, some media driven and some demand based, all of them the product of communicational work. This of course is constrained by many forces that cannot be read-off, altered, or controlled. Control is therefore a matter of trust assessment in the instant case or event. Increasingly, communication is mediated (shaped by mass media), and thus police communication that marks norms, social control, is both communicator or source and communicated about or subject of communication. I am concerned with contingencies and communication, communication by and about the police, the media as transformer and amplification, and meaning or intersubjective interpretations as well as the nature of the collective representation called "policing." A collective representation is real, external, constraining, and relatively durable, especially in a media-saturated era. The mandate of policing is rooted in changing images as well as the frozen scenes of memory, tradition, and experience. All interaction is dramatic since it must be interpreted, framed, and interpolated across situations, and involves equivocality (uncertainty about the source), noise (unwanted communication in that context), and information (a difference that makes a difference) that must be weighed for their action implications. These factors, represented by the police as sources of contingency, are objective and material, as well as subjective and intersubjective. The process of collective action, police actions, is a complex intermingling of factors. Objective realities and intersubjectively defined social realities are problematic, external, and constraining.

The information technology (IT) of police has potential as a source of their power and authority and as a source of failures and scandals. The structure and function of the police in Anglo-American societies has little changed since 1829 (when the British Parliament created the [London] Metropolitan Police), but there is sufficient evidence that information technologies and mobility capacities of the police have vastly improved. While most of the IT used has been means oriented (such as computer-assisted dispatch) and decreases the time needed to process incidents, some has been transformative (such as scientific laboratories and evidence processing) and increasingly is analytic (such as crime analysis and crime prevention strategies). These last have the potential to alter the incidence and prevalence of crime rather than reacting to it. These matters are dealt with in some detail in chapters 5–7.

Performances, images, and traces (the results of policing that are left on the bodies, selves, and surfaces of communities) are a selectively orchestrated drama in which the police have at best a marking role, sometimes a controlling role, and at times a directing role. The idea that policing is also communicated (about) suggests the role of the media in representing policing. The communications at issue may be mediated by technology, be face to face, or involve groups or aggregates affected at some distance from the source. Communication may heighten or underplay a given effect and can be either intended or directed, "given off," or emitted. Expressive action, communication about selves, and instrumental action, designed to achieve an end, are both conveyed by social actors, but sustaining a consistent performance is not equivalent to goal seeking or organizational efficiency.

Police organizations, seen in a context of dramaturgical organizational analysis, are themselves a rich source of individual and collective dramas of control, representing or signifying action, using conventional symbols of authority—costumes, settings, equipment, and technology—and take action where violence, hierarchy (domination and subordination), and struggle are likely. This metaphor highlights the execution of successful communicative action as well as failures, errors, or delicts that reveal the absence of preferred modes of being (Brissett and Edgley, 1990: 1–12) and previously developed remedies. Control dramas well and truly display the dialectic between audiences and performers in that cycles of crackdowns and tolerance, traffic law enforcement "blitzes" and "turning a blind eye," zero-tolerance policies and chitchats with the homeless, reduce social distance, and then increase it for different groups.

The police organize and allocate resources in line with tacit means (such as "routine patrol" concentrating on disadvantaged neighborhoods), explicit means (such as domestic violence arrests), and rhetorical strategies ("we practice community policing in this community"). By the distribution of order-keeping resources, including applying sanctions such as arrest, stops, tickets, and cautions, they create differential risks to population groups. What is called racial profiling is a gloss on such complicated processing of sanctioning. Tactics, the more explicit and proximal means to act in line with strategies, are shorter-term, changing, and easily altered activities. In community policing, many tactics, such as foot patrol, attending neighborhood meetings, and opening mini-stations, are employed. Any control strategy is profoundly moral because its operation reflects social resources, the norms and values available and applicable to a situation, as well as the intention of the participants to maintain the appearance of moral conformity. Matters emphasized may well suppress others. Police-citizen interactions are multileveled and fundamentally ambiguous in meaning. The story or the various competing narratives voiced may emerge only later.

The police undertake and manage other people's contingencies as well as their own, attempting to negotiate control. The police shape the uncertainty they manage, but they also reduce it by producing and marking consequential outcomes—police officers make arrests, stops, lay charges, serve warrants, collect money and seizures, and intervene to settle disputes. Sanctioning marks social norms and borders. These interventions are both instrumental and expressive, and because they are consequential, they sustain the illusion of control or the sense that intervention in a contingent situation is forthcoming or might unfold. Because the police actively and selectively produce messages seen as dramatic and can sustain their definitions of the situation up to and including using fatal force, they have power to mark and define contingencies. On the other hand, class, ethnic, and other social interests stabilize behavior and insulate people from attending to rapid changes and being mobilized. Status anxieties, based in lifestyle preferences such as religiosity (fundamentalism vs. Unitarianism), patterns of consumption (SUVs vs. small economical cars), and single issues (abortion, gay rights, social security) resonate culturally and are easily tied up in contests over morality, righteousness, and matters of status anxiety (Mills, 1956; Gusfield, 1986; Edelman, 1985). In other words, small matters of everyday life take on larger political significance when they are linked to ideologies or broader canopies of belief. As much as the imagery is quaint, issues of order, rise and fall, sin, salvation, redemption, and the afterlife remain as subtexts even in a secularized, commodified, and complexly configured society (Burke, 1959, 1965, 1989). The police play on the fear of crime and their accessibility, raising status anxieties and in their eyes at least increasing sources and strength of public support.

Policing selectively marks that which is notable, sustain it by repeatedly marking the same types of behaviors and making them visible to others, and re-mark on the sustainability of such conventions. The institution provides the language within which the risk or contingency is described. Exaggerated and simple police typifications are often cited as tools of the trade (Reiner, 1992). The clientele, customers, suspects, or targets are educated to format their questions and respond verbally and bodily to commands, requests, and suggestions. The interaction between audience and controllers is in many respects a ritualized expression of compliance, dislike, resentment, and other generalized sentiments. Through and by the police, society disvalues, scorns, and avoids. The police do not miss these messages, yet they are fundamentally ambiguous in that interpretation is always required to make sense of events.

Policing in action is something of a *game of control,* or risk distribution, rather than a rigid, rule-bound enforcement practice (Lemert, 1967). The unfolding of actions is guided, but not by formal, explicit enforcement and institutional linkages that are consistent and predictable. Applying the game metaphor to police actions and explicating their role in dramas of control in which honor and face are involved conceives of the strategic dimensions of social control as gamelike. Actors' choices, albeit shaped and controlled by external constraints, are a part of the emerging regulation of the interaction order. The consequences of actions are unknowable in any precise sense; the responses of others, especially when will is being imposed on them, varies. The tactical dimension of policing always looms large as it represents the social dynamics by which honor and shame are distributed within and across groups. In this way, the police dramatically use selective amplification to underscore the reality of crimes and disorderly behavior. They thus reaffirm rankings in the multiple moral hierarchies of an industrialized society. The notion of order, its constitutive parts and meanings, remains a shifter in the hands of the powerful to define and is often applied notionally after the fact to interactions of such complexity and nuance that they shall never be fully understood.

DRAMAS OF CONTROL

Dramas of control arise from scenes in which social norms are reaffirmed, either elevating or depressing their significance. Through dramas of control, whether the scenes entail reward or punishment, vertical and horizontal hierarchies such as those of gender, class, and ethnicity are affirmed. Other countervailing forces exist, but dramas of control stabilize society in the face of factual anomalies—if Americans are essentially good, innocent, and blessed by God, why do religious fanatics attack us? God bless America, united we stand (for what?). We now envision and perhaps remember such scenes, or are reminded of them via icons, filmed vignettes, or other aide-mémoire. Flags, a portmanteau sign of vast and ambiguous meaning, appeared everywhere following the 9/11 attacks on the World Trade Center and Pentagon. Control work is also accomplished through the rational strategic interaction that characterizes organizations such as the police, the rituals of control and etiquette of public intercourse, and the grand spectacles by which the big theaters of control, those with national and international scope, arise. This connection, the connection between imagery and action, is drawn out partially through memory and individual experience and partially through external and constraining collective representations of which the police are one. They represent themselves and are represented for us. Sociovisual space is a relatively new and ominous political arena for the police. They have always preferred to operate backstage if possible, to conceal information and selectively reveal it to their advantage. A sparse vocabulary exists to render visual politics, and little theory connects media and politics in an empirical or analytic fashion.

The dramas emerging in time in policing are social and collective as well as individual: they are ways in which society imagines, constitutes, and speaks to itself. Dramas reveal the meaning of selves and their acts, but their scope, historicity, impact, and dynamics vary. Communication genres, one being a drama of control in which sanctions are applied to a performer, or message formats produce recognized effects in audiences. Dramas of control introduce and represent "policing" in everyday life. Police funerals, graduations, award ceremonies, and even roll calls and appearances on television conceal underlying conflicts, disagreements, and negative feelings and sentiments. The most obvious examples of this are the funerals and celebrations at the death of a police officer and the relative quiet when innocent, unarmed people are shot. Lawrence (2000: 28) notes that of the 101 people shot by the New York Police Department in 1991, 90 in 1992, and 86 in 1993, only 5 percent were subjects of news stories in the city's major newspapers. Parallel figures for 1991 and 1992 for the Los Angeles Police Department and Los Angeles County Sheriff combined were 124 and 126, of which 17 percent were reported on in the major newspapers. Another way of stating this is that media attention, rituals, and public ceremonies are social gyroscopes that present somewhat ambiguous meanings and are differentially inclusive of events.

Policing is a drama closely linked to both high and low politics in a city and in a larger society. High politics deals with social order generally and political beliefs and actions rather than with individual violations of the law or disorderly conduct while low politics of policing deals with individuals and local issues of justice (Brodeur, 1983). Within a police department, high (questions of power, authority, and careers) and low (everyday gossip) politics exist as well. "Politics," the distribution of goods and services, who gets what, when and how, is shaped by socioeconomic and structural changes and individual experience and is now mediated. The resultant dramas of control are situated as well as macrosociological, and the police act in both the little (relatively private and backstage scenes) and big (public scenes, some with massive audiences) theaters of control. In

large part, this activity of dramatizing risk and threat evolves as police stip-
ulate their target groups (with ex post facto labels) and play to their audiences; control information, both concealing and revealing it; and deploy
rhetorics of control that sharpen their image and broaden the meanings of
their mandate.

In modern nations, the mass media are commercialized, driven by market share and ratings, and focused narrowly on today's exceptions as
"news" (Tuchman, 1978; Gans, 1979; Gitlin, 1983; Fallows, 1996). While
the written word, in the form of magazines, newspapers, and books, remains important to more educated readers, television sets the pace for the
understanding of matters cultural. Media find the police, crime, and criminals irresistible topics for stories, news, exposés, "live" reports, and featured dramas. This has been true for several centuries, but change in technological capacity and pervasiveness have altered the processing of media
and their immediacy in our everyday lives. The media in the last ten years
have become more mobile and worldwide in effect; they are transglobal in
capacity, twenty-four hours a day every day. They can rapidly film a scene
and send it worldwide via satellite. They increasingly seek to expose and
ridicule authority and celebrity as their basic diet—police fall into both
categories from time to time, as well as being the villains or victims in other
scenarios. Every drama has a countertheme, or "double plot" (Empson,
1973) that can be reversed to view it as "essentially" something else. A
comedy becomes a tragedy, a melodrama a farce; fame conceals hidden
flaws and unworthiness, and a fall from grace ensues. Crime news is brief,
snippets just seconds long, and dominates the local news. Politics at its
worst is a series of sound bites that are less than one minute. The media,
avowing neutrality and objectivity, in many respects play on distrust and
are cynically self-serving. The favored topics are its own activities. It is one
of the primary sources of social control. This theme is expanded below.

The visual has broader meaning and implications than are found
in the examination of television and films. The presence of the media and
the visual, screens in their several forms, increases reflection and self-
consciousness in the society. Screens and cameras seem to be everywhere,
and many are hidden to surveil and film people in public and semipublic
places, including the police themselves, who are monitored by their supervisors. Reflection on one's choices, both before and after deciding, is
increased by the presence of information, rationally expressed choices,
and information about past choices, all of which are symbolized and retained for reuse by information technology, both informally and formally,
in mass societies. The process of copying and screening, producing and reproducing synthetic versions of "originals," and their mass consumption,

has interactional implications. Images carry meaning and constraint from face-to-face social life and from the material world and challenge nominal notions of truth. Copying and screening alter the nature of the "other," the primacy of face-to-face experience, the locus of trust. These features, acting in high-tech, commodified societies, shape the meaning of the visual: not only is trust implicit, the "others" may not be seen, smelled, touched, or heard, or they may be media-created figures, celebrities with imagined lives.[5]

The interposing of visual media alters the relationship between an audience (an other) and a performer once bound by known, mutually shared expressive burdens. This has political implications. Local knowledge and transitory, or visual, knowledge compete. The nature, location, and social identity of the significant and generalized other (Mead, 1934) become moot. The fragile nature of trust, yet its necessity, may be the key feature of modern life. Arguably, as societies become more differentiated and complex, numbers, quantification, and measurement arise as a surrogate for order, control, and predictability (Porter, 1995). Media, often trivializing science and research, frame new social realities (definitions of the real and the significant) and other surrogates for understanding at a distance. Images flash on screens, which then can create erstwhile social realities. Each of these experiences presumes some level of self-awareness of being watched or interacting with others. Politics is shaped by these changes. Declining interest in politics, shrinking voter turnout, and politicians' increased use of the electronic media indicate a public politics of the spectacle driven by that which is created and viewed (Edelman, 1988: 7).

POLITICS AND MEDIA

A dramaturgical framework, emphasizing audience, performance, and theatrical aspects of everyday life, is therefore appropriate for examining changes in the relationships among media, politics, and interpersonal relations. In terms of the emerging forms of crime (cybercrimes, global crimes, terrorism) and changing images of crime, dramaturgy sensitizes us to what is seen and what is not. The most significant feature of this is that

5. Current theorizing of the media's role in politics and its effects on interpersonal relations in contemporary American society not only echoes questions about connections between modernity and viable democratic politics (Ortega y Gasset, 1932; Jay, 1973; Kornhauser, 1959; Marcuse, 1991) but sees the media as an insidious and even erosive cultural force (Debord, 1990, 1994; Gitlin, 1980; Edelman, 1985, 1988; Poster, 1990; Mitroff and Bennis, 1993; McGibben, 1993; Bourdieu, 1998). Clearly, politics is shaped by the mass media and by the dramatic engaging visual spectacles it presents (Edelman, 1988). Increasingly, "political" events are media-oriented events designed to be announced on television, covered by television reporters, and staged and managed to sustain credibility with the viewer.

the representation of politics is transformed by television into both a domestic monologue (we watch politicians talking) and a public matter. The abiding and troubling issue is that it is unclear whether this is a private conversation or a societal dialogue (Meyrowitz, 1985, 1992). This dramaturgical view of television is a structural view, a code for viewing relationships in society. Public relations and spin penetrate social life, and service industries using cable and Internet links make homes into offices and entertainment centers. These new forms of interaction are problematic and are now reflected and reflected upon. Politicians become capable of performing across registers (from MTV to formal lectures and debates), orienting themselves to the sound bite, the quick comment, and to grooming themselves for televised appearances. Public and private, like work and play, become blurred and intermixed.[6]

Rational-legal legitimacy depends on a cultural context of agreement concerning science, consent of the governed, courts, police, and bureaucracy itself (Merelman, 1998). Media ideology, while sanctioning the idea of rationality and reform, deracinates it and strips it of the values, norms, and basis of trust that sustains rationality (Merelman, 1998). "Stories," absent discussion of institutional structure and its bases in unexamined premises about good and evil, geared into the fundamental democratic processes of equality, justice, and security, and that minor reforms are needed to rectify the identified problem. Thus, while critical, the media sustain the status quo, fragment social structure, and decontextualize the here and now.

6. At some level, interpersonal processes are shaped by the mass media, and salient aspects of modern experience are derived from electronically represented images as well as from direct, sensate personal experience (Poster, 1990). Social roles are reflected and radiated by electronic technology, in image-creating machinery. Computers are personal meaning machines: personalized, named, decorated, displayed, signs of power and competence. The display of screened selves, perhaps being anybody, happens when one uses a computer. Selves appear both figuratively in the sense of seeing oneself on the screen indexed by words, and literally in that one sees one's words unfold, then they are reflected back powerfully and instantly on the screen. The words can then be altered, erased, edited, saved, attached, backed up, retrieved, sent flying off worldwide in an instant, and screened, if not read, around the world. Immortality beckons, as names, in the form of e-mail messages for example, are archived worldwide in computer memory banks. Electronic communication permits free play with identities and roles by allowing false addresses, hidden files, playful puns as names, and gamelike interactions (Heim, 1993), but may also permit new identities to arise and new social relations to develop (Kendall, 1998). The computer, with its directories and branches and files, like the banyan tree, penetrates deeply into consciousness. Unlike face-to-face communication, it is technologically mediated communication between electronically activated addresses, some of which may be false, mere numbers, or misrepresentations. This depersonalizes and mitigates authorship and obligation. E-mails leave traces, in the sender's and receiver's computers, but also in storage tapes, the servers, and of course anywhere any copy from one of these points is sent.

Central to modern political experience are media forms, or the ways in which the medium conveys the message. These stylized forms are informed by media logic (Altheide and Snow, 1991: 9). Think, for example, of the interview as a television form, created for an inexpensive response to an event, controlled and edited by the announcers and technicians at the station, brief and apparently thoughtful or reflective. Other events, staged or created by the media for their purposes (Epstein, 1974), are actually pseudo-events (Boorstein, 1987), sometimes with scandalous implications. Events may be re-created (by actors or graphics) or profoundly shaped by the media presence. Two profound examples are the filmed landing in Lebanon in 1991 impeded because the television lights blinded the U.S. Marines, and the obstructive presence of the media after the bombing of the Federal Building in Oklahoma City. More subtle processes, reviewed in chapter 4, are far more insidious.

Although television employs many genres and is indeed rich in intertextuality, often mixing genres (forms of art) and tropes (attitudes toward the content such as the ironic, the historical, the social scientific, or the poetic) (Fiske, 1987: 108–26; Fiske, 1991, 1994), it exploits its capacity to *simulate* realism. This simulated realism penetrates all the presented genres of television. Miniseries and dramas, live television, plays, news, feature stories and gossip, documentaries, and on-the-spot reports are mixed, adumbrated, coalesced, elided, and systematically confused as a means of entertaining. CNN runs "live" interviews, pictures data with the actual time when they were live shown at the bottom of the screen. The "attitude" or trope of television is overwhelmingly ironic, thus further confusing the viewer who does not know which of the "two sides" of a narrative should be attended to. In chapter 4 I draw out some of the implications of these practices.

Television, however, seems to have maximal effect when combining the realistic conceit (representing activities shown as "real") with its powerful technological infrastructure to broadcast recent or ongoing activities (Fiske, 1987: 4–6; Gitlin, 1980). It produces, it seems, a powerful counterfactual sense of "being there," but this being is almost entirely a deceptive fabrication (Bourdieu, 1998). The dominant media frame or governing principle ordering "watching experiences" complements realism as a trope or mode. Frames are "persistent patterns of cognition, interpretation, and presentation, of selective emphasis and exclusion, by which symbol handlers routinely organize discourse, whether verbal or visual" (Gitlin, 1980: 7). This framing activity, because so little of modern life is directly experienced, although it may be seen, reduces the dialogue between people and the media, muting voices and stories, as Gitlin (1980: 3) writes, "beyond recognition."

The media have political and aesthetic functions because they claim to "reflect" or reproduce "the world." This is the single great lie, a counterfactual assertion, made by the media in self-defense. They claim that they do not make the news, they report it. However, more accurately, they make the news, decide what is newsworthy, selectively emphasize, present, and context it, and in every way frame events and reproduce fields of meaning through which ideology becomes manifest and concrete (Gitlin, 1980: 10). Media create images, construct, manipulate, and "spin" images, all in the interest of entertainment and profit. Within the frame "television," the news is a technical redoing for entertainment, but the subsets of frames used are the working tools of media workers. The most important events, from a political point of view, are those created by media independently, or amplified beyond everyday realities by media attention, use, exploitation, and looping and relooping of their images of an event with political significance.

These images of political events may indeed change, their content may be modified, and the "story" may be grown over time. As such, a dance or struggle of images may ensue. In a loosely bonded and bounded culture (Merelman, 1991), interpenetrating of media and group relations increases. As a result, the core ideology of control, images of the police and "criminals," crime and disorder are sustained quite apart from debate, discussion, interpersonal acquaintance, and politics. The internal conflict within institutions remains to be played on as a source of new "stories," without a context.

The interconnections between media and politics are particularly relevant for police studies and a communicational theory of policing because policing both creates and reacts to communication and represents itself as powerful and authoritative. The police are the most common symbol of governmental authority in everyday life and the most commonly encountered governmental agency other than schools for most people. Yet most people have little direct experience with the police, and most of that is in the victim or service-based role. Mass media treatments of police and policing create a dynamic interplay between the social reality of policing and mediated versions of policing. Thus, the external environment of the police is not only constituted from figures acting in "naturally occurring events" in real time, but also includes a mediated, transformed environment that mixes or laminates social realities and times with events shown by the media. Further, as we shall see in the following chapters, the police

actively use and manipulate the media to suit their purposes. Their purposes may be organizational and in that sense self-serving, or they may be
by way of social control through the media—blaming, shaming, stigma-
tizing, and isolating an accused person in the public eye prior to any judicial undertakings. A mediated environment, politically viable, symbioti-
cally sustained, comes into being.

Media can frame events in many ways and can of course produce or create an event through their own staging. The term "media event," as used
by Dayan and Katz (1993), has a specific referent: televised ritualized activities that are massively ceremonial and socially significant and often created in anticipation of media diffusion of the event, such as the Olympics,
Super Bowl, peace conferences, or treaty-signing ceremonies. In 1999, the
massively ceremonial funeral of King Hussein was shown worldwide via
satellite. I use the term *axial media event (AME)* to reference a naturally
occurring event profoundly altered by television's diffusion of the images
of that natural event. The Rodney King beating is but one of these. Media
have great power to amplify the political significance of natural activities,
events that might otherwise be invisible and insignificant. Some media
events of an erstwhile banal character are *axial,* or historic, moments that
uncover the fault lines of societies, dramatic turning points in consciousness and collective life. These points entail a known and recognized systematic connection to the mobilization potential of axial-visual events
(Jaspers, 1953: 247–67). Media reflect and create these axial visual events
that portend change, whether ceremonially enhancing or reducing solidarity, while simultaneously engaging mass audiences in the meanings
that they unfold.

These AMEs, the result of media efforts, media work, have powerful
consequences. As we see in chapter 4, changes in the imagery and significance of organizations with long histories, such as the LAPD (Woods,
1973; Cannon, 1997), shape their policies, organizational leadership suc-
cessions, and effectiveness. The media also have an important "deviance"
amplification effects (Wilkins, 1965; Cohen, 1980) that converts errors and
falls from grace into big theater, entertainment, and, at times, spectacles
that enthrall millions.

LITTLE AND BIG THEATERS

Increasingly, it seems, little theaters of framing interpersonal conduct,
punctuated with failures, apologies, redemption, and little conferrals of
grace, are not nested in institutional protections. Occupational mandates,
including the discretion of the journalists, sustain a polite distance from

private conduct. While the police in practice rarely respect the common law restrictions on restricted access to private spaces and private "personal information," they are loath to have their practices, on street or in the jail, revealed. The backstage protects many things, not least of which is police probity and reputation (Holdaway, 1983; Young, 1991).

Thus, the "little theater" of errors, failures, and little defeats becomes a part of THEATER (Toobin, 1996) when the errors of Judge Lance Ito in the O. J. Simpson trial are revealed by jurisprudence critics, when Stacy Koon, the sergeant in the Rodney King beating, is critiqued by martial arts experts-trainers, and when LA police chief Daryl Gates is criticized nationally. In the JonBenet Ramsey murder, the errors of the detectives become part of an ongoing media examination of their practices, leading to the resignation of the police chief of Boulder, Colorado, and alternative versions of the crime by the parents, the police, and the media on television and in books (Schiller, 1999). The line "protecting" the backstage is now blurred, and the media play on the idea that they are now simulating the backstage as well as totally penetrating and analyzing the frontstage for an eager, naïve, and trusting public (even as public trust of the media plummets). Practices, jokes, especially ironic jokes, roles, and routines, taken-for-granted knowledge that underlies everyday interaction, are now scrutinized by the media as potential seamy misconduct and spoken of in pseudomoralistic tones by a "live" "reporter" or on film by a talking head. Crude remarks, gauche compliments, and slips of the tongue no longer merely let down the side or the team, seen as awkward moments of potential betrayal or role-compromise by team members, but as public events to be judged. They are judged as edited; as presented (re-presented) in formatted media genres accompanied by their narrative conventions governing talk and iconic representations.

A bit of little theater, now a part of THEATER that is memorialized, etched in the collective memory, talked about, shown and reshown, becomes one of a set of core dramas in a society. Core dramas, like the figure of the celebrity, a famous life without content, can be either international or merely local. Long-running core dramas, held together by mythic ideas and allegorical threads, may be called spectacles. Core dramas becoming international spectacles include the O. J. Simpson trial, the beating of Rodney King and the trials of the police officers involved, the investigation of President Clinton by the independent counsel and Clinton's impeachment by the House of Representatives in 1998, and Clinton's acquittal by the Senate in 1999. Local dramas, such as the death in custody of Mr. Alpha, discussed in chapter 8, resonate only regionally. Less explosive little dramas of control—arrests, traffic stops, community meetings, trials, hearings, bookings, and interrogations for example—also occasionally become public matters. Core dramas arouse sensibilities, fears, and sentiments, direct attention of both the participants and audiences to selective sanctioning by control agents, and convey encoded (complex and multifaceted) messages to mass audiences. While most core dramas engage individuals interacting together or in "embodied copresence," many dramas are products of media transformations of natural events, some of which are created by the media and framed for the audience in the absence of any direct lived experience. Mass media increasingly shape the meanings of social action. The primary or first ground of experience is regrounded by the media in what might be called "transformed reality," or simply "media unreality" (Mitroff and Bennis, 1993). Many of the media dwell on reflections on their own creations—celebrities, sports figures, sources of gossip and scandal, and their own minicelebrities, "anchors" and talking heads.

In summary, using the dramaturgical framework, the role of the media in social control and in shaping the role and mandate of the police can be articulated. The little theaters of control can be amplified by the media into big theaters, whether or not the media are there in the first instance. The passing dramas of the day, the mundanities that punctuate the nightly news and the newspapers for a few days, fade in the light of the current concern. When the media, especially television, seize on an event of importance to them and of putative import to their audiences, they can shape and sustain the story, especially if it is visual, into a focal point, a media event with political significance. Regina Lawrence's perceptive analysis (2000) of the politics of force, with a key concern for the Rodney King beating, provides powerful evidence of the shaping effects of the media and of the processes, interviews, headlines, feature stories, editorials, and experts' commentary that elevate the event from little or big theater, and move it into contention for status as a core drama or long-running folk morality play.

Rituals and public events reaffirm some aspects of order and suppress counterbalancing ideas and values. The lines of action displayed in a gathering contain rituals as "guides to perception," while the vulnerabilities of participants are sustained through exchanges of deference and demeanor. Organizational analysis of this sort requires linking conduct or behavior oriented to the others' judgments, subjective collective representations (of organizational action) that represent selves as subjects and objects, and organizations as constraint. Symbolizations of organizational action, because of limitations upon time, resources, and memory, must be severely edited versions of reality. They are dramaturgical, or context-specific, communications. Their value lies in their ambiguity and simplicity.

These points, taken together, suggest that the environment of the police is complex, "chaotic," unevenly demanding, a set of differentially organized networks or sources of contingency (Burns and Stalker, 1960). Coupling the organization to the environment, classification and labeling, signification and semiosis, the constant process of interpretation, uncertainty and its management, is an abiding concern of agencies of social control. I want to show how these basic processes have changed in policing in the last thirty years.

SUMMARY

Dramaturgy sees life as a kind of minitheater; it is a perspective that employs this theatrical metaphor, to explore the performances—the communication of messages and symbolic representations to an audience—that convey impressions that shape subsequent interactions. It concerns symbolic action that refers to what is represented as well as other matters and is predicated on trust. An encounter with a police officer initially is based on trust, but the interaction also echoes and relies upon what is known about "police" and "policing." Because action itself can convey a rich texture of ambiguous messages, some method is needed to pin down meaning or see how it is framed and encoded. Here, I use semiotics, or the science of signs, and frame analysis to explicate the structure of meaning that connects actions and structures. The concept of key, which indicates what is going on, or how the social reality presented is to be understood, is used to explain the realities that policing conveys and with which it lives. The problem of meaning is acute in societies that work with snapshot interactions, and where stranger-stranger communication or mediated communication (that which is conveyed by electronic means rather than in face-to-face encounters) is cheap and abundantly and virtually omnipresent. A society that lives in the present and only marginally in the future is condemned to suffer the pains and joys of the present. In many ways, the collective representations of our time are mediated; and it is through the "mediation" of dramas of control, little and big, that we "know about policing." Policing, in turn, is communication about contingencies and uncertainties and marks the meaning of events. The potential for police dramas, dramas of control, to become spectacles and change the meaning of policing has increased because of the vast speed and voraciousness of television.

TWO

ASPECTS OF THE ANGLO-AMERICAN
POLICE ORGANIZATION

INTRODUCTION

Policing as an organization is somehow understood, but rarely defined precisely. While the connections among uncertainty, drama, control dramas, and the drama of control, including both little and big theaters, set a framework for the analysis of collective action, the foreground must be the police organization, and that in turn hinges on a useful definition of Anglo-American policing.

A definition of policing and a sketch of police organization open this consideration of changes in policing, because they set the context for seeing the other changes in the media, technology, and the police role. A clear definition of policing elaborating Bittner's classic (1970, 1974, 1990) formulation is presented with the features of the subtype Anglo-American policing. Following the presentation of a working definition, I list sixteen features of Anglo-American policing. I believe that these pattern the nature of change and the symbolization, or representation, of changes unfolding in the past thirty years. In many respects, as recent research demonstrates (Fielding, 1995; Rosenbaum, 1996; Maguire, 1997; Greene, 2000), the structure and function of policing have little changed in the last thirty years. Indicative of the tensions and anomalies in policing, matters I call *contradictions* that arise from an evolving structure, sediments of past adjustments, compromises, and sentiments, are a series of claims made by the police. These are rhetorical moves that in brief, almost encoded, fashion elevate their power, virtue, even-handedness, modesty, and self-effacing nature and mark for appreciation their efficiency and accessibility as an organization. These rhetorical moves conceal as well as reveal and are in effect mini-ideologies that point to underlying unresolved contradictions.

DEFINING DEMOCRATIC POLICE

Like many key terms in social science—role, status, technology, stratification, crime, and social control—*policing* is more discussed than defined. It is an elusive term, and the search for a useful definition continues. No definitive source exists. Bordua's (1968) entry in the *International Encyclopedia of Social Science* is quite general. Maureen Cain's thoughtful discussions (1972, 1979) refined the definition to include state interests and power. *The Encyclopedia of Police Science* (Bailey, 1987) and the *Encyclopedia of Women and Crime* (Rafter, 2000) contain no definition of *police*. A thoughtful definition, Shearing and Stenning's (1985: 1439), emphasizes preserving order among people in a community, noting that ideas about this order may be widely shared or "imposed by a dominant group." A common approach in police studies and criminology textbooks is to offer no definition (e.g., Siegel, 2000), reduce policing to functions (American Bar Association, 1967; Siegel, 2000: 507–8), or rely on common sense (Reaves and Goldberg, 1996).

Let us begin generally. *Police,* a word with Greek origins that refer to regulating, governing, and administering civic life, connotes politics or the distribution of power (Stead, 1977: 1). Police functions, and agencies or groups performing them, vary cross-culturally and historically (Bayley, 1985; Becker and Becker, 1986). The democratic form of policing stands in contrast to totalitarian policing (as in the USSR under communism and the People's Republic of China under the Red Guard), authoritarian policing (as in states under martial law or semimartial law, such as Northern Ireland or South Africa prior to democratization), and sacred policing (as found in such Middle Eastern states as Iran, Iraq, Saudi Arabia, and Kuwait, where the civil law, even in secular states, has its roots in the Koran). Cross-culturally, the role of religion in defining and sanctioning police practice varies appreciably. Their current duties vary widely by local traditions and values. Police in the 1920s in America, for example, cared for wayward children, took responsibility for crime prevention, and covered a wide ambit of functions in large cities (Monkonnen, 1981, 1992; Appier, 1998). Clearly, democratic states vary in their concern for "high politics," and matters of "intelligence gathering" and use. Arguably, the German, Italian, French, and Japanese police have historically emphasized intelligence and monitoring of the civilian population more than those of other democratic states, and certainly more than the Anglo-American countries (Australia, Canada, New Zealand, the UK, and the United States). Bayley (1975, 1994) has noted differences in image, rank structure, and the division of labor with respect to powers and duties. The claimed American police mandate, reactive crime control, is but one of many possible foci—crime prevention, the control of citizens' movements and loyalties to the state, risk reduction, and security management.

A dramaturgical perspective on policing sensitive to identifying change must include more than designated public police agencies if it is to explain the distribution of formal ordering and sanctioning in society. These patterns have historical roots and are concealed by ideological canopies or beliefs about police functions and the police image. The illusion of control and the facade of order and control are always at risk when events surface that challenge the ideological canopy. Conversely, the subjective orientation of publics to the credibility of a performance—collective, team, or individual—remains problematic. These ambiguities suggest that police undertake dramaturgical work to sustain precisely this nuanced edge between violence, control, and order. In the broadest sense, the public police mandate is problematic because it must manage the edges of the public and the private in social relations. Much of police work, selectively maintaining such a working construction of the mandate, is backstage and unseen by the public. Like all institutions, policing is a mode of managing societal risks, of maintaining the appearance of control over the insoluble. This contradiction, perhaps a paradox, means that all institutions of necessity must create ideologies, or spin, to rhetorically obscure the deep and constant gap between expectations and performance.

Careful consideration of the similarities and differences in policing forces, nominally called "public" and "private," including budgeting, accountability, loyalty, territory, and use of force, is needed (Forst and Manning, 1999: 66–67).[1] Reiss correctly argues (1992b) that many policing agencies exist, that policing functionally is done by many organizations with quite different overall functions, using differing strategies and tactics, and that both public and private police use violence and regulate social life. The local American police, among many kinds of police, are not unique, and in some sense because of the local character of American policing, it is

1. The distinctions "private" and "public" police arise from ideal types, not empirical research, and close examination reveals the overlap of public and private policing functions (Johnston, 1993; Shearing, 1992; Forst and Manning, 1999). Perhaps the most significant differences are pay (much higher among public police) and its source, and direction of loyalty. Security, as an occupation, is oriented up, to the management and especially top management, rather than laterally to peers, as is public policing.

difficult to capture their functional range, let alone how many officers and civilians are employed (Bayley, 1992). Consider budgeting and accountability. Canada, for example, maintains a rich tapestry of policing. It includes contract policing carried out by local, provincial, and national agencies; several quasi-independent provincial constabularies (Newfoundland, Ontario, Quebec); a national police (nominally the RCMP) with strict legal limits on their mandate; and funding from several sources: local taxes and contributions, the Solicitor General's Office, and the provinces. This is a model of local-provincial and national funding and control that differs from that in the United States. Funding in the United Kingdom has shifted radically in the direction of Home Office financing since the Thatcher years, and Australia is being swept into a business model, heavily emphasizing downsizing, outsourcing, and contractual relations. Further, for any given problem, say dogs barking and running loose, a variety of agencies—public health, animal control, city parks and recreation, police, county and city units with the same function—may be involved in the "policing." The requirement for intergovernmental cooperation since the Crime and Disorder Bill of 1986 in the United Kingdom has further blurred the line of accountability as opposed to conventional agreements and local operations.

An Initial Attempt

A useful preliminary working definition of police is Egon Bittner's (1970: 39), which serves as the basis for most attempts to delineate policing analytically. Bittner draws on Heidegger (1977) and Husserl broadly as well as the jurisprudential theories of Hans Kelsen (1961, 1967) to ground his profoundly philosophical analysis. Bittner (1970: 39) defines *police* as "a mechanism for the distribution of situationally justified force in society." The police are required to stand ready to respond to all sorts of human problems when it is imagined that the application of force may be necessary at some point (Bittner, 1970: 44). Bittner adds that "the role of the police is best understood as a mechanism for the distribution of nonnegotiable coercive force employed in accordance with the dictates of an intuitive grasp of situational exigencies" (46). The ambit includes people unable to care for themselves. This definition, with its situational aspects, focus on violence, and "intuitive grasp" of a situation as the basis for intervention, combined with the absence of an explicit a priori legal dimension, is brilliant and penetrating. It has shaped two or more generations of police studies. Bittner's definition covers private police, many federal and state agencies that regulate health and safety (not called "police"), self-help groups, and paramilitary groups (Bayley and Shearing, 1999), as well as such agencies as private security companies, detectives, and reserve constables, regardless of their precise linkage to the state or the criminal law.

Violence or the threat of violence, applied situationally, is essential to police operations. It is seen as a (necessary) anachronism employed by the modern state, but the state, as claimed by Weber (1966: 5, 341 ff.), has no monopoly on legitimate violence. Here, Weber and Bittner differ, and Bittner certainly captures the current situation in the United States, where it is estimated that some twenty million legal guns are owned by citizens (Cook and Ludwig, 2000: 11), and the potential for collective violence from vigilantes and terrorists remains high. As Bittner conclusively argues, the law does not define "excessive force" (1970: 34, 38), and leaves it to local definition in many respects. But the action aspect is profound. Policing, he writes, is "above all making use of the capacity and authority to overpower resistance to an attempted solution in the native habitat of the problem" (1970: 35). In other words, it is the possible *resistance of citizens* and the right to overcome the citizens' initial formulation that drives intervening action, not the intrinsic features of the "native habitat" of the problem. Bittner's primary data and examples are drawn from field studies that elegantly describe the craft of patrol officers regulating mental illness, the homeless, and drunkenness in large cities. This strong ethnographic base ironically produces a misleading and partial picture of "policing" in part because he overemphasizes the detailed local knowledge and information bases of everyday patrol work, in part because he leaves the organization as a black box and in part because he does not articulate policing with the broader political economy directly. His work, although sensitive to the character of police organization and its view of information as semipersonal, private, and a resource (Bittner, 1990: 66–67), contains little data-based description or analysis of the internal workings of policing. He assumes that informal cliques—cliques that negotiate the vertical and horizontal flow of information and authority, of command and control, and of investigative work—exist. His is a view from the streets, and a rather stereotypical rendering of policing and officers' knowledge that rarely meets the high standard he assumes.

Bittner's definition requires additional clarification for ready application. Bittner, citing Kelsen (1961), argues that police violence is not applied without authority; it is legitimated ("authorized") and sanctioned by the state. This sanctioning is negotiated continuously on the ground and in public debate in a democracy. Violence serves interests. In that sense, the police's interests as well as the state's are served, regardless of the intuitive bases for the situational application of coercive violence. The actors' perceptions or consciousness, their definitions of the problem and its possible solutions, have no direct relevance to this praxis.

The interests of the state are thus not easily identified in advance, inferred directly from the power of any social group or from interactions. The police have political and economic interests in controlling sources of their prestige, and this takes different shapes in police segments, and is altered by unionization and style of command. The contemporaneous connection between the police use of force and legal grounds for justification is fairly recent (Bittner, 1970: 36). Deference to the law, as well as to other sources of order such as class, age, race, and gender arrangements, is a feature of police legitimacy. Compliance with the shadow of class and status interests is reflected in the law's enforcement. Inevitably, the powerful interests that sustain the state provide a tacit "authorization" for policing. Police objectivity favors the interests of the elites even in a democratic society (Manning, 1997b: 40–41, 101–2). This results from the ways in which the police have maintained the direction of law and the targets of violence in modern states.

Policing with force is something of an oxymoron in a modern welfare state (Bittner, 1970: 39). Metaphorically, the state will act by the same token toward itself (in the form of the citizens who constitute it) in a violent and punitive fashion, but more generally, the compliance of citizens and their unrecognized acceptance of force and violence directed at themselves must be noted. Symbolic violence, violence that "is wielded with tacit complicity between its victims and its agents, insofar as both remain unconscious of submitting to or wielding it" (Bourdieu, 1998: 17), is a reflexive aspect of postindustrial societies. "The function of sociology, as of every science, is to reveal that which is hidden" (Bourdieu, 1998: 17). This search for revelation entails at least probing the mechanisms by which the exercise of such symbolic violence is produced, both the more overt and visible sort and that which is protected or hidden. The operational solution of the police has been to focus on the marginal and weak, to seek to be accepted in their crudity of intervention on the grounds of necessity and time-framed expediency. The police, in short, are beneficiaries and guardians of symbolic violence. The police in every society are insulated in some fashion from those they police—by civil laws, traditions, legal conventions such as the common law, civilian review boards, and other modes of accountability. This is what Bittner elegantly (1970: 39) terms "bureaucratically symbolized communication." The police are armed and dangerous, and protection *by* the police is assumed, while protection *from* their actions, misdeeds, and mistakes is more problematic and perhaps less commented upon. The modes of review and accountability are many. Bittner's definition obviates the subtle political economy that shapes the police organizational mandate and assumes workers' (officers') compliance with commands (cf. Cain, 1972; Bayley, 1985: 10 ff.). Nevertheless, the outlines of the necessary features of a definition were set out.

Refinements in the Definition of Police

Maureen Cain offered one definition (1972) and modified it (1979: 158) to include the notion of state interests and power. A further refinement occurred with David Bayley's (1985: 7–11) definition: police are "people authorized by a group to regulate interpersonal relations within the group through the application of physical force."

Bayley adheres to (presumed) competence in the use of physical force as key, specifying the notion of domestic use to exclude "armies" (1985: 8) and "authorization" to marginalize organizations that use force outside legitimate authority. He focuses on "interpersonal relations" rather than on groups and power and excludes the specific political interests, their own or those of others, that the police attend to. What a "group" is and whether police in fact regulate only "interpersonal relations" exclusively within a given group is certainly an open question. A "group" such as an organized state differs from a tribal band or group with structured governance and begs the question of law, territory, and territorial authority. Like Bittner (1970, 1990), he acknowledges that threat of use of force differs from the application of force, but overlooks the fact that armies are used domestically in conditions of unrest and that policing takes place in revolutionary situations in which authorization is questioned and legitimacy at issue (Liang, 1970, 1992; Wakeman, 1995, 1996). Furthermore, "authorization" is vague enough to include private as well as public policing.

Other Attempts at Definition

These somewhat peripheral definitions are important because they are heavily ideologically freighted. They dramatize a few functions ("peacekeeping," "discretion," "law enforcement") and implicitly connect problematic matters (law, justice, and morality). While each feature in this list plays a role in the dynamics of Anglo-American policing, each is typically overemphasized to the exclusion of its opposite.

Let us consider the role of the law. Law is governmental social control (Black, 1976), or more specifically a language for translating everyday events into problems having to do with the rules and principles of the legal system. Given that much of what police do has nothing whatever to do with the law, or translating events into legal language (this occurs only in that rare event, the arrest), "law enforcement" is a small but important part of policing. Textbook definitions tie named functions (traffic enforcement, protection of persons and property, etc.) to notional legal constraints or argue that the police "maintain the law" (Roberg, Crank, and Kuykendall, 2000: 28); these definitions focus on "discretion," the empty hole in the doughnut. That is, legalistic definitions assume that the law fetters or guides decisions; such definitions address those decisions that the law guides without identifying all the matters outside the doughnut itself that shape deciding. The application of the law may include discretion, but the most salient lasting and important decision is whether to apply the law and which rule or rules to invoke. Those matters are not "discretion" because they are not fettered by law. Neither the law, law enforcement, nor "discretion" captures the requirements of policing, nor are they inadequate ideological conventions. The idea that policing is "law enforcement" is a misleading synecdoche since rather rarely do police invoke the law. Appeals to the law often mystify a situation of violence application because the law provides no prospective guidance concerning when it can be applied. Nor is the law the principal constraint on police actions (Manning, 1997b: 101; Bittner, 1970: chaps. 5 and 6; see Herbert, 1998, for a contrary view).

What about order maintenance? The assertion that police do maintain order is a truism and begs the question of whose order, and when (Wilson, 1968: 16–17). As Bittner (1970) and Shearing (1992) clearly argue, "order" is a relative, politically defined matter and varies widely among the areas of cities (Sampson, Raudenbush, and Earls, 1997). Furthermore, this notion of order maintenance sets out the police as primary, responsible, and symbolically accountable for something about which they have only the most pathetic or limited power to change: social organization (Banton, 1964: 5; Black, 1976). If it were not misleading, it would be arrogant, and it takes this face in the polemic *Fixing Broken Windows* (Kelling and Coles, 1996) and in writings that elevate the authority and claims of the police to a high art. It is quite clear that the zero-tolerance version of policing, as refined in New York City, became a useful tool to criminalize all forms of wandering from the path, literally and figuratively—including jaywalking, pornography sold in certain locations, the very existence of the homeless, the powerless, and the mad—and made *public policy* of the power to order and harass that the police have always wielded in the inner cities of the United States (Manning, 2001a).

What of morality? As American police are generally associated with morality, law, and violence, it is often mistakenly argued that policing performs some combination of these, with fatal force as a reserve power. The connections between law, justice, and morality remain problematic historically, analytically, and in practice (Black, 1976). Law, and law enforcement, may produce procedurally guided decisions, but these are not always fair or just, even by legal standards (Radelet, Bedau, and Putnam, 1992). Police in many respects operate with what Packer (1968) called a crime control model (not really meaning crime, but glossing the police function to all those matters of ordering that can be done with authority and power and without question). Morality is differentially reflected in law and in its enforcement, given the political influence of legislators, judges, police, and civil servants on the legal process. The application of the law is a dependent variable, a response to other social conditions, as well as an independent variable that produces effects (Black, 1980). And, as we see, the obligation to police is very wide indeed, ranging from dealing with those unable to cope with modern life to validating elections. *The New York Times* (November 12, 2000) showed a front-page picture of the Palm Beach, Florida, election recount with two officers standing in the foreground. What are they doing? Or are they being or representing something?

Similarly, the term "peace officer" is a created (misdirecting) oxymoron, suggesting that the officer is by nature and practice peaceful and the police task is peacemaking. Peacemaking can be profoundly violent, as the history of frontier U.S. marshals, bounty hunters, and the Texas Rangers reveals (Samora, 1979). The extent to which the police are feared, as opposed to supported, and trust in police vary by race and class (Cao and Stack, 2000: 73). The peace that peace officers keep is not a universally desired peace.

Are the police a "public service agency" producing "value added" products? (Moore, 1997). This question is cast in the rhetoric of social economics. For example, the euphemisms of economics and business connoted by the concept of "police management" currently used in police training institutes in Kentucky and Texas obscure the concrete and often primitive nature of the tasks to be managed. They equate response to market forces with service and even "efficiency." The citizen is a "customer" to be served, responded to, and thanked. She might even be a partner. But this clearly does not cover the political role of the police, their obligation to serve the state, not citizens, their use of coercive violence, and the absence of citizen choice or right to question the "quality" of service, the product, or the "salespeople." The police claim of "service" or crime prevention is unverifiable (showing that something is prevented is impossible), and calculating its value even more mystifying. The market-derived metaphor of policing as a profit-making business is crude, misleading, and poorly considered (Forst and Manning, 1999). Furthermore, it is not clear what their product might be since this implies a metric for comparison and ranking, and policing in general does not produce—it represents and re-presents contingencies.

A Working Definition

A definition of police should place the features of the police—their vio-lence, their constraint, their ordering and self-serving functions, as well as their "natural" dramatic potential and actuality—in the context of the politics of the modern democratic state. The drama of policing, it seems, requires both opposition and negation. One must consider what they do and represent as well as what they avoid or eschew and are prohibited from doing.

Liang (1992: 2) puts the idea of policing elegantly within the context of history and democratic values. What is expected of policing, he argues, is embedded in values that shape police actions and intentions. What they do and what they do not do are equally important. Liang argues that demo-cratic police should be legalistically guided, focus on individuals, not group politics, eschew terrorism (and counterterrorism) and torture, and strive to ensure minimal damage to civility. These are connoted by the term "democratic policing," whether such standards are met or not, and allow Liang to suggest the penumbra of policelike activities by citizens that shadow his definition. These include high or political police, self-policing, and counterterrorism. These types of policing stimulate resistance and self-help. These are necessary in a democracy, for without resistance and cries for justice, serious crime control may fade. These stipulations define the necessary penumbra surrounding a core definition of police. They refine the requirements citizens place on each other. Liang argues quite persuasively on historical evidence that it is through the resistance of par-allel and counterpolice forces that the need for a democratic police is sus-tained. The security police, the high police, and the various self-policing systems sustain the tension that permits the general strategies of demo-cratic, at least European, police—potential violence, divide-and-conquer tactics, threats of force, violence and deceit, and sustaining myths—to work over long periods of time (Liang, 1992: 14–17). These requirements, of course, become paramount in times of "crisis," when national security easily trumps individual rights, and fascism lurks in each new initiative of the government to provide "homeland security." I assume the implicit constraints on means or tactics specified by Liang.

Here is tentative working definition of *police*:

> The police in Anglo-American societies, constituted of many diverse agencies,
> are authoritatively coordinated legitimate organizations that stand ready to

apply force up to and including fatal force in specified political territories to sustain political ordering.

The above working definition, like all definitions, provides a set of "terms that clearly reveal the strategic spots where ambiguities necessarily arise" (Burke, l962: xx). By this I mean that each of the key terms in the definition could be subjected to a radical deconstruction. Definitions contain multiple facets, ambiguities that reveal social attitudes and institutional contradictions. Many agencies police, but few are authoritatively coordinated, that is bureaucratically structured to ensure compliance with command. Police legitimacy, as the next chapter discusses, is a negotiated acceptance of the scope of the occupation's claims, not an absolute or unchanging matter. "Standing ready" echoes Weber's terms (1966: 339) meaning that the threat of violence awaits and is there to be imposed if proffered solutions of the police are not embraced by the citizen. The specification of political territory is itself a problematic issue in practice, but in theory it is used to define the domain of police forces. The trends to transnational policing, in the form of agreements, task forces, and ad hoc "policing actions" as in Kosovo, Bolivia, Colombia, and Haiti, are with us (Sheptycki, 2000). "Ordering" is a political matter at root. By narrowing the scope of analysis to isolated items of performance such as arrests, interactions, or complaints, social scientists obscure the broader questions of authoritative ordering—for whom collectively and by whom the ordering is done—and certainly obviates the central question of organizational loyalty and its sources. Finally, what is constantly and systematically omitted in such definitional exercises is that the police are not neutral, nonpolitical forces without their own motivations, interests, ideological readings of events, and self-serving actions. When the occasional police scandal emerges, police become defensive and the media tend to elaborate and embellish the "official line" or narrative voice of the police, and the broader question of police interests is obscured or enveloped in allegations of individual corruption or malfeasance. "Political ordering" has no fundamental, acontextual, ahistorical definition. As Bittner (1970: 43) correctly points out, any action or group from which resistance might be imagined can be the target of policing. Thus mayoral candidate Rudolph Giuliani constituted "squeegee men" as a major political threat, along with the homeless, the beggars, and the street-based mentally ill in New York City. Later, the police were mobilized in a vast and systematic assault to "clean the streets" and take them back (without reference to who lost them) (Manning, 2001a,b). Of course, they are called out to sweep debris and dead animals from highways; retrieve cats from trees; chase large dangerous beasts on the loose (cattle, zoo animals gone missing, and wild game in city limits); and teach schoolchildren the great peril of "drugs." The most difficult question that is rarely asked is, To whom do the police owe their loyalty in a democratic society? While this is perhaps clearest in the UK, with loyalty to the Crown well understood, it is not so clear elsewhere in the Anglo-American world, where various notions such as "the law," sloganeering like "to preserve and protect" (what?), local icons, seals, and symbols on the cars, uniforms, and buildings all suggest clarity of purpose while obscuring the locus of obligation and accountability.

This emended definition of police seen dramaturgically is a term for ordering (Burke, 1962: xvii–xxv). It reveals central paradoxes of modern policing: the claim to control and coerce, to order fundamentally, in the face of the vagaries of the human condition, regardless of the willingness of the citizens to comply. The police assert, at least privately, the essential need for violence in a society that publicly eschews it and claims Victorian standards as a measure of civility (Bittner, 1970: 17). Ironically, a police idea that originated in the grand and elevating notions of restraint and deterrence developed in the late eighteenth century by Jeremy Bentham, Edward Chadwick, and John Stuart Mill finds its fundamental grounding in to-be-avoided violence. These paradoxes are outlined below.

FEATURES OF THE ANGLO-AMERICAN POLICE

Policing in the United States resembles the general Anglo-American model with respect to legal authority and its relatively local nature. It differs from policing in Australia, Canada, New Zealand, and the United Kingdom in important ways (Brewer, 1996; Bayley, 1975, 1985, 1992). I think some sense can be brought to discussion by explicating the similarities, rather than seizing on the differences at this point.[2] I believe sixteen features mark policing within the broad Anglo-American ambit.

Features

1. *Public policing agencies are diverse in size.* One of the most striking things about American policing is that the numbers of officers, the numbers of agencies, and the division between part-time and full-

---

2. Much of what is known about Anglo-American policing comes from studies of urban patrolmen policing in large urban centers. There is little research on state or federal police, specialized police and regulators, rural policing (whether on the small-town or county level) (Weisheit, Falcone, and Wells, 1999), nor on private policing (Johnston, 1993; Jones and Newburn, 1998; Newburn and Hayman, 2002). Young's work on West Mercia in England (1995) is a notable exception.

time employees are still being debated (Bayley, 1994; Maguire
et al., 1998). Because definitions—of part-time, reserve, full-time,
and sworn officers—are inconsistent, as are the samples of agencies (Maguire et al., 1998), and policing functions themselves are
variously defined (for example, some definitions omit agricultural
inspectors and OSHA and EPA inspectors but include the investigative officers within the armed services), there is little hope of
accuracy. All cited figures are estimates without known variance
due to sampling errors. The story begins with the noted difference between the estimates from the census and those from the
Department of Justice's Law Enforcement Management and Administrative Statistics (LEMAS) (Reaves and Goldberg, 1996)—
some 90,000. The census counts 560,799 officers and LEMAS
shows 649,037. In the U.S. in 1997, according to LEMAS, there
were some 18,769 local, 49 state, and an unknown number of federal agencies that "police." LEMAS shows some 90,000 federal
employees in some law enforcement function. It defines a police
agency as one with more than one employed full-time officer.
LEMAS said in 1997 that there were over 650,000 full-time public police officers, some 8.2 percent of whom were federal employees, and another 250,000 part-time officers (Reaves and Goldberg,
1996). This would mean some 900,000 in total. Civilians constitute 27 percent of police employees and have increased by 161
percent as a ratio to the population (O'Brien, 1996a: 197; cited in
Reaves and Goldberg, 1996: 127). Maguire et al. (1998) compare
LEMAS, the census, and a sample drawn by COPS agency, present a more systematic critique of the samples and biases of each,
and tabularize the several estimates. Adding omitted data,
Maguire et al. conclude (1998: 109–10) that there are in total
21,143 agencies in the United States: 14,628 local agencies, 49
state agencies, 3,156 sheriff-headed agencies, 3,280 special agencies, and an estimated 30 federal agencies. No one has been able to
firmly establish how many law enforcement agencies are federally
based. They conclude that "there may be as many as" 681,012
"sworn" officers in total: 383,873 in local agencies; 53,336 in state
agencies; 137,985 in sheriff-headed agencies; 58,689 in special
agencies; and 47,129 in federal agencies. Police organizations are
quite small on average, but the size varies by state (Reiss, 1992a:
61). Most police officers work in organizations of fewer than thirty
officers. The local agencies vary in size from a handful in departments serving small towns and villages to the over 40,000 officers

in the New York Police Department. Two county forces, Cook County and Los Angeles County, have between 3,000 and 5,000 (Reaves and Goldberg, 1996: 2). The UK has some 125,000 officers in 52 constabularies or forces. A variety of specialized forces, such as the nuclear and railroad police, also exist (Johnston, 1993: 114). Canada has 8 provincial police agencies, while the Newfoundland Constabulary, Ontario Provincial Police, and Quebec Provincial Police remain quasi-independent in operation and funding. Cities and towns throughout the rest of Canada are policed by contractual arrangements, funded at 70 percent by the Solicitor General's Office and the remainder by the provinces. Many local police functions are carried out by contract by the RCMP. The RCMP has powers to enforce specific federal laws in addition to its provincial policing responsibilities. Thus, it is an odd hybrid with the largest percentage of its vast resources committed to local policing, concentrated in Western Canada (it is the provincial force in British Columbia, for example), while enforcing selected federal laws and representing symbolically, albeit in a highly commercialized and mannered fashion, the nation (Dawson, 1998).

2. *Public policing is uneven in training and qualifications.* There are some centralized police training functions in all the Anglo-American countries except the United States, which does not have a national police college, force, or training system. In part, the paucity of development in the United States is a function, ironically, of the success of the FBI in dominating nationally based training in its academy. Police are trained in cohorts in local academies, and formal training requires at least sixteen weeks and usually an apprenticeship under field training officers. Hiring and promotional standards vary widely and are little influenced by educational attainment. Promotions by rank are few and arise when exams or boards are offered. All other forces within the Anglo-American ambit have systematic training in a national college, require retraining with promotion, have various schemes for rewarding advanced education, and have a nationally guided system for developing police leadership.

3. *Public policing is variously funded but tends to be grounded in local politics.* Police departments enforce a wide range of local, state, and federal laws as well as municipal regulations concerning parking, traffic, and the environment. American policing is shaped by known and applied local law and highly selected federal and ap-

pellate decisions concerning civil liberties and liabilities. The impact of the law is filtered by local traditions, but landmark appellate and Supreme Court decisions are closely attended. Police traditions and practices of ordering are locally learned, practiced, and refined and reflect (via training, recruitment, tacit knowledge, and learned practices) local standards of decency and propriety. Until fairly recently, police were likely to be born in or near the cities in which they worked, and lived nearby. This is no longer true except perhaps in medium-sized cities and small towns. The UK differs from the U.S. by maintaining a unified legal system, itself with variations in Scotland, Wales, and Northern Ireland. Australia, New Zealand, and Canada employ a weak variation system (strong national legal system with selected laws enforced by a federal police).

4. *Public policing historically stands in the executive branch of government.* Policing serves the executive indirectly, with the law as a mediating force, both protective and constraining. It is separated from courts and the legislature, yet in effect it "makes law on the street." Policing powers, de facto, are quite widespread and shared among individual citizens, private investigators, citizen self-help groups, private policing agencies, and occasionally, the military (national guard, reserves, and regular forces). Territorial limits or jurisdictional boundaries, once binding in Anglo-American policing, now are largely irrelevant at the federal level, since American law is extended and applied within foreign nations with startling impunity, and global and task force–based transnational policing is growing (Sheptycki, 2000).

5. *Policing in local agencies responds to overlapping governments and jurisdictions.* City, township, county, state, and federal laws are enforced by competing agencies. Police enforce a maze of contradictory statutes and regulations. The tendency to create small departments as suburbs grow into massive quasi-governmental mazes, rather than to create regional police, dramatizes the preference of Americans for local policing (Reiss, 1992a: 63). In fact, the constabulary system in the UK, the state and federal police in Australia, the federal police in New Zealand, and the patchwork of specialized police agencies in all Anglo-American countries (Johnston, 1993) mean similar local effects in law enforcement.

6. *Policing and its violence are embedded in the administrative structure of the modern state.* The state holds out violence as a means to coerce compliance only if habit and expediency fail. Police are ex-

pected to use the level of force needed to control a situation, yet not escalate disorder. The absence of visible police coercion is a sign of legitimacy and the effectiveness of informal controls (Banton, 1964; Goode, 1972; Black, 1976). Police violence is double-edged, as it can be turned against "respectable" citizens, as well as the state in revolutionary situations. On the state level, a variety of administrative means to regulate police, to provide remedies for complaints against them, and to review and evaluate their performance have been tried; none has long influenced policing. Many systems have been adopted and abandoned in large cities (Walker, 1994). The degree of dependence of the organization on the "environment," especially the police role in politics, and in political policing or "high politics" (Brodeur, 1983), is a central and unexplored question in police studies.

7. *Public policing grew from the regulation of city life.* Policing is adapted to observing and managing rare events and providing flexible and consistently graded response to emergent episodes. The police are a simple, flat inspectorial bureau (there are few levels between top and bottom; although rank differences exist, functional differentiation does not, in that most officers above the sergeant level are administrators) that patrols and responds to calls, investigates crimes, and reacts to other messy and unpredictable events. They maintain discretion in responding to events— whether to respond, how to respond, when to respond, with what level and kind of intervention—and they possess "original authority" in common law that protects the vast number of their decisions from review. Larger police organizations have a more elaborate division of labor and a large number of named positions, both of which differentiate police response.

8. *The police are bottom-heavy and reactive, yet mount periodic tactical crackdowns.* Consider the police's general organizational approach to resource allocation—holding back slack resources to cope with uncertainty (Thompson, 1963). Police in 1999 allocated 59 to 90 percent of their sworn personnel "on the ground" in shifts of eight to ten hours at a time, twenty-four hours a day, throughout the year (Hickman and Reaves, 2001: table 5). This figure has become unstable in the last few years and is decreasing, perhaps because of nominal (on paper or in terms of the funding source) reassignments of officers to "community policing." This allocation of personnel means—given holiday, overtime, and comp time, as well as disability and sickness—that whatever the desired strength on

each shift, and the total in a twenty-four-hour period, some four to
five times that number of officers must be employed to ensure full
staffing for a twenty-four-hour period. The work may be organized
on the basis of eight- or ten-hour shifts. The police react to calls
for service, further investigate those that are crime related, and
manifest minimal specialization. Some 5 to 8 percent are in detective work and other specialized units. The police are divided into
staff and line, with patrol as line and administration, internal
affairs, detectives, and the service division as staff. The top command and support are a very small part of the personnel, around
12 percent. Most officers prefer to remain in patrol, and city budgets constrain the available slots. The decentralized character of
Anglo-American policing makes policy-driven force- or precinct-
wide deployment, such as "crackdowns," attacks on "hot spots" of
crime, and zero-tolerance chimeras, quite problematic. Nevertheless, patterned, consistent, differential enforcement, profiling, and
"hard policing," e.g., frequent stops for traffic and other notional
"offenses," questioning and "intelligence gathering" or "community policing," are found in every major urban center in the Anglo-
American world. While the results, defined in a narrow sense of
increased arrests, are often striking in the short run (Wilson and
Boland, 1978; Sherman, 1990, 1992; Miller, 1998; Fagan and
Davies, 2001), the moral, political, and social consequences are
often unnoticed or unmeasured in this research (Rose and Clear,
1998). The concern with the welfare of the middle class and the
elites drives crime control research and obscures the longer-term,
powerful shredding and decimating consequences of short-term
attempts at "incapacitation" on truly disadvantaged people and
areas.

9. *Public police carry arms, some of which are visible, and use them.*
   Policing combines a visible and distinctive uniform with an astounding array of tools, including high-powered semiautomatic
   weapons and burgeoning information technology (Manning,
   1992b; 1997b: 102–6). These weapons and tactics have periodic
   display purposes, are rationalized as relevant to hostage negotiation rather than dynamic (nonwarranted) entries in drug cases,
   and are part of the rising militarization of the American police
   (Kraska and Kappeler, 1997). Police hold unique powers, even
   though fatal force is not restricted to the police in law or by practice, and stand ready to intervene variously in an open-ended
   range of social situations. Although it is clearly the case that they

fail to uniformly apply violence in moderation, when the rare
public and known shooting occurs it is often a public issue and the
basis for a media spectacle (Manning, 2001b).

10. *The police seek and avoid violence, both symbolic and "real."* The police differentially distribute violence to groups within the state, eschew its role in their work, conceal and deny its emotional satis-
factions and attractions, and sustain symbolic violence, or damage
to the interests of groups that accept violence directed at them
(Bourdieu, 1977: 44). Studies reveal patterned police tactics for
managing citizen encounters (Bayley and Bittner, 1986; Bayley
and Garofalo, 1989). These patterns suggest conditions under
which events may escalate, or require force, although official reports suggest that violent episodes constitute less than 5 percent
of police encounters (Alpert and Smith, 1994: 482). The use of
violence, ultimately sanctioned by the state, varies empirically
(Fyfe, 1988) rather than being, as Bittner claims, an "essential feature of the role."

11. *The police present many contradictory public and private faces.* Internally or backstage the police, especially the command segment,
emphasize control and service. Lately, warm and fuzzy, and meaningless, "vision" and "mission statements" and ostensive "core
values" lists are advocated (e.g., Toronto Metropolitan Police,
1997). This rhetoric clashes with visible policing practice and the
sentiments and concerns of the lower ranks. The basis for compliance to command is a mix of charismatic or personalistic authority
and rational-legal authority based upon expertise and experience.
Often, tensions arise between these modes of authority, in part because they are unevenly distributed throughout the organization.
Considerable autonomy and conflict exist within each of the divisions (usually patrol, administrative services, and investigative),
within the segmentalized occupational culture (management, supervision, and lowest ranks), and between civilians and police
within the organization. Unionization adds another important
source of internal conflict that can further divide ranks. Externally, or frontstage, for example, police exercise violence yet are
also shown as caring teachers of children in DARE programs and
strong defenders of the weak in cases of domestic violence; they
create and process information; they educate and negotiate; they
avoid work and are often overworked. A quick scan of any police
department's annual report, even just of the pictures on the cover,
will suggest this diversity: lost children being saved; men riding

high-performance motorcycles and other vehicles; schoolchildren being lectured; crime and accident scenes being managed; horses, dogs, and people mingling, smiling; and weapons and booty displayed in quasi-military exercises in the "drug war." Smiling officers of rainbow hue, white patrol officers in situ, and commanding officers in militaristic uniforms all glow out from the pages.

12. *Policing is dependent on citizens for compliance, information, assistance, and tolerance* (Mastrofski, Reissig, and McCloskey, 2002). To appear to control information, policing can and does occasionally employ information-processing tools, yet relies basically on interpersonal relations. In many respects, police are embedded in the social life of communities, but this embeddedness varies, based on the social composition of the area, its density, police strategies and tactics, and police traditions. Compare, for example, the policing of semirural England (Shapland and Vagg, 1988) with the imagery of urban policing (Bratton, 1998; Kelling and Coles, 1996; Fagan and Davies, 2001), or televised policing shown on *COPS, Law and Order, Homicide,* or *NYPD Blue.*

13. *Police officers generally work alone, in partnerships, or occasionally in small groups.* At times, they join in performance-oriented short-term teams to serve warrants, cordon off an area, or make massive traffic stops or sweeps of areas. In most cities they patrol, ecologically separated in time and space, linked via communications networks, and are rarely directly supervised (Jermeir and Berkes, 1979). Police workloads, the proportion of "free" or uncommitted driving-around time, and the composition of work tasks vary widely by time of day and day of the week, month, and year. Workloads are also shaped by local budgets, traditions, and weather conditions (Bayley, 1994: 39–44). The degree and kind of supervision vary widely (Chatterton, 1989, 1993, 1995; Van Maanen, 1983, 1984).

14. *The image and practice of the police is shaped by information technologies, and their work is shown on various screens.* We are assaulted daily with visual displays and mass media depictions of the police as both subject and object. They are increasingly knowledgeable and educated in the uses of the media and actively use videos of publicity, training, self-enhancement, and protection against suits, often releasing pre-prepared videos of incidents. The culture of simulation, surveillance, and control is developing informally and crescively within policing, rather than being guided by any central force or funding. The effects of the media, media use, and infor-

mation technologies are rather closely correlated with the size and location of the agency and the agency's accessibility to the media via media information offices (Mawby, 1999). The practice of policing is affected marginally by use of the World Wide Web (Young, 1999), the paperless office (Sellen and Harper, 2002), the fantasy of the all-knowing police car (Pilant, 1999), crime mapping (Rossmo, 2000), the 800 MHz radio capacity: features of an ill-considered fantasy future driven by technology, failed machines, incompetence, and inadequate training and without controls by law, finance, public sentiment, or intellectual critique.

15. *The Anglo-American police promote citizen-based demand, yet are occasionally overloaded.* The police are affected by technology, by roles and tasks of the participants in the police communications systems (PCS), and by their own ecology and interpretive practice. The publicly stated aim is to increase demand and provide service. They do plan some demand, such as for parades and demonstrations, and have elaborate plans for major disasters; they initiate stops and investigations; they control demand for investigative services by control over the personnel and overtime. But they are primarily responsive to called-in demand. Called-in demand is shaped. Police do this by screening, prioritizing, labeling 911, 311, and other calls, relabeling calls, shifting personnel, and altering their information technology. They are periodically unable to handle demand, thus sustaining their importance and power. Police develop and state organizational operational strategies, systematic allocation and mobilization of resources (personnel, equipment, time), and presentational strategies and tactics. The types of screens, roles and tasks, and technology used by the police are "buffers" for the patrol officer and serve to control and protect the officers from potentially overwhelming variation in demand and overload (Klapp, 1986). Overload is reduced in three ways: by screening calls and limiting the number of calls forwarded for further attention (the "gatekeeping" function); by downgrading the level of seriousness or urgency of a call or refusing to respond to the emotional tone or expressive content of a call; and by reinterpreting individual messages into universal or general categories of action for resolution. The last of these is accomplished by "policing by the numbers," or responding to vague calls by creating dispatching codes that set priorities officially that are ignored in practice. This also means that the power to control decisions lies largely with the lower participants—operators, dis-

patchers, and officers. These decisions are generally unreviewed except ex post facto in a crisis or scandal such as a refusal to provide service, a delay leading to serious injury, or a shooting.

16. *Police work has become more legalistic, complex, and demanding.* Several factors have made police work more legalistic. Courts have extended procedural guarantees since the Warren Court, even while expanding the explicit rights of the police. The prevalence of the Miranda warning, mumbled in rapid-fire order to suspects, has raised awareness of procedural protections, as has the media's scrutiny of errors and mistakes in arrest and charge. Increased technologies are in use, and the police have greater capacity to process forensic and other physical evidence. There is rising interest in using data to expand crime prevention, problem solving, and crime analysis. The workload at times in large cities is very heavy and stressful. It is likely that these features of policing are influencing recruitment and training, the division of labor within police departments (more civilian experts of various kinds), and career patterns. This remains a hypothesis.

Historical Shaping

These sixteen features of policing (Clark and Sykes, 1974; Manning, 1997b) reflect historical influences that shape what the police represent, what they do, and how they do it. The United States is a revolution-born, frontier, violent society with an individualistic, pseudolegalistic culture focusing on victimization, individual rights, and legal protections. Americans own twenty million legal guns—guns are everywhere, in five million households (Cook and Ludwig, 2000: 213 n. 11), owned by and differentially accessible to everyone (depending on the state). The society denies inequality as a part of the ideology, unlike the UK, and is stratified by both race and class. The fundamental issue in American society is the multiple effects of class and ethnicity on opportunity (Wilson, 1987). The American police mandate remains quite slippery if not "impossible" when based exclusively on the crime-fighting rhetoric. It has been claimed on the basis of local politics, professionalism, and crime fighting for many years (Manning, 1997b). Its latest rendition is cast in the fuzzy logic and rhetoric of "community policing," but its central contingency, the interface with its publics, remains demand management. The British police emphasize authority, the Crown, and traditional patterns of deference and demeanor, with more recently a crime control orientation. Other Anglo-American nations, as Merelman (1991) suggests, fall midway between these two polar types. Because police have focused largely on the two-sided claim of crime control and demand management, they are vulnerable to publicly known fluctuations in crime and in their capacity to control demand for other services. Insofar as they reflect the compositions of their communities and have political support, they are less subject to short-term crises.

INTERNAL CONTRADICTIONS AND PROBLEMATICS

The center of all institutions is a fundamental unresolved paradox that negotiation, symbolization, and rhetoric serve to obscure. A paradox is an irresolvable contradiction. Law deals with the problematic of property and mistakes; medicine deals with disease and its ultimate consequence, death; academics deal with ignorance; and the police deal with contingencies in crime, order, lifestyles, and trust and its manifestations. It may be easy to assert that the crime control claim of the police is an impossible mandate, but the thin and broad claims of police are both more difficult to assess and easier to obscure. This section outlines the contradictions of policing an everyday world. These are the public faces of the illusion of control and the bases for the constant tension between appearances and claims. I list these claims with some evidence to the contrary.

The police claim to:

Control order and disorder at all levels and at whatever magnitude. The central claim of policing—to manage and control social order and disorder in the interest of all, and definitions of how they are to be managed—vary by time, place, audience, and the race and class of participants. In England, for example, the low rates of violent crime, the low use of weapons in crime, the relatively stable class system, and the small minority population reduce the visible problem of crime. The coupling of a traditional insular culture that has not been invaded or conquered since 1066 with a monarchy as a symbol of authority makes policing less dramatic and uncertain work than in Canada or Australia. The crime focus of the American police (Manning, 1997b), a consensual point of reference in claiming legitimacy in the 1920s and 1930s, rendered them vulnerable subsequently to criticism for failing to control crime throughout the 1970s and 1980s. Realistically, policing rests on tacit consensus and, more importantly, on the public view that the police are autonomous or independent of base political interests, as an organization or as officers, and that they eschew attitudes that might conflict with the requirements of an objective, neutral force to maintain some amalgam of justice and order. In some respects, in times of change and conflict, traditional role models are revered and organizations find themselves admired and praised because they resonate with the past and with the imputed values of previous simpler times (Dawson, 1998: 53).

Do justice. Often, treating like cases alike, is conflated with the state and said to ensure justice. Given the loose links between law and deciding at every level, and the case-by-case ideology of the common law, this is a dubious if not absurd claim. The police role has little to do with legal justice directly, as they act as officers of the court whose sole role is to produce the facts of the case for judgment. The police, however, share with the common-law system the assumption that justice somehow emerges in the craft. The police claim justice as their working concern, but their efforts repeatedly and consistently target the powerless, the marginal, and people of color (Fagan and Davies, 2001). This is not entirely a matter of class or race. Cross-cutting classes, dividing them on occasion, are *fields* (of struggle)—objective sets of organized normative structures, e.g., science, the arts, and literature (Bourdieu and Wacquant, 1992). In short, the police operate within a class-shaped environment and are influenced by the fields and techniques they employ. The police operate in an environment that requires them to link vertical and horizontal ordering and interaction, often in a rapid, pragmatic fashion.

Be race-neutral in practice. The actions and the consequences of policing in America are racist in the sense that they are directed at the marginal and powerless, most of whom are people of color. The most explosive story of policing is the consistent, empirically demonstrable fact that in the United States in particular, everyday policing is about managing the lower classes and minorities, specifically blacks and Hispanics. It is almost impossible to disentangle rates of crime, arrests, convictions, and penal sanctions from everyday racism since it is argued by police that these groups disproportionately commit crimes, deserve surveillance, and are known for past records and deeds (both adult and juvenile). In an extension of this logic, they are more often stopped, questioned, and searched than other groups. Although differences exist within disadvantaged areas, those with high numbers of blacks also have high rates of arrests, convictions, and associated connections to the criminal justice system. Dark color is the key that sets off questions of trust, placement, and suspicion, and this premise is demonstrated in racial profiling. Racial profiling is the use of expert systems and documents that advise or encourage stopping people of a given "profile"—e.g., black teen-agers; a black man in an expensive foreign car; long-haired drivers of beat-up vans; a black driver in a "white" suburban area of a city. It goes to the explicit policy-driven attempt of agencies to direct discretion and increase, for example, arrests on drug charges (Manning, 2001b). Profiling of a less systematic sort is the heart of all policing— stops based on distrust, suspicion, awareness of people "out of place" in time or space, past experience, stereotyping, and other common typifications (Miller, 1998; Gordon, 1990; Walker, Spohn, and DeLone, 1996; Fagan and Davies, 2001). The data are overwhelming—people of color, no matter what their presence on the roads, work, or past record, are disproportionately stopped, searched, arrested, charged, and imprisoned (Meehan and Ponder, 2002a,b; Walker, Spohn, and DeLone, 1996).

Be a culturally, politically, and occupationally coherent and unified organization. The conventional wisdom in social sciences is that the police are dominated by a male, white working-class subculture on top of which is laid a "management" or command subculture (Skolnick, 1966; Crank, 1998). While the research has little to say about supervision, management, internal affairs, nonoperational civilians, and other experts within the organization, their influence, whether through policies, sanctioning for delicts, rewards, or leadership, is unexplicated. The role of gender, ethnicity, age, and even conventional religious values tends to be overlooked with a few exceptions (Haarr, 1997; Hunt, 1985; Martin and Jurik, 1996). Much research casts the "police organization" composed of sworn officers and others ("civilians")—diverse occupational groups—as equivalent to "the police" and that in turn to the patrol police culture. Affirmative action policies, diversity, equal opportunity employment, and the generalized political climate of the last twenty years favor or support hiring of those typically marginalized in the past: women, gays, minorities, especially people of color, and "senior" citizens. Nationally, 81 percent of sworn police personnel are white, 11 percent black, 6 percent Hispanic, and 2 percent others. Males make up 91 percent, females 9 percent (Martin, 2001: 403). It is perhaps best to see the police as a segmentalized occupation within an organization dominated by the ideology of the patrol segment and by the notion that policing is a craft and a job. In addition to the patrol-uniformed segment, there are at least three other segments in large North American departments—top command or management, middle management and frontline supervision, and investigative officers. These segments, which interact more intensely within themselves than among each other, are more or less oriented around rank.

Consistently and efficiently spearhead a unified and commanded effective assault on crime and disorder. The internal structure of police organizations is a source of uncertainty and sustains the language of contingency and risk. Police organizations—messy, complex aggregations of persons, technology, and matériel—are bound by authority, collective representations, symbolic labels that refer to joint action, conjoint interaction, goals, and objectives, and moral and expressive beliefs. They are both divided and dividing by rank-based segments, gender, ethnicity, age, and cohort experience. Although performing a mind-boggling variety of functions, they have

chosen at least from the 1920s to the late 1980s in America to represent
themselves as "crime fighters" engaged in "law enforcement," symbolizing
"protection," "justice," and "morality." They have a very complex association with the law, the state, conventional morality, and politics that they obscure with the blurring, mind-numbing, and often anodyne rhetorics of
crime control or "community policing." Any rendition of policing requires
metaphoric thinking, or seeing something in terms of something else, as
well as circumstantial thinking that is rooted in the situation.

   Sustain social integration. If police agencies "reflect" their communities
in terms of conceptions of order, justice, violence, seriousness of crime,
and the like, then their actions will consistently prove to be redundant. In
fact, they are not. The present police organization is a means for handling
contingencies, not producing redundancies. Police organizations are are-
nas in which conceptions of rationality are contested (Espeland, 1998).
While they symbolize justice and the law, they are internally personalistic,
feudal in their loyalties, and rather primitive in their conception of their
work and the citizenry. Differing bases of authority—charismatic,
personalistic, rational-legal, and skilled—are found within the force and
across forces. Organizational segments within police organizations
(Crozier, 1964, 1972) play variously on uncertainty. Their work in creating and managing drama is communications linked. The complexity of
embedded communication is pinned down to a level of ambiguity acceptable to participants (Weick, 1979, 1988, 1995).

   *Act as a "customer-oriented," service-oriented, pass-through agency re-
sponding to public demand.* The police operate as transducers, or interpola-
tors, that convert "raw data" or communications into "messages" and
"facts," or meaningful and useful units. Like all institutions, they reduce
and disaggregate information, sorting *noise* (unwanted or disvalued matter such as wrong numbers or repeat calls from nearby addresses), *equivocality* (trust in the sender—this varies when the senders are drunks, children, crazies, and people who do not speak English well or at all), and
uncertainty (the average doubt about the content of the message). Policing
is not information based. Processing calls is not a simple "pass-through"
function, or even "demand management," because police retain and create
uncertainties and sustain audience doubt about their responses. The
vague notion that citizens are customers ignores the fact that police must
constrain, arrest, coerce, and detain with impunity citizens in situations
that are not governed by the market mentality or rules that state that "the
customer is always right." Any occupation distances itself from its clients,
customers, or patients; some do so with more impunity and with more
elaborate language, such as elevating decision making to the "art of medi-

cine" or the craft of law. The degree and kind of distance are an empirical question.

Be universally accessible. Police encourage accessibility and advertise their sensitivity to demand, yet their accessibility, especially with the federally mandated 911 regional systems of organized response, means that the police potentially are overwhelmed by calls for service that they are unable to attend. Nevertheless, they claim a mandate to protect and serve all, or as is said on the streets, "you call, we haul." Their response varies by city, territory, time of day, shift, month, day, and year. The police information bases and skill level vary widely for given events. They have detailed plans for evacuation in the case of disasters, hurricanes, and floods, information on the location of explosives, gun shops, and accidents, but no information on drug markets (variations in quality, cost, dealerships, or higher-level dealers) or on gang formation or membership. Finally, police provide very little feedback to citizens, witnesses, victims, or families concerning outcomes or the state of developments in a case. The police are often ignorant as well in the sense that prosecuting attorneys seldom provide them with feedback concerning cases that are dropped, pleaded out (guilty pleas accepted for consideration), or successfully prosecuted. The police, it has often been noted, value secrecy and fear exposure of their team-held secrets (Westley, 1970). These factors, from shifting workload to lack of feedback and secrecy, increase citizen dependency and uncertainty. They make citizens' ability to predict police behavior difficult and rare, other than anticipating an initial response from a police operator (as is used in Detroit) "a unit has been requested."

These *contradictions* are of course partial truths, not lies. They haunt the police and occasionally burst into public issues. Their internal tensions and contradictions are managed overtly by presenting a unified front. Their ability to do so, in spite of consistent evidence to the contrary, suggests their power, their sacred roots, and what one might call their dramatic license (Hughes, 1994: 25–30). That is, they call upon their validated claim to a set of functions ostensibly tied to public security, and therefore concealed from further public scrutiny.

The police capacity to assert counterfactual "truths" repeatedly and publicly speaks to their legitimacy and enhances their authority and power. Even admitted exceptions or illegalities are claimed as rarities and aberrations, virtually unique in spite of their routine, conspicuous, and continuous occurrence (Lawrence, 2000: 33 ff.) This ideological hegemony in fact increases citizen dependency on the police. This dependency is much higher in disadvantaged and crime-ridden areas because such areas are "truly disadvantaged," lack collective efficacy, and are in many respects dependent on the police and other public agencies for many basic services such as ambulances, rescue, counseling, therapy, negotiation, and arbitration (Black, 1980; Wilson, 1987; Sampson, Raudenbush, and Earls, 1997). The public position of the police in the last eighty years, their claims to be a twenty-four-hour service agency at the public's call, has won them a mandate of service. However, with the move toward lessening social distance from the public, sometimes called "community policing," the contradictions between private solicitations of calls and demand and backstage private screening and managing of calls may come to the fore.

SUMMARY

The Anglo-American public police as a type has been redefined and several features of Anglo-American policing outlined. There is a considerable similarity in their functions. Underlying these features is a set of contradictions that plague the police from time to time, although some can be ameliorated. That many of the claims contain partial truths only underscores their partial truth and the role of ideology and social integration in sustaining a positive imagery. In many respects, the adjustments police have made publicly in the last thirty years are constrained by the decisions and drift of previous years. The fundamentals of policing, seen in the features and contradictions discussed here, have been parts of democratic policing since the early nineteenth century. The present is not an unfettered and spontaneous performance, but is enacted in and constrained by the shadows of almost two hundred years, an undefined police past.

PART TWO
PICTURING POLICING

THREE

MEDIA, REFLEXIVITY, AND THE MANDATE

INTRODUCTION

Since dramaturgical theory asks how organizational appearances matter, examines how they are symbolized and manipulated, and reveals the resultant ironies and contradictions, it must now take into account the role of media in shaping performances, credible appearances, power, and authority. The process of shaping the police mandate more than ever before is entangled in what people see and what is seen, as well as what has happened to people directly. Media's power is changing the meanings of "policing." The social form, television, is not just "watched," it is decoded or framed to achieve meaning; form and content interact. Drawing out this link between mass media images and the mandate can expand dramaturgical theory as well as the study of policing. The media and police are in a circular and mutually reinforcing relationship. Policing influences media and the media influence policing and its practices. This change in the role of mass communication indicates not only change in consciousness, but change in the structure of images as a source and aspect of social control and policing. I do not have evidence of the actual influence of imagery on police actions or consequences, only about the environment of images.[1]

As we have seen previously, the police operate in the context of contingency, trust assessment, and potential dramatic escalation. The dramas of

1. Charting the proximal connections between police and citizens, supported by ethnographic observations, and linking consciousness and action is another study, not mine (Perlmutter, 2000). The extent to which the media directly shape police consciousness is now being explored (Tuohy and Wrennall, 1995; Hallett and Powell, 1995; Press, 1991; Perlmutter, 2000; Lawrence, 2000).

control now are both immediate and distal, arising in a worldwide context (I heard about the Rodney King beating from colleagues in Oxford before I had seen the film myself). I argue here for changes in the quality and quantity of imagery of policing in the media; the presence of the media in everyday policing; effects of the way the police as collective representations are being portrayed, both generally and in respect to given incidents; and the pattern of media coverage. Having set the stage of policing in a dramatic world and the emerging role of the media, I want to turn now to the specific police-relevant aspects of the media and media-relevant aspects of policing. This chapter concerns changes in the police mandate, the relationships between the media and the mandate, as it has changed in the last thirty years. Their mutual influence, called reflexivity, its sources and consequences for policing, seems to be increasing in the last thirty years. I argue here that a fundamental change in policing in the last ten years and extending prior to that for more than twenty years is a result of the influence of the media. These propositions guide further discussion in this book, because they have global and transnational influences that remain only partially explored.

While it is clear that policing operates with a mandate and is a part of the division of labor, most of the research in police studies assumes the legitimacy of the police mandate and measures changes in identifiable aspects of outcomes, structures, or roles. This leaves unexplored the underlying structure of emotions, history, and local traditions of policing. It is typically and routinely atheoretical. The integration of media studies and policing has been uneven. The mandate itself is affected by the influence of media on citizens' expectations, their fears, and by the media's shaped and patterned discourse (Sparks, 1992; Altheide and Michalowski, 1999). It is perhaps a cliché to argue that the meaning of police work is political and the politics of the modern policing are shaped by television. Yet the assumption of most work in criminal justice, criminology, and police studies is that the police are "neutral" or "apolitical." The impact of media reflections of policing on policing and policing's impact on the media is in need of exploration. The perspective of television—ironic, selective, and a framing of encoded events as real—creates and sustains a media reality that would appear to shape policing. This "media work" is an aspect of the mandate because it creates imagery of the police as "an other" and imagery of the public as "an other" or "the other" of which police are aware. The relationships between these two mediated others is not yet clear, but it is an issue that cries out for additional careful attention.[2]

2. Television has been well studied, and some dramaturgical, semiotic, and structuralist analyses done (Fiske, 1987, 1989, 1991, 1994; Taylor and Mullan, 1986). The difficulty lies in measur-

THE POLICE MANDATE

The police mandate (Hughes, 1958; Manning, 1997b)—their socially validated moral obligations as seen by the public and managed by them—is a matter of claim and validation, a dialogue at best, and a dynamic process by which occupational power and authority expand and contract over time. In 1967 (rewritten in 1977 and then in 1997), I argued that the police had an "impossible mandate" because they claimed to control crime although crime, in many respects, was not in their command. Enduring factors include the age-specific birth and death rates for groups, migration and immigration, the political economy, governmental policies, and crime and victimization rates. The police tools—words, arrest, harassment, surveillance, and investigation—are constrained by law, custom, and resources. Yet the claim to professionalism, using statistics, science, and the rhetoric of education and training, as well as the traditional resources of tradition and awe associated with police and military, sustains public strategies and tactics and the myth of an active command-and-control front.

The claim that a police mandate based on crime control is unmanageable, or even impossible, does not sufficiently recognize the role of information technology and its spin-offs, the re-creation of imagery and information, and the direct and indirect effects of the media on the police image, police selves, and the mandate. Presently, especially in the largest cities in America, the police are agents of control whose mandate is mediated. Not only are crime and fear the leading topic for news and most features in newspapers and television, but policing itself has become more a matter of media concern—marking chiefs as celebrities, creating (or avoiding) front-page news, amplifying local scandals, and nurturing local crises that explode into national media spectacles.

The police are a compromising agency, not an eradication mechanism, but this notion collides with the binary world of television—of black and white, good and bad, failure and success, winning and losing (Fallows, 1996). The media can easily cast the criminal justice system as failed and burdened with procedures, while the media themselves can act expedi-

---

ing "effects" or impacts since attitudes are very indirect indicators of choices and behaviors, and little ethnographic work has been done on "how television means" or in what ways it achieves its many effects. While the television industry seeks audiences, and the programs are encoded and framed to engage viewers' attention, involvement and attribution appear to vary by gender and perhaps age and class (Taylor and Mullan, 1986; Press, 1991). Television is a grand dreamy projective screen on which things, selves, hopes, fantasies, dreams, realities, and constraints are seen. Not all the fantasies, ideological readings, and consumatory needs are produced by the industry. Perhaps most relevant to the analysis in this chapter is Gitlin (1980).

ently, staging their own "trials" and producing "gonzo justice" by intervening in and shaping the options of the accused at every point in the criminal justice process, especially prior to the arrest and charge of suspects
(Altheide, 1993, 1997).

While serving the state, the police also have a role in sustaining the pattern of social capital in a society and in maintaining their own credibility
and power. Clearly, the police perform controlling functions, ordering
both vertical and horizontal social relations. These ordering dynamics enable the realization of claims to the mandate. While in the past policing
functions, except for the occasional scandal, largely remained unseen, visible only to a few people with whom the police had steady contact, they are
now periodically visible and can be monitored almost daily in the media.
Note, however, that the content of the social "threat" and "disorder" that
loom visually shifts while the form (criminal sanctioning) and direction
(down) of governmental social control remains (Black, 1976, 1996). Thus,
the study of collective behavior supports an analysis of policing's rising
and falling fortunes and targets. The most important point about the shifting nature of police concerns is that their support of state interests does
not consistently wed them to the past, nor to the suppression of marginalized groups. They rather focus on either rising or falling groups as they
threaten the state's legitimate monopoly on violence and symbolic capital.
Police produce a public imagery of their activities grounded on an underlying commitment to and loyalty toward the status quo ante, whatever that
might be. This consistently places them personally in awkward positions,
when they must confront middle-class citizens in order situations, or in
traffic control, potential conflict with their "respectable audiences," and
they must police some public occasions, such as demonstrations and
strikes that they might personally condemn.

Notional independence is somehow associated with the law and justice
so that police passively undermine other efforts to make them more publicly accountable and selectively target groups for active control and intervention using the criminal sanction. The symbolic capital of the police
(collective belief in their credibility and in their legitimacy within the social order as well as the goodwill and resources they are able to mobilize)
results from maintaining the present pattern of vertical and horizontal ordering, and this is implicit in the contract between police and society. By
maintaining moral boundaries as they are drawn by the powerful (Bourdieu, 1977), the police sustain their own legitimacy.

Rarely, primarily in time of political upheaval, revolt, revolution, and
war, is the rather subtle management of order sustained by policing re-

vealed (Wakeman, 1995, 1996); institutional blindness grants the police prima facie credibility. The shifting focus of policing actions is obscured because the media in general rely upon and reproduce the official versions of incidents that they transform into stories (Lawrence, 2000: chap. 1).

In effect, the symbolic capital of the police is multifunctional. The police in their many functions mark the boundaries of society as seen by the powerful; by so doing, they reduce the social capital of the marginal groups. This is often done tacitly without awareness of the consequences of their policies or actions, and given the pragmatism of the police, they are frequently surprised at public concern or outcries such as those associated with the Giuliani policies in New York City concerning pornography, the homeless, panhandling, and jaywalking (Manning, 2001b).

THE MEDIA AND THE MANDATE

The media both glorify policing and seek to demystify and erode its authority by depicting it as brutal, violent, inept, or incompetent. That these may be incompatible has no lasting consequence. Mass media, however, set public expectations, amplifying scandal and police crimes, misconduct, and rule violation, as well as glorifying their ambiguous and sometimes liminal status (Chan, 1996; Surette, 1998; Kappeler, Sluder, and Alpert, 1998). Conflict between internal rules, regulations, policies, and procedures and external audiences' expectations is a source of tensions, and the police attempt to mediate the contradictions in these diverse expectations. Since the police claim absolute control and responsibility for public order (Young, 1995), police scandal, misconduct, and illegality are explosive: they raise questions about the veridicality of police claims and the safety and security of the community policed and undermine police sense of control, credibility, and competence. The relative role of the police in social control is left unexamined.

The police—their mandate shaped by changing urban conditions, their technology, and new modes of crime and social control brought about by new technologies—are working at regrounding themselves. Modern policing is an anomaly, for its traditions draw on medieval standards of honor, service, and valor, and the modern police oscillate between acting as a rational legal arm of the state, legitimated by state authority, and a charismatic, mysterious, personalistic, quasi-bureaucratic form. As police backstage(s) are penetrated and peeled like an onion (Holdaway, 1983; Young, 1991), and the police represent new threats to privacy as they employ computers in innovative ways, they are being stripped of the authority that arises from mystery, social distance, and idealization of performance that were the bases for everyday compliance; they are vulnerable. Understanding the interplay of social reality, risk, and tele-reality requires specification of the ways in which form and content shape public expectations and the police mandate. While the following examples illustrate some general principles of media logic (Altheide, 1997), others are less visible, implicit, and less easily studied.

Media perform an amplification function even while they add a new and growing level of risk to policing in police eyes. Media relations have become a systematic concern in large forces, rather than an ad hoc response to crises or scandals as they once were (Mawby, 2002). The media possess access to U.S. police records through the Freedom of Information Act. The police counter with complex request procedures and confidential records. The police appoint media officers and public relations agents and hire advertisers to promote their programs (Mawby, 1996). In the last ten years, the mobility of television cameras, and the resultant "live" on-scene news reports, has been enhanced by satellite uplinks that broadcast pictures worldwide. Citizens can report crimes to media and police via cellular phones, use video cameras to record crimes and disorder, and use computers to send files and information via the Internet. Journalistic ethics emphasize, especially since Watergate, antiauthoritarian and anti-institutional biases, and features of the industry, discussed below, emphasize speed, filling time on needy twenty-four-hour news channels, and blurring the line between "news" and entertainment. Easy, powerless targets, like Richard Jewell, the security guard who reported the bomb at the Atlanta Olympics and was charged with planting it by the media only to be exonerated after bringing a suit against the *Atlanta Constitution*, are easy media-created villains.

Television news in particular is a genre in which the police have preeminence. Nearly two-thirds of local news is about "crime" of various sorts (Glassner, 2000). National newspapers display less of this content, especially since the official crime rate fell in the 1990s (Blumstein and Wallman, 2000). The combination of the violence and implied violence of crime, with its putative "inexplicable" character, is attractive to viewers and stations seeking such violence, even if viewers are vexed, titillated, or shocked by it. The rarest crimes and the most unusual perpetrators are featured more than the routine crimes against property. It follows then that the most despicable crimes, violations of middle-class conventional morality, family values, and common sense are featured—incest, domestic violence, parricide, fratricide, and homicide of all sorts, and on the global scale, genocide and nationalistic and ethnic conflicts. These are the crimes about which police can do little; cannot prevent, do not see, and rarely encounter. Showing them as real, and constant, increases a sense of ambiguity, chaos, and risk. In this sense, community policing, which seeks to prevent and reassure, has aims directly contrary to those of the media (Sparks, 1992; Cavender and Bond-Maupin, 1992).

Police are perhaps experts in information control, but not experts in information gathering, synthesis, or analysis. They uneasily deal with journalists, hoping to contain or countercontain the effects of any revelation and to spin the news in their direction. Their strength lies in rendering and making redundant the "official narrative" about any problematic event involving the police (Ericson, Baranek, and Chan, 1989, 1991; Lawrence, 2000: 5). The extent to which police have information, can synthesize it, connect it to crimes and criminals, share it among themselves, and pursue criminal activity diligently is problematic, since their work remains profoundly reactive. The "reality" of television captures police as well, as actors, figures, performers, subject, and object of videos. The acontextual effects of television's treatment of crime—ahistorical, immediate, lacking depth, follow-up, analysis, or motive—makes the world a screen on which fears, hopes, and dreams, as well as risks to self and others, can be projected.

Police actions can be seen now in detail, close up and in vitro, as they unfold (or soon after), mediated by technology and separated in time and space from viewers. When shown on television, the police do not produce conjoint or shared emotional responses, even though they may elicit feelings of awe, respect, deference, or even mystery. The context has been changed. When reproduced visually by electronic means, scenes in which police authority is asserted have been symbolically transformed. Their power is not based on face-to-face interaction and lacks ritual context. One substitute for emotional identification and ritual solidarity as sources of compliance is authoritatively administered violence (Rappaport, 1971). Violence fills in for the absent. As the King film well illustrates, the application of democratic authority, especially violence, creates paradoxes, since power exists as long as it is not exercised. To maintain authority, the police routinely use coercive force, and out of context on television, the police appear as a dark and dangerous force: it is personal and immediate yet distant and abstract.

The implications of this news media–created environment are several. Police are seen more by the public and perhaps, using their new technologies, they see more. The media engage in more actions that debunk and penetrate backstage of policing. The media appear to believe that it is now their moral duty to penetrate privacy, reveal the backstage, and lay bare the little protections we offer one another in private.

COMMENT

From a theoretic point of view, pictures of or statements about policing as a system of social control are transformations in some fashion of the primary reality of police work. They are second-order observations. We do not know systematically how the increase in media attention and programs (Perlmutter, 2000: appendix) affects officers' behavior. In many ways, this impact can merely be indicated, or suggested, as I do in chapter four. When officers talk about their work, they can rekey it in many ways from that primary reality, and cues are available in that context to pin down the meaning or the frame employed. Language, of course, is always a double representation since it represents the speaker as well as what is spoken about (Bourdieu and Wacquant, 1992: 14). Thus, framing in the face-to-face context allows shared meaning to be checked against cues, negative evidence, and routine troubles within the frame (Goffman, 1974). The institutional structures within which the frame is located pattern and constrain choice and meanings. The symbolic capital of the powerful is safeguarded.

Media depictions, statements about policing as well as pictures of police work, variously framed, create the potential for paradox. Consider for example a picture of police smiling and talking to children on a playground, thus regrounding or defining police actions as charitable and altruistic. The meaning of this framing cannot be validated by the viewer because relevant cues and stimuli indicating whether this is reality may not be visible, can be edited out, or are not credible to viewers. In everyday life, close monitoring occurs. Framing validates the intended transformations of primary reality, but media framing, which favors the selective, ironic, and entertaining, often contradicts the experience of watchers including the police.

Reconsider now the arguments in the first chapter concerning the impact of television, especially interactions between television's institutional biases, form, content, and perspective, and viewers' perceptions. The reflexivity produces selectively induced blindness of the constraints of social structure. Local knowledge and direct personal experience are declining in importance in socialization, relative to media experiences. Television's display of expression, or play with the simulation of intimacy, potentially has alienating consequences. Television inverts, or at least blurs, distinctions between appropriate public and private relationships, in part because the information normally restricted to those settings is now widely disseminated by mass media. Mediated policing coexists with the natural events called policing, and both shape social control processes and the management of risk. None of this can be easily captured, so I suggest the power of frame analysis to suggest some further directions and research.

FOUR

THE DYNAMICS OF POLICE REFLECTION

INTRODUCTION

Changes in Anglo-American societies have produced contingencies to which the police have responded. These new and different kinds of contingencies have dramatic potential in their challenge and the response. While attention has been given to the impacts of surface changes such as the rhetoric of community policing, the reflexivity—connections between social change, the media, and the dance of images, including satellite-based television, the World Wide Web, the Internet, and commercial television—has not been well understood. The problem thus far is in many respects how to capture the impact of changing imagery, technology, and mediated communication and what impact this might have on policing. In the context of social change, the media role, when one includes the World Wide Web and related new forms of electronic communication, have expanded more than it is possible to fully understand. Police are to some unknown extent aware of media-generated expectations (Perlmutter, 2000). However, as Reiner (1997) points out, because of the blurred content and emergent genres in television, it is difficult to establish empirically whether the "content" of television includes more or less "crime-oriented" programs and what this means to viewers.

This chapter, using frame analysis, considers how policing is "seen," what the dynamics of this seeing are, and how the image(s) of policing has changed in the last thirty years. It is part of the movement toward mediated social control and its effects. The bulk of the chapter is given over to a frame analysis of how policing is shown. Using Goffman's *Frame Anal-*

ysis, I argue that policing is framed in four quite distinctive ways (recall the discussion in chapter 1). My aim in describing these ways of keying, and their internal and external variants, as well as the police-media dialogue, is to suggest changes in the complexity of the *visual environment* of modern policing.

- First, images may be keyed as "technical redoings," or transformation of the meaning of the images both by the mass media and by the police themselves. Such keyed images are shown on the mass media on news films of "on-the-scene" hostage negotiations, shoot-outs, and chases and are shown in police departments themselves as a form of monitoring and reviewing performances.
- Second, images may be shown as a form of "regrounding" of imagery. This results when motivations are reestablished by altering readings of the motivations of the figures shown. This occurs on the *Cops* television program and in police reshowing of visual evidence for use in court.
- Third, images are shown keyed as drama, dramatization, or scripted and planned re-presentations.
- Fourth and finally, images are keyed and rekeyed, as when policing is shown and talked about in chat rooms and Web sites used by the police and others for discourse about policing. I then discuss media-police relations and looping, reshowing images in new contexts, and the impact of police-staged realities such as the perp walk (the filmed escort of accused persons entering or leaving court) and the filmed warrant serving or dramatic search.

WHAT HAS CHANGED IN THE DANCE OF IMAGERY?

The imagery of policing is dancelike, but invisibly choreographed. Policing, of course, exists in at least two ways for everyone. First, it exists as an abstracted, distant representation with many connotations and denotations, an idea touched off by the word "police." This kind of knowledge is abstract and may be grounded by news stories, headlines, *People Magazine*, or the tabloids. Second, policing exists concretely either as memories and stories told to the police or as personal encounters experienced directly. This is what has happened to a person, their friends and relatives, in the course of their lives. One is the abstraction that patterns the mandate and the other is concrete and personal, but both shape public responses to police and policing. These two may not be consistent, and in this inconsistency lies a fundamental source of contradictions and public reactions to events. Granted that some considerable group of people have direct knowledge of police through friendships, kinship, or neighborhood, but most of what one knows comes from the media in the several genres now available—news, features, infotainments, shows featuring simulation and re-creations of policing like *Cops*, and dramatic shows. Blurred genres (books based on movies scripts, adapted from "real life"); docudramas combining dramatizations, reported events, and events that might have happened; edited pictures that show incongruous juxtapositions (Elvis Presley seated next to the Mona Lisa at the Last Supper); malleable forms (audio books) and confusing content (important local news is Dan Rather being sent to Afghanistan followed by a marathon runner with cancer, and ten minutes about the weather) manipulated by the mass media—all of these have become more diverse. Their social reality and consequence are problematic. Metaphorically, I refer to these changes as a "dance of images," a configuration that now surrounds us. The array of images that are available shape society's *sense of policing* as well as documenting policing practices. In this sense, the structure of images expands the range of attributions and meanings the public have of the police role, the mandate and conception of their duties.

This argument concerning the role of the dance of images at very least requires a review of the relationships between the media and social realities. I imagine a loosely articulated feedback model of media, social structure, and sentiments. In a communicational dramaturgical perspective, feedback loops are important because they provide the basis for reflection, correction, and revision. I take up here how recent changes have patterned the production of images, the experiencing of images, their content, the impacts of media on consciousness, the powerful effects of media's recycling of its own images and the tensions between the form and content of images. This outline will prefigure the next topics of the chapter, the growing role of mediated social control and the particular way in which images of policing both issue from and shape policing.

Image Production and Distribution

Images of all kinds are an effective way to communicate across time and space to diverse groups. The technologies of image production and the television industry are driven by economics and profit, providing entertainment as a commercial vehicle in a timely fashion, and with some sensitivity to "what sells" (Gitlin, 1983). The news, in particular, is a special, stylized, compacted, edited, formatted, and illusory type of television program (Gans, 1979). The news is something that is different, odd, or notable today. It is the retailing of differences, not facts, or even stories. The news is constructed from natural events, processed by the rules of the art of making a "good story" (Lawrence, 2000: 100–110), and generally concerned with the episodic, the brief, and matters that can be understood without an explicit context, background, or history. The "newsworthy" is identified in terms of its purported "story potential" rather than the contours of the natural event (Lawrence, 2000: chap. 5; Gans, 1979). Because the matters of interest are based on "beats," or contacts with official sources, most news becomes routinized (80 percent of the sources in elite newspapers are officials; Lawrence, 2000: 44) and reflects the efforts, through information concealing and spin, of the "official," sanitized, and normalized narrative (Lawrence, 2000). This means, however, that unexpected, nonroutine events—such as the Exxon Valdez oil spill, the Rodney King beating, the Stephen Lawrence investigation in London, and the repatriation of Elian Gonzalez—are not easily normalized. They may upset agendas, raise questions, and produce a concern for larger issues such as background, systemic causes, and solutions or reforms. Some of these events are filmed in situ, while others are reported later, and include film, photos, and live reports. The event in the natural world, my initial interest here, something concerning policing, is transformed by the sources and stories created, the technology of production, and the norms of journalism (assuming that these are relevant to celebrity interviewers, talking heads, and newscasters) and ultimately what sells.

Experiencing Images

It is well known that the direction of influence is not entirely from the media to the person or group and that past experience and memory shape the impact of images on viewers. Audiences are affected by media productions, but they also shape them in some indirect fashion by buying books, videos, and souvenirs, seeing films and plays, watching more television, and talking about it. There is constant resonance of media experience that is measured by surveys—marketing research, research on advertising and consumption—and shapes the choices presented to the audiences. Feedback loops seen either sociologically or within a system of televised images are complex and not easily measured. Perceptions and reality are distinguished, and this in part is a function of the complexity of the image shown. Watching television is not so much "watching" as it is a multifaceted experience combining social, psychological, and group effects with the intent and form of television. Many of television's effects are registered subliminally (Sparks 1992; Loader, 1997) or at least protoverbally, so that it cannot be easily captured and retrieved via words with precise, denotative terms and references. The meaning of watching, as noted in the previous chapter, varies widely by age, gender, class, and ethnicity (Press, 1991). Much watching is merely "being around" the picture, the sound, and the bleating commercials. Life goes on while TV chatters. Not all watching is active; the screen and sound may be merely background noise, a comforting occasional distraction, something that is just there. Sometimes, as one person said to me recently, "the television is watching you." On balance, of course, television is something of an ambiguous-context-bound set of messages—the stimulus or imagery is read off variously, sometimes as a source of displacement for vague fears, hopes, and anxieties, a calming influence for some, and a tense-anxious interlude for others (Sparks, 1992; Chricos, Padgett, and Gertz, 2000).

The Content of Images

It appears that with respect to content, the discourse of dramatic television is increasingly a discourse of fear (Altheide, 1997; Glassner, 2000) in which "crime" and crime stories of various genres play a featured, stimulating, and powerful role. Media and reflection are interwoven. Structure and sentiments are somewhat connected, but the connection is filtered through social relations; insofar as these are loose and massified, the impact of the media arguably increases. About two-thirds of the public in Britain obtain their knowledge of police through the media, without any personal experience with policing (Skogan, 1990: 18–19; Lawrence, 2000). While it is not possible to interpret the meaning of mass media in purely ideational terms because of concomitant changes in social structure (class, occupational, and educational distributions), high politics and governmental policies, and the economy that influence meanings, many media themes can be explicated, such as the high percentage of shows on television that are police stories (Perlmutter, 2000: 33–34). Whatever the content and form, the attitude of watching, like the attitude of television toward itself (metaphorically, of course), is ironic and ironicizing. The fundamental ambiguity of mass media treatments on television and in the newspapers is that television particularly is essentially an ironic medium that *cannot be satirized*. It is a constant series of self-satires, ironic clichés, a "cultural echo chamber" (Purdy, 2000: 10). Purdy (2000: 10) captures this profoundly when he writes that irony prevents deep attachment to values, culture, others, even to one's self, because the attitude produces distance, distrust, and doubt that anything could really be fair, just, or true or the like. The ironic stance of television is only increased by its own self-serving internal focus, its dehumanizing and vulgar commercials, and its preoccupation with its own activities (Miller, 1998; McGibben, 1993).

The Pervasiveness of Images

There are good reasons for being very cautious about the impacts of media on consciousness. The content of television, movies, newspapers, and magazines creates responses, and the audiences, other than that of television, in turn are stratified by education, gender, and race. It cannot be obviated that the level and quality of television viewing make it the principal source of our summated knowledge of the world—it is estimated that the average American watches four to six hours a day, or at least twenty-eight hours a week. This would mean that at an average life span of seventy years (watching since age five), an average American will have watched some one hundred thousand hours of TV in a lifetime (my estimates based on Perlmutter, 2000: 33). The nature of knowledge of policing is ambiguous, on the ground and in the mediated world. Central questions in common law and practice, such as what is "excessive violence," "civility," "racism," a "hate crime," or "racial profiling," are grounded in local conventions (Bittner, 1970; Klockars, 1994; Alpert and Smith, 1994). The definition of violence is local and quasi-legal, the distribution of these violent acts is unknown, and the rhetoric and practices of institutions are designed to conceal if not distort such facts, even if they are available. It is clear, however, that dramatic, scripted television exaggerates all the processes of criminal justice in the direction of simplification of the events and crime involved; trivialization, the victory of the good over evil in a short time span (twenty to forty minutes in prime time); level and kinds of crime; the level of violence (it is higher); the status and importance of the uniformed police officer; the relevance of justice and procedure; and the chronology of events. Perlmutter's analysis of awareness by young, suburban police officers suggests that they are aware that the police do not always get their villain; that not all processed will be found guilty; and that policing is about action and violent (especially violent), direct, individualistic resolutions to disputes (Perlmutter, 2000: 121). In another sense, however, television increases the feeling of "being there" for the officer who watches cop shows on television and knows the public do as well (Perlmutter, 2000: chap. 4). Increasingly, as I discuss below, the backstage of policing is penetrated and revealed, both by actual filming and by dramatic shows, which feature the real lives of the characters.

Recycling Images

Television represents society by producing stylized images, but it also represents images. Once an image is captured, it can be edited, reshown in a different context, fragmented and resized, put in a new genre (from news to entertainment to sports, for example), put in new context by juxtaposition, voice-over, or narrative, and sped up or slowed. All this can be done without any visible cues (traces that can be observed in the seen product, e.g., what is erased, omitted, recolored, or edited in some fashion) remaining. It is impossible to detect with the naked eye its "original" appearance. Consider a "natural" strip of activity, such as the terrorizing of women by men in Central Park in New York City in the summer of 2000. It was filmed by spectators. Still photos were shown on TV and featured in news stories in the New York City papers, and then the spectators came forward with videos and gave them to the police. Using the films, the police identified and arrested several of the villains. The film became evidence in the indictment. The *New York Times* then ran several stories on the event—the filming of it, how the filming led to the arrest of the alleged assailants—and showed pictures of the suspects now in jail. The *New York Times* then published an op-ed piece by ex-commissioner William Bratton (June 14, 2000) smugly noting the failures of the NYPD to control crime and disorder. This directed criticism to the current commissioner, Howard Safir, elevated Bratton's stature, and recycled the incident into the high politics of the NYPD. Jack Maple, the former deputy commissioner of the NYPD, wrote a similar piece in *Newsweek* a week later. In this case, a natural event is transformed into images, still and live; the imagery is reproduced in newspapers and on television in various genres; a story is written about the event and the imagery (filming of the event by citizens), and police actions are reported. The film is used as the basis for a grand jury indictment and as evidence for the prosecution; the arrest, charge, and indictment are the basis for another story (on TV and in newspapers) and an op-ed piece; and the mediated situation is now a part of this analysis in an academic book. Once shown, any media image (for example, several minutes of news film, such as a story about a police chase and fatal crash: an example of television's "realist" genre), can be reshown in either an identical or dissimilar social context. *Context* in this case means not only the changed keying within television (see below) but a change in genre, in channel (visual to print and back), and in format. An image shown, now reshown in another context, reframed by the media, enters a *media loop.* Looping, reshaping an image, is a common and perhaps essential media practice found on news, sports and feature programs, games, and talk shows. Media images are constantly recycled, reproduced in a new context, and reexperienced. This is the basis for the argument that television is highly self-referential (Miller, 1988). In many ways, it is a closed, self-reproducing world of competition and narcissistic differences. Events, once captured in images, can be altered in so many ways that a descriptive taxonomy would be necessary to sort them out. Media representation and looping both laminate or layer realities and interweave types of experience in a single visual experience. One sees and experiences several things at once. However, while each media genre is a form of representation, the rules by which genres are framed, converted from social activity to media event, and looped differ. Transforming activity into events and events into media looping, each creates differences. The differences that communicate are within the social world of television, not of everyday life.

Both Form and Content of Images Have Effects

In striving to connect the framing of television with experience and meaning, it is important to recall that both form and content are important considerations. Television has many genres or social forms within which its content is presented. Television is itself a kind of ironic frame around the world that claims "realism." As Goffman noted, this means that television often claims to be something it is not—the natural event. If we accept that it is a frame itself, a frame that commands attention and lodges selves, it is also true that what is watched is keyed, as discussed in chapter 1 on framing, in various ways. It can be seen as a benign fabrication, or a mere source of amusement, or as some transformation from the natural world that connotes other sorts of social reality. These realities range from drama, scripted and mannered, play or sport, through regroundings and technical redoings, as discussed below. Television presents and re-presents itself as many things—drama, news of a kind, live broadcasts (of sports and disasters primarily), docudramas and infotainment; these are thoroughly and consistently mixed, often in the same program.

Perhaps the richest field to illustrate this is the pre-9/11 preoccupation with the blurred lines between life and media realities. Some recent films and television programs illustrate further framing complexities and show the ability of the media to defend themselves by making ironic comment on their own tastelessness and intrusiveness. Television and the movies speak of themselves to themselves, while simulating concern for the average person who is a figure in the drama. Consider some examples of this. In *The Truman Show* (1998) the hero discovers that he has been and continues to be the subject of a TV show. Truman, a happy life insurance salesman in a seaside community in Florida that is actually a film set, does not believe that he is unaware of his life, which is in fact being framed as "make believe" by movie producers. The film shows people watching Truman on television as he goes about his business and passing comments on him. Then the viewer is watching him as if he were an actor in the film. Here, a key, a television drama, is rekeyed as a film of a television drama the hero of which believes he is merely "being himself." In *Ed TV* (1999), a blue-collar worker becomes the paid subject of around-the-clock filming of his life on a "reality program" that runs commercials below the picture, even during his love scenes with his brother's once-girlfriend. His "real life" and his "reel life" become entangled, and the meretriciousness of the TV executives is highlighted. They are scandalized that he feels his "acting" violates his privacy. *It's Garry Shandling's Show* (1986–90) was a comedy shown on cable TV that featured a talk show host appearing on cable TV. This show was keyed as a drama, in which a comedian and talk show host plays a comedian and talk show host on television. A slightly less complicated TV show is *Home Improvement* (1991–99), in which a comedian plays a home improvement expert on TV. In the spring of 2000, several "reality shows" were very popular on American TV, including *Survivor, Big Brother,* and *The House.* "Reality" shows are now divided into the twenty-four-hour running film Web site–type shows (a Dutch show being the most famous) and those that are real but edited, stylized, sequenced, set, and staged on remote islands by television networks and designed to become dramatic by virtue of the sequence of "survivors" who are voted out. This is a benign fabrication designed, within the context of television's ironicizing everything, to make money and attract viewers. Such productions are actually funded, directed, planned, designed, planned and created, edited, and cut before being shown, and, in the case of *Survivor,* were filmed at great cost in distant and exotic environments (into which film crews and television paraphernalia were brought) in order to create and sustain the appearance of reality. It was staged to appear to be something other than what it was. But what was it?

Television is in a sense a vast amplification and retracking system of images and snippets torn out of culture, time, even history. The ironic loop, or distancing from the content of images and scenes, and media recycling of images, showing and reshowing them in different and dubious unclear contexts, multiply the range of possible connotations.

MEDIATED SOCIAL CONTROL

The media, in their many forms, have become a salient means of indirect social control, or reaction to rule breaking, because they selectively affirm some rules as relevant, mark norms used to sanction "wrongdoers," and display the consequences of violating the rules. Because they are exaggerated, stylized, edited, looped, shaped by journalists' notions about a good story, the stories, whether news or dramas, bear only a tangential relationship to the messy processes that fieldwork reveals about the criminal justice system (Rubinstein, 1973; Van Maanen, 1974; Feeley, 1970; Walker, Spohn, and DeLone, 1996).

Consider now some examples of the intermixing of media, policing, and knowledge.

- In anticipation of media interest, especially in high-profile cases, the police will alert the media in advance about clues, leads, and suspects. They aim to dramatize their particular interests, rationalize their decisions, and anticipate criticisms. Thus, after the World Trade Center assault, the FBI announced it had twenty-seven strong suspects.

- The media respond to and amplify decisions in court and by the police before, during, and after the decisions are made, by interviewing police officers, attorneys, expelled jurors, and fired officials. It became normal practice to hunt down and interview jurors dismissed from the Simpson trial and show the interviews as evidence of the jury's mind.

- The media publish and/or broadcast passively received information as well as paying for interviews, evidence, and pictures. Media people directly process evidence and shape key facets of trials. Lawrence Schiller, a journalist, photographer, and writer, enhanced the audio tapes of interviews by Laura Hart McKinny of Mark Fuhrman for Judge Ito's court (Toobin, 1996). McKinny claimed they were the basis for a movie script she was writing about sexism among police in the LAPD. Schiller worked with Robert Kardashian to fashion a book and later a televised miniseries (see below). Witnesses, attorneys, jurors, and those on trial—e.g., O. J. Simpson, Marcia Clark, Mark Fuhrman, Christopher Darden, and jurors Tracy Kennedy and Michael Knox—tried and often succeeded in selling their stories.

- Key figures in criminal trials are subjects of the media, create the media "stories," are objects of media attention, and then use the law to prevent others from doing the same. Schiller persuaded Kardashian, Simpson's confidant, to reveal conversations and meetings he had attended; these become the basis for a book, *An American Tragedy*, written about the Simpson trial. This book became a television miniseries, also called *American Tragedy*, with a script written by Norman Mailer, with whom Schiller collaborated on *The Executioner's Song*, the book and film about Gary Gilmore. *American Tragedy* appeared on ABC-TV on November 12 and 15, 2000. Simpson had previously sued Kardashian in civil court in an attempt block the showing of the film and sued ABC to prevent its showing. Both cases were denied, and this information is shown on the screen at the beginning of the miniseries. A *New York Times* reporter who covered the trial plays himself and has a few lines. He wrote about the differences between the miniseries and the "actual" courtroom and his personal experiences reporting the Simpson trial in the *Times* (November 12, 2000).

- Media "talking heads" create commentary on local and national news and are part of the discourse and definition of the situation. For example, during the Simpson trial, Alan Dershowitz, a consultant attorney for the defense and a Harvard professor of law, was shown on a small screen from Boston, defending the Simpson decision and criticizing the LAPD for its errors in handling forensic evidence. Dominick Dunne, writing a roman à clef on the Simpson trial, also appeared weekly on *CBS Evening News* and mornings on ABC's *Good Morning America* as a commentator on the trial.

- Visual media are used extensively in trials as graphics and as simulations; some hearings are entirely media guided.

- Lawyers for the LAPD officers accused of beating Rodney King— Stacy Koon, Laurence Powell, Timothy Wind, and Theodore Briseno—asked the FBI to enhance the audiotape from the King beating and reedit the video of the beating taken by George Holliday from his balcony. Lawyers for the defense played portions in slow motion to the jury; segments were edited out by KTLA, a television station in Los Angeles (where it was originally shown) to emphasize King's movements toward Powell before Powell shattered King's face with his Monadnock PR-24 aluminum baton.

- Media buy stories and control the release of them over time; e.g., Lawrence Schiller bought the pictures of Gary Gilmore's execution and sold them; he also had a similar agreement about posttrial pictures with Simpson. This plan was abandoned (not for reasons of taste, but because the European satellite networks refused to buy them after public outcries were heard after the not-guilty verdict).

- Court cases are filmed, edited, and used "live" and on-line as well as edited for *Court TV.* Confessions are now shown in a TV show called *Confessions.*

- *Court TV* showed taped snippets of the beatings of King and Reginald Denny (a white truck driver beaten in the riots following the acquittal of the police who beat King) during the trial of the men who beat Denny, editing and juxtaposing the King and Denny beatings as part of the same "story."

- New technologies permit direct on-line and satellite broadcast of events—trials, chases, arrests, riots—across the world in minutes. The exchange of information by many channels on matters of social control is faster and flows through many more channels than thirty years ago.
- The media can now quickly and efficiently loop and reuse images produced for other purposes. These images can be altered without any visible evidence of change. No original exists as a basis for comparison; a digital image can be erased without a trace.
- The media coverage of important criminal justice matters in the United States ranges from news, features, interview shows, and talk shows (e.g., *Geraldo, Hard Ball*) to feature films, miniseries, documentaries, and combinations of images impossible to verify. Film from actual news is used within the context of feature films. Meaningless, banal labels such as "suggested by real events" or "based on facts" or "based on a true story" are shown preceding feature TV films.
- Through VCRs and tapes (e.g., those sold by Simpson about his trial) viewers can repeatedly watch anything.

Because television was not an immediate presence in events thirty years ago, the media could little influence and anticipate responses to "deviance" and "control," shape decisions, actively press for and determine outcomes, differentially amplify aspects of social control (exciting chases, high profile, rare events, etc.), mix genres and frames (entertainment, "reality" TV, reconstructions, and deconstructions), and shape police decisions especially in high-profile, publicly known cases (Corsiaros, 1999). There is prima facie evidence that the media set public agendas, in part by their editing and dramatizing of aspects of cases, in part by choice of "experts" and stories, especially in high-profile cases (Lawrence, 2000: chaps. 5, 7).

In short, these changes in the persuasiveness of the media and their lurking anticipatory role—both their increased presence on scenes and the increase in number of available channels and sets—are indicative of a new imagery by which we know policing. Mediated visions provide the context (often obscured intentionally) and show more crime and crime stories. They shape the process of control of "news" at every point, yet deny they are part of the social construction of the news. The media have an unquenchable thirst for trivial observations about untoward events. The media often touch off deep associations and assumptions about the nature of social order and disorder, social integration, institutions and their functions and mandates, and even vexing existential questions about the continuity and meaning of lives. They entertain, largely though superficial elevation of empty celebrity lives, excite, dramatize, and then comment on their entertainment, explore the excitement about the excitement that they have identified, and then comment upon and recycle the entertainment, the excitement, and the trivial lives. It is not clear whether the media "reflect" society's interests and feelings, or whether they produce the very things that they attribute to the "audience." The effect and impact of the media are in constant debate; what is known is the changing content of the news with respect to policing and the reflections of its work in other media and therefore what is read and seen.

HOW THE POLICE ARE REFLECTED IN THE MEDIA

Now it is possible to suggest the dynamics of police reflection using frame analysis. These processes are aspects of the mediated environment in which police work. Television links activities with produced imagery to mark the political or the exercise of power. What is needed is a perspective that links the media form and content and the often-implicit context of police imagery with its social and political role. Clearly, any frame can be violated or negated and the context of viewing can change interpretations (Press, 1991). The first division, between primary or natural activity and activity that has been rekeyed as make-believe—"television"—is certainly blurred. Furthermore, the internal dynamics of framing, how meaning is keyed and rekeyed so that a change in frame is occurring, specially in drama, can be profoundly confusing.

Any media image converts or transforms a face-to-face interaction into a *representation* of policing, but it lacks context. If we think of images of policing as "strips of activity" that are framed, or given new meaning, they can take on at least five new keyed meanings (Goffman, 1974: 47–77). In each section, I divide the uses into mass media uses and internal police uses. Within any frame, drama, technical redoings, regroundings, and other keys can be used that indicate that what is seen is variously a "contest" (man against the elements; detectives against the villain); a ceremonial encounter (a confrontation of good versus evil in the form of police and criminals); a technical redoing (keyings can be contained inside each other, as the above suggests); a make-believe play keyed as a contest between good and evil (by narrative voice-over); a demonstration of the utility of helicopter pursuit; and an entertainment (shown on *The Wildest Police Chases*). These are audience-based inferences about how a strip of imagery is interpreted. While dramatic renderings are the most common keying, technical redoings and regroundings are more subtle ways in which one kind of reality is transformed into another.

Technical Redoings

Some images of the police are framed as technical redoings (Goffman, 1974: 58), in which activities are transformed by being filmed and given another meaning. They are rekeyed as having a meaning other than that intended in the original filming. Included here are surveillance films of both police on duty and citizens; fixed monitoring of citizens (CCTV); court TV used for documenting decisions; police filming of raids, warrant servings, crime scenes, and evidence; tapings of interrogations, bookings, and stings; citizens' videos that become "evidence"; and filming of police scenes (chases, hostage situations, beatings, crime scenes) by news cameras either on foot, in vehicles, or in the air.

REDOINGS IN THE MASS MEDIA. Police appear frequently in the local nightly news.[1] They are figures of authority in their work roles and frequently appear in uniform (although detectives, whose "uniforms" are plain clothes, are most likely to be shown) and in televised versions of their work, both fictional and actual. At the scene of an emergency, police and other agents of control (soldiers, fire personnel, EMS technicians, and ambulance drivers) are typically asked by a "reporter" to explain "for our viewers" what has happened, what is happening, what will happen, and why it has happened. Respondents produce an idealization of their actions, often followed by a cynical media portrayal of the trusted authority's incompetence, failings, or misconduct (Surette, 1998: 14). There is an ongoing tension between reliance on officials and official narratives that simplify and compress complexity and the antiauthoritarian norms of public service, exposé, and crusading journalism (Ericson, Baranek, and Chan, 1989, 1991; Mawby, 1999).

Most news is routinized by institutional forces, the discourse about crime that is dominant, and the limits upon knowledge due to information control of the police and other officials. When an event becomes widely known and repeatedly featured, reshown, and written about, it becomes a basis for agenda setting and for broader reconsideration of practices. Some events become widely known via actual media filming on the spot, some by videos made by citizens or police themselves, and some as a result of media explosions of attention when the "story" breaks. The root source and the

1. This section has been influenced and shaped by my reading, very late in the day, of the very careful and impressive work of Regina Lawrence (2000) on the politics of force.

media response differs when an event is prominent in itself rather than merely the product of "news gathering as usual." Clearly, the beating of Rodney King was one of these events.

The past ten years have seen at least ten scenes of these types shown and reshown as part of a story line that counters official normalization (Lawrence, 2000). I include in this number some shown live, such as the Riverside helicopter chase (December 1998) filmed by a news helicopter; the beating of a black man by some twenty officers in Philadelphia prior to the Republican convention in July 2000; the shooting in San Diego of a suspect televised by a television helicopter; and the 1997 Cincinnati beating (Kaminski and Jefferies, 1997). Some were filmed and shown later, such as the Central Park terrorizing of women, and some became media events after the fact. These include an number of shootings of unarmed citizens: the Riverside incident involving Tyisha Miller in January 1999; the shooting of Amadou Diallo, an unarmed African immigrant, forty-one times in January 1999; and the Patrick Descombes shooting. Two unarmed Hispanics were pulled over and shot dead in New Jersey, one incident in the racial profiling drama in that state. Other events widely described by the media were the sodomizing of Abner Louima; deaths in custody (see chapter 9); and the unfolding Perez scandal (revelations of corruption, planting guns, perjured testimony, and criminal indictments of officers on drug dealing, bank robbery, and assault in 2000) in the LAPD. These events—big theater—are now more present as a result of the mobility and rapidity of media work—new helicopters on scenes, handheld cameras, satellite feeds, and new rapaciousness for "news" to fill twenty-four-hour stations and CNN-like channels. The events more quickly become big theater. These are seen as real representations of policing, part of the larger picture of policing in general. The images and discourse are looped and seen again and again, used in feature films, court television, news programs, and movies, and discussed on talk and interview shows. They are international events, shown worldwide within hours of their occurrence. Yet they retain, I would argue, fundamental ambiguity because of the complex stimuli the media bury such "stories" in and the distrust of the media by the public, patterned by race, class, and gender. The reality of policing in this way is a mediated reality and must be seen as such.

One example of this—the media response to the events, a few stories, and then a gaping silence, as in the case of the Louima beating—cannot be disentangled easily from the rapture of the New York papers with Bratton's "crime war" and Giuliani's support of policing. However, when crime was reportedly less, rapture was reduced and demonstrations emerged against the police after the savaging of Diallo. Violent incidents are generally seen as exceptions and not representative, the product of a few bad cops, aberrant, and something for which swift and sure punishment will provide a remedy. They can be seen as fundamental signs of violence, corruption, racism, and ill-supervised police who are part of a larger pattern of institutional racism, once one considers several of the fundamentally defining features of the events: they all came to public attention and led to media explosions, investigations, indictments, arrests, and court cases, all (except the Philadelphia beating) involve white police officers shooting, killing, beating, or torturing young men of color. With the exception of the two officers convicted in the King beating and the two in the Louima rape, either all the officers were found not guilty or the charges were dismissed. If the circumstances were reversed, white citizens being set upon by officers of color, or shot by officers in color in "gang squads" or "tac squads," it is unlikely that public and judicial opinion would be so consistently supportive of police violence.

INTERNAL POLICE USE OF REDOINGS. The police use of videos instituted for one purpose and in due time serving another indicates the influence of visuals on controlling, evaluating, and providing police services. Traffic stops for drunk driving (captured once an officer with a video camera mounted in the car stops a driver) are used as deterrents and controls upon an officer's behavior.

Filming of police work serves to monitor the police as well as citizens. Cameras have been used for more than twenty years to surveil police charge offices, jail cells, and holding rooms. Stationary cameras view the inside of jail cells and lobbies. Films and video are now used in routine police work—booking prisoners into jail, transmitting images and records from police stations to court or jail, sending fingerprints and photos electronically to the FBI, and filming police raids and critical incidents.

Films can be used to support police claims, deny liability, establish evidence, and influence juries. Some police actions are filmed outside the car. The South Carolina incident (discussed below) was inadvertently filmed from the patrol car of the officer who assaulted a black woman. He was shown dragging her out of her car after stopping her on a highway. New Jersey State Police promised to have video cameras in all their vehicles after "race profiling" was charged (*New York Times*, June 16, 1998). Florida's Volusia County and Maryland state troopers and police in thirteen states and over three thousand jurisdictions are being monitored for the proportion of blacks stopped (Jack McDevitt, personal communication, October 7, 2002). The issue of racial profiling continues to be debated, in part on the basis of data gathered by the police on their stops.

Four Detroit-area police departments have microphones and cameras in at least one patrol car. Statewide, it was estimated that 25 percent of the cars are video equipped (*Detroit Free Press*, March 26, 1995). Videotapes are also used for supervisory and disciplinary purposes if a citizen complaint is made.

Police increasingly use mobile digital terminals (MDTs) that combine a screen, a computer, and a handheld microphone (it serves as either a radio or a telephone) (see the next chapter). Rather than hearing information sent and returned via the radio, officers now see their inquiries as well as responses to them on one of several screens (with menus) accessible in their vehicles. Unlike radio transmissions that anyone tuned to the police band can hear, MDT transmissions are seen only on the sender's, the immediate backup's, and the recipient's screens. The calls and their disposition can be brought up on the screen by other officers—a parallel to listening to the assignments on the radio. The work of police patrol, people work that is sensory at base and was once done almost entirely face to face (Rubinstein, 1973: 224–25), as a result of MDTs, cellular phones, radios, and laptop computers linked to mainframe computer records, is now in part electronically mediated and experienced at the second remove by police.

Police also use video cameras to monitor public and quasi-public citizen behavior. Quasi-public behavior is now captured without permission by cameras in many settings; shopping and traveling are filmed by cameras, mounted and often hidden. Cameras film people in shops, subways, parks, train stations, squares, supermarket parking lots, and malls, and at stop signs and lights. Some surveillance is temporary, such as that of crowds at a demonstration, strike, or riot, and some is semipermanent, such as the video cameras installed in Washington Square in Greenwich Village, and at all ATMs, convenience stores, and banks. The tapes are used to identify and circularize pictures of suspects and as evidence in court. Leisure activities (such as at football matches and in parks) are filmed often by hidden cameras and used in zero-tolerance campaigns to suppress "disorder." Such secretly filmed records, edited and monitored, may be used to find villains, shown for purposes of identifying and naming suspects, and used in court as evidence. CCTV in England has been used to monitor bus stops, train stations, town squares, and other busy places, in part as deterrence and in part as a data-gathering and prosecution screening device (Brown, 1995; Norris, Moran, and Armstrong, 1998; Haggerty, Huey, and Ericson, 2000; Newburn and Hayman, 2002). Jones and Newburn (1998: 62) cite an estimate of more than 150,000 CCTV or public surveillance cameras in operation in the UK.

Regroundings

Some police images are framed as regroundings, or transformations of the meaning of the scene, by altering the purpose of the film with reference to the *motivation* of the participants and the audience (Goffman, 1974: 74). Regroundings in the media are such things as the use of police images in feature stories and talk shows; films used to shame drivers (fixed points at stop signs); *Cops; The Wildest Police Chases;* infotainment shows; training films (illustrating how to make a traffic stop, do a surveillance, book a suspect); and by extension listservs, chat rooms, and Web sites that contain images of police in action and other police activities. Some television shows use "real police work" to demonstrate, e.g., how forensic evidence is evaluated. Policing is regrounded as activity performed to entertain, as in *Rescue 911*'s confusing reconstructions of rescues using voice-over, actors, bits of film, simulated sets, and dramatic, tension-producing music.

THE MASS MEDIA'S USE OF REGROUNDINGS. Police infotainment shows such as *Cops* sustain the framing of police work as real (Surette, 1998: 67, lists ten such programs from 1989–91). These shows are simulations, stylized, designed, and marketed versions of policing, commercial products, not cinema verité. Brief, often violent and dramatic, episodes are selected from hours of film to display producers' notions of what the public wants to see. The *Cops* show is actually a theatrical performance, a simulation of police work. The presented shows are carefully edited portraits featuring selected scenes chosen by the producers of the show, censored by the officers shown, and reviewed and edited by senior administrative officers in the departments in which the episodes are filmed (Hallett and Powell, 1995). Scenes of police violence, racism, and incompetence are edited out, and the sound and pictures are modified to obscure the most brutal scenes and exchanges. Edited versions of chases and encounters "too hot" for TV are sold via ads on television and the Internet at the *Cops* Web site (www.Cops.com). An analogous program on "live" policing is shown nationally by CBC, the Canadian national television service.

Somewhat less edited and stylized, but drama nevertheless, because they are filmed for that purpose, are two types of shows. The first is the "fly on the wall," a genre quite popular in Australia (Hatty, 1996; Chan, 1996) and the UK. Examples include Frederick Waisman's films of policing in Kansas City, Graef's (1982) *Police* series, Fleming's (1995) *Scotland Yard*, and Beriff's (1994) *The Nick*. In December 2000 (James, 2000), an edited, stylized docudrama, complete with music—"a structure that copies episodic television" of the NYPD homicide squads in Brooklyn—was presented in a three-part "reality series." The reporter wrote, "[if the se-ries] weren't so artful it wouldn't be disturbing; unenhanced reality, how-ever upsetting, rarely makes great television." This "enhanced reality" erases the line between reality and fiction. The most famous of these is an Australian film, *Cop It Sweet*, that showed brutal beatings of aboriginal people. Roger Graef's *Police* followed officers, some on the drug squad, planning strategies and tactics, and executing them through several weeks of episodes. A second, similar genre, also unseen in American prime time, is "real time" policing shown as it happens. Such a series of programs on policing in London, Manchester, Hampshire, and Newcastle was shown on London's ITV as *Police Action Live* (the tape was delayed thirteen sec-onds to allow censoring if needed). This is the cinema verité approach of having a camera accompany officers in their work. The London showing of policing on the streets was well received although it showed the boring and mundane aspects of patrol in a large, lively city. It was not repeated, al-though public reception was positive (Mawby, 1996). This same approach is used in East Lansing, Michigan, where the local cable community access channel showed several hours of police patrol from the passenger's per-spective. The videotape—with raw and unedited conversation between the officer and the cameraperson accompanying the flickering, wavering pictures of substandard quality, and with noise and granularity—"spoke" realism.

INTERNAL USE OF REGROUNDINGS. Police increasingly use visual evi-dence in their work. In this sense, they are communicators, showing them-selves and their work, rather than being the object of, or communicated about by, the media and citizens. Police are aware of the power of visual evi-dence in defining and constraining their role legally and in supervising their on-the-job behavior.

The LAPD, as shown in the O. J. Simpson murder trial, uses video cameras to document possible damage done at a crime scene (most fre-quently a problem at sites of drug raids); it films the crime scene, the col-lection of evidence, and the evidence itself in major crimes. The Australian Federal Police, investigating corruption, films and makes audio tapes of all interviews with suspects using repeated cautions, films instances of brib-ing officers that are presented in court, and films the serving of all search warrants. The Royal Commission on Police Corruption in Australia in 1994 received evidence from the police and others in a "fully telematic" courtroom where visual evidence was entered, retrieved, and displayed on monitors at the tables for counsel, and where international satellite con-nections were used to gather evidence from witnesses on several continents (Nigel Hadgkiss, Australian Federal Police, personal communication, January 1999).

Policing Shown in Dramatic Images

Police images, of course, are framed also as drama, as fully scripted undertakings. Drama, the third type of transformation, is a scripted, planned, edited, stylized, designed presentation intended to produce an anticipated emotional effect on an audience. These dramatic renderings include feature films, TV films, plays, cartoons, television series and miniseries, videos produced by the police for public relations purposes (such as those done by Community Policing in San Diego), and faux training films produced as ironic reactions to actual training films (Meehan, 2000b: 108). Additional variants of this are media-police "control-containment games," police manipulation of the media, and dramatic events that leap the bounds of everyday policing and become axial media events (AMEs), or political spectacles.

DRAMATIC IMAGES OF POLICING IN THE MASS MEDIA. Policing is the subject of a varying, but large and disproportionate, number of television shows in addition to the news. It is not clear what the popularity of these shows represents. They have been dominant in the last thirty years of television, challenged in the drama genre only by Westerns and soap operas for sheer popularity. They certainly combine a socially constructed postindustrial style of risky narratives, perhaps substituting for the absence of risk and active challenge in everyday life, displacing everyday anxieties. They remain real because fear of crime is more highly correlated with television viewing time than with reported victimization (Chricos, Padgett, and Gertz, 2000).

Police programs on television vary in their content, and presumably in their influence and claims to represent "reality" or sundry realities the most common show has content rather closely connected to folk models. As Sparks notes (1992), others are more complex or innovative. The fictional policiers (police series, feature stories, and films) share a basic syntax borrowed from folktales—a syntax of problem and resolution, in this case a sequence of heroic conflicts against evil culminating in resolution through the victory of the good. As a basic social form, the police dramatic program stimulates base feelings and sentiments, generic arousal, not specific emotions. This is perhaps because the media themselves are "cool" media into which many feelings, anxieties, and hopes can be read. Television is a screen onto which one's life, dreams, hopes, and fears can be projected with impunity.

Clearly, there are subgenres of the ideal type of "police drama." For example, Mawby (1996), drawing primarily on British television, suggests one useful typology of televised police shows. Perlmutter (2000: 133–48) lists all televised shows featuring the police in 1947–94. I modify Mawby's list to include American versions of the shows when they exist. There are at least three types or subgenres of dramatic police shows: fictional police dramas (*Z-Cars, NYPD Blue, Hill Street Blues, Law and Order, Homicide,* and others); police information public service shows, shows in which crimes are depicted or reenacted with requests for the public to come forward with information (*Police 5* in the UK and *Crimestoppers* in North America); and "crime scarers," which focus on unsolved, mysterious, and unusual crimes (*America's Most Wanted* and *Unsolved Mysteries*).

Police are featured in glossy mass media Sunday inserts as heroes, complete with makeup, staging scenery, and close-up pictures in uniform. *Parade Magazine* (Wilson, 2000) showed a smiling "police officer of the year," who "battled three masked gunmen in a crowded Las Vegas bar. Outnumbered and outgunned, he fought back—even after being shot 8 times." At the bottom of the lead story is a note: "Cover photograph by James Sorenson, taken outside Flamingo Las Vegas Resort Hotel & Casino. Grooming by Jack Matthews." The shooting was in Mr. D's Sports Bar, but the picture was staged and the officer groomed in front of the Flamingo.

Inside are stories of eight other nominated officers. Their accomplishments ranged from beginning reading programs and beginning a "dad's skills" program, and rescuing a teenager in distress in a "runaway car," to throwing a grenade to protect officers on a raid and killing armed holdup men in banks and convenience stores.

Cartoons also portray police. For example, in a March 1998 cartoon in the *New Yorker,* a uniformed officer was shown in front of a shooting gallery with a sign reading "41 shots for 5 cents," a reference to the slaughter of the unarmed Amadou Diallo on the streets of New York City in February 1998.

INTERNAL POLICE USES OF DRAMATIC IMAGES. Some police visuals are used for fairly banal public relations. For example, the Portland Police Bureau (Oregon) (http://www.portlandpolicebureau.com) and many others maintain Web sites that include maps, diagrams, statistics, and pictures. The FBI placed some 16,000 pages of case files on the Internet at (www.fbi.gov) and plans to post a total of 1.3 million pages. This is said to serve public requesting information under the Freedom of Information Act. The FBI also has a hyperlink to its stolen art Web site (www.fbi.gov/majcases/artheft/art.htm). The San Diego City Police (www.sannet.gov/

poli) and Chicago Police Department (http://www.ci.chi.il.us/CommunityPolicing) have prepared elaborate videos to be given out to publicize their community policing programs. The Chicago police have a large media budget for advertising on radio and television, preparing and distributing their tapes to neighborhood associations and the media. A recent article on police Web sites, now prominent among some two hundred million Web sites registered with search engines, showed they were descriptive, linked mostly to the FBI, and self-promoting in their content (Dykehouse and Sigler, 2000). About 5–6 percent of criminal justice agencies maintained them as of 2001. The most linked sites were the FBI, the Police Officer's Internet Directory, and www.copnet.org.[2]

Police are using the Internet and intranet for a wide variety of functions, including posting sex offenders' names and offenses (used in Kansas); a Web site featuring people who do not pay child support; an Internet search engine (www.lawintelrpt.com) to arrestees' home addresses in Philadelphia and San Antonio (Scott, Brock, and Crawford, 2000). Lists of Web sites in law enforcement are featured in all current criminology textbooks, provided with CD-ROMs, and listed in articles (Scott, Brock, and Crawford, 2000). A number of brief handbooks list Web sites and the uses of the Internet for teaching and training (e.g., Nesbary, 1999). None of these articles explores how and why these sites are established, their use, or their applicability to everyday police work.

Not all police use of visuals is representational in the direct sense; some rely on abstraction and simulation to depict crime, calls for service, or the social characteristics of an area. Some city police (e.g., those in Lansing, Michigan; San Diego, California; Dallas and Austin, Texas; and Chicago, Illinois) are using geo-mapping of call or crime reports to produce graphics, tables, and maps of crimes, calls for service, and neighborhood characteristics, thus rendering microscopically the aesthetics of a "neighborhood," police precinct, or entire city. These visuals are used to inform citizens of their current problems at neighborhood meetings.

Police training uses visual and audiotapes. Training is a way of framing instances of misconduct (Goffman, 1974). Horrendous and humorous examples of officer-citizen interactions have been taped and circulated among police departments and are somewhere between rehearsals, training, and demonstrations. They can be seen as technical regroundings, as drama, or as redoings (Meehan, 2000b: 110; Goffman, 1974: chap. 3). At least two publishers—Prentice Hall and Wadsworth—now offer interactive CD-ROM-based training devices, and a training Web site has been

---

2. See also www.officer.com, a police resource Web site.

posted (www.crimescenes.com). These films and interactive CD-ROMs
walk the viewer through crime scenes, asking them for solutions, referring
them to relevant databases, and focus on presenting a case for indictment
in court.

A mixed-genre approach is taken by police in Lansing, Michigan, where
a cable television program, *Join the Team,* is shown. It is composed of segments—films of a ride-along with a Lansing officer, safety tips, and a
question-and-answer segment where citizens can express their concerns.
The question segment is created by city employees going to neighborhoods with handheld cameras and filming citizens' questions that are then
answered by officers in the studio when the show is being produced. It also
has "skits," or semidrafted topical acting out of right and wrong ways to respond to drinking, trick-or-treating, and holiday shopping.

INTERACTIVE IMAGES. A fourth type of framing of police images occurs
in newsrooms, chat rooms, and interactive Web site with policing as a topic
where exchanges are playful or disconnected from an explicit instrumental aim or goal. Because one is free to choose identities and names in most
of them (some are controlled by passwords and security devices and limited to members and subscribers), communication takes place as play
(J. Young, 1999, on alt.law-enforcement), and pictures, sound, and words
are exchanged.

POLICE–MEDIA RELATIONS

Police manipulate media and vice-versa, but the police have grown in skill,
in resources, and in willingness to engage with and to engage the media in
the last thirty years or so. They now anticipate public reactions and try to
manage "damage control" (Chan, 1996), engage in media contests, stage
events for the media to use, and are changed by media criticism.

In the *Report of the President's Crime Commission* (1967) and in *Criminal
Justice Standards and Goals* (1973), the police were urged to appoint media
officers to improve police-media relations. In part this arose from the violent, undisciplined, and publicly revealed police riots (Stark, 1970) of the
late 1960s. The assumptions of government spokespeople were, it appears,
that more information is better, that framing events in the best interests of
the police would improve their media relations, and that in the nature of
things, more interaction and exchange would be to the advantage of the
police (Latterell, 2000). These are, of course, highly moot points. In the
last thirty years, the police have added training for filmed appearances,
media spokespersons, and audio- and videotapes as part of public infor-

mation for newspapers and television, and faxes, e-mails, and attachments for rapid transmission of information to the public.

According to Mawby's (1999: 281) survey of police in the UK, the police approach to the media is becoming more "proactive" and less reactive. Some cities send police information officers directly to scenes to preempt if possible the framing of the activity as the media begin their search for a "story" (Latterell, 2000). While media have monitored police calls on scanners for many years, the police now monitor the media. The most elaborate example of police media monitoring is the twenty-four-hour pressroom in Scotland Yard, the London Metropolitan Police Headquarters, which includes on one wall a bank of televisions monitoring national and international news coverage. Three facets of police-media relations are distinguished here—direct consulting with the media in their dramatic presentations; contests with the media; and direct manipulation of the media with respect to technical redoing called "news."

Police Advising the Media on the Dramatic Construction of Policing

The first television programs in which it was publicly known that the police advised the producers were Jack Webb's productions featuring the LAPD: *Dragnet, Adam 12,* and *Badge 714* (still being shown in reruns). LAPD chiefs "Jack" Hormel and William Parker advised Webb about the image of the LAPD they required to be portrayed. In exchange, the LAPD supplied technical assistance for the production of the shows (Gates, 1996: 325–26). When he became chief of the LAPD, Parker hired the first police department press relations officer in 1951 (Gates, 1996: 44). Chief Daryl Gates, perhaps ironically given his insensitivity to racism and police brutality, continued this media-sensitive tradition. According to his autobiography (1996: 326), Gates appeared as himself in at least two episodes of *Hunter* (a show about the LAPD starring ex–Rams football star Fred Dwyer) and assisted in the televised announcement of the arrest of two men charged with the beating of white truck driver Reginald Denny in the LA riots of 1992. Gates, perhaps an unusual example, appeared during his career as a serving officer, as a fictional police figure in television shows, as himself in fictional television shows, and as himself in news and news conferences called to dramatize his own decisions.

Police Contests with the Media

Police differentially release news and bulletins to one newspaper or wire service and not a competitor. They refuse at times to release information on suspects, cases, or "leads." In the early days of press relations in the London Metropolitan Police, officers in each police district, called "district liaison officers" (DLOs), were appointed to provide information to the media. They were soon nicknamed "Don't Let Ons." The police in general work to convince the media to falsely report "facts" to protect or enhance an investigation. Police also arrange press conferences to make the national news, limit the information provided on the topic, and selectively mention the assistance of other agencies (Nigel Hadgkiss, Australian Federal Police, personal communication, March 1999). Similarly, local police make tapes listing crimes to be accessed via telephone and limit reporters' access to other facts (as in Lansing, Michigan). It is not surprising that the Australian Federal Police receive training in self-presentation—how to answer questions, how to deal with the media, what to wear (even to the color of tie and shirt)—thus emphasizing the thin line between performance, acting, and self-presentation on the one hand and duties on the other (Hadgkiss, personal communication, January 1999).

Nowhere is the political nature of videos more exposed than when the police use them in media wars and political debates over their practices. The containment and countercontainment game can lead to charges that the police have intimidated the media (Lawrence, 2000: 57). Police are sensitive to and respond to media allegations with press conferences and press releases. Police have become more media-wise, using videos of criminal acts to present in court, but perhaps they have endangered their "nonpolitical" position by seeking publicity. In many respects, as Janet Chan (1996) has shown, the media orchestrate sequences of responses to negative and potentially damaging revelations that threaten the police claims to absolute propriety (Young, 1995). The police respond with "containment moves," attempts to maintain the original framing of an event, usually that of the police (Hatty, 1996; Goffman, 1974), rather than the media's readings. After his success at controlling the officially reported rate of crime in New York City, Bratton was featured on the covers of *Time* and *Newsweek* in the early months of 1996. He resigned or was fired by Mayor Giuliani because, according to *Newsweek* (April 7, 1996), he was taking too much credit for the reductions in crime in the city and had received too much publicity. There were also differences between them concerning policy and control over the police department, as Bratton himself admitted. Bratton's version (1998: 303) is not inconsistent with this reading of the politics of his stepping down.[3]

Although increasingly police undercover operations, such as stings and

3. Former police officers can engage in debate with new chiefs or commissioners as when both Bratton and his former deputy, Jack Maples, criticized Commissioner Howard Safir's handling of the Central Park incidents in op-ed pieces in the *New York Times* June 14, 2000.

crackdowns and sweeps, are filmed, filmed evidence, because it is easily modified and open to interpretation when used in criminal prosecutions, remains problematic. Even the admissibility if such evidence is questionable. The admissibility of videos from a secret taping of Mayor Marion Barry of Washington, D.C., was debated. Barry's lawyers claimed the recording was entrapment. It was debated in the media and in the courts before his conviction. The Lansing, Michigan, police in 1998 filmed the entire raid of an after-hours club, including the interviewing and booking of suspects, and released it to the local television station after complaints about brutality and civility were made by several people arrested. Warren, Michigan, police filmed the police at a hostage scene at which a schizophrenic who threatened police was shot and intended to use it to fend off civil suits by the dead man's family (this occurred during my 1996 fieldwork). In South Carolina, a state trooper was filmed by his own car-mounted camera accosting a woman in her car, opening her car door, pulling his gun, dragging her out, and then arresting her. She had apparently questioned his authority when he asked her to get out of the car. The film of the assault was shown on national television, including *Good Morning America* (GMA). The following day, the director of the South Carolina state police appeared on GMA with another videotape, showing an officer writing a ticket being sideswiped by a hit-and-run driver and knocked to the ground. Passing motorists pursued and stopped the truck driver, who was subsequently arrested. Admitting the errors of the officer shown the previous day, the director wanted to bring attention to the courage and dedication shown every day by the South Carolina State Police, and the respect they command from the average citizen (GMA, April 23, 1996). On the other hand, the police, when it is expedient, refuse to have their activities filmed and reshown in court. The Chicago Police Department in November 1998 was under pressure to film its interrogations after police failed to convict the white men charged with the murder of a young black man, but the department refused.

Police Stagings of Events for the Media

Police use and manipulate the media, and the relationship is often symbiotic. Consider some longer-term strategies, more elaborate stagings, and scriptings produced, directed, and performed by the police for the media. The police participate in media activities, some of which are planned and staged explicitly for the media, such as raids, warrant serving, "buy busts," and "street sweeps" (Gates, 1996). These then become the basis for a "live" televised "news conference."

A most dramatic instance is the "perp walk." Police often plan to "walk" a prisoner into and out of court to focus public attention on the prisoner's often-shabby appearance—humiliated and led in handcuffs, and taken and collected in a police vehicle, often with lights flashing. This is designed to show police success, increase public confidence that the police always get their man, and to reveal the shame (and guilt) of the prisoner.

These walks can backfire when the person is shown to be innocent (as was the harassed Richard Jewell, accused bomber at the Atlanta Olympics in July 1996) or is shot on the spot (as were Lee Harvey Oswald and, in 1984, Gary Doucet, an accused kidnapper and child molester) or if other untoward events occur. The case of O. J. Simpson's first arrest scene was ambiguous, as Simpson's lawyer persuaded the LAPD to take off the handcuffs they put on Simpson before they led him to the car. This was all filmed and reshown by the media.

Another strategy of the police is alerting the media to be present at an arrest or warrant-serving scene, exposing a person's police encounter to national publicity. The Royal Canadian Mounted Police frequently call the media to witness, film, and broadcast their activities and have sold the worldwide rights to their images—uniforms, pictures, souvenir icons, and films of their elaborate horsemanship show, the "musical ride," to Walt Disney (Dawson, 1998). For example, in March 1999, the RCMP, who are the provincial police in British Columbia, searched the home of Glen Clark, the province's serving premier (and the only National Democratic Party head of a provincial government in Canada at the time). The search, which was filmed by the media, was incident to an investigation of corruption in issuing a gaming license to Clark's neighbor. *The Toronto Globe and Mail* (March 4, 1999), in a media loop, printed a story about the media's presence and a picture of a distressed Clark taken through the front window of his house as the police searched. "It was not immediately clear how BCTV managed to be on hand when the RCMP arrived," said the story, but it is likely that the RCMP alerted it, either directly or indirectly. The *Globe and Mail* obtained a copy of the tape and reported that as the RCMP approached the door the cameraman turned on the high-intensity television lights and flooded the porch. "There's three from the RCMP and two media [people] behind us," the *Globe and Mail* reports that the first officer at the door announced. The television reporters said they were just in the area on the odd chance that something newsworthy might happen.

Media involvement complicates policing. In September 1998, after the London Metropolitan Police failed to find and convict the murderers of Stephen Lawrence, a black youth (Cathcart, 1999), the report on the matter that condemned the police was widely covered. Protests, led by his parents, prompted a reinvestigation, a public televised apology by Paul Condon, the commissioner of the metropolitan police, and charges of institutional racism by the media, activists, and the family of the murdered man. The family refused on television to accept the public apology of the commissioner. An investigation headed by a judge rendered strong evidence that suspects were overlooked, evidence was mishandled, and racism was present in the investigation from the beginning. These kinds of spectacles may arise regardless of the presence of filmed evidence of the matter, but the media amplify and continue the story, now using their own films and staged interviews (Reiner, 1999: 35). In another British case, media attention on the accused mass murderer Rose West was so great in 1994 that her lawyers argued (unsuccessfully) that she could not have fair trial. In the course of this investigation, journalists eavesdropped on officers in pubs, followed them, set up hot lines for clues, suggested new lines of inquiry, interfered with evidence gathering, bought stories connected to the investigation, and interviewed witnesses before the police did. As Mawby (1999: 278) summarizes: "a media-driven investigation threatened, with a press corps undertaking parallel inquiries to the police and conducting a trial by media." The converse also occurs, when media, police, and researchers become entangled. According to one fieldworker in the Ericson, Baranek, and Chan studies of media and police, the police secretly taped the interviewers' interviews and tapped the researchers' phones.

There is a limiting case in which the suspects, or victims, or targets of policing strike back and create a media event by calling a cameraman to stand ready, or use their Web sites to publish police names, addresses, and phone numbers. This active self-help was done famously in the Elian Gonzalez case, when the boy was seized to be returned to his father and eventually to Cuba. The family alerted and paid a freelance photographer to stand ready to take a picture if needed.

Six-year-old Elian Gonzalez had been rescued and brought to the United States by the Coast Guard after the boat carrying him and his mother from Cuba sank and his mother died. The police raid on a house in Miami, Florida, at dawn, April 22, 2000, to seize him and return him to his father was filmed; one key photo, reproduced locally, nationally, and internationally on television, and in newspapers, tabloids, magazines, and the elite press, shows the boy being held by an armed police officer in combat gear, including a bulletproof vest, who is pointing a semiautomatic assault rifle at two people from whom he wrenched the boy. What was the context? Who was the officer holding the boy? What police force was involved? What was the basis of the warrant? Who took the picture that was widely circulated and published on the Internet? What did this scene show? The natural event was immediately big theater. The punctuating event, ending with Elian's return to Cuba with his father, was but one of a series of scenes and acts in a long-running media-sustained melodrama-spectacle. It was a synecdoche again for police violence and terrorism (unannounced violence in the name of politics).

It was subsequently revealed that the event took place in the house of the relatives of Elian who had secreted him and refused to yield him to police after federal courts had ruled he should be returned to his father's custody, and he was being held by the fisherman who originally rescued him. Many appeals were made.

Federal officials planned the raid, expected to find weapons in the house, and armed the raiding party, which entered through a crowd of demonstrators supporting Elian's remaining in this country.

The picture was taken by a freelance photographer, Alan Diaz, who knew the family and had been invited by them to the house in anticipation of a raid; Diaz was stationed in the bedroom where Elian had been hidden. Diaz sold the picture to the Associated Press, which then sold it and distributed it. Another widely circulated picture, also by AP, shows Elian with his father in a house in Maryland, and en route to Cuba, smiling.

The pictures and the resultant dynamics of the Elian case had consequences, although at the time, the context was unexplained in media renditions of the raid. It echoed in international relations between Cuba and the United States and in Florida politics. The mayor of Miami replaced and subsequently fired the city manager, the former police chief, Donald Warshaw, for failing to inform him in advance of the raid. Warshaw was then indicted for embezzlement and fraud for using a credit card furnished him by a charity when he was chief. He had been called a heroic opponent of corruption during his time in office. The ethnicity of the participants added fuel to the conflict, bringing in the high politics of anti-Cuban forces in Miami. The new chief, Raul Martinez, was the first Cuban chief of the department. Cubans, pro- and anti-Castro forces, the local politics of ethnicity and ethnic succession in the police department, and international diplomacy were all affected. Such a case, in which the high politics of policing are touched off, is further escalated by the pictures taken, cropped, edited, and sold, appearing on the Internet, in magazines and newspapers, and on television. The pictures appeared internationally. These dramas are not entirely in police hands.

Citizens as well as the police use videos in everyday social control activities. Seeing may not be believing, but it is a powerful tool in persuasion to bring incidents to police and court attention. For example, two Michigan school districts have equipped more than half their buses with sound and video cameras that the drivers can monitor. Several citizen-produced videos have led to criminal investigations and arrests—the most famous being that of the beating of Rodney King. Recently, films have been used in criminal cases: of a burglar stealing women's underwear from a bedroom drawer and of the hazing of Marine recruits. In a more proactive mode, an African American ex–LAPD officer cruises around Los Angeles with fifteen thousand dollars worth of video equipment in his van, hoping to film an illegal stop and/or search. Citizens have used videos as a means of protecting themselves against criminal charges, the most infamous being Dr. Jack Kevorkian, the master of assisted suicide in Michigan, who has given police videos showing people killing themselves without his presence. He has not avoided being charged and tried three times for homicide. He was indicted for and subsequently convicted of second-degree murder in March 1999 because he "killed" a man with Lou Gehrig's disease and gave a copy of the videotape to the television program *60 Minutes.* The death was shown on the most popular American television show in prime time on November 22, 1998. In November 2000, an ex-radical, on trial in Los Angeles, now living in Minnesota as a housewife, posted on her personal Web site the names and addresses of officers in the LAPD involved in her case (*USA Today,* November 19, 2000). She claimed they lied about the facts in her case.[4]

FEEDBACK AND LOOPING

Having described the diachronic (time-based) and synchronic (cross-sectional) aspects of the media-police relation, I want to address some additional aspects of change that arise from this interaction.

Feedback and Change

Within the media, recycling of themes occurs. Books, such as Joseph Wambaugh's series on the LAPD, including *The New Centurions, The Choir Boys,* and the *Onion Field,* became the bases for a television series *(Police Story)* and three full-length films. Media sitcoms and action police stories are converted into TV miniseries and movies, such as movie parody

4. The repeated revelation of police mistakes on big screens and in dramas on *Court TV* weakens the protection of ideology, of institutional misrecognition in courts (Bourdieu, 1977: 5–6), and contributes to tensions within the occupational culture. Like the repeated use of sting operations, it weakens trust in the police (Marx, 1989).

of *Dragnet*. Police movies are used as the basis for TV shows, and movie scripts are adapted into books. Ex–police officers recycle themselves in new roles, playing police officers in films and on TV. As these sequences illustrate, the media amplify their own effects.

Consider examples from New York City in the early 1970s. Informants reveal corrupt officers' behavior to an NYPD internal affairs unit, and they are featured in hearings. An NYPD officer, David Durk, provides background and interviews for a series on police corruption published in the *New York Times*. A report on police corruption is published commercially (Knapp, 1972) after the city issued it. One of the informants, Frank Serpico, was featured in a book by Peter Maas, *Serpico* (1973). The book was made into a movie starring Al Pacino. Serpico was later charged with corruption himself, resigned in disgust, and commented on subsequent corruption and violence scandals in the NYPD (including the Abner Louima beating in July 1997). In the late 1970s, several officers involved in the "French Connection" case (stolen heroin evidence) resign; one, "Popeye" Doyle, is later the subject of the film, *The French Connection*. Robert Leuci, a detective on the case, turns to writing and publishing detective novels. Robert Daley, Commissioner Pat Murphy's executive commissioner (in charge of press relations) writes Murphy's biography, a police novel based loosely on his period with the NYPD, and several other novels drawing on his experience. Daley rewrites at least two of these books for feature films.

Here is another media sequence, this one based on the work of reporter David Simon of the *Baltimore Sun*. Simon wrote and published an ethnographically rich (although misleading) book, *Homicide* (1992), on a year's work of two squads of homicide detectives in Baltimore. Charting their work day by day, following a set of cases through the lengthy book (some five hundred pages), Simon produced a penetrating and realistic picture of the work. His book was reviewed in the *New Yorker*, went into a trade paperback, and eventually became the basis for a long-running television show, *Homicide*. The television program became the basis for a picture book, *The Making of Homicide* (1998). Simon worked as the chief adviser to the show. The network program *Frontline* also showed a program on the filming of one episode of *Homicide*. One of the officers he observed while writing *Homicide* became a colleague and fieldworker, coauthor of a second book, *The Corner* (Simon and Burns, 1997).

Media use of police material is adventitious, cynical, and relatively unconstrained by ethics (Fallows, 1996). If one medium reports a story, that story can be quoted as a source, considered valid "news," and discussed in other media. The veracity of the story is of no consequence, since the second story is about the first story, and responses to it, not about the events, or reported facts (if any). Newspaper stories are written about stories previously covered by other media, and that coverage is itself another iteration of "news" (Kurtz, 1998). These stories-about-stories, no more than gossip, are often highly embedded and are constituted as news, news about news, and a feature, and may be then featured on *Dateline, 20/20, Hard Copy,* or *60 Minutes.*

Media coverage may produce changes in police practice. There were claims in the media that as a result of publicity surrounding the Rodney King incident, the Los Angeles police had changed their behavior. They now have ethics discussions at roll call, at which officers are warned to be careful or "they'll be roomin' with Stacy" (Stacy Koon, the sergeant who was convicted in federal court in connection with the beating of Rodney King and served a sentence) (Herbert, 1996). There has been a reported decrease in baton beatings, use of Taser guns, and shots fired since the King beating. Data from the LAPD suggest reduced violence in arrests, reduced use of fatal force and batons, but a substantial rise in the use of pepper spray (Kappeler, Sluder, and Alpert, 1998: 269 ff.). The program *Cop It Sweet* had an important role in changing policy in New South Wales. It led to new reform legislation, changes in training practices, and attempts to control violence. The Graef film *Police* led to reform in the treatment of rape victims and was a turning point in depicting policing realistically and in a convergence of public approval and police sense of their work (Mawby, 1996: 13). It is impossible to exaggerate the impact of the video of the police beating of King on subsequent events, including the riots that followed the acquittal of three of the four officers who savagely beat him, their subsequent retrial on federal charges, the Denny trial and suit, Daryl Gates's resignation, the appointment and failure to reappoint Willie Williams as chief, and the unfolding power politics of Los Angeles. Bernard Parks, named chief after Willie Williams was not reappointed in 1998, set out to deal with corruption and fired and reassigned officers. This led to strong resistance to his reappointment by police unions. He was not reappointed, and in October 2002 William Bratton was named chief of the LAPD.

Loops and Looping

Not only does television format and frame activity, it loops and rekeys and transforms activity so that realism is a putative and relative term meaningful only in comparison to some other frame. News is now often visual (very few words are spoken in the average half-hour national network newscast), assembled from images, still pictures, graphics, and film culled, snipped, and enhanced by technicians, subeditors, and producers, and by other imaginative re-creations and simulations of newsworthy scenes, events, and conversations.

These programs in turn are looped and become the putative basis for tomorrow's news, today's differences—reported before and after being printed in the *New York Times* or the *Wall Street Journal* or *USA Today.* All of these, because they reprint unsubstantiated stories printed by other sources, participate in vulgarizing and making a cartoonlike caricature of human vicissitudes. They are then reported in slick nominally "news" magazines, such as *Maclean's, Time,* and *Newsweek,* and "feature" and human interest–based publications like *People.* The loop is joined when the stories about them and the stories about the stories are commented upon in the general-interest monthlies. These feature stories on how celebrities react(ed) to the stories and the stories written about the stories written about them in other media. This print media material about police, basically a recycling of gossip about the media itself, by Sunday is massaged by pundits on CNN, other networks, and local stations. This material, now again "new," becomes tomorrow's news (Manning, 1998). The sequences are varied. Media loops arise from the events; films resulting from the trial; stills used in feature stories, interviews created in feature stories, each becomes a kind of HTML to the other. The nightly news is used to tout feature programs, especially those with current faddish interest such as *Survivor;* and in prime time the networks feature made-for-TV films on the Waco raids and the murder of JonBenet Ramsey. Police-made film also becomes a useful loop within a media loop. Many police-produced videos, or news films, in turn, are given to television stations, looped or recycled, and shown on the news, feature programs, and documentaries.

Media consistently seek to broadcast "close-up," intimate views of "newsworthy" activities featuring violence, terror, blood, mayhem, or potential violence. These events and media events, self-reflexivity and system-reflectivity, can at times coalesce to change the social image of police as well as some aspects of themselves. Any event, it would appear, as a result of television's massive attention and impact, can be transformed from an everyday matter into an AME. These once-real-world natural events are recoded, converted using television's code, so that the boundary between personal experience, audience experience, and politics is blurred and diminished.

Media events are interwoven tightly with actual events. The revelations of misconduct via the media have become an almost essential feature of the modern definition of a "scandal." In the O. J. Simpson murder case, Detective Fuhrman testified, and subsequently was found have perjured

himself. This raises questions about the credibility of other evidence he
has presented. The media publicized it and interviewed the chief of the
LAPD, Willie Williams, who deployed damage control tactics and announced on TV that the LAPD is investigating all of Fuhrman's previous
cases. Fuhrman retired, and returned to take the Fifth Amendment. A
lawyer for a defendant now in prison as a result in part of Fuhrman's testimony filed an appellate court brief to have his client's case reheard. The
Simpson trial was a riot of media loops.

Citizen "feedback" is stimulated by the omnipresence of images. In an
unusual twist on videos, the mother of a young man saw him on local television news robbing a convenience store (captured by the store's hidden
cameras). She called the police and her son was arrested for the crime.
America's Most Wanted has led to the recognition and capture of several
wanted people every year since its inception.

Self-produced visual media also penetrate private officer-citizen relations and are reframed as prefigurative or as a warning of mistakes at work.
In this sense, videos are analogous to war stories—they capture aspects of
the work about which one should be cautious (Shearing and Ericson, 1991;
Meehan, 2000b: 112). Videotaping of violent events, for example, by
police, private citizens, and the media, is now quite common (Kappeler,
Sluder, and Alpert, 1998: 146). Citizens' taping led to police actions and
accusations of police malfeasance in the Rodney King beating and the
Central Park terrorizing crimes. The private films taken by citizens in the
Central Park episode were used to identify and subsequently arrest suspects. Political consequences, loss of appointed and elective office, suits,
civil and criminal prosecutions, and loss of credibility if not authority follow upon public showing of the film of these events. Social control, response to deviance, is exercised not only interpersonally by agents of control, but indirectly, via media and visual modalities. The responses of the
media shape institutions and institutional practices.

COMMENT

Aside from the interesting analysis of Perlmutter (2000) in a small Wisconsin town, we do not know in any detailed ethnographically grounded
fashion what this new environment of images portends for policing. What
changes in reflection are indicated by these examples of depictions, feedback, and response to policing? The technology has made rapid the dissemination of videos from police, newspeople, citizens, and other agencies
(private corporations such as banks and supermarkets). The number of
channels and sources of imagery have increased vastly, not only via cable

TV, but because of home videos, pay-per-view, DVD and laser discs, and image-producing capacity on PCs. International coverage of events is now possible, of media-created events, spectacles, and news. The content of the media has shifted toward more police shows (Perlmutter, 2000: appendix); about half the local news shown on TV is about crime, and 30 percent of local newspaper stories deal with crime. As Altheide shows (Altheide, 1997; Altheide and Michalowski, 1999), "crime" is but one of several themes in the media-generated "discourse of fear."

New genres have appeared that blur drama and other kinds of framing. A *New Yorker* cartoon ridiculed this by showing an announcer at front stage saying: "The part of the players will be taken by the audience tonight." The overall impact of this is to increase the speed, dissemination, and impact of police imagery in the last thirty years, as well as to mix me- diated and direct experiences.

Perhaps most telling of the changes in police-media relations are the police-created media events and the spectacle. The media events— the walk-out, the press conference—the differential sharing of "news," the cultivation of media "outlets" (and vice-versa), and the training and use of professional consultants to sharpen police presentations are new. These moves and countermoves in the game of media relations are not all of a piece, nor are they uniformly successful in presenting the police view of a story line (Mawby, 1999), but they are new features of policing since the early 1970s.

The ambiguity of the effects of media on policing arises from many sources. Some of them are: distrust of the media many report as they get most of their news from it; the cynical view of media people of their own work which suffuses their reporting and candid remarks (Fallows, 1996; Purdy, 2000); the ironicization of much of modern media presentations; and the driving force of sponsors and pressure groups on what is shown (Glassner, 2000). I have argued that internal dynamics and rekeying take place as well as ambiguity in the appearance formula of those shown. This media work and mediated communication sustain the fundamental prob- lematic of contingency and ambiguity that in turn generates drama. Per- haps in yet another way, drama is a means to pin down meanings as they rapidly change—simplifying, stereotyping, typifying, and making formu- laic matters not easily captured in factual, referential discourse.

Remarkable research by Jacobs (1996) and Hunt (1996, 1997) on reac- tions to the Rodney King beating using focus groups and content analysis of Los Angeles newspapers reveals that what was reported and how it was "seen" and evaluated varied widely, with African Americans taking a very negative view of the King beating and trials and the African American newspapers taking a more critical view of the events and judicial and political responses (Lawrence, 2000). Similar findings were reported by Kaminski and Jefferies (1997) in a survey of attitude change as a result of the televised beating of an arrested African American in Cincinnati. African Americans were both more negative in general about police violence and less likely to become more negative following the showing of the arrest.

While the "reality" of policing is constituted from many sources, some of which arise from actual participation in the police world and some of which do not, media amplification creates powerful potential for feedback and change. The feedback among media, authors, audience, and police (in their several roles as authors, media figures, officers, producers, and technical advisers) requires further exploration. The connections called reflexive, between social sentiments, roles, selves, and opinions and the media, are complex. The growth of the media and the increase in "police shows" suggest that media influences compete with personal experience to form a visually stimulated "sense" of the police and policing. Police experience themselves and their significant others in and by media, especially television. The visual is an important feature of police work, and the visual media play roles in both social control and in the control of policing. In these examples, the line between back- and frontstage, the private and the public, the formal and the informal, and varieties of reality is blurred, indistinct, and intentionally confusing.

Some speculation about the direction of effects on policing in the future is included in the last chapter of this book.

PART THREE
TECHNOLOGIES AND INFORMATION

FIVE

THE CAR AND DRIVER AS THE BASIC
POLICE TECHNOLOGY

INTRODUCTION

The contingencies of policing, some mediated, some praxiological, and some a part of their own beliefs and ideology, are a world of social reality and organizational realities. The broader picture or imagery of policing, created and sustained by commercial forces as well as the police themselves, seems a long way from the view from the streets. Police technologies historically have developed to increase the probability that the police will be present when the untoward arises. This reification and ideological commitment to the "road officer" means that enormous time, effort, and expenditure have been devoted to the car and driver, and amazingly little on what is done in the car and why.[1] The story then of car and driver is synecdoche for the story of modern policing—a reification of concern that blinds the organization to its options. Ironically, the growing ambit of policing and the police's increased capacity to anticipate or rather rapidly respond increased public expectations of their capacity and willingness to cope with citizen-defined emergencies.

This chapter therefore shifts focus and level of abstraction to put the reader in the car with the driver. Even though many forms of patrol, including horseback, foot patrol (alone and accompanied by dogs), bicycle, moped, motorcycle, and armored personnel carrier, are used now and have

1. Related policies and procedures—high-speed chases, shootings at fleeing suspects, uses of the car to punish and damage suspects, and ironies often concealed by the ideology of the entrepreneur acting with discretion (a bad pun), often with little training in driving, pursuit driving, shooting, or chases in general (Alpert and Fridell, 1992)—are little discussed.

been used in the Anglo–American police world, the car and the driver have been the center of the complex symbolism of policing since American police became motorized in the 1920s.[2]

In this chapter, we look up and out from the car, rather than down from the subtleties of rapidly changing postindustrial society. Since the driver and the vehicle bound the immediate world of policing, the vehicle produces a narrowing and blinding worldview that obviates many alternative realities, many of which impinge upon policing as an organization. While the fundamental technology is interpersonal skills and talk, it is in the car that the policing experience is shaped for officers, and there all officers begin their careers. I want to begin here with the concrete, the here and now, this center of policing, and then consider more abstract issues—of technology, of technological innovation and change—as dramas. In the ideology of the job, everything, in some sense, begins and ends in the car.

THE POLICE VEHICLE: THE 1970S

Look now at the standard police vehicle, a rather wide four-door sedan, of the 1970s. Although cars could be personalized to some degree, they were rather spartan, utilitarian vehicles.[3] Clearly, then as now, some differences could be found between large and small departments and between typical patrol cars and cars that had been "personalized" or modified to accom-

2. Police, like people in all occupations, refer often to a mythical "Golden Age" in which the present vexatious problems did not exist, even the villains or difficult clients or customers were acquiescent, and the lower participants had the support, understanding, and total empathy of those above. In my fieldwork in London in 1973, officers were aware of the decline in what they perceived as the independence of the officer. They noted the growing distrust of colleagues and the public, use of violence and tools by both officers and villains, and the decline in capacity and joy in employing wit, shrewdness, and verbal skill. These officers had begun to patrol under the old fixed-points system, which required patrolling in an order so that their sergeant could anticipate and monitor their movements and occasionally meet them (unexpectedly). They were now (spring 1973) subject to the new layered-response scheme. Only recently had they acquired personal radios connected to the local subdivision. Forcewide radio was monitored only by area cars in the division, and 999 calls from metropolitan police headquarters were not monitored in the subdivision. They viewed themselves as being on their own, whether on foot or in a vehicle, but with colleagues and the public near at hand.

3. I have made extensive use of long memos from Albert J. Meehan, Amanda Rigby, and Jenny Young. These documents are original ethnographic descriptions that reflect on changes in the interior and equipment of the police cars. Meehan (personal communication, February 22, 1997) recounted these observations based on his extensive fieldwork and field notes taken in seven cities over nearly twenty years. They were the basis also for a footnote in *Police Work* (Manning, 1997b: 215–16 n. 15). I entered comment and reordered the presentation to describe the car's appearance, the equipment for the car carried by the officer and the officer's personal equipment. "Personal," as Meehan notes, is an elastic category.

modate officers of higher rank or special functions, such as warrant-serving "tac cars." Picture an ideal type rendering of these earlier vehicles:

[Police] . . . cars [then had] no air conditioning, AM/FM radio, power locks/ windows, or rear defrosters. The standardization and simplicity were obvious even then, with absence of many standard features—no electric clock, matching stylized upholstery and colorful appointments, nor special exterior or interior sporty chrome or paint trim. Metal screens between the front and the back were common, but not standard. Seat belts were used, if provided. Front and back seats were hard, and bench; and the back doors had no interior handles. The communications equipment was limited to a force radio (with a few local channels and limited to the department's jurisdiction) and a personal radio carried by the driver. Radar units were not standard equipment. Three sets of lights were available—running lights, the rotating top, or bubble, and front fog lights. The color of the vehicle was standard, usually black or white or black and white. In London, area cars were a dark blue, and the minicars were light blue and white (hence the name "panda"). The types were few: pandas (mini-Coopers), area cars (four-door Rover sedans) in London, and traffic cars. In most large cities in the U.S. most visible vehicles were the "black and whites" of standard size, shape, and power options. They tended to be large, wide, roomy inside, and slow to accelerate, although they had high top-end speed and torque. They had large, inefficient, straight V6 or V8 engines and rear-wheel (two-wheel only) drives, and a "police package": four-barrel carburetors, dual exhausts, and modified running gear including a more rigid suspension, antisway bars, and heavy-duty shock absorbers. Unmarked cars were used by detectives, but were known as standard issue in both countries—plain, unadorned cars with often a large searchlight or extra-long distinctive radio aerial. Chevrolet Caprice and the Ford Crown Victoria—inexpensive cars with the largest interior dimensions that meet (since 1974) federal fuel and safety standards—were and are in widespread use.

There have been a number of changes to the interior and accessories of the car.

THE POLICE VEHICLE: 2002

The police car in 2002 is impressive: a medium-sized sedan, a highly visible vehicle with distinctive paint and trim, decoration, lights, siren, heavy-duty tires, and identifying markings.

The cars in general are smaller, lighter, and faster than those of the 1970s and handle with greater ease at high speed. Under the hood is a very powerful engine capable of high-speed acceleration, long periods of low-speed operation, and carrying heavy loads. The car is also equipped with heavy-duty bumpers and shock absorbers, and its interior is specially fitted. It has distinctive color and trim and displays the logo of the jurisdiction it serves as well as perhaps a motto or epigram, a distinctive visible number (sometimes including the division and unit number), the rank of the driver if he or she is a supervisor (but not if below or above that rank); and usually "Call 911" painted on the rear quarter panel. The cars have more standard equipment and power options: air conditioning, power locks/windows, cloth bucket front seats as well as safety screen, usually of thick plastic, between the front and rear, with a little sliding door. Mechanisms for communication and passing objects between the front and back seats are in place. The cars are equipped with shoulder and seat belts. Their bumpers are heavily reinforced for pushing and ramming. The car's wheel base and interior dimensions are smaller, although more variation in size, models, and makes for squad cars exists, too. Many types of vehicles are now in use and called "standard." Some are front-wheel, some rear-wheel, some four-wheel and positive-traction drives. Some cities have distinctive traffic cars with special markings, equipment, and lights. In West Mercia, England, Range Rovers are used to patrol the motorways, and BMWs are used as well. The Michigan State Police use Jeeps, Ford Mustangs, vans, and SUVs in highway patrol. The campus police at Michigan State University use a Chevrolet sport model and four-wheel-drive deluxe Jeeps, as well as the standard issue four-door Ford Victoria sedans and unmarked cars. With the changes in seizure laws that allow local police to seize with impunity vehicles even notionally implicated in drug crimes, police in many departments, especially detectives and drug police, drive a wide variety of seized cars.

The car, in any case, must be checked out in both senses of the phrase prior to being driven. This is a police routine that binds car, driver, and partner prior to and at the end of every shift.

Checking Out the Car

Police cars are in almost constant use throughout the day and night; when not in use, the car is usually warm and sitting in a cramped parking area adjacent to or under the station. When an officer comes on at the beginning of a shift, after roll call, she or he will enter the car only after checking it visually inside and out for any defects, equipment malfunctions, dents, or missing equipment. She or he tests the lights and siren and starts the motor. If the car has a video camera, it is turned on and the microphone tested. The officer also checks under the seat, in the trunk, and on the front and back seats for left items, either of a prisoner or of the previous driver, such as evidence, especially weapons or drugs. An officer checks the trunk for the standard equipment (see below) before depositing any equipment there. In practice, since many cars in large cities have malfunctions of various kinds—loud mufflers, dents in the doors, seat belts that do not work, unpredictable radios, or a faulty exterior loud speaker, yet are running—the concern is whether the car can be driven and is no less functional than it was on the previous shift. The car may then have to be repaired, gassed, or washed before the shift begins—when the driver reports in to the dispatcher as being "in service."

When the officer slides into the front seat and settles behind the wheel, the car's interior, especially at night, commands attention. It is a bright, compelling visual display, with quite seductive features. It is disorienting at first to see the amazing range of lights, gadgets, and bells and whistles that dominate the interior. Entering the driver's seat of a late-model police car (usually a Ford Crown Victoria or Chevrolet Caprice), one is assaulted by a large dashboard of lively glowing lights and dials and specially mounted instruments perched on swinging arms from the dashboard or in the console between the seats. The gadgetry filling the car presents some issues that require consideration.

First, consider the lights. In addition to the immediately noticeable glowing and somewhat familiar gauges—odometer, tachometer, and fuel, speed, and heat gauges—are switches set in the console. These include switches to control eight to ten kinds of lights, two kinds of sirens (wail and whoop), and the radio (to change both channels and volume). The car's lights and sirens have become more complex and specialized. The visible exterior lights are highly variable, given the now popular "Christmas tree" rack of lights on top.

Next, look at the other equipment in the front seat. The computer screen and keyboard fill the area between the driver and passenger. Usually in big cities, a mobile-digital terminal and screen glows at the driver's right (or left in the UK), mounted on a moveable arm. A shotgun may be mounted between the seats (space requirements and political correctness mean that shotguns if carried are now relegated to the trunk in most cities). Most cars in London and in large North American cities carry guns (in London they are locked in the glove compartment). In some cities, officers carry their aluminum batons in a holder to the left of the driver on the dash. It dangles, ready. If the car does not have a mobile digital terminal (MDT), typically a radiotelephone combination is set in the center of the dash. Radios, some with wider range and channels for specialized units and some on 800 MHz, have become more complex, with better range, more channels, and enhanced features, and a radar unit may be mounted on the dash. To the right of the steering wheel, mounted on the dash with a Velcro holder, is the radio microphone. Some cars, "camera cars," have a video camera mounted below the rearview mirror and a small monitor for the video unit.

Third, think of how cramped quarters are if the patrol car has a portable computer, or "mobile work station" as they are called in Toronto (Sparrow, 1993), and the absence of flexibility in the use of space.[4]

Fourth, consider "personal space." Loose equipment, such as a clipboard or logbook, may fill the passenger seat if there is no passenger. There is no room for personal belongings between the seats, except up and behind the radio–lights–siren console that is lodged between the seats and behind the driver's elbow.

Even the trunk is full. The trunk can contain the video recording unit, radio and computer signal transmitters, or an automatic vehicle locator (AVL) unit, in addition to the standard complement of flares, door openers ("slim-jims"), spare tire, and tire-changing equipment. The officer may also keep her or his personal equipment in the trunk as well (as will be discussed below). In Toronto, the equipment also includes a medical aid kit, flares, reflective vests of bright orange for traffic direction, and a biohazard response kit.[5]

In Action

The in-car setting presents a truly dazzling array, especially when an officer is in action, when road and traffic noise increases, lights and screens flash, and the radio bleats insistently. These sounds compete with casual conversation, although officers can monitor the radio and talk, picking out their call numbers of important messages while driving and talking. The lights and sounds of even routine patrol present a rather demanding set of stimuli for the casual observer, or "ride-along." This engaging action field requires systematic framing and reframing of attention, action decisions,

4. There are several unresolved, fundamental issues. First, officers are not trained on the computer systems and have to master them on their own time. Second, as the computers are in theory "portable," the question of whether officers can take them home and use them off duty remains. Third, the databases accessible from the work stations are still quite limited in Toronto (Young and Rigby, 1999).

5. According to Bill Terrill (personal communication, March 2000), who observed policing in Indianapolis, officers who drove their patrol cars as their family transportation reported that they were sometimes embarrassed that the trunk was full of equipment such as a stroller, car seat, or other necessities for carrying children. They were also loath to transport drunks and sick prisoners for fear that they would vomit in their cars and leave a lingering stench that might compromise the pleasure of family outings.

and fluctuations in attention between the interior of the car and the external environment.

Thus, imagining the dispatching process as it is seen from the front seat is essential to understanding patrol work. Meehan (personal communication, 1998) provides an elegant and parsimonious description of the dispatching process in a Midwestern suburb, which is consistent with my recent experience observing dispatching using MDTs:

> After the radio transmission, the responding officer, and the assigned back-up officer, receive a message on the MDT screen which provides: a) the address; b) an incident number; c) time the call was received and dispatched; d) the incident crime code [if relevant] and a literal translation of the code (e.g., 0310 robbery with firearm); and e) the name of the business if the address is non-residential. The officer then presses the "en route" key on the terminal, which records the time the call was received from dispatch. This triggers a series of four screens [the officer can move between them by pressing a "display message button"] . . . providing information. [If the department has entered this information. This varies by department and by the time required to enter information and update it]. Screen one indicates the general vicinity of the address (cross roads) . . . and any "general alerts" such as "storage of flammable liquids, audible alarm system." Screen two displays contact information which provides the last five dispatched calls to the address by date, incident code, and report number. It also displays the names of managers and owners if the address is a business. Screen three contains standardized police alert codes such as "attack dog," "guard," "weapons present." Screen four "police notes" [pertaining] to past police relevant activity at the address entered by department personnel (e.g., person is mentally ill or drug dealing. . .). When the officer arrives at the scene, pushing an "on scene" key acknowledges arrival and records the time on both the MDT and CAD [computer-assisted dispatching] system.

It should be said that the skill and comfort of officers in driving *and* using this equipment vary. Even if the MDT is "down" or inactive, the screen blank, and the radio dead, the routine demand conditions—driving, observing, making do, noting, and registering—persist. The capacity as well as the willingness of officers to effectively use the many tools, from weapons to interpersonal skills, varies, as does their willingness to experiment in order to become more competent.

Having examined the car both outside and inside, first the car of the 1970s and then the present multifaceted vehicle, and seen some images from the front seat, it is important now to shift attention to the officer and the equipment she or he carries to and from the vehicle at the beginning and end of every shift.

THE OFFICER AND EQUIPMENT

Personal Equipment: The 1970s

Outwardly, the police uniform and personal (carried) equipment have changed little in the last thirty years.[6] Because the occupation is conservative, small changes become symbolically charged and the old ways get sentimentalized.[7] Even the minor decorations on the police uniform have meaning and convey symbolism, as the recent eruption of flags (post-9/11) on everything suggests.[8]

The basic equipment carried by the officer has been augmented since the early 1970s. H. Taylor Buckner, once a police reserve officer in Berkeley, California, described one version of the patrol officer's standard equipment in 1967. It was an awesome collection of weighty tools (Manning, 1997b: 215–16 n. 15). Buckner (1967: 230–31) lists the astounding weapons he was required to carry as a reserve policeman:

6. The introduction of artificial fibers, lightweight wools, and wash-and-wear permanent-press shirts has certainly made the wardrobe more comfortable. On the whole, the uniforms, in part because of the introduction of people of various heights and shapes, have become more varied in subtle ways. Within the police world, because "dressing in" (putting on the uniform) is taking on the role and the self, and because of the identity indicated by the very visible and dated look that a uniform now conveys, the uniform has powerful connotations. Putting on the uniform is a secular ceremony of role transition, something like the dressing ceremony a matador undertakes prior to a performance. Even if done at home, it is freighted with emotion and meaning. The gun or guns worn are something of a synecdoche.

7. For example, in the 1970s, black officers argued that they could not wear their caps because they concealed their Afros, a curly, thick hair style, while supervisors cited them for being out of uniform if seen without a cap. The size and style of caps, for example, connote status. Malcolm Young, who served in the Newcastle and West Mercia constabularies in England, notes how rich and meaningful were the caps and helmets worn:

> In Newcastle, for example, we had worn a guards' style cap and despised the traditional helmet, for we were required to be at least 5′10″ and most were taller. Helmets were therefore said to be reserved for the "dwarfs in the sticks" who needed assistance simply to look taller. Then again helmets were also in use in the despised borough forces, for they took in "gnomes" as small as 5′6″. Soon after amalgamation, however, the helmet became standard uniform issue to the whole force. At South Shields in the early 1980s, a sergeant formerly with Newcastle Police still wore his old guards' style cap on nightshift to make his own ritualistic statement that "since the amalgamations the job's fucked". Worcester City officers were still regretting the loss of their highly decorative helmet in the early 1980s, for such symbolic forms of self-identity have a deep hold on the imagination. And though the Cornwall County force had long since vanished in an amalgamation with Devon Police to become the Devon and Cornwall Constabulary, the 1988 programme of the Cornwall Police Choir tells how it was "founded in 1956 to celebrate, the following year, the Centenary of the Cornwall Constabulary, [and its] members still proudly wear those buttons and insignia [lapel badges] on their choir uniforms". (Young, 1991: 33)

8. Wearing pins and medals is restricted to those won while serving in the armed forces or the police. No other decoration is permitted to mar the uniformity of police appearance, although the marvelous and rich imagery produced by the many pins, badges, and honors worn at formal occasions by a senior police officer can be quite eye-catching (Gaines, 2001).

The authority of the uniform alone is not sufficient to control many situations, which the police encounter, so the police officer is fitted out as a weapons systems with a variety of weapons useful in various situations. An officer will routinely carry a .38 caliber revolver and spare ammunition, a 12 to 14-inch truncheon, club or baton, a flashlight, handcuffs and keys, call box key and a whistle, a notebook and pen, a citation book, an arrest book, possibly a two-way radio. In addition, he may carry a spare gun, a "come-along" or "bear's claw," brass knuckles, a blackjack, a confiscated switchblade knife, a palm sap, a canister of tear gas or a more potent chemical weapon depending on his own preferences and the rule of his department. . . . My uniform, which does not include a radio or any additional weapons, weighs almost twenty pounds.

In addition to these weapons which are carried on his person, his patrol car may well contain a shotgun loaded with four rounds of "oo" buckshot (9.32 caliber pellets per round), additional ammunition, a 26" baton, a riot helmet, a small law library, copies of the department's regulations, forty to fifty types of report forms, flares, blankets, first aid equipment, chalk, measuring tape, a two-way radio, red light and siren, and a "hot sheet" of stolen cars and license plates. [See Laurie, 1972: 75–77, for the equipment of the London officer in 1970.]

When walking out to the car, even in 1972, an officer usually carried additional equipment, some of it required, some of it personal. Here is a description of equipment carried to the car some twenty or twenty-five years ago in Big City (Meehan, 1992, 1993, 1994):

Officers carried their hand held portable radio . . . nightstick, flashlight and a clipboard [with] spare report forms, the "hot sheet" of stolen cars, the briefing sheet, and always on top, the patrol log (or "cheat sheets"/"my lies"). . . . Their belts were lighter: a gun, handcuffs and spare rounds (6 in the gun and 12 extra bullets). Officers . . . carried their "drop gun" or "oh shit" gun along with a blackjack . . . and "sap" gloves—gloves with lead or sand around the knuckle area. Some carried pocket knifes and switch blades. . . . [Suburban officers] were more likely to carry briefcases to their car. . . . This created a very "professional looking image." The briefcases typically contained extra report forms . . . some had their "pads" dating back six months to a year; a copy of the rules and regulations for the department; a transistor radio (older cars . . . did not have commercial radios in them) and personal items like books for school. (Meehan, personal communication, 1998, based on his fieldwork in Big City)

Personal Equipment: 2002

By 2002, the police officer's equipment, both official and "personal" (what is viewed as needed to do the job in addition to the official equipment), is more numerous, but has become lighter and more compact. The net effect of this additional equipment is to hinder movement and mobility, as well as to weight the officer heavily around the waist.

The police officer carries virtually all the items listed above as well as many others such as pepper spray, two extra clips of ammunition, gloves, and a CPR mask. Officers now carry equipment in and out of the car in duffel or sports bags or briefcases. Included is "standard equipment" that varies across departments, a personalized set of tools, and perhaps a personal cellular phone.

Meehan describes (private communication, 1997) what is carried to the vehicle by an officer beginning a shift in Midwestern suburban department in the late 1990s:

> [Clipboards, always a standard piece of equipment, have changed]. Clipboards are . . . a small metal box, slightly larger than the standard size of paper and a half-inch thick. The officer's belt contains a gun (with 16 rounds plus 2 extra clips each with 15 rounds), metal handcuffs (sometimes 2 pair), plastic cuffs, portable radio, pepper spray, a collapsible baton (which has replaced the nightstick) and a video microphone transmitter (if the officer is driving a camera car). . . . Officers may also carry their own personal [metal flashlights] . . . a mini maglight and many wear pagers (largely used by family members and friends and bypassing the communications center). . . . Body armor, or "the vest" is common today. . . . The technology has changed to make it lighter weight, more effective, less cumbersome and more comfortable. . . . [If] officers are required [by city regulation or state law] to be EMT or medical first responders, they carry in the car a defibrillator and a medic kit. All officers carry a PBT (portable breath tester) for testing drunk drivers [usually in the trunk]. In addition, officers carry duffel bags. . . to store other items such as: binoculars, cellular phones, tape recorders, portable scanners (to scan bordering jurisdictions), plastic latex gloves (AIDS related), additional guns and rounds of ammo and . . . nightstick as well as gifts for children . . . either victims of crime or "nice kids."

One of the most interesting issues that has arisen as equipment has become lighter and more compact is that the traditional unofficial weapons of the trade—the heavy multibattery flashlight, used as a cudgel; the thick leather boots, or "shitkickers"; the metal clipboard, or "knee knocker"; and perhaps a "throw down" gun have all become lighter, more compact, and easier to carry. The brass knuckles, the sap, and the lead-loaded billy club are considered too awkward, cumbersome, and dated for rapid deployment. The car, fists, and feet remain the most commonly used tools of the trade when violence is needed.

Equipment and the Self

The basic police unit features the body of the officer in uniform, equipped. This is an ensemble, a front. An interesting example of the fit between self and front is found in Tracy Kidder's description (1999: 53) of "Tommy O'Conner," a small-town officer profiled in the *Atlantic* and later in Kidder's book *Hometown* (2000).

> He wore a blue shirt with sergeant's stripes on the sleeves, dark pants, black boots and a clip-on necktie (because the real one could become a noose).

The drama of his appearance in full regalia is not lost on Kidder or O'Conner. Kidder (1999: 53) writes:

> All uniforms make the people in them seem easily understood. [Emerging onto the streets] leather creaking and hardware softly jangling, he rolled his shoulders and held his arms bowed out a little from his sides, as if he fancied himself a weight lifter and gunfighter all in one. The impression he made, of confidence and force, wasn't altogether wrong, or unintended. But in fact he rolled his shoulders to adjust the protective vest he wore underneath his shirt, and all the equipment on his belt forced his arms out from his sides.
>
> About ten pounds of hardware hung from his uniform—pistol, pepper spray (the safest means to subdue suspects and mental patients who have begun to fight), pouches full of ammo and rubber gloves, two pairs of handcuffs, a kielbasa-sized flashlight . . . and a P-24 baton.

The modern officer symbolizes power and authority, whether we consider the uniform, the equipment, the walk, or style of self-presentation, or the tasks undertaken. There remains a bit of the sacred, and therefore the officer is "awesome."[9] The outer package, the car, conceals the uniqueness of the driver, his or her equipment, and the potential for violence.

---

9. Yet the total accumulation, the entire ensemble, acts as an impediment to quick movement or even walking more than few steps, and it is clear that the modern police officer remains more like a cavalry officer, tentative and awkward when off the horse, masterful while on it, than a comfortable strolling neighbor. When on foot patrol in large cities, the police are still encumbered with equipment and heavy accessories suited to and developed from the tradition of motorized patrol. State police use costumes, such as the wide-brimmed hat and boots, that quaintly echo the uniform of the pre–World War I cavalry. He or she also symbolizes technological mastery, with a radio squawking periodically even as he or she talks to citizens, unlike the officer of the past, who carried only a personal radio when walking. Even when riding bicycles, many of the present police look like wobbling elephants or whales atop the tiny, dwarfed machines, rather than accessible fellow citizens. When the computers in the cars crash or the radios go out, the car is out of service and often has to be driven across town to the radio repair shop and left for several hours while it's being repaired. While the move to make police more accessible and to reduce social distance between the police and the public—"community policing"—moves ahead, the equipment, uniform, and shoes in particular resemble another era, and are suited to motorized patrol, not walking.

SUMMARY

The appearance, comfort, and number of accessories in and on the car and driver have changed in thirty-plus years. What do these changes signify about the contingencies and drama of policing?

In many respects, police functions remain quite static—responding to calls for service, one at a time, in some priority determined partially by the call takers and dispatchers and partially by officers (Sparrow, Moore, and Kennedy, 1990: 43). The distribution of time given over to various tasks and the work does not seem radically different from that of the 1970s in large cities, but there are indications that the workload is heavier. It is possible that the addition of community policing functions adds to the time spent by sergeants in supervision rather than paperwork (Stroshine, 2001). Nonetheless, an officer spends virtually all this time in a vehicle, some of which is "personal," with the exception of breaks and occasional visits to places (parking empty police cars that would otherwise be out of service is a misleading practice that does not always indicate an officer is walking). The car serves as office, break room, a sphere of privacy for naps and snacks; it represents the status and authority of the driver.

The car and driver are arguably more comfortable and safer. This is a result of equipping police cars with common amenities as well as the AVL, video cameras, seat belts, screens enclosing the back seat, power locks on the doors, and better driving and handling characteristics. The intense and brighter lights for road stops are certainly more noticeable and may reduce accidental deaths of officers making traffic stops. Officers can now patrol in various styles, colors, and models, and consume currently trendy models as well as any upper-middle-class citizen. There are more options to motorized patrol for an officer who chooses those, or for a neighborhood that wants a change.

There are more communicational channels in the car. The channels available now include the equipment in and attached to the car; the range of communicational and coercive devices carried by the officer; and the portable equipment officers coming on duty bring to the car. Specifically, these channels now include more lights and sirens; more powerful and linked personal and car radios operating at higher megahertz; the cell phone (private and departmental in some cases); the MDT-phone-radio combination; the radar unit and the video unit (each of which can be tracked from central sources); and the AVM when used. The video unit is perhaps the most insidious from the officers' point of view, because it includes a voice-activated microphone and a camera inside the car that can be turned to the back seat (to surveil prisoners or passengers) or the front

seat. CAD, which just emerged in the early 1970s, has now become virtually universal. This in effect means closer monitoring and more rapid and
context-sensitive response than were possible thirty years ago, as well as
the potential for heavier workloads because of reduced pass-through time
and fewer lost and/or screened-out calls.

There are more information sources, such as databases available to the
officer in the car (or any officer using a personal digital assistant, cell
phone, or computer-phone combination). These include direct access to
the department of motor vehicles; the various patterns of calls by time,
neighborhood, address, unit, etc., that can be reproduced on the MDT;
lists of warrants or local data on crimes, arrests, and the jail; and in some
departments, regional networks of wanted and arrests.

Descriptions of present-day police work (Ackroyd et al., 1996; Meehan,
personal communications, 1997; Young and Rigby, 1999), as well as my
own observations and interviews, suggest increased technological dependence of the officer. This means in practice meshing both with colleagues
who share these communicational channels and with the public. Nevertheless, independence and dependence, especially in North American officers, remain in tension, and officers swing from one to the other, depending on their sentiments and the situation at hand. Swings between denying
the actual considerable dependence of the single patrol officer upon colleagues and the public and the elevation of putative independence, even fatalism, indicate a fundamental value tension among patrol officers.

The car—the patrol officer's office—like all modern offices, is being
shaped both symbolically and materially by technologies, especially information and communicational technologies.[10] The officer's personal equipment and departmentally sanctioned equipment are more diverse, lighter,
and more likely to be electronic and computer based. Technology changes
organizational structure to some degree (see the next chapter), and it also
stimulates organizational and interpersonal transformations because complex, interrelated, communicational processes require cognitive work.
Policing may well catch up with the microserver revolution in time to be
behind in the transition from the Internet to wireless communication. As
Weick (1988, 1995) writes, there are necessary imagined processes that unfold in the mind of the team or person using the technology. The question

    10. Ironically, as Meehan (private communication, 1998) notes, this car-self-contained-office-
unit continues, in this time of community policing, to isolate and protect the officer from the community, enables paperwork to be accomplished, and provides privacy and insulation from external distraction and new time demands. Another strange construction is used on the job—one is
"out of service" when attending a call, writing up paperwork, and dealing with a complaint or
problem, while "in service" when driving around with no explicit assignment.

is whether the mental work, the imagination of the police, is bringing the new web of communication—dense, complex, and uncertain—into mind.[11]

11. On the horizon loom other innovations such as the experimental car in Texas that has four cameras feeding it images. The driver can monitor the front and rear of the car, as well as the back seat, and can combine all three images on one screen (Pilant, 1999). A few cars also have fax facilities, allowing them to acquire warrants via affidavits, receive them, and send back results via fax to the courts. Two other technological developments that have not been taken up are the "heads up display" above the head of the driver like a jet pilot has to project the road ahead, and the "robo-cop" helmet with a built-in computer developed in England. A third innovation, which I believe has great promise, is the palm pilot, or hand-held organizer–computer–cell phone and Internet connector. These are made by a number of companies—Handspring, Sony, and Compaq—and were selling for prices from around four to five hundred dollars as of December 2001; they could be used as cell phones, to keep records and logbooks, and to send messages and files, including incident reports. They have the same advantages and disadvantage (from a management point of view) as do cell phones or mobile work stations. They are flexible, cheap, and useful but can provide a degree of disconnection from the centralized command and control system.

SIX

HORIZONS OF TECHNOLOGY

INTRODUCTION

Information technologies epitomize the police's belief that the public expects technology, through its mysterious power, to solve social problems; thus, the idea is very much part of modern police reform efforts (see Fuld, 1971; Leonard, 1980; Tien and Colton, 1979). The rhetoric and the reality are widely separated. But in technological mystification lie claims to power, authority, and control, and hence dramatic potential.

ORGANIZATIONAL CONSTRAINTS

The complex links between social structure, contingency, and uncertainty are generally thought to be reduced by technological means, and this in turn is claimed to be the road to improved service, quality, and effective public service (Moore, 1997). Thus, changes in the last thirty years would appear to have reduced pass-through time, simplified operations, sped up all aspects of police work, and perhaps moved the police toward the paperless office (Sellen and Harper, 2002) and "just in time" budgeting and planning (Gates, 1996). This is a dubious claim, but it nevertheless has priority of place among American values and the ideology of police reformers. In this mediated age, technological innovation means increased demand and cries for reform predicated on new infrastructure based on rationality, measured outcomes, and systematic feedback. The police, having claimed a mandate on the basis of service and responsiveness, have seized on technologies that have little impact on crime control, order maintenance, or the quality of service rendered, but this effort is a part of the process of imagining the future (Dunworth, 2000; Abt Associates, 2000).

Technologies are envisioned and enframed. The dominant police strategy of adapting, shaping, and using some innovations and safely embedding them within the present structure has had consequences unacknowledged in the programmatic writings of reformers and consultants on the impact and future of IT in policing (Sparrow, Moore, and Kennedy, 1990; Dunworth, 2000). These writings are suffused with optimism. They contain summaries based on limited research on the use of specific systems needed or in place (see, e.g., Dunworth, 2000: 389, on laptops and MDTs); hopeful statements inconsistent with actual use and impediments thereto (Dunworth, 2000: 397); and turgid statements or observations that contradict the general tone of the writing (Dunworth, 2000: 379, 398). Furthermore, the limited recent research based on case studies that project the extent of use focuses on command hopes and rhetoric and remains cautious in spite of rather chaotic conditions even in the most well managed and directed departments, such as San Diego's (Abt Associates, 2000).

Technology possesses something we might call a *poetics,* or aesthetics, that reflects how it looks and feels, its shape and design, as well as its material presence and functional capacity. It speaks, or signifies, and communicates therefore to audiences. But this communicative aspect is an idea, an idea that must be realized in the future. As Bruno Latour (1996: 23) has written, all nascent technological innovations are "fictions" that require imagination, for they do not exist until they are created, planned, debated, interpreted, used, and finally made part of work routines. Further, as he says and as I explore in the next chapter, technology studies require that one move from the expression (that which points to something) to the object, the matter pointed to (its content), holding in mind the interpretant, or that which completes the sign. The object has a meaning as imagined and as a matter of practice or use. The potential tensions between idea and action should be part of the analysis of a technology. To study technology one must move from signs to things and vice versa (Latour, 1996: 80). When writing about technology and technological innovations, we are involved in translation (finding out what technology means) and back-translation (speaking to the users of their uses). Observations describe and create the object.[1] Furthermore, the world of technologies has been trans-

---

1. In this and the following chapter, I draw on the fieldwork of Abt Associates, my own work, and reports on police technologies by Dunworth (2000); LeBeuf (2000); and Soulliere (2000).

formed basically by the digital revolution, and our names for devices no longer denote their full functions.[2]

ONE HORIZON

Each technology competes for time and attention with other means and is judged by somewhat changing pragmatic, often nontechnical, values—its speed, its durability and weight, and its contribution to the officers' notion of their role and routines. New equipment is generally introduced without experimentation, clear expectations or standards, or proper repair and maintenance contracts, and often IT facilities are purchased by the state or local authorities for multiple purposes and are neither vetted, contracted for, nor acquired by police management or budgetary officers. The absence of knowledge of IT has made police vulnerable to vendors (Abt Associates, 2000: 163), changes in city or county policies, or the serendipitous collocation of officers who have learned IT on the job and found a niche (Abt Associates, 2000: 72). Police administrators have welcomed publicly each new technological innovation since the telegraph and alarm system as a solution to deep and abiding organizational problems such as discipline and corruption, as well as vexing problems of law enforcement and crime control (Manning, 1988, 1992b; Sparrow, Moore, and Kennedy, 1990).

Adjustments to technology seen only from the management perspective obscure some other important dynamics. The shifting interest of police in IT hinges on the fit of technology with the chief *contingency in* the mandate, the *focus* upon presence based on an inspectorial bureaucratic structure, and the *theme* of responsiveness. These in turn illuminate the fundamental limits on police data—its raw, concrete, just-gathered-at-the-front-end quality. The primary contingency has been viewed as sustaining or increasing mobility and secondarily as some loose combination of deterrence and apprehension. Looked at in budget terms, technological innovations in mobility and weapons dominate, followed at a great distance by tools for data processing of crime-related materials, training, and finally transformative and analytic tools such as software for expert systems, crime mapping and analysis, and all aspects of statistical analysis. In summary, *IT has been fitted to the extant structure and traditional processes of the police organization, and these organizations have little changed* (Greene,

---

2. For example, a "cell phone"—now called a "personal digital assistant"—has an Internet interface, e-mail and fax sending and receiving capacities, games, a scheduler, a simple calculator, diaries and journals, phone and address books, and various other internal functional capacities never before associated with a telephone.

2000).[3] We can see this by a quick review of police-relevant technological developments in the United States.

A SECOND HORIZON

In order to examine the emergence of response to innovations, a time perspective is required. Early innovations in police IT came in large part from external pressures and/or reform-minded chiefs. IT innovation, seen in the context of traditional policing strategies or routines—e.g., heavy organizational investment in crime control, random patrol, and on-the-street decision making—can be examined in five stages: pre–World War II; post–World War II; the LEAA stage; the NIJ experimental policy-driven stage; and the local innovations–COPS stage. In each stage, the aim was to facilitate more rapid response to reported incidents, especially crimes, and at some remove to improve the quality of the police response to calls, upgrade record keeping, and integrate various databases (Tien and Colton, 1979; Dunworth, 2000: 380–98).

Stages of Innovation

Pre–World War II (1890–1939). Prior to World War II, the telegraph, call box, and telephone, followed by one-way and then two-way radios, each altered the shape of police patrol and with it the potential for close command supervision of officers (Colton, 1979; Tien and Colton, 1979). Each technological innovation was welcomed as a breakthrough in scientific policing and seized upon as a managerial tool enabling enhanced coordination and discipline of patrol officers. The development of the Uniform Crime Reports (UCR) under the FBI became a staple of police self-promotion and self-evaluation. These early innovations also gave a precise content to the "crime-fighting," "scientific," and "professional" imagery sought by police reformers such as August Vollmer (Carte and Carte, 1975), Bruce Smith, and O. W. Wilson (Stead, 1977). Throughout this period, the police also increased their "scientific" or laboratory capacity, in part based on information technologies that decreased processing time for the transfer

---

3. I omit developments in special weapons and tactics and lethal and nonlethal weaponry. Arms have been an important area of innovation: new weapons and force-application techniques such as nine-millimeter and ten-millimeter and semiautomatic machine pistols, Taser guns and training in the martial arts, aluminum batons such as the Monadnock PR-24 (nunchakus are used in San Diego), and laser-guided weapons and night scopes are widely used. One of the most innovative and little studied (in North America) types of technology innovation is discussed in chapter 4—the use of video cameras to film police cars, jails, traffic, reception desks in police departments, and the public via CCTV in city centers in the UK; such films are used to evaluate policing.

of information. From the 1930s on, the process of complaint investigation and responding to citizens' requests was facilitated and accelerated by the combination of the two-way radio and centralized radio dispatching.

Post–World War II (1945–67). Widespread diffusion of the telephone and greater automobile use now escalated the problems of police response to incidents, increased demand, and extended their responsibilities (Bordua and Reiss, 1966; Reiss and Bordua, 1967). Police leadership took a public position of commitment to full service and response to all calls while encouraging (by traditional delegation of authority and working conventions) informal management and rationing of calls for service by dispatchers and officers. The spread of suburban living expanded the distances and costs involved. It is possible that public expectations also rose, shaped by police self-promotion, and that belief in the ideology that defined the police as a twenty-four-hour service agency with the implicit motto "you call, we come" became widespread. Demand grew, until the American public became the most demanding citizenry in the Anglo-American world (determined by calls per capita). By the late 1960s, interest grew in using computers to collect, organize, and systematize calls to the police and to respond sensitively with appropriate and measured resources to the level and kinds of reported problems.

The LEAA era (1968–80). The Law Enforcement Assistance Administration (LEAA), an agency designed to pass out block grants to states and fund social research to support law enforcement, had many functions. Its primary accomplishment in the technological realm was sponsoring computer-assisted dispatching (CAD), a system by which calls were entered, categorized, dispatched, and monitored by computers and where computers assist initial assignments. The presidents' crime commission had argued in 1968 that a national emergency number was needed and 911 was adopted by the FCC and AT&T (Dunworth, 2000: 385), but the idea took many years to be accepted by police and local governments. The first full-time computer assisted system of dispatching was installed in the Saint Louis Police Department in the 1960s (Larson, 1989: 28). Prior to that time, all records were done by hand, often literally handwritten, and departments maintained files that had to be directly handled and kept in huge record-keeping rooms. Further systems, computer-assisted record keeping, collection of information and dispatching, combined with a simple, well-publicized, three-digit number—911 in the U.S. and 999 in the UK—were introduced in Chicago in the late 1960s and in the West Midlands and Strathclyde constabularies in the UK in the mid-1970s (Hough, 1980). By the early 1970s, as a result of LEAA funding, a few large departments (New York, Detroit, and Chicago among them) had adopted

CAD systems. The progress in the use of 911 was slow, in part because it was tied to changes in dispatching itself, with only 17 percent of departments using it by 1980 and some 85 percent by the late 1990s (Dunworth, 2000: 381). The typical CAD system is the center of the records-keeping system with respect to external matters (and can be, but is not always, linked to the internal databases such as criminal records and arrests and to databases used in crime analysis). Around 1980, "enhanced 911" (or E911) systems appeared (Larson, 1989). An E911 system displays the address and number of the phone from which a call was made and permits the operator to hold the line while the problem is investigated. Further, an enhanced system permits checks of addresses, review of previous calls from that number, and simplifies data gathering from callers. By 1989, 89 of the 125 largest cities in the United States had enhanced 911 and 36 states were required by law to adopt it after 1989 (Larson, 1989). In the next few years, 911 numbers and funding became a national requirement.

The rise of NILECJ and NIJ (1974–present). By the mid-1970s a federally designed research agenda emerged. The National Institute of Law Enforcement and Criminal Justice—once a division of the LEAA, now a division of the Justice Department and renamed as the National Institute of Justice—attempted targeted innovations: a series of experiments and quasi-experiments. These exercises focused on a series of studies of critical areas in policing designed to provide cutting-edge empirically supported innovations. They funded research on simplifying detective work by developing "solvability factors," advocating crime analysis units, reducing random patrol by implementing schemes combining directed patrol (patrol assigned to a set of sites, or to duties for a given shift) and random patrol, managing demand by setting call priorities, and rationalizing drug law enforcement by introducing task forces (Manning, 1979b). By the late 1980s, experiments involving computer applications, expert systems, and network analysis for drug enforcement and community policing were funded. In many respects the Reagan administrations reduced funding for research and focused on the control of violent crime.

The COPS period. In the last fifteeen years, federal funding for police research, apart from the massive Crime Control Bill of 1994, has been reduced sharply and shifted to more modest research projects and program evaluations. The Crime Control Bill, which established support to local police departments to hire new officers in support of "community policing" (Maguire et al., 1998) and evaluate the spread of community policing, poured money directly into research for evaluation (Dunworth, 2000: 399–400; Greene, 2000). The authors of the Crime Control Bill avoided defining community policing and stating what adding a hundred thousand new officers on the streets meant. It was an occasion for reflection upon the needed information systems if community policing were to be realized somewhere. These facets of information systems include, according to Dunworth, crime analysis, management information systems (MIS), integrated records and databases, community involvement, and intelligence gathering (information gathered prior to an incident) (Dunworth, 2000: 399–400).

More recent developments (1996–present). Consider some of the IT innovations in the last six years. The internal configuration of response remains unchanged. The same operators answer calls from different numbers (311, 911, seven-digit service numbers), sometimes transferring them to other call takers, but use the same system of allocating cars. Local funding for new technologies has replaced large federal grants. Many important innovations have been devised and adopted by local police forces. Many large departments, such as those in New York, Boston, and Detroit, having introduced a second generation of mainframes with associated software, are now attempting to integrate decentralized servers for some databases. New wiring and terminals, modified databases and access points, creating compatible software, and reprogramming and installing decentralized server systems must, as in all large organizations, be considered in determining future operating costs of all departments.

The Pattern

In each stage, the advances were unplanned, politically driven, and centered around an imagined efficient force that in fact was traditionally organized, committed to a professionalized model of practice, and (while emphasizing crime control) devoted primarily to the appearance of service via demand management and reactive patrol.

A THIRD HORIZON: TYPES OF TECHNOLOGY AND CURRENT DEVELOPMENTS

A time perspective allows for one means of assessing the police response to technological innovation. Another way of viewing the relationship between the police and technology is to review the progress made with respect to the various existing types of technology. If we cluster the technology available to the police into ideal types, five types of technology with salient features are currently in use: mobility technology, training technology, transformative technology, analytic technology, and communicative technology.

Mobility Technology

The consistent leader in expenditure and maintenance costs for technology are *means of mobility*. These technologies increase rapid and flexible patrol. The focus is on the capacity to allocate officers to areas and poise them to respond. The role of material technology in this connection has changed little since the 1930s except for increases in the speed, number, and types of available vehicles.[4] This cluster of technological advances grew in popularity with the recent emphases on satisfying citizen demand, presence, and availability. As a result, the car and driver are the core material technology of modern policing: a mobile office, an insulated compartment, a retreat, and a work setting, a place in which patrol officers may spend from eight to twelve hours, a focus of conditions of work and union contracts. The costs of random uniformed patrol are the fundamental and abiding costs of modern policing, and it is estimated that it costs $600,000 to maintain a car and driver in operation for a year (Bayley, 1994).

Training Technology

A second area of technology is *training*. These are systematic means to modify people—their attitudes and behavior (officers themselves as well as the public). They vary but tend to be brief and combine in class-lecture learning with field training with a field training officer (FTO). Little is known systematically about the content of police training curricula, but the core remains physical and symbolic (shaming, harassing, conditioning, rapid response to orders) and to a lesser degree academic learning about the law, diversity, and cultures, interpersonal relations, and problem solving. Training modalities also include educating officers in crowd control procedures for managing SWAT, hostage and antiterrorist activity, and training in noncoercive persuasive techniques such as mediation, and hostage negotiation. Field training tends to be highly variable, a function of the skills and interests of a senior and respected officer, and produces highly variable skills in young officers (Fielding, 1988).

Transformative Technology

A third area of technology consists of *transformative* devices used to extend the human senses and present technical evidence in scientific form. This area of technology is one that has seen great advances in recent years as a result of general scientific progress. Most of the advances are processes for

4. In the last few years, citizen contributions to the San Diego police department, for example, have allowed them to develop a quasi-autonomous division-based bicycle patrol.

refining, enhancing, and reviewing criminal evidence. Police cars are often equipped with video cameras, allowing police to capture, in video and audio, their interactions with suspects. Forensic scientists, once restricted to fingerprint evidence and blood typing, are now able to identify individuals by their DNA or place them at the scenes of crimes using a variety of trace evidence (e.g., hair, fiber). The FBI and some states are also creating a DNA bank of known felons convicted of certain crimes. These have enormous potential to extend police power as well as to augment civil liberties of the accused and wrongly convicted.

The Boston Police Department has computerized its mug shot database. Police are able to compare fingerprints via computer, taking mere minutes, versus the visual comparison of fingerprint cards, which in the past could take weeks if not months. While the percentage of municipal police departments with their own Automated Fingerprint Identification System (AFIS) is small (9 percent) (Reaves and Goldberg, 1996), the FBI is sponsoring the use of computerized fingerprint files for on-line checks of criminal records. Technological advances in this area are embraced by police as being consistent with the professional crime fighter image, even while they continue to complain about failures in technological support and often lack the skills to properly use computer software

Analytic Technology

A fourth area of technological innovation in policing is the introduction of *analytic devices:* those designed to aggregate, model, and simulate police data to facilitate crime analysis, crime mapping, and activities in aid of crime prevention. Police have made advances in the last thirty years in their ability to acquire, store, and aggregate data. Some of these innovations are quite remarkable, such as the purchase by Charlotte-Mecklenberg police of thirteen hundred laptops (defined as personal equipment for use at home and work) and the handheld computers used by motorcycle officers in San Diego. Seventy-nine percent of municipal police forces staffed by one hundred or more officers in 1996 used mobile computers or terminals in the field (Reaves and Goldberg, 1996). The access to such data in the field has been shown in a few studies to increase productivity (e.g., Chan, 2001). Meehan and Ponder (2002a,b) suggest that use of the MDT for "running plates" varies with ecology, the race of the citizen, and the age of the officer.

Collection, storage, and retrieval of data by police, however, do not mean that the data are used for analytic purposes. Perhaps the technology of greatest interest to the law enforcement community at this time is *crime mapping,* in large part due to its ability to facilitate problem solving and community policing via the identification of areas with repeat calls for service or other underlying problems. Depending on the software used and the skill of the data analysts, crime mapping can be used to identify the locations of crime incidents and repeat calls for service, make resource allocation decisions, evaluate interventions, and inform residents about criminal activity and changes in such (Mamalian, LaVigne, and Groff, 2001). Despite the overwhelming interest in this technology, research indicates that few departments (13 percent of those surveyed) use any computerized crime mapping (Weisburd, Mastrofski, and Lum, 2001).

Where crime mapping is used (typically in larger urban police departments with greater resources), one of the most important innovations has been the *crime-analysis meeting*, first introduced in the NYPD, and adapted by departments in Hartford, Connecticut, Boston, and other venues (Silverman, 1999). In such meetings, data on crimes, gunshots, traffic problems, calls for service, arrests, drug problems, and problems of disorder are displayed. In monthly meetings in Boston, for example, PowerPoint presentations are used to project maps, pictures, tables, graphs, and animated figures onto a screen while officers present a narrative to an audience of top command and others. A book is created and rehearsal used to polish the presentation. Questions are asked and officers are urged to use the problem-solving scanning, analysis, response, and assessment (SARA) model and present results. Districts rotate in their presentations, and sometimes a special presentation is made, such as a report on a recent successful drug raid and seizure. In these meetings, a management approach is combined with data and feedback and evaluation to integrate the technology-derived data with practice and accountability.

Communicative Technology

The fifth type of technology consists of communicative devices used to diffuse information to the public at large rather than to gather in and analyze data. The external network of communications centered at the police department has been radically expanded and made more sensitive in the form of the Internet, the World Wide Web, and changes in the screening and allocation of calls to the police using 311 and 911. Technological advances in this realm have allowed, if not greater direct contact with the public, greater sharing of information with the public. For example, the Hartford (Connecticut) Police Department has provided seventeen computers for community groups to access crime reports and other data (Abt Associates, 2000: 82). Distribution of banal information that had previously been done through newsletters, handouts, ads, or meetings can now be distributed via Web sites and citizen-accessible terminals (as in Hartford and Chicago). San Diego has the capacity to distribute warnings (of tornadoes and other disasters) to local areas via e-communication, faxes, and telephone (Abt Associates, 2000: 54) and alert officers via e-mail to their laptops.

A recent article on police Web sites (Dykehouse and Sigler, 2000) showed that about 5 to 6 percent of criminal justice agencies now maintain sites registered with search engines. One use of the Internet involves the posting of crime information for citizens. Police are able to use their departments' Web sites to show maps, diagrams, statistics, and pictures. The FBI in June 1997 placed some 16,000 pages of case files on the Internet and plans to post a total of 1.3 million pages. This is said to serve a public requesting information under the Freedom of Information Act. Other uses of the Internet include posting the names and offenses of sex offenders in several states, a Web site featuring people who are delinquent in their child support payments, and a search engine to find arrestees' home addresses in Philadelphia and San Antonio (Scott, Brock, and Crawford, 2000).

Some departments use the Internet, e-mail, and visuals for information and educational purposes. The San Diego and Chicago police have created elaborate videos to be given out to publicize their community policing programs. The Chicago police have a large media budget for advertising on radio and television, preparing and distributing their tapes to neighborhood associations and the media. Communication technology has also created newer, more efficient forms of communication among officers. E-mails are generally not favored within police departments, even when available, for direct orders or commands because of the lagged or temporal feature of the communication. That is, messages may not be read, and another rule must be created and enforced requiring acknowledgment or response to e-mail. E-mail communication, as well as that afforded by cellular or digital phones, does have advantages, however. Chan's (2001) study in Australia showed that IT has facilitated information sharing among officers, accountability, and improved communication, resulting in a more cooperative and positive work atmosphere.

A FOURTH HORIZON: THE PRESENT

The fundamental police concern is typically with processing demand for service, not storage, retrieval, analysis, or even record management per se. Policing runs in a crisis mode and is overwhelmed with the present, impending, or possible crisis. Each information technology at first competes for space, time, and legitimacy with other known means and is judged in policing by somewhat changing pragmatic, often nontechnical, values— its speed, its durability and weight, and its contribution to the officers' notion of the role and routines. New technologies are put into use untested and without arrangement for the maintenance that will inevitably be needed. In other words, innovations are taken up on an ad hoc, here-and-now basis. Some IT facilities are purchased by state or local authorities for multiple purposes and are not vetted, contracted for, nor acquired by police management or budgetary officers. The absence of knowledge of IT has made police vulnerable to vendors (Abt Associates, 2000: 163), changes in city or county policies, and the handful of officers who have learned IT on the job and found a niche (Abt Associates, 2000: 72). This has increased maintenance costs, made replacement expensive, and created an array of incompatible databases and systems.

Large American urban police departments, in spite of evaluations showing the minimal role of computer technology in crime control and resource allocation for over twenty years (Tien and Colton, 1979; Manning, 1992a,b; Dunworth, 2000), continue to introduce second- and third-generation mainframe computers, buy a variety of software and work stations, and acquire a new round of complex and expensive information technologies. Large departments are facing a crisis in interfacing their outdated mainframe computer systems with new decentralized servers for specific functions and linking them in some fashion without loss of efficiency. Less costly innovations—laptop computers, mobile digital terminals that combine computing, radio, and telephone communication capacities, and cellular phones—have been introduced.

Fieldwork and interviews by myself, Dunworth (2000), and Greene (2000) in large North American cities suggest that departments have acquired new information technologies, and most departments possess:

- Many nonlinked *databases* (CAD, criminal records, other management data, fingerprints, visual images such as "mug shots," and many paper files). The RCMP in 2000 had four hundred databases and four work stations with partially compatible software (John L'Abbe, personal communication, June 18, 2000). The range of accessible but nonlinked databases is large and growing. These include record management (budgets, personnel, workload, and payroll) as well as external records—of dispatching; crime analysis, and geo-coded data; UCR/NIBRS systems (the latter being virtually nonexistent in practice); criminal and offender records; and various investigative records (detectives' work, case records, statements, evidence, and court decisions if any)—that typically are not integrated with patrol-generated data. Capacity to gather and process data quickly, to store them in an accessible and orderly fashion, and to develop vast files of fingerprints, criminal records, lab reports, arrest documents, and case files is considerable. The growth in storage capacity without access and use reveals the tendency to acquire systems without a clear standard or purpose and without considering the complexity of interface, collocation, and analysis. At times, this strains the memory capacity of departments, and computers crash or lack functional memory for peak time operations (Greene, 2000).

- Numerous *software* systems (ArcView, for geo-coded material; Pop TRAK, for monitoring problem solving; specialized programs for workload management; many spreadsheets for accounting and noncriminal records maintenance) and work stations equipped with many kinds of word processing and other software. Research suggests that they are rarely and poorly utilized (Dunworth, 2000; Abt Associates, 2000; Manning, 2001b), that data transfer is awkward and flawed, and that departments have diverse work stations, always including a sprinkling of Macs and IBM clones that do not speak to each other.
- A *Web site* with descriptive materials, some data on calls for service or crime patterns, and hyperlinks to other Web sites.
- Decentralized terminals allowing minimal data access to citizens in neighborhood terminals as in Hartford; laptops in Charlotte-Mecklenberg; mobile digital terminals with a phone and text base in other forces. Few terminals permit direct access for officers or citizens to detailed maps, selected printout, or on-line data because the databases that can be accessed are limited to recent CAD data. Questions of privacy limit access to many databases.
- Multiple and incompatible channels of communication from the public to the police and within the police department. These now include Web sites, e-mail, cell and land-based phones, "snail mail," personal visits and face-to-face encounters, networked communication via fiber-optic cables, paper documents, and e-files sent as attachments.
- Inconsistent user and backside *technology interfaces:* several servers, diverse and uneven mainframe access. Perhaps as a result of the ad hoc accretion of these via purchasing, the influence of vendors, trends, and failed innovations, police have disparate information technology clusters that are not cumulative in their effects.
- A tendency to use mapping information for short-term tactical interventions without "problem solving," in Boston and New Orleans (Jack McDevitt, personal communication, May 17, 2002).

In summary, even the most advanced forms of communicative technologies have been backfitted to the extant structure and traditional processes of the police organization. As of 2001, no police department had refined a systematically integrated collection of technologies to facilitate problem solving, crime prevention, policy analysis, or community interfaces (Abt Associates, 2000: 150–65). Chan's work (2001) on the Queensland Police Service, however, finds subtle changes in time use and skill levels among younger officers, as well as a positive attitude to computer-based innovation. Dunworth's review (2000) suggests that in general none of these are operational in any police department, and that the fundamental dimensions of community policing—interface with communities, interorganizational links, workgroup facilitation, environmental scanning, problem orientation, area-based accountability, and strategic management—are nowhere to be found well developed. There is little evidence that thirty years of funding technological innovations has produced much change in police practice or effectiveness. Furthermore, much of the present research on IT is intended to imagine the horizon for technology rather than to solve the fundamental infrastructural problems of training, skills, database merging, and software compatibility associated with transforming and rationalizing policing. Questions such as how to enhance the capacities needed to transform policing toward crime prevention and problem solving, developing links to the Internet and other agencies, and designing Web sites and public data access are scarcely discussed outside the world of police researchers and consultants.

ENCOUNTERS AND THE PRIMARY INTERFACE

These types of technologies require people work, or the process by which the computer becomes a useful connection to the work and the world. The people work required to use technology fully varies by the type of work, and policing is an essentially craft-based job of interpersonal management. Most discussions of information technology omit the context in which the worker and the machine confront each other (exceptions are the insightful and systematic work of Barley, 1983; Meehan, 2000b; and Zuboff, 1988). A close look at the impact of technology must move beyond attitudinal studies—bleak surveys with low response rates and ambiguous results—and *observe the actual context of use*.

Three kinds of *technological encounters* arise, and the nature of the interaction that is produced differs in meaning. Let us begin with the encounter and move back to the routines of the job on the ground.

Encounters

The first kind of technological encounter found in patrol policing is with technology used *pragmatically* and immediately by police once they decide it is relevant, a handy resource for control and discretion, and responsive to their routines. These technologies include forensic tools, weapons, and breathalyzers, as well as the several databases linked directly to the radio and MDT. The second kind of encounter is with technologies that more actively shape or, better yet, *interactively shape* decisions and choices of patrol officers. These include the radio, the MDT, and the CAD system (including MIS and records). These are seen as untrustworthy, too abstract and distant in their relevance, and perhaps threatening. The latter may be marginal or variable in effect, depending on officers' workloads, traditions, and departmental mission—service-, traffic-, or crime-oriented (Meehan, 1998: 231; Mastrofski and Ritti, 2000; Mastrofski, Ritti, and Snipes, 1994; Wilson, 1968; Wilson and Boland, 1978). Harper (1991) has suggested that the computer is a source of power to detectives in the UK and a threat to villains. It is useful to intimidate them into confessions and revelations in connection with a criminal case. The third is *technology that merely shadows the job:* IT with relatively little perceived operational impact that enhances strategic planning, management decision making, allocation of personnel, criminal intelligence files and reports, and the machinations of internal affairs. Almost all the technology associated with transformation and reform of policing—in the rhetoric, "community policing"—is of this sort: distant, irrelevant, trivial, and somewhat mysterious nevertheless. These technologies are "phantom technologies," misunderstood by officers, inaccessible to them, secret and often producing data sets encoded by software that makes the files literally unique and, even when connected, incomprehensible (Tien and Colton, 1979; Manning, 1989; Nesbary, 1994). In many respects, the "technologies" of problem solving, crime analysis, and prevention, crime mapping and other more analytic tools, are honored in the abstract but seldom if at all used by officers. Examples in the literature of problem solving are usually carried out, defined, managed, and written up by outside experts—researchers and consultants, not serving officers—or are hypothetical (Goldstein, 1990).

The Processing of Information and IT

Officers on the ground shape information technologies to their purposes. This is the primary interface. In order to understand information processing, or fact-information-knowledge transitions, in police departments, a natural history approach is needed. That is, the process of gathering and "input" must be traced from the call through the incident, the record, and the consequences, and on through the feedback and evaluation of the outcome (if any). This requires a somewhat rambling walk through the information processing "system" of a city police department.

Dispatchers, operators, and officers and their uses of the format (the computer file into which the facts gathered from the caller are placed) and the format of MDT textual messages or "radio talk") shape data input. The service categories, the names and numbers used to order the data, e.g., dispatching by the numbers, are a result of design decisions made by the computer engineers who installed the system. Generally, a format will include information about at least six items: (1) the caller, perhaps a name and address; (2) the call (time of day, day of the week, etc.); (3) the operator (an ID number given to the incident, the time the particular operator spent processing the incident); and (4) the incident itself (once accepted as a valid call by the operator), its classification and routing. When the dispatcher has assigned it to an officer, the format includes (5) the assignment number and (6) information on what, if anything, was done on the scene (the detail here depends on the feedback of the officer to the dispatcher) (see Manning, 1988). CAD processing serves to screen and allocate calls to dispatchers responsible for a given area of the city, to record assignments and current workload of officers, and permit brief (a few weeks at most) storage of records on a mainframe computer. More elaborate systems, such as those in Chicago, can hold several screens of information, or windows, ready while the call is being processed. In effect, message-call-job processing functions to screen and evaluate calls and to assign work to officers. Message processing is not a simple pass-through function, as approximately one-half the calls received do not leave the communications center or at least are not formally received by officers (see Toronto Metropolitan Police, 1997). Many departments do not keep systematic records of the outcomes of the call or require only such meaningless notations as "service rendered."

The patrol officer is the symbolic center of policing for both the public and the organization and the source of virtually all raw data, aside from that gathered in investigative work, in the organization. To understand how "data" become "information," we must accept that policing data is primarily tailored on the ground, processed, shaped, formatted, and entered into official records by the officer. Policing is defined throughout the organization, from top to bottom, as a practical craft, done in the here and now, one that partakes of the immanent crisis mentality. This input process must be considered the fundamental nexus for reformulating police use of IT.

It is perhaps churlish to list all the reasons and obstacles to the easy adaptation of IT to the present craft, especially as these are well known by all police command personnel. As has been pointed out above, given the inspectorial and response-based nature of Anglo-American policing, it is not surprising that the response is valued more than the context of the response, or indeed the further uses that might be imagined once the incident is "closed." It is well known that few quality controls are in place to monitor and validate recorded raw data. Sergeants and/or booking officers may question arrest data, as district or Crown attorneys may later, but unless a crisis arises, the quality of the data is of little concern. Bittner (1970: 57) notes that the internally applied complex rules and regulations defining discipline, including dress and demeanor, contrast to the rather cliched and vague recommendations concerning dealing with citizens. Only the discharge of firearms is closely monitored (Bittner, 1970: 101); the LAPD, for example, has no database on use of force or violent incidents other than the officers' written reports (Lawrence, 2000: 221). An organizational crisis brought on by responses to a fatal shooting, failed hostage negotiations, or a high-speed chase leading to death(s) precipitates scrutiny of once-processed raw data that has become information. This is the state of the art.

On-the-Ground Pressures: The Natural History of Facts and Information

Because pressure is placed on officers to respond to assigned calls, be available, and return to service in reasonable time and handle incidents in "normal time" (the time expected for officers to be out of service handling a given type of incident), much that is "known" is not recorded for official dispatch records. It may be recounted in stories, recorded in cars' logbooks, or captured in radio or MDT transmissions (themselves kept only briefly before the tapes are recorded over). Sensitivity to the protests of officers who view themselves as vulnerable and subject to capricious discipline means that supervisors are unwilling to implement and enforce problematic policies like mandatory arrest polices in domestic disputes or zero tolerance of drug dealing and selling in designated areas. As a rule, data about the *context* (what the officer thinks about what happened, its relation to previous incidents, patterns observed, ways that future calls might be handled and why) of an incident are omitted from written records. The nature of the incident, as defined by the officer, once framed and formatted, is the core knowledge and other matters are "fringe" (see chapter 10 on this process of abstraction from the natural event). Some information—e.g., information on restraining orders—is avoided or not written down because such knowledge and failure to act may make the police as an organization and individual officers vulnerable to lawsuits. Officers involved in awkward situations such as a shooting, chase, or serious beating of a citizen are inclined to confer privately before writing reports to "get the story straight" (Manning and Hunt, 1991) and may be advised by sergeants about how to write up an incident. The somewhat problematic issues of testimony, potential perjury, or disciplinary action and liability always shade the present encounter.

If an incident is written up, it remains problematic in the eyes of officers. All paperwork, because it contains an abstract perspective rather than the clinical or context-dependent features of the original scene, is discredited or distrusted. While creating and distributing work forms is only about 13 percent of work time (Mastrofski, Snipes, and Parks, 2000), the increase in formatted menus for arrests, field stops, and potential racial profiling is notable. The emphasis upon personalized authority and information, when combined with secretive guarding of knowledge and expeditiously completing tasks without paperwork, means that "street decisions" are largely unreviewed and unreviewable. Only under certain specified conditions does police knowledge become shared, reproducible, and held collectively in accessible organization records. On the other hand, a well-written report is one that is elegantly parsimonious.

These recorded materials are kept in diverse storage areas (some in warehouses outside the department itself) and in decentralized, nonlinked systems. Many officers, from my observations, have limited grasp of the capacities of the computerized facilities in their cars, minimal or nonexistent access to or use of mapping and printers, and almost no knowledge of software and terminals—computer skills are seldom acquired through police training. Like the rest of us, they are often unable to understand and correct texts and messages after error messages appear.

Once processed, the data are deposited in databases, but these may not be linked to any other databases. For example, dispatch records and detectives' records are not articulated in any department I know of in any useful, planned fashion. Unlike the classic bureaucracy that features centralized, formatted, and accessible stored records and files, police keep their data highly decentralized. It is a complex network of sources, linked by trust, secrecy, private information, and loosely connected data banks. Data are organized around case numbers and records in other organizations—courts and laboratories, for example—as well as in the property and evidence storage rooms of the police; they are written in different programming languages depending on when the database was created and the programs written and installed. Information is sedimented into a few richly textured and coherent islands and isolated from other islands of information.

Only under certain specified conditions—usually when a crisis such as a beating or shooting that receives public attention, or a decision by an operator or dispatcher that causes injury or death, focuses police attention and draws together police resources—does police information become accessible, understood, generally shared, reproducible knowledge held collectively in organization records. This means that data sharing is not possible unless it has been planned as an aspect of the original system. Once databases are organized, it is very difficult to reorganize them, especially after staff or consultants have left, retired, or been transferred. Little effort is made to systematize information from the several databases for future analysis or planning purposes (Nesbary, 1994). There is a policy-absent reason for this as well, for police commanders eschew responsibility for forward planning and rationalizing and linking databases because they believe the action, and discretion, is on the ground. The unwillingness of command personnel to specify in advance the nature of information needed and to ensure that it is gathered and processed means that most police information remains aggregated, context-dependent knowledge. This reduces command responsibility to supervise and blurs lines of accountability.

If data are entered, and accessible, officers decide when and how to use them. They view much of what is transmitted as an aspect of monitoring and surveillance of their work, rather than "support." Refinements in the 911 system, such as E911 (to track the addresses and numbers of callers) and MDTs that allow officers to review their calls and calls assigned to others, as well as calls to that address for a selected period of time, are used periodically to check on officers' work productivity. Officers on the ground differentially trust the information they hear or see from central communications. That which they trust, mostly criminal, warrant, driving, and vehicle records, are always viewed as appearing too "slow." MDTs have always been viewed with ambivalence (Pays, Boyanowsky, and Dutton, 1984). The most common effect of installing MDTs with direct links to motor vehicle and criminal records is that officers can "run plates" almost endlessly and show "productivity" (Meehan, 1998: 231–34).

Officers, especially detectives, see information as a source of power and influence. They also tend to personalize it and define information as property. The uses and distribution of information raise questions of politics, questions of power and authority. I refer here to the sergeants who run daily report production; officers who produce maps; programmers and civilian computer experts, and accountants and fiscal officers who control disbursements. Data are power, and changes in databases and access to them have potential for creating political conflict. In investigative units, very little case-relevant information is shared except among partners because clearances are based on knowledge and are bases for success. Pressure to create automated or at least systematic case management is increasing as a result of police incompetence in media-enhanced politically sensitive cases (e.g., the botched case of the murder of Stephen Lawrence in London, and the brutal sex-murder case against Paul Bernardo in Ontario), and best represented now by the English system, HOLMES, used nationally for major incidents.

Within the organization, organizational features, as well as the content of messages, amplify the asymmetrical aspects of information flow and processing. Police calls are numbered sequentially, and they can be easily re-called by neighborhood, area, time of day, or type of call. If, however, one wants to reorganize calls around an analytic category such as household composition, percentage of rentals, or juvenile gang activity, major reprogramming must be undertaken.

Obstacles to integrated justice systems that encompass police departments are profound. Unfortunately, goodwill efforts to systematize databases and access meet with (well-known) obstacles. Data may not be online or are entered by hand periodically. Routine computer failures, "crashes," and slowdowns, as well as routine maintenance problems, handicap information system maintenance. Often, the cost of expert advice is too high or in-house people too few to cope with routine demands of maintenance, updating, and innovation.

Dunworth (2000: 398) observes that there are entrenched information processing systems and data at local agencies; difficulty in coordinating interagency projects; limited understanding of technological issues and capacities; needs for systems to be private and secure; fundamental interagency differences in recording/reporting systems; and a shortage of information technology professionals (Dunworth, 2000: 398). He further infers from his fieldwork that internal record-keeping systems are local and not linked and are kept mostly in paper rather than in electronic files. The records themselves are gathered and maintained in part based on legal and civil liberties protections that vary by record type. Servers and mainframes are awkwardly combined, and there are no universal formats or software for data integration. Among the police and civilian employees, there are few people who understand and can operate, maintain, and repair the extent systems and very little actual interest in doing so.

SUMMARY

The nature of police information, gathered in a context, means that innovations in technology do not have results consistent with an engineering-based information-driven conception of the impact of information systems on organizational efficacy. The primary contingency of policing, the focus and theme of modern policing, patterns the work. A review of the types of technology that have been attractive to police suggests that mobility and weaponry still are considered the fundamentals and that training is least innovative. The transformative devices and new analytic devices have promise. A history of IT shows that a great critical mass of data or facts and some information are being gathered with no purpose, aim, or consequence. The core of policing, the patrol function, sets and determines how, why, and where what information is obtained, how it is processed (in large part), and what is and can be done with it. The introduction of new and more refined information systems is inconsistent with present practice. Future shifts toward prevention and software, mechanics, or equipment alone will not accomplish problem solving.

A movement is now under way in policing—imaging and imagining the pathway to future, intelligence-led policing. The exercise of imagination requires hearing what is not heard as in jazz or music generally (notes omitted, coming in before or after the beat, improvised riffs that take off "between notes"), seeing what is left out or added in as contrast (as in Picasso's figures), and looking beneath the surface of words to practice and tacit knowledge. This perspective must be created. Absent a perspective, we are left with mere observation, and thus the need to see the *enframing* (how the technology is seen and what it is intended to do) and the *dramatics* of technology (how it is selectively defined, used, interpreted, accommodated to ongoing routines) as an ongoing process.

Some of the many consequences, so far as we now know, of IT innovations are described in the following chapter, where I take a process-oriented and dramaturgical view of technological innovation. There, I will address also the processes by which police technology is *symbolized* or represented, and changes associated with IT innovation in patterns of authority, division of labor, role relations, teamwork, and expressive aspects of police patrol work.

SEVEN

PROCESSES: INFORMATION TECHNOLOGY AS A SOURCE OF DRAMA

INTRODUCTION

Uncertainty has a place in organizations that is often embedded in past practices, ideologies, and histories—stories—and is not always the subject of overt dialogue. It is clear, however, that the introduction of IT to policing is a multistimulus, a *dramatic statement of some kind,* requiring a response from within organizations. Such statements cry out for counterstatements, and they are found in police organizations. Nevertheless, little is known about how this process of adaptation to technology unfolds, especially since the police organization conceals its actions as much as possible, in spite of media mendacity and rapaciousness. In line with the unfolding story thus far, it is clear that the introduction of new technologies, those in the family of IT, have been introduced at great cost and with great publicity in the last thirty years, but the attitude of the police and of most scholars remains surprisingly hopeful, but without empirical support, even as the century ends (Dunworth, 2000: 412). What is needed is a closely observed analysis of technological innovation that combines the aesthetic and instrumental aspects of technological innovation. Pfaffenberger suggests a series of stages and a natural history of technology as a means to identify the challenge of technological innovation and the response to it, or, in Burke's (1989) terms, a statement and counterstatement. Organizational response to new information technology in urban Anglo-American police departments has a natural history that includes phases of entry, liminality, adaptation, resistance, and reconstitution (Pfaffenberger, 1992; Manning, 1992b). This scheme focuses attention on the stages and dynamics of adaptation to technology, but it also suggests that active forces shape technology and that the process can be both a cause and an effect of organizational change (Thomas, 1994). I begin with a diachronic, or time-sensitive, analysis and end with a brief synchronic, or non-time-sensitive, analysis. Thus history steps into the future. We now turn to an analysis of the ways in which police organizations adapt in time to technological innovations. An analytic framework encompassing the social organization of policing is needed to understand the impact of new technologies.[1]

THE ROLE OF INFORMATION TECHNOLOGY IN POLICING

We have seen the features of policing outlined in chapter 2 shape the emerging processes by which they cope with new uncertainties, especially those brought on by new transformative and analytic technologies. While there are limits to the consequences of new IT, they do produce an internal dynamic best described as a dialectic among change, adaptation, and response.

In theory, centralized command and control in the police operate via the radio, routines, procedures, rules and regulations, and close supervision (Bordua and Reiss, 1966), and these communications are monitored and recorded. This notion, tied to the central theme of responsiveness, has not changed in the last thirty years, but policing has expanded to include a broader notion of the mission. This is the rhetoric of community policing. This rhetoric has proceeded without substantial changes in demand management—roughly speaking, dispatching systems—in all but a few large departments such as San Diego and Los Angeles. Any form of community policing is seen as an add-on to the core function of responding to calls. The guiding conceit is that communication links patrol officers on a given channel to a single voice of authority, produces official records of decision making, makes the police more accountable, and permits civilian review and audit, especially of major events. To the extent that traces, electronic or paper, remain of these communications, they can form part of a reconstructed record used in internal affairs investigations, departmental hearings, media inquiries, or legal proceedings. This is the public face of police rationality and IT. Themes in the patrol subculture and in middle management counter the dominant meanings attributed to police work by

1. The myth of the inherent rational development of information systems has been recently challenged, as have assumptions of rationality about the impacts of technology (Orlikowski and Baroudi, 1991). The idea that systems evolve in some predictable and uniform way is not supported by empirical studies (Hough, 1980; Manning, 1988, 1992a). Politics and history as well as the specific material technology at issue must be considered.

top management. This may be a generic adaptation (Kunda, 1992). Unfortunately, none of the several sophisticated ethnographies of patrol work (Rubinstein, 1973; Van Maanen, 1974, 1988; Ericson, 1982; Herbert, 1998) carefully examines the subtle processes of compliance associated with police command or the varying role of the new technologies in this dynamic. Technology, often seen as the sole driving force for change, is but one element in a complex game of work control and supervision. Technology in policing has not been well described. Furthermore, unfortunately, the veracity of Bordua and Reiss's observation, made more than thirty years ago, remains: "there is no detailed empirical description of command processes in a police department" (1966: 68). This means that we have snapshots of patrol work in big cities, we have brief cases studies of some technologies, and we have very little understanding of command and control and the internal politics of policing.

Clearly, the development of IT is related to the thrust to create managerial accountability based on the techniques and rhetoric of profit-making organizations, emphasizing cost control, efficiency, and decentralized, lean functions (Chan, 2000: 2). The combination of external scrutiny of costs amid budgets is complemented internally by audits, cost accounting, complaints, performance indicators, and evaluations. IT, in short, is a window into the functioning of policing, as well as a potential for increased quality of public service.

A dramaturgical analysis should take into account how changes over time, both within and across segments, produce change, and how resistance is fostered, reduced, or increased by the dialectic produced. While policing is a pragmatic, instrumentally focused occupation, it nevertheless has a "moral" core that is quasi-sacred, and sentiments attach to aspects of the work including routines, tools, and especially personal tools (the car, gun, badge, handcuffs, uniforms, nightstick, pepper spray, radio); the tools tend to become a sign of personal identity and self and are thus relatively sacred to officers. Even more distant tools routinely employed, such as cell phones, mobile digital terminals (MDTs), and handheld personal digital assistants (PDAs, which combine the cellular phone with the Internet, e-mail, pagers, and other functions), strikingly illustrate personalization, introjection of selves, and aesthetics.

TECHNOLOGY AS A SIGNIFIER

"Technology," when seen semiotically (recall chapter 1), is a signifier without an obvious signified or referent, but it can be associated with many connotations and perhaps many denotations depending on context. Its

Four Meanings of Technology in Police Organizations

OVERT MEANINGS (DENOTATIONS)	COVERT MEANINGS (CONNOTATIONS)
1. Regulation (statement)	
	Organizational control emphasized
	Ritual used to stabilize uses
	Status quo asserted
	Old content placed in new formats
2. Adjustments (counterstatements)	
a. Countersymbolization	Meaning redefined by those without it
b. Counterdelegation	Technology acquired nonofficially
c. Counterappropriation	Disarming and obviating technology
d. Sabotage	Destroying or stealing the technology
3. Technological reconstitution (restatement)	
	The code remains unchanged
	More of the same uses and activities
	Surface changes appear
4. Technological reintegration (statement)	
	The social field is modified
	Role shifts occur
	A new ideology of use develops

multiple meanings indicate the adaptations organizations make to the introduction of technology. The accompanying table shows four distinctive, yet overlapping, meanings of technology. Semiotically, each is a signifier attached to a different signified. This produces a sign. There are thus four signs, each labeled "technology": *Technology 1* represents processes of regulation of technology; *Technology 2* represents technology as a source of modes of adjustment; *Technology 3* refers to the reconstitution of technology; and *Technology 4* stands for processes of social reintegration.

All four technologies as signs exist within any police organization. These four meanings each reference a cluster of paradigmatically organized, associated overt meanings of "technology." By "overt" I mean that they are generally understood and recognized in rhetoric and descriptions of operations. The term "paradigmatically" indicates an analytically created cluster of words or expressions with similar denotative (content) meanings. The four paradigms signal both positive and negative similarities of meanings of "technology," while concealing relevant dissimilarities. Selected covert meanings of technology, or connotations, are shown in column two of the table; both covert and overt meanings are illustrated in this chapter. The identified meanings work within a set of objective and subjective forces, or a social field—in this case, policing. The policing field has four paradigms, each of which contains a type of technological discourse—"statements" that generate "counterstatements," or opposing symbolizations (Burke, 1962). Statement and counterstatement take place within an organizational context.

Let us examine the four overt meanings of technology—regulation, adjustment, technological reconstitution, and technological reintegration—in the police organization. Reintegration is discussed specifically with respect to expected changes in patrol roles and tasks. This is a metaphoric framework within which to explore the range of responses to technological innovation. They may not appear in the order in which they're presented, and even if one stage is necessary to produce another, it is not a sufficient condition.

FOUR OVERT (DENOTATIVE) MEANINGS OF TECHNOLOGY
Technological Regulation

Technology 1 refers to the regulation or routinization of technology by those who introduced it. Such regulation can be simply defined as the processes by which technology manifests itself as evidence of the organization's formal authority system. It leads to efforts to maintain the present organizational stratification system, to suppress alternative uses and definitions of technology, and to sustain connections between the present and past social arrangements. Here are several examples of technological regulation in police departments.

When adapting computer-assisted dispatching (CAD), a British (BPD) and American (MPD) force placed sergeants in the role of dispatcher to make assignments to officers face to face and via two-way radio and computer, thus reproducing the traditional vertical flow of command. Radio dispatches are meant to be heard by an officer "as if it were an order from the chief." The communicative model remains the face-to-face "command and control" idea borrowed from the military.

Record keeping in these two departments and all others with which I am acquainted employs the previous formats, even though computer-based formats are used for dispatching. In both departments, the vehicle log contains the essential data on officers' activities. The computer printouts of "runs" for a given precinct from the police communications center in the MPD are incomplete. It omits precise information on actions taken. It contains no details concerning what, if anything, was undertaken on the scene, the disposition of the assignment, the credibility of the callers' descriptions of the event, and the validity of the initial classification of the assignment by the dispatcher and/or operator. It simply affirms that an assignment was made and carried out in some fashion.

When serving a warrant in Dallas County, Texas, officers can use fax machines to produce records of the contents of a search, and leave a copy with the householder. In Houston, Texas, criminal cases are electronically filed directly with the district attorney's office, yet officers employ the same formats and observe the previous lines of authority. Electronic transmission of files and documents speeds or facilitates a process, but it does not enhance the quality of a document or its contents.

This is a process of "officialization," or using the form regardless of the content, and the technology is merely an alternative mode or vehicle for dispensing with the incident.

In Houston, where a dispatching system attempts to differentiate police response to calls for service by their seriousness and potential for further risk, the police use minicomputer terminals in precincts to check the progress of 911 calls directed to that precinct. Officers telephone callers and request feedback on the progress of the event and significant changes in the level of need or danger. They can decide to terminate nonviable calls. While the enhanced feedback capacity of the computer permits more rapid control over priority setting, decisions remain on the ground.

In San Diego, California, and Reno, Nevada (Abt Associates, 2000), tracking systems were designed so that officers could show when they were engaged in problem solving ("out of service") and to report the content and outcome of the work. In San Diego, most files were opened and never completed, not sent on to crime analysts, and of little value in assessing the extent of ongoing problem solving. In Reno, software was designed to take officers through the scanning, analysis, response, and assessment (SARA) model (Abt Associates, 2000: 104), keep records of problem-solving activities, location, type of problem, and officers and supervisors involved. However, in Reno data that might be relevant to the exercise are largely unavailable and crime analysis is not done. "Scanning is mostly based on personal observations, analysis in support of problem-solving typically unsystematic, and assessment is often lacking due to unavailability of data" (Abt Associates, 2000: 11). In other words, the tracking system does not work and is not used, and the data available—when they are available— are meager; outcomes are not monitored and assessed, and the tracking operation is largely symbolic.

In the five case studies done by Abt Associates, only one department, San Diego's, had a working crime analysis unit. In Hartford, police had no access to raw data; in San Diego, the STAT report (a description of calls by division and address) is not utilized, and the Abt report concludes that there are few rewards for crime analysts, and that they are not trained. The CompStat-like systems in Hartford, and Boston use "crime analysis" as short-term descriptions of reported crimes, which are then used to deploy officers tactically, as in the past. Officers are assigned to deal with immediate crime-based incidents, not problems. Although the data used in

Boston, for example, include such diverse things as gunshots fired, most frequent sources of phone calls for service, traffic incidents, and homicides, they are treated as naturally occurring, police-needed delicts that require action in traditional tactical fashion.

A perhaps more serious way in which regulation occurs is that the present IT sets the limits and constraints on innovation because memory, software capacity, and fields available for data entry are limited. Databases are not linked. For example, although the San Diego department records field stops electronically, the police can only use ten characters in three fields—age, race, and infraction. Similarly, while Massachusetts state law requires that data on traffic stops be recorded for purposes of monitoring possible racial profiling, the Department of Motor Vehicles records the data (from handwritten records of stops made by officers) in a field of only nine characters, five of which are for coding the basis for the search Thus the formatting omits the context of the stop, and the decision of the officer, not an analytic scheme, becomes the basis for recording the data.

"Technology" in these examples marks and reaffirms the extant field of authority, typical modes of domination, and the present distribution of power. The information technology associated with CAD and management information systems (MIS) installed for strategic planning, information storage and retrieval, and on-line responsive capacities (Tien and Colton, 1979) is encoded within traditional structures.

Adjustments

The introduction of technology produces responses or counterstatements in organizations, which are associated with Technology 2. When adjustment occurs, it commonly takes one of four forms—countersymbolization, counterappropriation, counterdelegation, and sabotage (the last of which is not included in Pfaffenberger's scheme)—but it is not clear at this point in fieldwork what conditions might produce one or the other. Members of organizations can elevate its absence through countersymbolization, obtain aspects of the artifact (such as access to computer functions) without being responsible for it through counterappropriation, or reduce its value by disarming the feature having relevance to their work through counterdelegation. These responses may be episodic and exploratory and may "sediment" into a dominant mode in time. Let us examine each of these counterstatements.

COUNTERSYMBOLIZATION. Organization members countersymbolize a technology when they redefine the meaning of its absence, thus using that absence as a marker of their own exceptional status within the organization.

This usually occurs in the more powerful segments of the organization when members choose to bypass the technology yet assert their status.

In a small suburban Texas police department, the chief refused to buy, possess, or learn to use available computers to review available departmental information. However, each morning he arrived with a cup of coffee in the cramped deputy chief's office to gossip and ask his deputy to show him the computer-generated reports on the previous night's events, reported crimes, and personnel changes. The police chief of another suburban Texas town refused to have a computer in his office, and required all reports to be given to him in hard copy (not sent via e-mail) and expressed in under two pages. In San Diego, although the deputy chiefs all had computers, they were nearly the last group to receive them; it is not known whether they were used or for what purpose (Abt Associates, 2000: 60). In these cases, the top command maintains the mystique of distance and command and defines the absence of a computer, and communications via means other than the computer, as a sign of power.

Each innovation can be the occasion for drama, as one informant told me in my Canadian study. "I sent an e-mail to the deputy chief and the chief [of a large metropolitan force]. I got no reply, but soon a memo appeared: 'There will be no e-mails sent directly to the Chief.'" Other versions of this are "do not reply to the sender of this message" when it is sent out from above to those below. In Charlotte-Mecklenberg, Reno, and Hartford, e-mail addresses were assigned to officers, but used only internally if at all (Abt Associates, 2000). E-mails from citizens are not accepted in any police department I am aware of, although they seem a promising way to increase information flow and feedback. Social constraints on technology are thus marked.

Investigative work and intelligence units generally are outside the patrol-based CAD system. Both are given greater status in policing than patrol work, and the absence of a radio marks and symbolizes these differences. While many detective units use computer files on previous arrests and convictions, they are used reactively, in the context of a known suspect (Simon, 1991). Other research suggests computers are useful to investigators with respect to coercing suspects and informants, frightening them with the putative power of data and information police may have (Harper, 1991). This activity rather strikingly makes the point that instrumental and expressive aspects of IT cannot be separated.

Intelligence units are rarely linked directly to the CAD system and rely on secondary and tertiary information processed by command or investigative officers (Manning, 1992a). Crime analysis and crime mapping units are in general isolated physically and symbolically and rarely directly consulted. Boston, I found in my 2002 fieldwork, is an exception to this generalization.

The events recorded in CAD data are treated as responses to an ahistorical series of unrelated events, disconnected from long-term problem analysis and planning and underutilized in strategic planning activities. Most CAD systems cannot be linked to other databases and are used essentially as on-line monitoring. Conversely, no one can retrieve incidents if the data are not entered into computer files in the first instance, or if they are entered by a problem label, general term, or analytic category that is not formatted or built into the software. Thus, new software designed to aid problem solving, if compatible with the hardware and software of the mainframe, still may require some programming to assemble "problem" items if their tags are not conventionally used, such as crime, incident, arrest, or evidence files. The lack of articulation of intelligence and investigative functions and information files with CAD suggests that these functions are perceived as inconsistent with the focal concern of policing, the here and now happening on the street. Given the claimed potential of information technologies in intelligence and drug law enforcement, it could be argued that the lack of sophisticated integration of CAD with intelligence functions reveals the ambivalence with which computer-based (record-keeping) information technologies are viewed. The point is that while the organization buys software and databases and installs them, they are systematically unavailable differentially within the organization.

Dallas patrol officers in the late 1990s developed a test: a countersymbolization and appropriation strategy that might be called "the Alamo run." A patrol officer would bet that he or she could drive a patrol car (without official permission) from Dallas to San Antonio, have a Polaroid picture taken at the Alamo, and return within the eight-hour shift. Fellow officers would call the runner on his or her cellular phone if anything untoward took place on the officer's assigned territory and cover the calls in the officer's territory while he or she was on the mission. In East Haven, Connecticut, the chief of police announced that cellular phones were being removed from police cruisers because they were being used to call 900 numbers that offer sexually explicit conversations with women. The calls were costing about seventy dollars a month (*Law Enforcement News,* September 15, 1992). A former FBI agent reported to me that phones in federal offices (DEA, FBI, etc.) in one large Midwestern city were altered to block calls to 900 numbers.

COUNTERAPPROPRIATION. Technology officially denied to members of some organizational segments can nevertheless be acquired. Officers may access information technology—e.g., pagers, laptops, personal cellular phones, and personal organizers—through nonofficial means.

The use of cellular phones requires some additional clarification and background, as they are a somewhat anomalous development. The cellular phone was introduced to policing in the mid-1980s, when it became inexpensive and compact and regional phone networks and towers were built. It was adopted in several departments to facilitate community policing programs and is increasingly popular. The intent was to give the community policing officers a direct means of communicating with people in the policed neighborhoods. In Flint, Michigan, a sergeant supervises fifteen officers, each with a cellular phone, who carry out crime prevention and community policing duties. By 1991, the cellular phone was standard equipment in patrol cars in Dallas and widely used in Houston. They are spreading rapidly in Texas to specialized units such as vice and narcotics and among supervisory personnel. In Detroit, they are given to command officers of the rank of inspector and above and installed in cars. Pagers and cell phones are common throughout the Midwest and used by officers at all ranks. The cellular phone is now used in patrol cars and by supervisory-level police (up to the rank of deputy chief) in many middle-sized American cities (among them Lansing, Michigan; Madison, Wisconsin; and Midland, Beaumont, Waco, and Amarillo, Texas). Some suburban Michigan cities (such as Auburn Hills and Warren) have phones built in to the MDT.

Cellular phones are issued to patrol officers, top management, and some specialized units. Cellular phone behavior is very difficult to study because not only do many officers at the sergeant level now have department-issued cell phones, but also because many officers carry private personal phones and tuck them under the visor on the driver's side, in their bags, or in the trunk of the car. Personal phones are used at breaks and on duty to make personal calls. While generally departmental cellular phones are issued to command officers and not patrol officers, cellular phones are now inexpensive and are bought and used by patrol officers to carry out departmental and/or private business during working hours. These phones may be analogous to the second handgun carried by many officers. Although not officially provided, they are tacitly approved or overlooked.

Cellular phones are growing rapidly in use and are less costly each year to operate. The number of cellular phones in the United States has risen from some 340,000 in 1985, to 8,000,000 in 1992, to 110,000,000 in 2000, to 128,000,000 in 2001 (http://wireless.fcc.gov). (Predictions are poor: it was expected that there would be as many as 10,000,000 in use in 1995, and over 20,000,000 by 2000.) Exactly how many are now in use in police departments is unknown, but they are one source of rising demand as measured by calls for service, and special procedures are being developed to process cell phone calls.

Counterappropriation certainly proceeded as officers used the phones to call friends and sex hot lines, avoid supervision, reduce runs by handling complaints by phone, or avoid work—and these all sometimes produce spectacular results. In many respects, cellular phones created ambiguous indices of their evaluation. Cellular phones are used at both the top and the bottom of the command structure, and some were privately purchased to use with pagers. The PDA is portentous, if bought and used by individual officers for use on the job. Yet their meaning within the command–rank structure is unclear because absence can indicate loyalty or failure to acquire a new status symbol outside organizational boundaries. Additionally, any police computer can be used to browse the Web, play games on "company time," do homework, send e-mail to friends, and so on. Some of the long hours many officers spend at desks are filled as they are in other organizations—playfully.

COUNTERDELEGATION. If a technological feature threatens the distribution of power in a field, and threatens the power of the particular segment to which it is "applied," the process of counterdelegation is a likely consequence. One indication of this is disarming a technological feature. Perhaps the most obvious example of this is neutralizing the buzzer indicating a seat belt is unattached by connecting the two parts of the belt together permanently under the driver or by disconnecting the wiring to the buzzer. This allows officers to stop, leap out, and act quickly in line with their core notions of the role and to disregard safety concerns or command wishes to reduce injury rates. The Los Angeles Police Department experimented with several laptops to find a model that would survive being thrown out the window if an officer at work had to answer a call quickly. During the late 1990s, when police departments were experimenting with both car-installed MDTs and laptops, special hardened cases were developed to protect the in-built computers in case of crashes or emergencies. These roughly doubled the cost of the computer, in part because the extra protective shells caused the computers to overheat absent special and costly cooling. The size, awkwardness, and difficulty in inserting the computer in the entrance portals meant that many were broken—this may have been sabotage or merely an attempt to realign the laptop with patrol practice.

Consider now further examples of counterdelegation.

The automatic vehicle locators (AVLs) used in vehicles in Saint Louis were designed to provide a sector quadrant location for any equipped police car. They were intended to monitor movement and increase the safety of officers who might be unable to respond to a radio call by providing a signal independent of verbal radio communications (Larson, Colton, and Larson, 1976). The newly equipped cars disappeared—cars were "lost" and could not be relocated. Dispatchers made radio inquiries to establish the cars' positions and could raise them after some time and relocate and enter them anew on the grid. Interviews with officers revealed the unseen dynamics behind the recurrent pattern of "lost" patrol vehicles. Officers perceived the AVL as a Big Brother control and surveillance device and determined to foil it dramatically. The officers discovered that if they switched off the engine while crossing a bridge, the car's signal would disappear at the communications center. They would be "lost" and could not be relocated until they reported their current location. Once off the grid, officers could respond and reposition themselves by reporting a false location and continue to be a phantom misleading "blip" on the dispatcher's screen. Such behavior sits just between sabotage (see below) and counter-delegation.

MDTs, basically in-car computer-radio-telephones, can be manipulated by not entering information or "police notes" intended for others, not distributing information known to others after having been dispatched to a call via MDT, and typing in misleading information about one's present location, intentions to attend a call, or arrival time. The editing of MDT messages is doubtless more common now since the scrutiny and publication of MDT messages between officers after the Rodney King savaging (Cannon, 1997; Meehan, personal communication, 1999). Attention to what is recorded and written on this channel will also be precipitated by the new interest in patterns of profiling and race-based stops and searches.

The radar gun, issued to clock speeders, can be converted to a self-protective service instrument. Officers in one central Michigan department who wanted to sleep on the night shift would back into an alley or parking lot with the patrol car facing out and the radar gun on. When another car approached the beep of the radar gun would alert the officer to a possible visit by a sergeant (Meehan, personal communication, 1999).

The cellular phone seems to be emerging now in departments such as those in several middle-sized upper-middle-class cities in Michigan with MDT–cellular phone combinations. Supervisors use output from MDTs at the end of the shift, and cellular phones as management tools, to monitor "production." The supervisor can check when the microphone on the MDT is converted to a cellular phone, see the number called, and use output such as traffic stops, tickets, and vehicle checks to supervise and advise officers about how they should improve their "activity."[2]

In spite of apparent standardization of record keeping, mainframe and other computer software may be incompatible. In Los Angeles, for example, the new laptop computers introduced in 1989 could not interface directly with the LAPD's mainframe computer. Officers continued to come into the precinct as in the past for breaks, to complete paperwork, to exchange gossip, and to "download" their diskettes to be converted via ASCII language and then "uploaded" onto the departmental mainframe (National Institute of Justice, 1993). In San Diego, a new handheld computer is used by motorcycle officers to write field reports, traffic citations, and other official reports. It is also linked to the Internet and can transmit files for printing via infrared rays. The computer is kept in the saddlebags of the cycle when not in use. However, when officers began to use the computers to surf the Internet for amusing (primarily sexual and pornographic) Web sites, command officers ruled that all computers must be brought into the precinct to be recharged and the contents of all files downloaded. This was both an instance of counterdelegation and an attempt by the command segment to reconstitute the technology.

These examples suggest, as does the traditional manipulation of radio information by patrol officers, how the process of valuing sense making on the ground is elevated over electronically mediated communication. For example, officers use radio silence to maintain autonomy and to play with radio messages (most are in fact socioemotional in content; see Meehan, 1998: 243). In command-communication centers, call takers and operators play with the video display screens and menus. Call takers, dispatchers, and officers send obscene jokes, lies, and embarrassing messages to each other. Although such play lodges expressiveness in the social structure of the organization, it is also a source of uncertainty and autonomy (Manning, 1988: chaps. 3, 4, 7). The evaluation and feedback features of CAD, when intended to function as surveillance tools, are reduced in salience.

New meanings of the technology emerge. On the one hand, workers use IT for their own purposes, not the organization's, using it to maintain discretion and autonomy and to add a playful dimension to the work.[3] As

---

2. In a large Canadian force I studied in 1999, some five to ten tickets a month were expected, and eight a day is considered "easy" when using a radar gun. Ticket production is seen as "activity" and indicates an officer is attentive, interested, and actively monitoring the environment.

3. New IT can shape organizational learning insofar as these technologies alter work routines and norms of production, output, and competence. It is possible that on-line inquiries to the de-

noted above, they certainly weaken the overt use of official control. On the other hand, management may collude in some ways, either to avoid confrontation or because they share the ambivalence of officers on the ground to technological innovations. As Chatterton (1991) notes, supervisors and command personnel are often ignorant of computer techniques and overlook the patrol officers' resistance to using computer files for strategic planning. They turn a blind eye as long as the appearance of compliance—e.g., turning in required paperwork—is maintained. Implicit collusion between workers and management is probably a common feature of overt conflict resulting from the introduction of new technologies. While the official paper and record keeping maintains the appearance of conformity, responses create a dialectic of meaning. Clearly, drawing sharp divisions between management and the worker is misleading when collusions arise. Much like other forms of corruption, cooperation is necessary to truly dismantle management controls.

SABOTAGE. A fourth adjustment is possible. Sabotage, literally putting in the boot, based on the lower participants' occupational culture and contrasted with the culture of management, signals a loss of command authority and power. A variation on counterdelegation, sabotage can take the form of direct destruction of machines, work stoppages or slow-downs, strikes, increased union activities, and associated bargaining demands. Rather than compromise, sabotage is a form of overt and sanctionable resistance to it. This tactic is usually touched off by feelings of loss of job control or rapid changes in the conditions of work. If successful, this means that the technology in question is neither reconstituted nor reintegrated.

Simple, even impulsive, acts can render a technology impotent (as anyone who has spilled coffee on a keyboard well knows). Dunworth notes the frequency with which laptops malfunction or are out of service (Dunworth, 2000: xx). Kevin Haggerty (based on Ericson and Haggerty, 1997) reports (personal communication, February 3, 1998) that an officer in a fit of pique poured graphite on a keyboard to disable it. Radios are left off, on other channels, or inoperable for periods of time when officers choose to be unofficially out of service. The most striking examples of sabotage involve the clever dismantling of in-car video cameras. These cameras,

---

partment of motor vehicles increase pressures on patrol officers to produce, and that computers increase pressures for more efficient records management by detectives (Harper, 1991). See the careful studies of Barley, 1986, 1988; Suchman, 1987; Zuboff, 1988; Barley and Orr, 1997; Thomas, 1994; and Latour, 1996.

mounted behind the rearview mirror at the upper center of patrol cars' windshields and equipped with a voice-activated microphone, can be shaped to officers' routines. A writer riding along with LAPD officers noted that immediately upon leaving the precinct, the officers disconnected the video camera "linked to a sealed box in the trunk containing a 12 hour video that is part of a new experiment" (Rayner, 1995: 32–33). The camera was immobilized, the officers said, because it symbolized undue surveillance and was installed merely "so they can beef [make complaints against] us." Once the camera's eye was blinded, the two patrolmen checked their MDT for new calls (Rayner, 1995: 33).

More systematic sabotage occurs by simply failing to supply resources to support certain functions with ostensive importance. The criminal intelligence division of police departments is often not sent information to organize or synthesize and has no access to "raw data." In effect, the unit is sabotaged by lack of current and relevant information. Internal affairs units stand often in the same kind of relation to patrol and must resort to creating their own leads.

Technological Reconstitution

In technological reconstitution, the apparent or surface features of the work change, but the underlying code, rules, and principles that determine when a message has meaning in a context remain unchanged (Eco, 1979: 31–32). This transformation is not necessarily consistent with the current lines of authority.

MDTs were introduced in several large American police departments, such as those in Dallas, Detroit, Houston, and Los Angeles, in the mid-1970s. They were expected to increase officer efficiency, reduce paperwork, and reshape the nature and quality of police response. In practice, officers use the MDT reactively as described above and proactively once on a ob, much as they do the radio. They use it to determine current vehicle ownership, license, or registration, or the validity of a driving license, and to inquire of the police department, NCIC (a vast, unedited FBI database of outstanding warrants), or any area-based data source, about an arrest record or outstanding warrant. These information bits are requested and trusted because the MDT speedily produces useful crime-related data. Ostensibly, MDT is faster, and speed is taken to indicate efficiency. On the other hand, the potential for reduced paperwork, checking drivers, autos, and suspects quickly, and providing valid information may increase use of the MDT and improve morale (Meehan, 1998: 231). The ambiguity of claims for technologies when first introduced is illuminated by the present situation in large departments in which some are abandoning and replacing MDTs with laptops. Charlotte-Mecklenberg, which had 275 cars with MDTs, is now equipping officers with personal laptops or "mobile work stations" that can be used in the car or outside. Most medium-sized and smaller departments are now making the transition to MDTs and 800 MHz radio systems. Both MDTs and laptops or work stations provide the same data and are equally isolated from most of the other databases in the department.

Detectives in a suburban Texas police department use computers as word processors to write their summary statements of investigations and enter them directly into the police records system. The deputy chief in charge of investigations, when asked how detectives used the resultant additional time, answered: "They work more on their other cases." Since most detective work is paper processing and producing paper clearances, and the differential attention to cases is determined for the most part by internal factors judged by investigators, computers may permit detectives to allocate newly available time to other cases (Brandl, 1992). Reducing pass-through time and shifting to other less solvable cases is efficient, not an increase in efficacy. New police radios require very little power, transmit on a variety of channels, and can lock on to any of more than eighty channels. However, most police departments in urban areas are still unable to communicate on-line, share records, and cooperate in ongoing cases or investigations. Vice and narcotics units do not monitor the general (usually area-based) police channels and argue that their channels should be dedicated, restricted to their use to protect secrecy as well as provide rapid access to an uncluttered radio channel. Increased channels and more sophisticated electronic communications ironically sustain and amplify the long-standing communicational anarchy among police in urban areas.

While using cellular phones (some connected to MDTs), officers take alternative routes around crowded airwaves to obtain information. This may not be shared with other officers. Cellular phones are used by patrol officers to check on details of a call with callers, to verify assignments, to discover if an incident remains ongoing, to discuss jobs with other officers, and to verify information with the communications center. They are also used for informal officer-to-officer communication. Officers can call other agencies, such as social welfare, other police agencies, and EMS directly from a cellular phone, rather than requesting that police operators make the call. They are used by supervisors to coordinate field actions if radio channels are crowded or useless because the radio frequencies of participating agencies are incompatible; by vice and SWAT units to communicate secretly about a raid or surveillance (they assume that police radio channels are being monitored); and by deputy chiefs to inquire about or advise concerning an ongoing issue or problem reported by middle-level officers and sergeants.

Technological Reintegration

Once a counterstatement arises, attempts, often visible, can be made by those in power to maintain the social field and to reintegrate the organization. They seek to "bring the artifact back into the controlled and ordered space of regularization" (Pfaffenberger, 1992: 30). This means that normalization and social control processes reproduce the previous vertical order and may again restrict the range of meaning of technology. New technology is not an "open text" that can be endlessly rendered. The dialectic may reshape aspects of traditional patrol officers' roles, given this staging of response.

Management, using CAD, can now monitor officers' activities via on-line or "real time" performance data generated by computers, MDTs, cellular phones patched into the main radio channels and recorded by the mainframe computer, and other recording devices. An enhanced 911 system, which enables a communications center to block a line and leave it open until an officer arrives to investigate an incident, can produce anywhere from twenty to forty jobs per unit on a shift during which the officer is under (relatively) direct radio supervision. According to my 1979 fieldwork in Detroit, the average appears to be closer to twenty a shift than to forty; the average may have changed in the intervening years.

While efforts have been made to reintegrate the cellular phone—in the past ten years, police organizations began to monitor cellular phone use and incorporate data from cellular phones into official records—it appears to decrease the surveillance and sanctioning capacity of first-line supervisors and middle management. The cellular phone, like e-mail addresses if circulated to the public, tends to make individual officers more accessible. It affects organizational routines by accelerating them, by making decision processes more visible, and by substituting external telephone–based demand for individual officer decisions, random patrol, and citizen contact. While the cellular phone has been normalized as a part of the command and control hierarchy, it is not fully embedded in the routines of policing. It can be used to circumvent the communications center and increase private phone calls on the job. It is cheap, requires few new skills, and can be easily carried and concealed.

Technological reintegration is not equally problematic to all officers. Routines created by officers to cope with technologies may be invisible to supervisors. These include using laptop computers and MDTs, not sharing their inquiries and the results of those inquiries with their colleagues, following up on calls (driving to a scene when not dispatched as a backup unit) without accepting them, and increasing their "activity" by running the plates of cars parked in motel and hotel parking lots. These cannot be monitored easily by command officers who notionally determine what is officially known. The semiprivate nature of cellular phone communications makes it unlikely that these routines will be widely known and shared. Managers cannot include this new content into the organizational culture at the middle and top because they do not directly experience it. Command use of cell phones is simply an extension of command activities, as anyone attending a meeting with a chief can attest, but cellular phone use by patrol officers is a modification of procedures. The integration of cellular phones with MDTs produces an organizational record and changes the potential for organizational supervision and sanctioning for improper conduct.

The primary efforts in integrating the cellular phone are not direct, but a consequence of another innovation, the introduction of MDTs to some cars in the 1990s. When integrated with an MDT, the cell phone's transmissions produce an organizational record and change the potential for organizational supervision and sanctioning for improper use. With such an integration, the independence effect of the cellular phone is reduced. MDTs, with direct links to the computerized records in the state department of motor vehicles (vehicle registration, license plates, and drivers' licenses), NCIC, and departmental files of outstanding warrants and stolen cars, facilitate rapid checks on moving vehicles and are productive of tickets, seizures, and arrests.

These new information-based technologies fit or are fitted to the occupational ideology of the patrol segment. Officers believe that information is central to their work, that more is better; they admire and trust only those technologies that streamline their work in the short run (reduce paperwork, decrease inquiry time, provide a sense of control for the officer). Officers do not equate information technology with useful and valued knowledge. IT symbolizes many ideas and is a condensation symbol that on close examination explodes with internal complexity and contradictions (Turner, 1969).

In many respects, the drama of technology in policing is a struggle between management and the worker for control of the work setting, its pace, and its associated output. This is true in all work to some degree (Hughes, 1958). Organizational controls on the worker (primarily the lower participants) and the forms of resistance they elicit, including a turgid occupational culture, are manifest in many bureaucratic organizations (Crozier, 1972). They are reproduced in cross-section in all departments. Many patrol practices, examined over time, can be seen as moves in a drama of work control that require tacit teamwork from patrol officers, and at times their sergeants, to sustain an impression of propriety to audiences (the public, colleagues, sergeants, command officers). Some collusive actions between various audiences and performers arise because policing is believed by all to be risky and highly uncertain, clinical work best understood "on the ground." It is occasionally very dangerous, creating work-related anxiety and stress, but the anxieties and uncertainties inherent in police work are amplified by the patrol-based police ideology, which asserts the abiding dangerous character of policing. Police teamwork reveals a pattern of clinging to rigid procedures in the face of risk, work uncertainty, and the need to exercise authority (Skolnick, 1966; Van Maanen, 1983).

SYNCHRONIC ANALYSIS
Cross-Sectional Analysis

The above-mentioned examples and analysis rest on a *diachronic perspective*, one that assesses change in symbolization and function of IT over the past thirty years. Technologies, all four types, even within the same type of organization, produce different dynamics, and present a different face when examined diachronically, as above, or synchronically (looking at an organization at one time). The case of the cellular phone suggests that the technology was beginning to stimulate adjustments (countersymbolization, counterdelegation, and counterappropriation), but that it had not yet been fully reconstituted nor reintegrated. If this drama is seen synchronically rather than diachronically within a police department, the meanings of technology change.

Michigan City and Tanqueray in Synchrony

In two Michigan cities studied in 1997–98 (I'm calling them Michigan City and Tanqueray, although those aren't their real names), the technology can be viewed synchronically. The aim here is to see how the organizational segments relate to each other and the technology over the course of innovation. If technology is a symbolic statement, what counterstatements emerged in these two cities?

Countersymbolization occurs in Michigan City because older patrol officers complain that the young officers are losing their street skills or not developing them because they are searching the screen and using the computer for information rather than acquiring it through observation, memory, stories, or interviews. Command officers do not use it routinely, nor do they have it in their cars or at home, unlike the force radio. The differential distribution of the equipment—it's installed only in a few cars, and not in command cars—means that high status is associated with being off the center, and support of computing is theoretical, rather than based on command officers' usage. Counterappropriation, or obtaining the technology unofficially, is used for social communication, or expressive reasons—to chat, joke, gossip, and orchestrate breaks and meals (about 50 percent of the messages). Counterdelegation, or disarming or minimizing the MDT, is found. Officers don't use it to report some of their activities to shield them from supervisory review. Technological reconstitution is apparently proceeding in Michigan City because officers now alternate between the radio and the MDT in communicating with fellow officers. Some information can be put out as an all-cars bulletin, but at other times kept or only broadcast on the radio. The information in the MDT (screen one) is sent only to the officer dispatched and the backup officer, not to others. Thus, the meaning of patrol communication varies for the radio and the MDT. Rules have developed in the department. According to one interview (Meehan, 1998) officers "don't criticize the department on the air, don't complain about people in the department, and don't say anything you won't want your wife to know." The MDT data are used to increase accountability (a product of reconstitution) and play an important role in evaluation and supervision in Michigan City. The ability to control and segmentalize the work assignments, alternate channels for information requests, and share or not share general information (with a choice of channels on which to do it) increases uncertainty in communication among colleagues. Because the tapes for the video cars are not monitored, they are sometimes left outside the machines or reused without renaming the days and times; the cameras and/or the microphones are "inadvertently" turned off during a stop.

Reintegration has not really come to pass here. New communicational channels such as MDTs do not change the underlying code of police working these organizations: reactive, law enforcement–focused, historical responses to suspected violations. The proactive use of the MDT appears to be context dependent rather than a general feature of the MDT technology. Low workload and supervisory concern for showing "activity" may increase use. In Tanqueray, the struggle between the subjective forces at play in the field, the segment-specific values and job control perspective of the patrol officers, and the objective factors of the information transmission capacity, speed, and value for loosely crime-related activities, and the structure of accountability into which the MDT was linked (countywide database and the CAD system) create conflict between segments and subsegments within the force. When the force size is small, as it is in Michigan City, Western (see chapter 10), and Tanqueray and the workload relatively small, tickets are an easy source of revenue and a sign of activity. The relative celerity and ease with which license plates can be run or traffic stops made, especially when these are linked to the mission of the force and are a source of revenue (Meehan, personal communication, 1998), facilitate adaptation and use of new information technologies.

The context of adaptation is important. New forms of reconstitution and reintegration of technology are partially dependent on the resources available, the demand conditions of the environment, supervision and evaluation, and the workload as constituted on the ground. Unlike these small cities, in large cities, such as Detroit, where the workload is high, the total number of personnel has shrunk by almost 25 percent in the last eighteen years, the proportion of serious incidents requiring reporting is much higher, and the use of MDTs is voluntary, there is much less proactive work. Not least of the pressures to avoid running plates or outstanding warrants is the huge number of them, while the chances of collecting the fines are low.

RHYTHM AND RESPONSE

In general, in the last thirty years, the growth in means of communication and channels has made police work more demanding and complex and tied the officers more directly to the communications center.

What changes in organizational authority, skills, roles, the division of labor, teamwork, and expressive aspects of the work are unfolding in patrol work? Does it produce new contingencies for patrol officers?

Authority

The newer versions of IT, MDTs, and cellular phones may further the currently limited capacity of the command segment of police organization to monitor, supervise, and control the actions of field officers. Presently, in cities such as Dallas, where all patrol units are equipped with cellular phones, officers can avoid the central command structure and recording devices by directly communicating with the public or colleagues via the cellular phone from the car. In Dallas, cellular phone communications are not recorded and cannot be retrieved for use in disciplinary hearings, nor used by the courts, the media, or citizens to reconstitute events. By this token, cellular phone communication will weaken indirect and ex post facto supervision of officers. Officer-to-officer communication, either face to face or by radio or phone, and some upward communication or "feedback," alters the nature of accountability and serves to maintain officers' face with superior officers. On the other hand, phone records can be used to monitor officers and hold them accountable, and phone scanners can be used to locate and listen in to private conversations among officers. In some sense, however, formal authority of command officers is reified by information technologies. Elaborate modes of collection of calls and operator-based allocation of incidents, electronic monitoring, printouts of patrol activities, and computer-coordinated taping of calls for service and radio calls undercut sergeants' willingness to engage in close supervision (Van Maanen, 1983). It further segregates command officers from line workers and from middle management.

More decentralized information processing, made possible by laptop computers, cellular telephones, and MDTs, grants autonomy and a measure of discretion to patrol officers, while the fiction that centralized control is enhanced by information technology is sanctified by middle and top management. While command officers publicly state that IT expands their capacity to command and control officers, the research literature, with some exceptions, argues that the police are a "paramilitary" bureaucracy without examining the tenuous nature of compliance (for a clear statement of the complexity of compliance, see Reiss and Bordua, l966). Officers, meanwhile, can reconstitute many features of the technology and maintain their modes of work control. Viewing power relationships in a dramaturgical fashion, one can infer that the social field of power relations has changed, giving patrol officers less discretion, yet a bit more autonomy, some additional skills, and marginally more control over uncertain outputs.

Skills

Police officers are rarely trained in the use of the new technologies they are expected to use, and those who are not likely to use them are never trained (detectives are not trained in driving, patrol workers do not learn about how to run a wiretap, etc.). Classic remarks were made by the chief in Western (see chapter 8) when he noted that moving into community policing was such a high priority for the organization that they had no time provide training. On the other hand, San Diego has focused on training even in the use of electronic equipment, but it is a clear exception. Innovation is crippled by the failure of most police organizations to train officers in technologies (even word processing), to reward good use of those technologies (especially by ambitious and rank-promotion-oriented officers), and to alter such standard practices as reactive dispatching and holding operators and dispatchers to meaningless measures like response time and pass-through time. The most useful and important distinction is perhaps a pragmatic one. It is possible that in time officers will acquire skills as result of using an integrated, decentralized "command center." Routine use of MDTs, for example, could increase patrol officers' transferable skills. Integrated modules of technology in the patrol car, especially the new combination of a mobile digital screen and a computer, could be to the advantage of patrol officers in maintaining work control and autonomy. Furthermore, as cohorts enter policing with previous training and comprehension, and computer-literate officers take on administrative roles, greater openness to IT will result. The relative skill of officers can give them an advantage over those lacking skills.

Defense technology (the transfer of which to the public sector has been ongoing since the Vietnam War), helicopters, night vision cameras, high-powered weapons, Ninja Turtle combat outfits, and SWAT teams, all of which are glamorous and seductive to both police and the media, insinuate themselves increasingly into the standard organizational armamentarium. These are the backstage innovations that appeal to many officers, feed into the "war mentality," and on occasion make impressive displays of police power for the media, e.g., in hostage or terrorist circumstances. The question is not whether technologies of all kinds, especially information technology, will shape police roles and routines, it is which roles, to what extent, with what content. The movement toward abstract models of policing, one aspect of this change, is addressed in chapters 9 and 10.

Roles and the Division of Labor

Within patrol work in large cities, an informal division of labor emerges in time as a result of knowledge about the skills and interests of given officers (Walsh, 1986). There is little formal recognition of skill. Some officers are capable in violent situations, some are good interviewers keen on developing informants, while some are eager to make arrests. Still others are skillful in handling domestic disturbances. The task cluster performed in patrol is differentially affected by IT. Communicational skills, based on IT and cellular phone use, enhance and also stimulate sociotechnical talk, or discourse related to and arising from work tasks. The connections that result, both expressive and instrumental, segregate officers into social worlds based on shared problems. These social worlds—segmentalized universes of discourse, subcommunities of discourse—contribute differentially to routines and to shaping the content and form of organizational memory (Brown and Duguid, 1991). If innovation is to continue, feedback and memory are essential. One of the most striking findings of Janet Chan's work in New South Wales (2000) was that younger officers had been formally trained in the use of computers, used the IT more, and en-

joyed it more, while officers above sergeant level had no training; the few
used it had taught themselves. Even in this case, the young officers found
the computer useful to do things more quickly—run plates and check on
outstanding warrants, the jail population, and arrest records—rather than
to do innovative problem solving.

Teamwork

The new IT, especially the cellular phone, alters officers' teamwork opportunities and facilitates some colleague relations. It allows officers to
communicate directly and privately with other officers across political
space: e.g., precinct, city, county, state, and national boundaries. They can
alter political jurisdictional boundaries through personal decisions: e.g.,
calling for assistance from officers from other police organizations. This is,
of course, also a benefit and could increase officers' safety since radio
communication across police departments is often impossible because
channels are not shared. It would appear that these communicational processes could draw officers closer to the public by facilitating direct communication and verification of calls. The pattern of direct communication
between beat officers and the public mimics the community policing
movement's emphasis on police officers developing interpersonal skills
and being in contact with citizens in non-crime-generated encounters. On
the other hand, it could move officers toward increased colleague dependence and loosen connections between patrol officers and their publics. It
also can potentially change relationships between patrol officers and specialized units who can be alerted directly, without the use of the main communications center, and with first-line supervisors who can be reached
privately. This decentralizing movement suggests that role realignment or
organizational learning is occurring.

Expressive Activities and Gaming

All work activity has both an expressive or stylistic aspect and an instrumental aspect. Expressive or affective symbolization resulting from emotional catharsis or frustration associated with new work tools adds new
dynamics as well. IT gives rise to symbolic statements—e.g., office jokes,
memos, cartoons, oral cultures (Meehan, 2000b: 130)—characterizing the
nature and content of new, technologically shaped work processes, as well
as a means by which they are bounded, defined, and controlled. It does appear that the availability of the cellular phone changes the nature of expressive games (Goffman, 1967, 1969). Deference to a line and a face, and
the expressive order that lies behind it, can be privately orchestrated. In
instrumental terms, it adds to the modes of communicational deception

that permit the evasion of institutionalized rules and procedures about reporting, feedback, and legal liability. Widespread use of the cellular phone, like many other mobile communication devices, decentralizes some power and creates new communicational routines, but it also disconnects a channel from the official organizational memory: a comprehensive computer record of reported patrol activities can no longer be produced from the ongoing flow of activity. IT thus reduces feedback and police capacity to tailor new and more flexible and innovative responses to complex, unfolding events. Dialectic between control and autonomy is produced.

Risks and Contingencies

The introduction of new technology, signaling new routines, rules, and contingencies, also presents new risks for those at the bottom of the police hierarchy. Because the various instruments are used repeatedly to communicate with other officers, IT changes sociotechnical interactions (work-related talk) and the dynamics surrounding work tasks, especially in the car and the communications center. IT almost by definition changes the number of channels through which mediated communication occurs. The complexity of the new MDTs creates a data-saturated environment for the officer, and priorities become more difficult to manage and maintain. Communication can flow, and heavily mediated communication can isolate the officer from the sights and sounds of the outside world. Although the basic equipment in any vehicle is considerable, some vehicles—for example, those on traffic patrol—include extra lights and equipment for dealing with stops and road accidents; radar, cameras and microphones, MDTs, individuals' laptops, and PDAs. Even small matters repeatedly intruding can affect performance. The balance of noise, equivocality, and trust in communications may be more difficult to ascertain when some cues, e.g., the sound of voices, microphone clicks, and laughter, are obviated or omitted from digital communications.

The risky aura surrounding IT is not restricted to the resistance that arises because of new skills that are required, the inherent complexity of a computer and related software, or a simpleminded Luddite ideology. From the perspective of those on the ground, what is useful, trusted, and tolerated arises directly from pragmatic use. Is it quick? Is it relatively trustworthy and valid? Does it allow me to cover my mistakes or obscure my ignorance and errors? In short, does this new machinery facilitate and simplify my routines? While this perspective dominates most police organizations, Chatterton's work (1989) suggests that if the sergeants take on board the technology as a useful tool, they can better guide, direct, and evaluate officers and can penetrate or make transparent some of the patrol officers' more egregious work avoidance practices. Top command (Young 1991, 1992; Hunt and Magenau, 1993) seems largely out of touch with the everyday uses and consequences of information technology and more concerned with avoiding scandal and being found culpable for foul ups and mistakes. As James Q. Wilson noted (1968) more than thirty years ago, there is more concern about the officer who gets into trouble and embarrasses the department than about the level of crime.

Although Dunworth's work (Dunworth, 2000; ABT Associates, 2000) suggests a huge and rather significant gap between capacity, implementation, and use of virtually all information systems and tools, Chan's case study in Australia (2000) suggests that changes are emerging. Officers reported being more aware of the surveillance and review potential of the new IT, and making officers more accountable for their actions. While officers noted that there were more data and more potential for analysis and problem solving, they also reported that they had too much data (facts and raw factoids) and too little information (useful and meaningful materials). In line with Ericson and Haggerty's (1997) findings, they felt they were a mere pass-through agency for insurance claims. Chan's respondents (2000) conveyed an attitude of hopeful optimism about the changes brought on by IT in New South Wales. A changing sense of the "technology game," as she calls it, suggested that Bourdieu's concepts of habitus (learned modes of responding to uncertainties) and the cultural capital (available resources) of policing were changing. This preliminary research suggests that policing is becoming less hostile to IT and that the technology game can be seen as a challenge rather than an oppressive force. This optimism is not conveyed in studies done in the United States.

One observation about change supported by research (Pays, Boyanowsky, and Dutton, 1984; McRae and McDavid, 1988; Nunn, 1993; Meehan, 1998; Chan, 2000) is that the impact of MDTs is primarily on traffic enforcement. LEMAS data show that two-thirds of local police now use CAD (Dunham and Alpert, 1998: 53). Call takers can alert dispatchers to an important call coming by pressing a "hot button" and sending it, alert them by voice or phone call of a call, and the dispatchers can also alert cars using radio before they send out a dispatch via the MDT. Because it is connected directly to central communications by more channels (radio, AVM, MDT, force and personal radio, perhaps cellular phone, and video and audiotapes), it is possible to respond more quickly to calls.

There is great ambivalence within policing about the value of any given technology, especially information technology. Some of these negative feelings surround the distrust of such machinery, and the connection made within the police world toward surveillance and monitoring by supervisors. While management advocates the global positioning systems, automatic vehicle locator systems (AVLs), and MDTs as a source of safety, there are some reservations concerning the stratification by rank with respect to use and facility with IT. Cars in general, including the police car and its innards, are increasingly computerized and complex, and breakdowns can arise from more machinery that requires repair. The costs and infrastructure needed for routine upgrades and repair have not been recognized and continue to be sources of periodic crises. While the rhetoric emphasizes imminent advances in technology and their links to community policing, the gap is vast and the utilization of capacity minimal.

In summary, a look at rhythm and response suggests very subtle changes in policing's use and adaptation of information technology. The capacity is increasing rapidly, but the capacity of various systems generally is not integrated or based on a systematic plan, and changes in IT are creating ironic anomalies. These surround the introduction of new systems of data gathering while abandoning others, innovating without evaluation, and engaging in suits with failed contractors for past failures (Jack Greene, personal communication, January 18, 2001). The lack of expertise in contracting with providers of information technology is apparent and very costly to departments (Abt Associates, 2000: 163).

THE DRAMA OF CHANGE

Police organizations remain a useful setting for observing unfolding technological dramas, alterations in traditional roles, and the management of contingency. Technological regulation and associated reconstitution, in tandem with processes of symbolic counterstatement, are manifestations of the balance of power in police organizations. Although other forces, such as societal and internal patterns of racial and gender composition, may change policing, innovations in the form of computer-based information technologies hold great future potential for producing change. Nonlinked databases, noncompatible hardware and software, and the uneven distribution of computer skills mean that information technologies do not integrate police organizations, but rather produce a web of interconnected social realities and divisions. The nature and kind of organizational transformation that evolves for various segments and status levels is unclear. These changes, it is expected, might alter authority relationships (since these pin down meaning and provide sanctions against variations in traditional deference and compliance), in colleague relationships (since changes will alter sociotechnical interactions), in accountability (since new routines may obscure or alter external audiences' capacity to sanction organizational performance), in skills that may be transferable, and in the division of labor.

This analysis suggests that police officers, while at the bottom of the hierarchy, if not in control of the balance of power, assert their power in spite of increased use of IT. Patrol officers' counterstrategies are aligned against the shaping constraints of information technology. Patrol officers' powers remain only slightly diminished by attempts of command officers to alter the current balance of power with new information technologies. IT differentially affects segments within the police and the various roles performed (detective, administration, and patrol roles). IT is shaping detective work, budgeting, and planning, and it is linking police departments with other departments, government agencies, and academics through listservs, Web pages, electronic bulletin boards, and chat rooms on the Internet. It serves to widen the information net, but probably does not increase its depth. Many of command's initiatives are met by workers' responses. Each overt meaning of "technology" is multivalent, and contains the seeds of its own transformation (Pfaffenberger, 1992). Regularization and reconstitution of technology permit patrol officers to introduce new means of controlling the pacing and character of their work. The extent to which this continues and the dynamics it reveals require further research.

An increased number of channels through which officers can choose to work once the CAD system has been mastered is a source of autonomy. More modes of communication are given status, used, and emphasized; e.g., e-mail in a department typically raises the question of universal access and reply obligations when rank's privileges are violated (flaming the chief, sending large numbers of e-mails to command staff, refusing to read e-mails from supervisors, deleting or "losing" them). The fact that officers can communicate directly with DMV, social services, citizens, or other officers via cell phones or directly with the MDT without the knowledge of other officers reduces interpersonal primary social control among officers and uncertainty about what one's colleagues are doing and where. Symbolic status–enhancing or status–reducing matters that alter the prestige of organizational segments are associated with access or lack thereof to databases, software, and servers. These can either elevate or reduce the status of given segments. Speed of inquiry serves to expand choice if officers use MDT effectively. However, most research suggests that patrol officers, like other workers, aim to control rather than to increase their "output." This suggests that officers will convert any time saved through the use of the MDT into doing more of the usual: routine reactive patrol and responding to calls for service (Parks et al., 1999). Officers may also increase their autonomy as a result of mastering computer word processing.

Research also suggests that officers are increasingly sophisticated in applying word processing, in entering computer-driven formatted statements, and in filing electronic records (e.g., of warrants, charges, and arrests). Some have written miniprograms for simplifying their work. In time, computer skills may be more widespread at the bottom of the police hierarchy than among middle and top management.

The introduction of cellular phones into policing may be an exception to the generalization that sees information technology as inevitably embedded in vertical and horizontal authority structures. It appears that police responses may be a function of the combination of a command-and-control ideology and loose coupling at the bottom (Weick, 1979). The cellular phone has the potential to slightly elaborate characteristic dilemmas in such inspectorial bureaucracies. Whether it will reshape patterns of authority and provide a problematic point of discretion remains to be seen. Since officers already have considerable discretion and are at considerable risk of punishment for errors and delicts known to management, the eventual character of this technology's social space cannot be easily predicted. Differential knowledge of the uses of new technology, such as the cellular phone, like the computer and the MDT, characterizes police cohorts and ranks within the organization. Length of time in the organization as a well as time in rank or position divides those at the top and middle from those on the bottom.

While they increase the "visibility"—organizational traces produced and recorded as a result of patrol officers' activities—and expand modes of organizational control over the worker, very little transformation is taking place. Slow erosion of traditional policing practices certainly has occurred, and public expectations of speed and response have perhaps increased as well. It is not clear whether expectations have risen faster than police performance, nor whether the quality of "service"—interactions with citizens in the informational, victim, or witness role—is better. The center of the police information system is not the communications center, but the officer. Information technologies have been used to speed up processing primarily in record keeping, evaluation, and monitoring of patrol. In spite of its radical potential to realign assignments—i.e., to alter reliance on reactive policing, redistribute workload, reshape authority, and even facilitate long-term strategic planning—IT has had restricted use.

The fascinating theme in recent changes is not the actual use of new information technologies. It is rather that the police departments are imagining the future, seeking to outline directions, more than moving to a master plan or agenda.

COMMENT

On balance, the technological drama suggests that IT has produced more of the same sort of policing—reactive, clinical, incident focused, and personalized, but perhaps a bit faster. It has probably not substantially changed the practice, but little systematic evaluation research has been done since Colton (1979), other than Dunworth (2000) and ABT Associates (2000). This pattern of innovation without evaluation also suggests that the dominant institutional clique within policing and research and funding sources within the government sponsor and support IT and "scientific policing" in the abstract, but they are less concerned with measuring and assessing how implementation proceeds, what IT affects, and the extent to which it changes the quality of policing, citizen satisfaction, or even performance. Further analyses, case studies, longitudinal and comparative organizational studies, and systematic survey research are needed to clarify areas of conflict and response as well as agreement and mutual facilitation where IT is involved. In addition, studies of other forms of technology (see note 1 to this chapter) will augment our knowledge of police technologies and resultant dramas.

The natural history approach suggests that the next phase of innovation will be based on a movement from a local large mainframe (a standalone server) to local and regional servers linked by optic cable or telephone lines. In time, processors that systematize and distribute data on the World Wide Web will be adopted in police organizations. They will then bear the cost of their retrograde vision and limited resources. This means that the local developments now being pushed in virtually every police department in the Anglo-American world—to update software, obtain more computer-based services and access, and to streamline local systems—will shortly become obsolete. The future will include officers linked to each other and the Web via cell phone–palm pilot connections that will make the tension between centralized command and control and decentralized deciding on the ground quite profound.

Like the risks of technologies, the capacity of the police to monitor and control their technologies is a matter of debate. The risks to individual privacy are great—the FBI's Carnivore software can monitor the Internet; governments at all levels have vast databases of information on individuals; individuals are monitored by hidden cameras; DNA tests and similar tests are increasing, as are the databases based on such testing (Marx, 1989; Ericson and Haggerty, 1997). The potential is surely much greater than it was thirty years ago, and the skills and technologies available far cheaper and easily accessible to even small departments. As Nogala (1995) notes, the capacity to intervene, prevent, and monitor is far greater now, especially in invisible modes of monitoring and surveillance—via Internet communication, satellite-based phone systems, and computer monitoring. The entire notion of privacy and individual rights, based on the nineteenth-century idea of privacy and protection, is undergoing such radical changes that it is difficult to assess the threats. The enduring devotion of the police to the here and now and the event-driven nature of policing mean that systematic observation and crime prevention, hinging as they do on premonitory design, are very unappealing and slow to make a change in police practice.

There are promising developments in the wider use of computers and software for policing, and there is continued exploration of such areas of concern such reduction of paperwork, increased arrests, and the diminution of conflict in some public order enforcement situations through the use of technology. Proscriptive brochures point out (Sparrow, 1993) that information technology makes it possible to rationalize local knowledge, connect incidents to shape "problems," standardize the amount of information present when a call is answered, and facilitate information flow up the line. Capacity and potential differ from actual practice. The social context within which resistance is created and sustained, the segmented occupation, the diversity of employees in the police organization in critical roles, the strong overall and shared ideology about "good police" work, all support resistance to technological change.

PART FOUR
POLICE ROLES AND CHANGE

EIGHT

POLICE ROLES AND CHANGE

INTRODUCTION

We have seen that uncertainties are made more problematic by the media, that the big and little theaters of control are created in large part by the media, that technologies only slightly modify the practice of policing, and that the internal dynamics of adaptation are seldom discussed when urging reform. As changes in social structure unfold, policing is adapting, but slowly and in terms of the historical constraints that it has honored, including its claims to being of service and servicing demand. The interacting forces that are most changing policing—the media, the rise of new IT, and the emergence of community policing (CP)—are moving policing in inconsistent directions and causing tensions in management and in the patrol officer's role (Turner, 1976, 1978, 1990). Thus uncertainty moves closer to the workplace and the role.

In this chapter, the nature of compliance and legitimacy during an organizational transition in a police department is explored ethnographically, using a case study of community policing in Western (a pseudonym for the Midwestern city where I did fieldwork). Reform and reorganization in Western, including four chiefs and three deputy chiefs in seven years, were constant from 1992 through 2001. Policing reform, especially "community policing," has implications, it appears, for performances, routines, and teamwork, but also for the drama of control and command. When drama moves from the little theater to big theater, tragedy lurks.

THE POLICE ROLE AND CHANGE

The police role itself is a source of patterned contingencies that are coded in occupational knowledge (Chan, 1996; Sackman, 1991; McNamara, 1967). Interactional dimensions of policing, especially the police role, illustrate aspects of the dramaturgical scheme—stabilization of performances, routines, and roles; altercasting or identifying and naming the audience; seeking performances that sustain the appearance of consensus; and creating those depictions and allusions that ground social control. The basis for comparison with the patrol role is the investigative. Investigative work is dependent on the information gathered—the quality of the on-the-scene interviews with witnesses and the thoroughness of the immediate investigation (Greenwood, Petersilia, and Chaikin, 1977). Workload and cases cleared are context-bound (Simon, 1991). The importance of police cases is defined retroactively. If the media and command personnel become aware of the broader ramifications of a case or series of cases, political focus can change them into "big cases" (see Simon, 1991). Inequities among cases and in patterns of case processing (number of investigators assigned, type of effort mobilized, length of the investigation, and even the particular investigator[s] assigned) are assumed among police. However, it is very difficult to predict which case at what point will become the focus of media or political attention. Although the environment is composed of a variety of events, and some of these become "cases," the initial typification of the case by the officer or by the detective can be redefined (Waegel, 1981; Sudnow, 1965).

The following evocative quote from Reiss identifies the recurrent problem of the patrol officer (1971: 3):

> Patrol work usually begins when a patrolman moves onto a social stage with an unknown cast of characters. The settings, members of the cast, and the plot are never quite the same from one time to the next. Yet the patrolman must be prepared to act in all of them.

Arguably, CP adds new dimensions to the problem set faced by patrol officers and perhaps the encounters they must manage dramaturgically. Some studies suggest enhanced morale results for CP officers (Greene, 2000: 339–42), although these studies are few. Studies of CP suggest apparent changes (Greene and Mastrofski, 1987; Rosenbaum, 1996; Fischer, 1998; Fielding, 1995; Brodeur, 1998; Skogan and Hartnett, 1997; Lyons, 1999) and an ongoing tension between the public front and the activities of officers (Parks et al., 2000; Fielding, 1995; Greene and Mastrofski, 1987; Rosenbaum, 1996; Skogan and Lurigio, 1998). The CP role is a new en-

semble. Given the new uncertainties arising, it is necessary to trace connections between the patrol officer's role, external audiences, and internal
expectations. The means studying how managing uncertainty is done
through routines, repeated behaviors that accomplish tasks, and joint performances, or teamwork, both of which sustain loyalty and underlie collective performances.

Traditionally, the patrol officer is expected to act as a buffer, translator,
information channel, and receptacle of information and fact, all the while
scanning the environment for information that should be either processed
at that time, or processed and passed on subsequently to investigators, internal affairs, juvenile officers, or vice officers. Much remains in the officers' memories, unwritten. The decisions faced are complex, fateful, and
persistent.

The patrol role has *decision-making features* displayed repeatedly
(Mastrofski, Worden, and Snipes, 1995). These include the centrality of
autonomy and discretion with respect to a set of limited functions—those
involving encounters with the public (this is in effect an index of organizational power) that are either initiated or a result of a response to a
call. The autonomy of the officer, although constrained by tacit standards
within the department and organizational reward systems, i.e., what is
counted and what is worth doing, is manifested in decisions made to
intervene, and how to intervene, and with what intended consequence.
Since the decisions taken are typically "low visibility," and most are unreviewed, the net effect is to empower the officer as a gatekeeper who ac-
cesses and sets in motion the criminal law. Officers' decisions are very
consequential in the lives of citizens and in the quality of life of neighborhoods and communities. The initial decision to stop and arrest sets in
motion fateful mechanisms producing stress, economic loss, and possible
punishment. The decision is binary: intervene or not, arrest or not, ticket
or not, etc. Furthermore, police decision making is more complex than
other legal decision making. The less serious the offense, the wider the
choice of actions. The conduct subject to policing control varies widely
from highly trivial untoward behavior to crimes of the utmost gravity.
The perceived triviality or gravity of an act or event will almost certainly
have implications for judgments made about whether to enforce or not.
This decision, however, is not entirely a binary choice—action or inac-
tion—for the question of *how* to act is equally important. Police can
choose to do nothing, refer to other agencies, give advice, warn, threaten,
formally caution, or arrest.

The contingencies, risk, and uncertainty confronted daily must be reduced to manageable proportions, fit standing patterns of behavior in the

force, meet the expectations of immediate supervisors, and be carried out with some style. Recall that police work is learned in an apprenticelike way; that it is a craft with uncertain contours; that styles and tactics vary widely and are accepted as such; and that one's personal style, if any, emerges in a dialectic between past experiences (such as the armed services, one's field training officer, and one's past partners), and one's present situation (such as one's current partner and the task at hand). This description of the patrol officers' role is a microcosm of the police communication problem more generally. Patrol officers look "up" hoping to avoid trouble and not have things come back to them, while command staff look "down" as well as "up" and "across," hoping to produce compliance and have it reciprocated, and to connect performance expectations, technology, and supervision within the organization with interorganizational relationships in a chaotic, turbulent external environment (Geller and Morris, 1992). Both of these segments, mediated by the supervisors' role, are concerned with how to create and manage compliance from publics, the external environment, and sustain the morale and autonomy necessary to mobilize work effort.

Historically, the police have tried to insulate—through various social and political mechanisms such as recruitment, training, punishment, and transfers—officers from alternative sources of influence and demand (Bordua and Reiss, 1966) while directing, guiding, and supervising their performance. Conversely, the patrol officer trades a bit of autonomy for commitment and loyalty.

New kinds of uncertainties and drama are introduced in this chapter concerning the impact of team policing—a reform with the explicit aim of altering the role and the audience—on patrol officers' roles, routines, and loyalties. The uncertainty perhaps inherent in the patrol role is made denser in periods of change. Both command and patrol officers experience change. In this change process, police command draws on traditional charismatic authority and rational legal authority—authority based on procedures and the law (Weber, 1966). These forms of authority—charismatic-personalized leadership and rational legal leadership—are often contradictory and in tension in practice (Hunt and Magenau, 1993). Police command is little studied (Bordua and Reiss, 1966: 68), and the relationships between command and patrol officers' work are still unclear. Magenau and Hunt (1989: 547) remark that "surprisingly little attention has been given to understanding the process by which police roles are shaped." The reform studied here presents officers with self-presentational and teamwork dilemmas that must be managed. Of major interest in the context of communicational-organizational analysis are the conflicting sources of the police role, which highlights the problematic nature of a team (and audience), teamwork, and how teamwork is to be carried off.

POLICING AS TEAM PERFORMANCE

Policing is an engaging show, an interactive drama, based both on loosely connected teams performing in diverse settings and on individual officers, but it also requires moral support, tacit public cooperation, and ongoing public trust. Policing, and its symbols, actions, and material culture, connotes a shared sentimental definition of the situation and a collective representation (Durkheim, 1961) by which the police as an entity are known, but it is also an agency of law enforcement, social control, and violence. These are all resources. The enactment of policing signifies authority, but is dependent upon repeated interactional accomplishments for success. The audiences confronted and managed vary widely, in spite of the ideology of policing, which splits the world into two categories, the good and the evil.

The arena for this preparation and performance is public-police encounters. Interaction requires mutual monitoring and collaborative performances—activities that influence other participants. When coming into others' presence, we attend to signs that indicate their orientation. These signs and interactions are based in setting-specific cues and rules. Once an organizational performance is proffered, moral commitments are or are not made by an audience to the emerging joint performance. Through interaction over time, routines and sets of behavioral moves (or parts) develop. Social relationships emerge if the same parts are played repeatedly before the same audience. Since extension in time and place is a criterion for "organization" as a dramaturgical concept, the same organizational audience is located in settings with potential teammates, and repeated strategies and tactics of interaction are displayed. These are constraints on dramaturgical choice. A *front,* or those matters of material costume, manner, style, and interpersonal tactics used to convey a performance, it should be clear, can be institutionalized and guided by conventions such that audiences easily recognize it using only parts of the *repertoire;* e.g., an officer is recognized by a uniform, armament, manner, and other equipment.

The "audience," seen from the police view, looking outward, varies widely, is unpredictable, and yet is essential to success. As argued in chapter 1, the police are a "service" organization with a "people work" technology, whose organizational boundaries and authority require at least as many resources to maintain as do those of "law enforcement" or "protecting and serving." The primary arena for marking boundaries and setting vertical and horizontal alignments is public-police encounters. An infrastructure, material resources, personnel, management skills, and organizational strategies and tactics are also required. These, taken together, make possible the concrete enactment of the mission and the symbolization of the mandate.

Internally, performing for the same organizational audience, located in repeated scenes and familiar settings, produces potential teammates and strategies and tactics of interaction. These are the analogue for the growth of a "professional etiquette" (Hughes, 1958) and are constraints on dramaturgical choice.

Policing is based partially on teamwork. Teamwork, as Goffman notes (1959: 79), is a joint performance by individuals who cooperate to stage a routine and maintain a projected definition of the situation. It is threatened by miscues and responses to failed or potentially failed (collective) impression management. "Team" and "teamwork" are *performative terms*, not functional descriptions of normative consensus, agreement on purpose or means. These minimal requirements for interaction do not imply mutual orientation to a shared goal or purpose, and while situationally constrained to carry off an interaction, a situated performance does not necessarily serve an organizational objective or goal.

Such peer relationships and teamwork are critical to policing because officers believe themselves to be engaged in risky work, fraught with uncertainty, a work that is somewhat stigmatized and set apart from other types of work. They work largely either alone or with one other officer and look to their peers for symbolic and real support (Jermeir and Berkes, 1979; Van Maanen, 1974). The occupational culture resounds with themes of uncertainty, authority, and dependence, and these are seen quite differently by patrol officers below the rank of sergeant and those holding ranks of sergeants and above. The culture insulates police against the environment, especially the uneven demand, the differential evaluation of cases, and conflict with the public. To some degree the "overdemanding" nature of the role (Goode, 1960) means that threats to self and peers from errors must be constantly managed. In practical terms, the occupational culture is revealed in the teamwork in which officers periodically engage.

On the other hand, shared meanings derived from the occupational culture, work routines, and face-to-face teamwork among small groups of officers and negotiated orders of agreement provide informal bases for coherence and stability (see Manning, 1988: chaps. 6, 8). Internally, this means that the work is characterized by cliques, cabals, informal groupings that are a reaction to this uncertainty and provide proximal control over work-generated risks. These cliques may be based on gender, race, cohort status (when one joined the force), or rank, although they tend to crosscut rank. Power devolves to those who control and define the nature of the uncertainty faced by the organization, and this may not inhere in the command structure, given variations in leadership and loyalties (Jermeir et al., 1991).

Policing is both an individual and collective performance, based on face-to-face interactions, public deference, and societal validation of the collective representation. The process of interaction is the product of policing, and the consequences of these interactions are the most consequential outcomes of policing.

Policing is about the *aesthetics and politics of appearances* even though most of the work is done in often banal and futile interactions, rather than in dramatic confrontations and crime control (Rubinstein, 1973; Mawby, 2002). The law remains an important resource, as do status-, gender-, and class-based power differences. Communicational skills, the craft of the work, remain essential to interactional control (Mastrofski, Reisig, and McCloskey, 2002). Given the control theme of police work, police will act to sustain a focused definition of the situation with audiences (Reiss, 1971: 3). The police management of appearances involves several distinct audiences (Cain, 1972; Preiss and Ehrlich, 1967; Young, 1991: 189). Most attention has been given to encounters between police and unruly citizens, one of the several audiences they must manage. But the several audiences are layered outward figuratively like an onion from colleagues in the police world to quasi publics linked to the police world but standing outside the organization's boundaries, other criminal justice agencies, and the "respectable public." The primary symbolic opposition—the disrespectful and disrespectable, the criminals, and other groups denigrated with brutalizing labels—are ironically closest interactionally yet the most distant according to public morality. The respectables in the community are the invisible support of police. The undifferentiated public are a significant audience not seen, or served directly as in the past, either as victims, witnesses, or offenders encountered in reactive radio-dispatched work. The rhetorical elevation of the citizen to a "partner" involved in the "coproduction of order" may shift the salience of the citizen-as-audience. They are to be mutually engaged with police in the service and community emphasis in CP, including proactive problem solving.

This previously projected "other" (the person in the encounter) must become more differentiated and appears in new settings, interaction arises around new problems, and in collective meetings as well as in encounters in streets or private dwellings. This change in audience, setting, and problematic means that an individual officer may no longer be expected always to be "in charge" or take control. Interpersonal tactics and routines required when intervening and controlling, or even responding to a complaint, differ from those in which the police are but one party in a negotiation, or in a problem definition session. In theory, and perhaps in practice, this empowers community members and reduces police authority. From an organizational point of view, as Bordua and Reiss note (1967), the management of interaction sustains the boundaries of the organization as well as marks the limits of political legitimacy (see Mastrofski, 1998).

Yet, policing displays a fundamental irony: the police enact a collective drama that they can only partially script, cast, and organize. Except in rare public order situations such as riots, disasters, and rebellions, "policing" as social regulation or governmental social control is performed by individual officers in complex public and private situations in which the necessary public cooperation essential to sustain a routine may be absent, minimal, or dubious. Performances may fail, and fronts may not adequately be combined with setting and routines to sustain a single focused definition of the situation. The "fundamental irony of policing," that it represents itself as a militaristic organization based on command and control yet is everywhere carried out by isolated individuals making highly subjective decisions, produces consistent internal dramaturgical ambiguities because the collective drama, as seen by police supervisors and top management, may frame required duties differently than do patrol officers. In many respects, the dominant view of police work is represented in the ideology of the patrol officers—"police work is on the streets" (Holdaway, 1996). Implicit demarcation of team ("us") and others ("them") is a fundamental division in the drama of work (Hughes, 1958), yet always somewhat problematic.

Police emphasize symbolic dependence on others, symbolized by trust in the context of work uncertainty and "common allegiance between colleagues" (Holdaway, 1996). Police teamwork may be disrupted or fail through failures of coordination between police (team) and public (audience) or within the police team through betrayals or dramatic failures within the police team or as a result of coalitions between criminals and the public or criminals and the police. Policing, in spite of possessing vast potential (lethal) force, is particularly vulnerable to the vicissitudes of interpersonal drama, encumbered as it is with maintaining the impression of undertaking, managing, and reducing societal moral burdens.

While symbolic resources supporting the claim to legitimacy may be abundant and violence stands as a remedy, the police generally seek to avoid violence (Klockars, 1994). Police appeal to signs that enhance conformity—the flag, city, and state symbol; they conceal actions inconsistent with moral circumspection and maintain highly stylized routines for interacting with the public, suspects, victims, and the media (Mawby, 2002; Mastrofski, 1995). Through these routines, they emphasize claims of honorable and dutiful character. Thus, performances are tied to audiences, and successful performances require the management of information, settings, and fronts as audiences validate them. The police task is complicated by the several factors noted above, especially teamwork, as well as the "audience" problem. Organizational change with respect to sources and kinds of demand can interpose new routines, roles, and audiences, all of which affect teamwork.

REFORM AND COMMUNITY POLICING IN WESTERN

While police in Western are deeply engaged in a drama of control, their strategies and tactics have changed. The "professional model" of policing so brilliantly articulated by Reiss and Bordua, and the dilemmas it has produced in the context of recent social and political change (Reiss, 1992a), is now being transmogrified. The symbolic vehicle by which this reform is rationalized publicly is denoted by the sponge term "community policing" (Cordner, 1995). The dynamics examined in this case study are produced by the local version of the transition from "professional policing" to "community policing."

CP is grounded in ponderous and glittering generalities. For example, Trojanowicz, a leading promoter of CP (Trojanowicz and Buqueroux, 1994: 6–7), lists ten elements in "community policing": a developed philosophy of policing; full-service officers; personalized policing (focusing on knowledge of people in the beat); broad law enforcement; permanent beat assignment; decentralized decision making and local responsibilities; proactive, preventive policing; partnerships with the community; and problem solving. However, a number of strategic and tactical innovations have resulted from attempts at police reform (Cordner, 1995; Green, 2000). CP is realized through a wide array of tactics (Skogan and Hartnett, 1997: 7). The role of the officer in a CP scheme is to act as a relatively visible and available watcher, based nominally in an area, representing dedifferentiated social control. The officer strives to manage disorder, control crime, and produce some level of order maintenance. The community, for its part, is expected to provide problem concerns, information, support, and feedback. In some sense, they should provide the filter and screening of problems to focus police actions. The police are expected to respond to citizens' concerns whether expressed at meetings, rallies, in person, or by phone. A variety of strategies and tactics can be used to distribute services. CP advocates reject the mobile, shift-based, specialized, distant, and crime-focused mode of policing.

The Setting

Western, a city of some 127,000 in a metropolitan area of nearly 400,000 (1990 census), employs 101 civilians and 268 officers in its police department (14.9 percent minority; 73.4 percent men), most of whom were hired in the mid-1970s.[1] The department hired 90 new officers (1996–2000) and expects a 20–25 percent attrition rate by 2005. The department began a reorganization when Chief A was named (from within) in 1991. The city has a large industrial and educational base and is a center of state and local government. It covers thirty-three square miles. It has long been a center of the auto industry and is known as a union town with a strong UAW presence. A large university is nearby, and a community college is in the city proper. It is a highly educated population. Over 18 percent of Western's population is African American, and over 7 is other minorities, most of whom are Hispanic. Its official crime rate dropped modestly (4 percent) in 1996, and its murders from 1996 through 2001 ranged from nine to sixteen. Western is governed by an elected mayor and area-based elected city council. Chief A is a white male with twenty-nine years' experience who held the chief's office for some six years beginning in 1991; he has a master's degree in criminal justice.

The eight years discussed here in some detail, and especially the last three years, have been punctuated by public, potentially damaging police-initiated incidents, political protest, and almost constant reorganization. The saga includes, by the end of 2001, Chief A and his two successors, three assistant chiefs, two acting chiefs, and one acting deputy chief. A complex story unfolds, in which the following play roles: Acting Chief 1, who was Chief A's successor; Chief B, who succeeded Acting Chief 1 in 1998; Acting Deputy Chief 1 (who later became Acting Chief 2 and subsequently Chief C), who succeeded Deputy Chief 1. (Deputy Chief 1 served briefly under Chief B. Also included are miscellaneous captains who were shifted around, forced to resign, reassigned, and retired. The sequence is thus: Chief A (with Deputy Chief A), 1991–97; Acting Chief 1, 1997–98; Chief B, 1998–2000 (with Deputy Chief B); Acting Deputy Chief 1 (to be in time Chief C); Chief C, 2000–present (with newly reap-

---

1. Please refer to the preface and appendix B for details of data gathering in the fieldwork connected with this project.

pointed Deputy Chief C). In the eight-year period, the department had three appointed chiefs; two acting chiefs; three assistant chiefs; and one acting assistant chief. Six people held the two positions of chief and assistant chief in the eight-year period.

Reorganization in Western

In 1991, shortly after his appointment, Chief A reorganized Western's police department. An advocate of Trojanowicz-style CP (see below), he created a dedicated CP unit and a network center and targeted a few areas of the city for nonevaluated CP "experiments." The plans to decentralize command began with the opening of the new West precinct building in spring 1996. To set in motion his reforms, Chief A had first appointed a study group of officers of several ranks in 1991. He followed with an implementation group (mostly higher command officers) charged with carrying out the changes recommended by the study group. Several training sessions of one to two days introduced the concept of community policing to officers.

In 1991–92, some of the pressures to reorganize were financial. Thirty-five officers had been lost through retirement or resignation in the previous few years. There was a long-standing conflict between designated community officers and "road" or patrol officers, based on stereotypic ideas and beliefs—the notion that CP officers shirked work, went to amusement parks with kids on duty, attended neighborhood meetings and ate cookies and drank punch, and were not crime oriented. They were seen as very autonomous, and this, with the idea of a low CP workload, created envy. The CP officers were seen also as a political force, a clique who had the attention of the chief. They were also sponsored within the department by a core of dedicated officers, several with master's degrees. The road officers saw themselves as the backbone of the department, overworked and underrewarded, the thin (and getting thinner) front line of crime control. The work of the CP officers, patrol officers thought, was not only counterproductive and socially irrelevant, their absence from the patrol rota meant additional work for the present patrol. A rallying point for opposition to CP was the nationally celebrated success of one CP officer in an experimental program in one area in the city. During a transitional period, a CP unit was assigned to an area of mixed residential and business use. The sergeant working there was personable, immensely successful, and popular in the neighborhood. He was featured in several national television and radio programs, was referred to in the newspapers as a success story in the city, and symbolized visible accomplishment for CP. His success created envy not only because it suggested the public support for CP, but because he was no longer a team player, playing to the public rather than to his police colleagues.

The Second Reform Move

In 1995, having experimented with community policing officers (CPOs) as a separate unit with supervising sergeants for some three to four years, Chief A made further changes. Approximately ninety patrol officers, covering twenty districts, now were to work four days a week in ten-hour shifts. This change to 4/10 with ninety officers contrasts with the previous pattern of 110 to 120 officers (or more) working fourteen districts in eight-hour shifts. The community policing unit and "CP" (the named position) were removed from the organizational charts. Key loyalists—community police advocates, sergeants, and lieutenants—were promoted. Over this period, Chief A developed a changed concept of CP based on teams. The area-based team concept became the CP vehicle in spring 1996. The chief remained committed to the CP approach as modified via his experience. In Western, team policing became the delivery modality, the public face of a strategy of decentralized, citizen-guided, service-oriented policing. The new plan, both the changes and the unchanged factors, played a role in the drama that followed.

The communications system of the department—the allocation and prioritizing of calls for service—was unchanged. The regional 911 telephone system, a patchwork of several police, fire, and EMS dispatch systems in the area (including Western's), remained. Dispatching practices, informal understandings, and priorities were unaltered. Supervisors did not provide dedicated time for CP, nor relief for individual officers from calls to develop problem solving. Some change in the overall workload may have occurred (see below). Some other technological innovations were in progress. Criminal records became available in several locations via terminals, motorists could make accident reports in either precinct, and laptop computers were being introduced to provide direct digital communication with records and other units.

The core idea of Chief A's second scheme was area-based teams. Notional teams were to be assigned to areas within each precinct. Each precinct (two, East and West, had some control over resources and decisions) had ten teams and was headed by a captain and two lieutenants. Teams, not shifts, were to become the working basis for local policing. Each precinct listed officers by team and shift with voice mail numbers; sergeants could now use voice mail to send messages to an entire team or shift. A hot line and a media information line were updated daily to include information on criminal incidents, community meetings, and current police issues. Lists of officers in teams and neighborhoods were printed and distributed, but the lists led to complaints because of reassignments of officers and foul-ups in the voice mail system. In spite of uneven performance of the voice mail in the West precinct, it did increase sergeants' workloads.

The East precinct was in the headquarters building, scheduled for a move to a separate facility in three years (in December 1999, renovations were completed). Officers assigned to West enjoy a remodeled, light, and airy former school with a basketball court, offices, meeting and conference rooms, and computer facilities. The twenty problem-solving teams include officers formerly assigned to the CP unit, traffic, K-9 duties, the detective bureau, and patrol. The formerly designated community police officers retained the CPO title. In the East precinct, six teams had one CPO, one had two, and three had none. In West, two teams had two, one had one, and seven had none. These latent identities, based on past as-signments, continued to be a basis for reference and interaction. One ser-geant headed each team but did not serve on the same shift as all team members. For example, the designated head of the team, a sergeant, may be on days and have only one teammate officer on the same shift since the other team members were on afternoons or nights. Sergeants were ex-pected to hold team meetings at least once a month, and officers were paid overtime to attend if off duty at the time. This in practice was not done, and the overtime was used as a reward by the sergeants.

Some reorganization of the other officers was attempted. Detectives were designated as precinct based and assigned nominally to teams, but re-tain considerable independence. Special operations, criminal sexual as-sault, and crimes against persons units remain in headquarters, as well as K-9, the regional drug squad, the administrative component (records, personnel, the jail, the chief's office, and internal affairs), and traffic. The special operations division retains prestige and considerable independ-ence, remains outside the team-based structure, and symbolizes active crime control, raids, warrant service, surveillance, and dramatic interven-tions. Special ad hoc squads, composed of officers who are rotated through under acronyms such as "COPS" (Community Oriented Policing Ser-vices), still exercise extraterritorial authority and operate across the city, carrying out raids, serving warrants, and making arrests and investiga-tions. The traffic division successfully resisted disbandment as they had ceremonial and control functions as a result of the proximity of the state capitol building and grounds. These specialized units work at their own agendas, at their own speed, place, and time, with no coordination with the CP teams. In short, the "team policing" idea was operational only among patrol officers, and there were no formal means for coordinating investigations, special operations, warrant serving, raids, or detective work generally with the teams.

Tensions and Reforms in Western

Establishing team policing in Western had organizational consequences, several of which have implications for the role played by patrol officers and the roles of their supervisors. The tensions in the role (Gouldner, 1960a,b) and destabilized reciprocities—e.g., between supervisors and their squads, among community police working given areas who were reassigned, between detectives and their headquarters units—signaled the tragic dimensions of the reform as well as eroding informal, interpersonal, trust-based exchanges that solidify and enliven organizational life. In Western, problem solving and teamwork were rationalized as the basis for reorganization. Yet the basic notion that policing is individual, discretionary, practical, direct problem management in a face-to-face or emergent tactical solution, punctuated by the occasional risky chase or confrontation contrasts markedly with—and often may be in conflict with—group-based, mutually cooperative teamwork seeking to prevent or ameliorate problems. Since officers may be involved in both teamwork and call response at a given time, the decisions made "on ground" affect long-term personnel needs and resource allocation. Both practical and ideological constraints are operative. Patrol officers felt an increased burden of work as a result of the reorganization. In effect, since the team concept is overlaid on unmodified random patrol-based areas (defined initially by workloads), and with equivalent or less support from specialized units, team-based problem solving creates additional obligations, contingencies, and unrewarded responsibilities for those officers. Conversely, CP was believed to result in the withdrawal of some officers from the road. As Chief A noted dryly, "There is a perception of overwork out there." Fewer officers are routinely on the road as a result of attrition, reorganization, and reassignment. All officers are expected to answer calls and service uneven citizen demand. Officers continued to expect each other to carry their load, to cover for colleagues who are out of service, and to range widely within the city to pick up work if and when needed. Research also suggested that officers rarely stayed within their assigned areas or even precincts, and ranged widely especially as "backups" on potentially difficult calls.[2]

2. It is impossible to determine the workload of patrol officers in the department at present; thus, changes in workload resulting from the reorganization can't be calculated. Although calls received are recorded and records showing calls dispatched could be obtained, the disposition of the call by the officer is not a full record of each officer's work. Officers take calls assigned to oth-

The little training that was given provided no basis for systematic problem solving, organizing, or meeting with neighborhood associations. The training for CP lasted a few days and was given in the academy for new officers, yet patrol officers were aware of command expectations that they should engage in proactive problem solving and team activities. "Problem solving," using a SARA (scanning, analysis, response, and assessment) model or equivalent, the practical dynamics of joint or team policing, and crime prevention are only words, ambiguous or misleading terms they have heard or read.

The dominant political segment in Western, road officers, saw real police work as crime related and rejected CP as not real police work, as it was in their view not crime focused. They denigrate current and former CP officers. They find little of what they imagine to be team work that is consistent with their ideological construction of police work. The imagery of police work is the "professional model" in Western, an imagery shared by most of the patrol officers and sergeants and some of the command officers, including Deputy Chief A (an appointee of the previous chief, he frequently silently disagreed with Chief A).

Nevertheless, team policing caused reflection on old approaches to patrol—"push things around, move 'em out of your turf, clean up the work at the end of the shift." Problems were place specific—one could push problems into another precinct, across the river, to a nearby township, or to another district or beat. This pattern of "isolate and control" worked in Western; a freeway and a river divide the city (they are boundaries between the East and West precincts), two radio channels exist, and there are strong demographic differences between East and West (e.g., the percentage of owner-occupied housing is much higher in West). A senior patrol officer, now retired, disagreed with this territorial strategy and claimed he did not want to "work for Atlas" (i.e., move crime, people, and problems around); he wanted to "work for Orkin" (i.e., exterminate vermin). He saw the job as crime control. Of course, the Atlas approach he attributed to team policing is consistent with the old notions of narrow responsibilities to maintain one's own turf and ignore displaced crime or problems that transcend several districts. Crime prevention, or community cooperation, was

ers, share work, swarm at certain calls that are unofficially attended, create work—traffic and juvenile stops, interviews, and surveillance—and attend calls off their beat and even out of the city. A preliminary investigation of workload during the study found that only about 40 percent of the officers kept a reasonable and valid logbook recording their work. Officers who claim the workload has increased or decreased may be reflecting their own experience, offering an opinion, or making a political statement. The felt consequences of the reorganization of Western varies by precinct (East vs. West), shift, beat, and team, as well as reflecting the individual work styles of officers.

not discussed in focus groups, although the department had targeted several areas in the city for concentrated efforts—harassing prostitutes and drug dealers and placing barriers to reduce traffic flow. These "crime-fighting" efforts and projects (usually targeting crack houses) of the COPS program (special task forces in community-oriented projects) are governed by traditional tactics.

Challenges to the Traditional Patrol Officers' Role

Fieldwork (see appendix A) in Western suggests that at least seven aspects of the police officer's and first-line supervisor's roles were made problematic by the two reforms and reorganization: changes in routines; altered socialization; confused supervision; confused evaluation; weakened teamwork; new patterns of job control; and eroded loyalties.

ROUTINES. The routines officers learn are formatted, metaphorically and literally, and serve to pin down procedures in complex, interpersonal "people work." Through routines, officers manage to combine autonomous action and avoid supervision. Routines, as Goffman (1959: 16) reminds us, may coalesce in time into a role, a set of audience (and performer) expectations associated with social status. Learned often through apprenticeships with a field training officer, the patrol role ideally fits the scenes, fronts, and settings in which it is manifest.

Some twelve core routines are practiced by officers in Western: a traffic stop; a juvenile stop; an arrest; a search of a car; a drug (or any other major crime) investigation; handling a domestic or order disturbance (loud party, neighborhood fight); searching for a missing person; interviewing and questioning a person (victim, suspect, witness); intervening in a street fight; taking a report (stolen car, missing person, burglary); making an inquiry via radio about a warrant, criminal record, or vehicle; and going in and out of service (taking a break or finishing a shift). These are taught in the academy and reviewed by FTOs (field training officers, who ride with probationers). Consider working traffic. Routines (and subroutines) for making a safe and effective traffic stop—checking operator's license, motor vehicle registration, and outstanding warrants; making a simple investigation; doing a breathalyzer; filling out a reports; and questioning suspects at an accident scene—are soon well known. These become the basis for characteristic strategies and tactics of interpersonal control, teamwork, and impression management. Officers learn routines by observation, emulation, and personal experimentation.

Team policing required new routines, many of which had to be invented, made up like a piece of jazz. These routines include organizing, planning, chairing, and finding a location for a meeting; mobilizing and nurturing a block club or neighborhood association; teaching a DARE class or giving a speech; answering questions about police policy and procedures; defining, analyzing, solving, and tracking a social problem (especially one requiring paperwork and planning and defying immediate closure); networking with city agencies; working as a school officer; doing an analysis, including maps, of crime trends in an area; providing information to a neighborhood (e.g., via a newsletter, handout, or newspaper); and advising citizens on the security of their homes, businesses, and schools. None of these is explicitly taught to officers, and they have little if any opportunity to observe others performing them. They have few role models, either positive or negative, from whom they can learn.

SOCIALIZATION. Western officers are subjected to a harsh and intense sixteen-week socialization in a regional academy hosted by a community college. This is followed by apprenticeship learning. Young officers learn by adopting stylistic variations, "dramatic realizations," that highlight activity with signs intended to confirm impressions the officer and teammates wish to convey to an audience (Goffman, 1959: 83). In many respects, one's partner and sergeant are role models, along with the FTO, for what works and why. These emerge pragmatically. Older officers don't want to be involved in CP activities, so younger officers are assigned to CP. They can choose a new assignment every three months, but assignments are based on seniority. While the content of the formal academy training remains unchanged, and the new strategy has not been reflected in changes in specific on-the-job training in Western, ad hoc seminars and focus groups on performance evaluation and community and team policing, along with a series of incidents, heightened awareness, and ironically reduced morale. In Western, command officers (in private) and Plea for Justice, a political action group critical of the police for violence and deaths in custody yet supportive of CP, both question the adequacy of police training.

REWARDS AND EVALUATIONS. What counts? Officers learn routines, strategies, and tactics that comprise a style of work reflecting their assessment of what counts. What counts is not always counted, or recorded, nor easily counted, and it varies within and across squads and segments. In patrol, the focus is on handling the call load. The routines stand for active or reactive control: traffic stops, arrests, and other crime-related activities (Rubinstein, 1973; Walsh, 1986) punctuate the otherwise sporadic call load. What counts, as Rubinstein (1973) and Van Maanen (1983) have exquisitely described, encourages officers to learn routines from other officers for accomplishing repetitive tasks. These emerge with practice, usually during field training, and are rewarded both informally and formally (Bayley and Bittner, 1986; Mastrofski, 1995). An ex-captain characterized practices prior to the reorganization: "We [patrol officers] know what counts, and we know how to do those things that count [traffic, etc.]. We go to a familiar fishing hole [a location where it is easy to write tickets]." A lieutenant said, "Officers don't like to just walk around and chat; they like it when it is 'I talk, you listen.' Officers know how to make a stop, shake someone down [search them], make an arrest, or take someone to jail, but they are uneasy when the job is not control." The official redefinition of patrol work from answering calls and random patrol to these routines plus problem solving, team work, and team meetings, means that team policing creates new expectations for filling time and uncertainty about what counts. Old routines no longer firmly undergird roles. Clearly, the changing of routines affects what counts, unless the sergeant and the officer supervised are in tacit agreement about the extent of commitment to the team policing concept. In Western today, evaluation criteria are uncertain. Formal consideration of modes of performance evaluation (what counts, why, and how) are under way. At present, team policing emphasizes problem solving, but few sergeants have any grasp of it, of how to teach or evaluate it. It has not been translated into clear expectations by supervisors. Patrol practices and habits remain, and crime is the preferred focus, a source of risky activity and excitement.

SUPERVISION. How is what counts translated in supervision? Past supervision by sergeants was based on a resource-exchange model of giving and receiving favors and mutually negotiated obligations between sergeants and officers (Van Maanen, 1983). Working on the same shift day after day, usually in the same precinct with the same partner, officers learn their sergeant's expectations. The sergeant is a source of personalized accommodation to the authority structure of the organization (Van Maanen, 1983). Face-to-face supervision, decisions about assignments, the quality of paperwork, and one's "production" are carried out with the same sergeant who rotated on the same shift with his or her squad. Supervision in Western has changed. As Reiss and Bordua (1967) pointed out some thirty years ago, the transition to a communications-based system of dispatching and assignment alters supervision and makes it more a matter of negotiation than of direct observation or guidance. It is virtually always after the fact.

LATENT IDENTITIES. Latent identities, such as the age, ethnicity, and gender of individuals holding sergeant and middle management ranks, can produce conflicts and status discrepancies with officers. Recently promoted young sergeants supervised veterans; Hispanic sergeants were subject to harassment; one female captain was constantly transferred over the years of the study from precinct head to human resources and to another administrative role. Several affirmative action and discrimination suits were filed against the department. Supervisors remained ambivalent about the new organization and some were very negative—usually covertly, sometimes publicly and in city council meetings. Sergeants were unclear about what they expected of their officers and what command officers expected of them. Officers are profoundly ambivalent about supervision, complaining both about the absence and the presence of sergeants. Sergeants, for their part, were unclear about what is expected of them. A sergeant could serve both as a shift sergeant (some shifts do not have a sergeant, however) and a team sergeant. Sergeants were not in the routine, predictable, face-to-face communication with members of their squads or teams that was provided when roll call and shift meetings were held and when the force all started and ended their shifts from the same building (attached to the city courts and city hall). Problem-solving groups (a notional idea) were to develop solutions on the ground and follow them through from initiation to closure. They did not. There was no consensus among the sergeants about the new philosophy and reorganization plan, and they had little or no experience in group problem solving. On the contrary, their experience, like that of their officers, has been individual problem solving with little direct help or supervision from others. Sergeants made assignments to individual officers—e.g., to write tickets from 2 to 6 A.M. (parking on the street is prohibited during those hours); to check on a complaint sent down from the chief's office; to check on truants during the day and (juvenile) curfew violations at night. No record was kept of CP projects, problem solving activities, or outcomes. Sergeants were unclear about the idea of problem solving. At least one sergeant refused to be directly involved in problem solving, especially in community meetings. He challenged the lieutenant to order him to carry out CP. "Order me . . . tell me what to do." One sergeant said in a focus group meeting: "I have no idea what 'problem solving' means . . . how can I tell anyone how to do it?" On the other hand, some senior officers and a handful of sergeants are quite adept at public relations and problem solving; they develop and solve their own list of problems and report them to the newspapers and researchers. One successful team-oriented sergeant works in the same area in which the previous media-praised CP officer worked. In a focus group, he called himself a "shit magnet." He attracted a lot of work via phone and voice mail and learned how to distribute it. Sergeants and lieutenants who are apt problem solvers now have increased workloads and broader responsibilities. For the majority of officers, particularly those in the West precinct who lacked sergeants who encourage teamwork or problem solving, it was police work as usual.

TEAMWORK. Rank-and-file officers define policing as teamwork, yet in fact face-to-face collective action is quite rare. Often, if and when an officer requires assistance, it is forthcoming. It is a default option, since officers prefer to solve incidents without paperwork and return to service (meaning being available for the next call, but in fact being out of service until then). The interdependence of officers is dramatized in public order situations and in risky situations, especially when an officer is in personal danger and might require backup or prompt assistance. Shift work—the fact that squads headed by a sergeant rotate together through a predictable sequence—and precinct-based patrol, as well as the common pattern of two-person cars, integrate and reinforce mutual concern and obligations. So teamwork in Western, as in most departments, was unusual, but visible and important.

Teamwork, an integration of skills, marks the dependence of the officer who works alone on colleagues as well as on the skills and backup of specialized units. Teamwork in community policing in Western was being redefined, but not in a fashion that was visible to officers on the job. Sergeants no longer share a shift with those they supervise. Some supervisors saw officers face to face only at monthly team meetings. Lieutenants in the West precinct split days and nights rather than territories, while East lieutenants divide responsibilities territorially. While the idea of a team suggests leadership and direction, few (at least two in the East met monthly with their teams) give explicit guidance or feedback. Many officers did not see the arrangement as "teamwork," because they did not share goals with other team members, or feel they are just assigned to a "problem solving team" without content or duties. The reported level of communication between team members varies from team to team. One sergeant kept a "team book" in which he entered problems.

PATTERNS OF JOB CONTROL. The focus of the patrol officer historically has been job control—defining and controlling the workload and the conditions of work defined fairly narrowly. Police unions are very strong at the patrol officer level and define their interests as job control and con-

trol of the conditions of work (pay, hours, benefits). Unions presented operational obstacles to policing reform in Western, as they do elsewhere.
The union-driven personnel policies of the department are based on written and negotiated legal contracts that define how and when open positions will be filled. Some requirements were modified as a result of negotiations between the city and the patrol officers' union in the early 1990s.
For example, 80 percent of the designated community police officers were
new hires in 1997. Officers may change divisions every three months, and
pick assignments, transferring in and out by seniority, by union contract.
Sergeants cannot control transfers and assignments, and officers can
transfer from teams or areas. Union rules give preferences to senior officers. Officers who do not like their sergeant (team head) can transfer to another precinct and/or division. These factors meant that most CPOs were
and are young and inexperienced and that high turnover is characteristic
of officers in team policing areas.

LOYALTY. To whom is an officer most loyal? The loyalty question highlights the performer's "expressive responsibility," or obligation to share the
team's definition of the situation (Goffman, 1959: 79). The problem of loyalty, a correlate of team policing, remains. Loyalty and teamwork are traditionally linked (at least situationally). A team as a problem solving and interactional unit is problematic under reorganization. Questions of loyalty,
symbolizing the personalized form of authority, suffuse modern policing
(Bordua and Reiss, 1966). The loyalty question arises when traditional
modes of interacting that produce personal loyalty, such as roll calls, joint
work on incidents, exchange of work duties arising from rotating shift
work, and tolerance, are changed by new work routines. Loyalty, like trust,
and the significant audiences outlined above, is configured something like
an onion, but is reinforced in interactions. These constraints lead to political negotiations and in-fighting among the top command (down to the lieutenants) and work dilemmas for the officers and sergeants. New routines
have emerged, and self and work are in new juxtaposition for most officers.
Tactics for coping with the uncertainties while maintaining the appearance
of loyalty and compliance were developed during the reform process.

Tactics for Coping with Emergent Challenges

Officers in Western responded to the reorganization in several ways.
These are coping mechanisms for "sustaining the show" (Goffman, 1959:
34), as well as strategies for managing organizational change.

Redefinition of the work. Some officers redefined the job using their
present skills, expecting that that would produce predictable results. They

patrolled and continued to answer calls for service, but added a routine to make visible their problem solving activities. One officer drove to the gates of a large factory, parked, and observed the prostitutes and made arrests when they propositioned men coming off the night shift. Some officers embed old practices in new visible activities and apply new labels. COPS teams plan busts of drug houses and sweeps and neighborhood stops. They focus on visible crime control, symbolized by street-based drug dealers, crack houses, or prostitutes—on matters they can handle using the old routines. They can devise, execute, and complete their strategy without fear of dependency on citizens. Ironically, they call on the shadow of previous forms of authority to mobilize actions, now under the CP rubric. Supervisors (lieutenants and captains), as part of the exchange, argued that they had to "give 'em something that's fun in exchange for doing the community policing," as one captain said. In other words, some conflation of the two forms of policing occurs in given role performances. These were part of the CP strategy in Western.

Creative paperwork and self-presentation. Some officers took a few minutes out of the car, made a few inquiries in a neighborhood and labeled it a project. They continued to mention it to their sergeant as an aspect of community policing. One officer spent several days trying to convince an elderly alcoholic man not to drive his car. Many paper projects were never realized but could be reported on at team meetings if and when they were held. Like drug officers whose work is largely invisible unless they make an arrest, officers could continue to construct and sustain a burden of mythical "problem solving." Other officers mentioned what they intended to do (future projects being discussed).

Minimalization. Most officers simply carry out minimal team duties, seeing them as an extra burden laid on top of their current obligations—answering calls, controlling crime, keeping juveniles and petty criminals in line. Fielding (1995) shows that CP officers are caught with a fundamental dilemma because they work with a role definition provided by their colleagues and traditional policing, answering calls and keeping their numbers up, but they are expected to attend meetings, call on shopkeepers, and display their presence by "showing the flag" (parking the vehicle and walking). They also are aware that the public has been convinced by years of police rhetoric that policing is fundamentally about "law enforcement" and reactive "crime control."

Work as usual: no team, no problems. In the sergeants' focus groups, only two admitted to understanding problem solving and how it was done. One reported actively solving problems himself but did not give examples of how he assigned problems to others, supervised them, or evaluated results. The officers' focus groups produced one example of problem solving, and the remainder of the officers could give no examples, or named complaints passed on from their sergeants or the chief's office as "problems" they were expected to solve. The concept of a team had little reality to them, and it appears to be in a formative stage in Western. Problem solving is done, but defined as residual; a label for a variety of work arising from sources other than radio calls.

Keeping busy. In a given shift, from three to five officers are working in a precinct covering some ten beats. Practically speaking, they cover the entire precinct because calls are distributed by precinct, and officers cover calls out of their areas, backup officers from other precincts, and fill in when work is heavy in another district. Area-based policing is an administrative fiction since officers are more off their designated districts than on them (Reiss, 1971: 99). It is quite easy to maintain work or avoid it depending on one's style. Absent direct assignments, no time remains for problem solving.

Sergeants' countertactics. The successful team sergeants who organized responses to problems retained the old territorial notion of policing— "keep 'em [lieutenants] happy and off our backs" and "push things around." Others, as noted above, had no clue about community policing.

These views of reorganized policing in Western represent a "bottom-up" perspective, one that looks at the reform as it affects patrol officers, rather than the vexations and frustrations of command officers. The officers' perspective, combined with cynicism about command leadership, rejection of current trends in policing, and ironically sensitivity to groups critical of the police (the Plea for Justice movement), was one index of low morale.

THEMES OF IRONY AND VULGAR TRAGEDY IN WESTERN

In many respects, the leadership and reform efforts of Chief A were a vulgar tragedy. Reforms in the Western Police Department led, in the eyes of the patrol officers, to undercutting their authority and their role, changes in their audience and rewards, and erosion in the traditional pattern of feudal or charismatic leadership and compliance within the organization. Combined with new routines and challenged authority at the middle-management level were changes in the overt, media-based imagery of the organization. This led to a questioning of leadership and whether Chief A was just an ironic interlude, a romantic gone wrong, or a tragic figure, fatally flawed, a hero who was fated to crash and burn. If we see the natural history of this reform as oscillating between a tragedy and a comedy, different kinds of irony, given a hero's fatal flaw, we can see that it is double-plotted (Empson, 1973), maintaining both genres as possible readings.

The Enigmatic Hero

Chief A resigned on 1 August 1997. Let us step back from the story and examine the key figure and the political and media-shaped processes that lay behind this (probably forced) resignation. Chief A was an intense, driven man who had a self-defined mission. He had an air of tension and anxiety. He listened to some of his command coterie (many of whom did not advocate community policing in any case), and was worried that he would be fired. He had been appointed by the current mayor, but considered himself weakly placed politically and vulnerable with an election coming in the fall of 1997. In part, his self-preoccupation and isolation meant that his eventual resignation was less than "tragic," in the sense of posing a fatal flaw, and more a function of failure to heed advice and take active part in controlling officers' practices. The reorganization weakened Chief A's authority and his ability to command; external events also contributed to his demise.

Events: Little and Big Theaters

Several factors, over the 1992–97 period, elaborated by the local media, played a role in Chief A's resignation. They had an orchestrated, cumulative effect, even though they were very diverse in their content. Among them were:

A series of dramatic murders. These included a seventeen-year-old shot in the head in a drug dispute; a nineteen-year-old shot in a fight after a traffic dispute; and the stabbing of a seventeen-year-old in the heart in front of her mother. The eleven murders in 1996 were, however, a three-year low. In March 1997, a series of near-fatal shootings (of three African American teenagers) were characterized as an ominous sequence by newspaper and television coverage.

Killing of citizens by police. Nine citizens were killed by Western police in thirteen years, three of them in 1996. Those killed included a schizophrenic former mental patient who burned down his house and threatened officers at a distance and was shot by a police sniper; a Chicano shot dead outside a motel as he threatened officers with a BB gun that officers thought was a rifle; and a Chicano who threatened officers with a knife.

Violent deaths in custody. Two violent deaths in Western police custody took place over a two-day period in February 1996. The death of "Mr. Alpha," an African American man diagnosed as psychotic and in care became a national story. He died of congestive heart failure as a result of being hogtied with plastic restraining ropes and sat upon by three officers in his cell. What followed included an internal investigation (no fault was found), an FBI investigation (no fault was found), a civil suit (lost by the plaintiffs), and eventually a suit against the Western Police Department brought in federal court (the suit claimed forty million dollars in damages and costs, but the family was finally awarded twelve million). The federal trial featured a future candidate for governor and was widely covered in the press and on television. The second death was that of another African American man, "Mr. Omega," who died in a nightclub parking lot after being wrestled to the ice-covered ground in below-freezing weather by club bouncers. They sat on him after constraining him with plastic handcuffs with his arms behind his back. Police arrived soon after and called EMS. He died later in a hospital. The police were absolved of criminal responsibility by investigations of the county prosecutors' office in the later case and the U.S. Department of Justice in each case. The first death, with other events, touched off the Plea for Justice campaign, which demanded the hiring of more minorities and reforms in the complaints procedure.

A series of dramatic protests. The Plea for Justice movement began as a result of a protest about the failure to establish an East precinct station, community policing, and the deaths in custody. The protest arose in part because of perceived changes in the CP approach—changes to a team organization from a specialized CPO unit; a new COPS agency grant to the city and the university. These were in part instigated by a former associate of the Community Policing Institute in the university who leaked information and memos to the movement. Her aim was to sustain the work of Trojanowicz and others. The comments of opponents of the dissolution of the special CP unit when quoted in the media were vague and unclear as to what the source of concern was; they spoke only of their support for CP and fear that it might change. From what to what was never specified. Plea for Justice mounted protests, including a march on city hall and group appearances at several city council meetings. The chief and officers in uniform attended one council meeting and spoke on their own behalf; the leader of Plea also spoke at that meeting. Plea continued to function through 1999 and then was silent.

High politics of policing. The high politics of policing involves managing external audiences and matters of funding, legitimacy, leadership, and competence of police as debated publicly. Managing the crisis were the mayor and city council members. In the fall of 1996, the minister who headed Plea, two members of neighborhood associations, a member of the police commission, and a local television pundit appeared on an open-mike call-in show. The content was remarkably "propolice"; callers criticized the minister for increasing tensions. Chief A did not appear, nor did any members of the department. In December 1996, the mayor of Western responded to pressures from Plea for Justice by producing a plan to increase minority representation on the force and the number of officers living in the city; construct the East precinct building; revise the civilian complaints scheme; form a police community forum to meet yearly beginning in April 1997; and create the post of a deputy chief responsible for community relations (this was never done). The protesting group was angered that it was not consulted on these proposals and through July 1998 actively claimed racism and rejected the mayor's reform proposals. The police community relations forum met in April. Two years later, another new chief instituted a series of forums on race profiling (see below). As of May 2002, none of the other changes were realized.

Gassing strikers and the city council's response. Perhaps the most dramatic of the incidents was a response to the police gassing of union strikers. In May 1997, fifty riot-equipped Western officers used live tear gas canisters (borrowed from the nearby university police, who had kept them on hand since the 1970 campus demonstrations) on one hundred union strikers assembled at the gates of a factory. They were trying to intimidate those going to work or prevent them from entering (both "scab labor" and union members). The gas drifted out on prevailing winds into a quiet working-class neighborhood and gassed families and children. Neither the mayor nor the chief made any public comment, nor took responsibility publicly for the decision. The police circulated an official apology via leaflets a few days later. The police claimed that the strikers refused to move after being warned via loudspeaker. The Western City Council and the city's police commission both held investigations. Video evidence shown to an investigatory commission appointed by the mayor revealed that the strikers did not appear to hear the warning. An academic quoted in the newspaper said that although he wasn't there, he felt the gas was used consistent with police practice. One city council member was quoted in the newspaper saying the police were "acting like Nazis" when they used the gas. The council publicly absolved the police of responsibility after an investigation.

In summary, although all of these factors were critical, the gassing of union workers in a strong union town was the turning point in police-community relations. It touched off the high politics of policing that focused on the chief. After retirement, Chief A became an associate in the Regional Community Policing Institute, employed to guide departments toward reorganization and a CP style.

REORGANIZATION AND RESPONSE IN WESTERN

These dramatic events dominated the local news, along with general articles of praise for community policing and cooperation with neighborhood associations during 1996–98. Overt media attention is one part of the uncertainty that the organizational crisis created. The community and the police department have responded to these events. What lay behind these events in addition to the uncertainties produced at the role level in Western?

Western is probably no more divided along class and ethnic lines than any other medium-sized city. Public enthusiasm for community policing in Western remains. The divided community and city council criticisms of policing in Western are less severe than in many cities, and violence, drugs, and gang activity are quite modest. Three of the city council critics of the police were not reelected (one did not run), and one was reelected. The mayor resoundingly won reelection, and the police were not an issue either in the election or through the fall of 1998. Divisions in support for reform among top command remain.

The resignation of Chief A was followed by a national search. During the search period Mr. Sausage, a former police captain with a "street cop's mentality" who was popular with the "troops," was named acting chief. He subsequently applied for the chief's job and then abruptly withdrew a few months later. Mr. Jones, a black man who had worked once in a small town near Western and was police chief in the capital city of another state, was named chief in Western. Mr. Jones is called here Chief B. The appointment of Chief B made some political moves possible. The previous deputy chief, a critic of community policing and of Chief A, retired. The previous acting chief, Mr. Sausage, also retired when Chief B was named and approved by the Western city council; he became a school police officer. In a September 1999 interview that was part of my fieldwork, Mr. Jones stated that his goals were to bring some discipline and order into the organization (including rewriting procedures, rules, and regulations); increase diversity; and bring standards to hiring across the board (he participated directly in all hiring, from the janitors to the deputy chief). At the time of his hiring, Chief B had persuaded the deputy chief who had opposed Chief A to retire. Chief B argued that the previous reorganization had weakened the department—and began a rewriting of the policies and procedures, a review of the general orders, and a reallocation of officers to patrol from desk jobs. He participated in all promotional and hiring interviews, and spoke of the need in newspaper interviews of crime control and solid patrol-based service. He was in some ways a traditional chief with more traditional emphases on patrol service and crime control in his early days in office. He reassigned all of the serving captains, promoted to fill one captain position, and forced two captains to retire. The retirement of the deputy chief and two captains, combined with other promotions, changed the face of command. Three of the four captains, four of the ten lieutenants, and two of thirty-seven sergeants were educated at the nearby university, were advocates of CP, and now surrounded the new chief. Chief B named a new assistant chief, who took a leave to attend the FBI Academy and then accepted the chief's job in a city in another state. Captain Streets, a very active, lively, and enthusiastic supporter of CP, was then promoted to acting assistant chief. Just after Chief B took office, two officers chased a young black teenager into a basement and sent in a dog, which the suspect shot. The two officers entered the basement and shot and killed the suspect. The subsequent FBI investigation reported that it was done according to procedures. Abruptly, after slightly more than a year in office, Chief B resigned to take a job in the corrections department of another state. Captain Streets was then named acting chief while another national search was undertaken. He retained the assistant chief. Captain Streets applied and was appointed chief. He is here called Chief C, the third chief in three years, and is in his third year as Western chief (as of May 2002).

SUMMARY AND TRANSITION

This period of crisis and reorganization unfolded in a department that remains in flux (see this chapter's epilogue). Some thirty-three new officers, about a third of the patrol force, have been hired since 1998. The degree of public enthusiasm for community policing in Western, especially among members of neighborhood associations, divisions among top command, and the resistance of patrol officers are all salient in this story. The tactics of patrol officers and countermoves made by supervisors reproduce the game of supervision and control in most departments. Union constraints on officer assignment and contractual provisions for officers to make choices play an important role in Western, because they shape the allocation of personnel and the "fit" of officers to role, territory, and audience. Tension about the content of the role is exacerbated by union rules and personnel practices that set the job control interests of officers against the interests of middle management and top command. Change at the top has a ripple effect and adds to the uncertainty of patrol officers who feel vulnerable and in need of support from the top command officers. The low morale and considerable resistance of patrol officers remains. The absence of new hires due to budget constraints and crises has had a morale effect, as has the loss of officers due to retirement. The Western department is facing a major demographic transition as the large hiring cohorts of twenty to twenty-five years ago depart and new officers are slowly being hired.

At the patrol and first-line supervisors level, roles and routines are linked to organizational authority and loyalty. Community policing, in many respects a movement to reduce social distance between police and public, may have the somewhat predictable consequence of lessening loyalty and weakening commitment to organizational norms (Bordua and Reiss, 1966; Bordua, 1968).

Uncertainties of other kinds can be identified from this case study. Command authority was questioned in Western. Changes in patrol work—namely added routines and obligations—in supervision, in the kinds of teamwork expected, in the focus of evaluation and command expectations and strategies, blurred the always negotiated traditional bases of authority and the tacit bases for teamwork. The bases of command authority are shifting and unclear, especially with four chiefs, including the predecessor of Chief A, serving in less than eight years. Transitional periods such as these exacerbate the contingencies in trust in leadership that exist when the *person*-in-the-role is nearly as important, or more important, as the role occupant. The police officer's personal authority is modified. The changes in Western made abundantly clear that the officer is not obeyed because of "legal authority," symbolized by uniform, badge, gun, and equipment, but because of interpersonal presence, the support and concern of the public, and the lurking presence of other officers. Such interdependencies are rarely admitted. Neither are the cognitive changes evolving in the definitions of the public. The authority of supervisors was questioned and they in turn questioned their own legitimacy. Although the traditional bureaucratic police role implies discretion, freedom of choice, and options in controlling disorder, highly dramatized in the occupational ideology of the patrol segment, patrol work is governed in fact by a concrete logic that emphasizes job control, security, protection of personal time, and freedom from close supervision. On the other hand, the denial of dependency, the wish to be commanded (at least indirectly) and subject to clearly stated and applied performance measures and evaluation, and efforts to control and limit the level of effort, are central concerns of patrol officers (Hughes, 1958). The boundaries of the police officers' role were blurred in Western, as they are in any community that experiments with community policing. The team structure, combined with proactive policing and problem solving emphasis, left the sources of the officers' authority in audience terms unclear. The change appears to be from almost total concern with immediate colleagues' evaluations (Cain, 1972) to team orientation, and from team to community orientation. These are transitions in audience, routines, and role conception. Familiar and perhaps comforting connections between routines, roles, and status are made problematic, rendering also unclear the moral burdens of mutual obligation between team members and a team and audiences. Changes that emphasize initiative in problem definition and solution require police teamwork and proactive elaboration of the role. These blur the outlines of supervision, and the individual officers' capacity, including well-developed and understood routines and tactics that serve above all to control the workload and to minimize or avoid work.

Policing, viewed within the communications-organizations framework, sees the police role and teamwork, repertoires and joint performances developed with audiences, as central to a working consensus that facilitates performance and impression management. This points to the importance of examining the impact of organizational change and transformation not only of the instrumental, goal-attaining aspects of work, but of the expressive and symbolic aspects (Barley, 1986; Zuboff, 1988; Manning, 1992a; Thomas, 1994). Nevertheless, the precise nature of team loyalty, dramaturgical discipline, and circumspection altered during the course of the reform are unclear. Organizational authority and supervision are being altered and the definition of team is being nominally refashioned. These interpersonal adjustments and choices, perhaps emerging as patrol tactics, indicate structural changes. Whereas in the past known routines, teamwork, and the game of avoiding supervision were learned and simulated by watching others work, formally defined teamwork in connection with problem solving alters this role learning and audience definition.

Thus, in many respects this study echoes the findings of other research. Every instance of community policing–based reform, even in the most successful examples—San Diego; Portland, Oregon; Chicago; Saint Petersburg; Indianapolis; Richmond, Virginia—shows the departments' resources still heavily invested in maintaining the symbolic presence of routine patrol (Parks et al., 1999). This tension between apparent service and reducing social distance in other ways remains because police organizations remain publicly committed to serving callers yet are stretching their personnel to engage in problem solving as well. Without more personnel, a differential response scheme that leaves officers some time to locate and define problems, or the intervention of sergeants, community policing problem solving means an increase in workload with no additional compensation or rewards. Several modifications, including problem solving by officers during an overlap of shifts (in the late afternoon) and distinctive job descriptions for community police officers, have not solved the workload problem in these departments. These findings suggest that the basic processes described here are found more generally in this period of transformation and reform.

EPILOGUE

Captain Streets had been promoted from lieutenant to chief in five years. His core command staff is highly educated and committed to community policing and has risen through the ranks during this transitional period. They stand with the chief. He has an advanced degree from a local college, is an advocate of CP and a student of the subject who has also studied at the Kennedy School at Harvard. He teaches CP and criminal investigation at a local college. As Chief C, he appeared before the city council and reaffirmed his commitment to CP, and in the fall of 2000 held a series of open seminars across the city on racial profiling, calling on an instructor from the local college to lead the discussions. This received very favorable press in the local newspapers and on television. One other public event remained little theater. The police, in cooperation with the city, in November 2000, moved a group of homeless people from a vacant lot in the Kennedy School tradition of "fixing broken windows" (broken people are of no interest). The core of the CP advocates in Western now hold the rank of lieutenant, having risen from patrol officers at the beginning of Chief A's term of office. The implementation of the program, including the absence of problem solving and role definition, the lack of organization of personnel within the team (shift differences), and unresolved differential attachment to the philosophy of CP by some sergeants and command officers continues to engender uncertainty.[3]

3. Joseph Schafer's recently published book (2001) on a similar city reports problems similar to those outlined in this chapter. His data show that the organization failed in a transition to community policing; it suffered from problems in staffing, morale, consensus, training, evaluation, rewards, and the accountability of officers to supervisors, the absence of content in the community policing efforts, and the negative view of both the philosophy and practice of CP in the organization by the officers on the ground. The high levels of education of those above patrol officer rank were correlated with support of the philosophy of CP. Unfortunately, the book does not discuss any public events or violence that discredited the "philosophy" of CP, whatever that is. The book has hopeful and positive spin and tone, and remains resolutely optimistic and supportive of the efforts of the organization, in spite of clear evidence that it was a massive failure with reference to educating, converting, and socializing officers, and training them and mobilizing them to do community policing. The book contains no examples of what community policing might refer to, examples of its being done, nor the strengths and weakness of whatever practices are covered by this gloss. In fact, given what was reported in the book (without validation) about community policing "projects," they were the product of little or no time spent, and evidence of time available suggests it was scant, given the call demand management orientation of the patrol officers (chaps. 7–9). This remains a very good case study of the failures of implementation, given an earnest and long-standing attempt to change a police organization.

NINE

RISK, TRUST, AND REFLECTION

INTRODUCTION

This chapter concerns the place of trust in policing and how changes in the media, the technology, and the role are altering the meaning and indicia of trust in policing. I argue in this chapter, by way of a summary of the implicit grounds for the argument thus far, that social change in policing over the last thirty years can be understood only by examining the background of trust and changes that are now ongoing in policing.

I use the example of developments in crime mapping and crime analysis to suggest some of the ongoing changes. While crime mapping builds on the primary data of policing, the "natural event," as described by the officer in a logbook or in a transmission, it is now possible to re-represent the event, say a burglary call, in some six or seven levels of abstraction away from the initial encounter between officer and the event. These range from simple aggregation of events by time or address up to the simulation and model building incorporated in "expert systems." The "disconnect" between the everyday world of policing and the trust-assessment that it must entail has not been fully appreciated by advocates of technological change (Dunworth, 2000); officers have been seen as blameworthy for their resistance to new forms of data analysis.

THE JOB AS ASSESSING TRUST

The police are suspicious, and suspicious especially of suspicious-looking people, those who look or act different from the norm in the context in which they are seen. They seek, note, and frequently investigate incongruities in people, place, time, and activity while on patrol. They might ask: Is the person out of place here (e.g., a suburban white teenager in a disadvantaged area of the inner city)? Why is traffic at 2 A.M. on a highway slowed to a crawl? Why are two teenagers playing catch in the middle of the night? Why does a dog continue to bark at night? Police work with the incongruity principle, monitoring changes in appearances of places, routine, and the activities of habitués. In many respects, changes in sound level and smells alert them (Rubinstein, 1973). Within known areas of "trouble," they may drive more slowly, stop and talk to people, search them; and the same procedures are used when a particular sensitivity is in the air as a result of a series of crimes of a type, newspaper publicity about crimes, or roll call alerts about particular crimes, places, or persons. While some known areas of crime are patrolled routinely and repeatedly, some may be publicly identified as "crime ridden," thus lowering the level of trust in such crime- and disorder-heavy areas. When on traffic patrol, officers look for drivers driving at high or low speeds, wavering in a lane, or making frequent lane switches or poor and jerking starts—each of which can indicate a driver who has stolen the car, or a youthful unlicensed driver, or an impaired or drunk driver.

But action must be done and it must be seen. A paradox is inherent in a universally distrusting posture because it paralyzes one in interactions and isolates police from others. Therefore, we must recognize that it is only in stories and mini-ideologies that officers "trust no one." Trust can be transferred to technologies. In this regard, consider the expanded capacity of police to monitor traffic using fixed video cameras at stop signs and to link them to computer-based ticket-issuing software. Here, trust is obviated and delegated to a machine that processes all violations regardless of context. Any technological device, such as binoculars, night vision devices, cameras, microphones (concealed or not), listening devices of various types, wiretaps, or software that intercepts "signals" of deviance (like FBI's Carnivore software), that extends human senses also reduces the role of trust by setting some arbitrary and fixed standard for defining crime, disorder, and malfeasance. The same is true of increases in mobility over space and time such as the advent of police helicopters, airplanes, diving equipment and boats, and other specialized transport vehicles. These extend the presence of the police and permit them to penetrate areas previously unexamined or rarely examined. Databases with analytic dimensions produce standard formats for wanted and missing persons, and these are more likely to be shared in local networks using faxes and secure computers. These change the context within which trust is involved from immediate to mediated and from individual to group reciprocity and trust.

Officers trust each other at least notionally and categorically, and the ideology of patrol states that one can always count on backup from colleagues, even though experience tells officers that that is not always true. They carry out situated performances, make plans and execute them, communicate at a distance via radio–telephone or mobile digital terminal (MDT), often without a rich context or nonverbal cues, act and react in risky situations such as fights, raids, hostage situations, and chases, anticipating the moves of the other, and carry out joint deceptions in and out of court (Manning and Hunt, 1991). It could be said that stability in social relations arises from repeated assurances through routine actions that trust exists and is rewarded and valued. Clearly degrees of trust differentiate officers within the police world and citizens within the world of citizens (Van Maanen, 1998).

Trust assessment—determining the degree to which individual others are trustworthy in promise, word, or deed—is required not only in patrol, but in specialized policing. Narcotics officers reported that you should "never trust an informant, . . . don't let them get over on you," but they were required to trust informants operationally in virtually every investigation in order to produce a truthful affidavit for a warrant (or at least not to utter ascertainable falsehoods), to provide information on movements of dealers and drugs, to take money in and drugs out when making a controlled buy, to vouch for the agent if he or she is to be "duked in" (introduced as a prospective buyer or seller of drugs to dealers). The most problematic and rarest instances are salaried agents who are expected to go "underground" for a long period of time without frequent contact with a control agent. These long-term investigations that seek conspiracy charges or try to locate "big dealers" are fragile and usually are abandoned or fall apart because far too many elements are problematic (Manning, 2002b: 221). One of the most frustrating aspects of detective work is in persuading witnesses to give statements or depositions and, more importantly, to testify in serious cases. In high crime areas, this is a particular "art" of threat, persuasion, and coercion, but ultimately investigation requires trusting the person to render an honest statement and to appear in court when summoned.

Trust is fundamental in message processing in the police communication system (PCS), because the channels used—telephones, MDT, fax, and/or radio—lack the nonverbal context that enables the framing of a message and the purposes of the sender (e.g., Whalen, Zimmerman, and Whalen, 1988; Zimmerman, 1992a,b; Whalen and Zimmerman, 1998;

Garcia and Parmer, 1999). Conversational analysts (just cited) have attempted to explicate the effects of the order of requests, trust, the sequences of asking and response, the complex nonverbal component in managing conversations, that are displayed in calls for help. This is a micro insight into trust as an invisible matter or background condition to talk. Trust is critical in determining whether a call is answered, entered in the system, dispatched, or attended to. Trust emerges as an issue at the beginning of the process when operators must decide if the caller is

- credible in general (not crazy, drunk, or a child);
- telling a valid, current story (not a dream, a vision, a fantasy, or perhaps a systematic delusion, a hope or something from the past);
- describing an instance that properly needs police attention (not more appropriate for handling by social services or some other city agency);
- giving information that is worth repeating (this can have several contours);
- providing enough valid information to entertain the call.

The working rule of operators, very fearful of condemnation for failing to process a call, is "send everything down." Calls are both upgraded and downgraded (in terms of their seriousness and priority as stated in the initial call record) by call takers and dispatchers as well as by officers (Nesbary, 1998). Feedback from officers serves to recategorize the calls, thus adding to the notion that callers are not to be trusted about what they say about the nature of the event they are calling about. Trust remains problematic when officers, who are sent three to five messages an hour, need to determine by their priorities whether a visit to a scene is needed, what is required to close the incident, and if it might require police intervention. On a scene, the officer attempts, using all of his or her senses, to determine what has happened and what should be done—and generally assumes that control must be produced. The context of such interactions is highly determinant, and invariably a range of tactical options is considered, albeit quickly (Bayley and Bittner, 1986; Davis, 1983; Mastrofski, Ritti, and Snipes, 1994).

While mediated communication and communicational channels have increased, trust is still shaped by time and space. Patrol officers prefer taking action and bringing closure—pragmatic on-the-spot solutions, rather than time-consuming, paperwork-based negotiations or even problem solving encounters. This mini–ideology, shared generally within policing, obviates establishing a depth of trust. Some people are seen again and again. Time defines their existence as regulars or repeat players. Repeat players establish working relationships, whether with "criminals" or villains or with fellow officers. Through time, trustworthiness is (or is not) built up through interactions with other officers. These interactions—properly transactions—are indicated by patterns of exchange of information and arrest credit allocation (Manning, 2002b), in raid parties joined, in "gifts" of prisoners and evidence, in shared cover-ups (Manning and Hunt, 1991), and in managing violent situations such as fights, chases with crashes, and shootings. These are often epiphanies for young officers.

While trust is shaped by the space in which it occurs, space is also shaped by routine actions that take place there, as well as typifications attributed to those actions. Every city has its area known for disorder at various levels. These levels are of course relative, and the areas may sport punks on skateboards with their dogs, harmless squeegee men, or dangerous armed felons. These dangerous areas are routinely heavily patrolled, and patrol interventions in the city will cluster there. Routine arrests and raids, sometimes in "hot spots," sometimes a result of tactical policing, build up collective or organizational memory, and stories develop that are told to other officers (Herbert, 1996). Indications of an area's rich and rewarding history, from a police point of view, are to be found in the abundance in official records of traffic stops, investigations, calls for service, reported crimes, loud parties, dogs on the loose, missing children, domestic violence, and other service-generating matters. These are the dangerous areas (Klinger, 1997).

The moral topography of a city, the mental partitioning of space, differentiated into "good" and "bad" areas, shapes the workload expected of an officer, the nature of that work, the implicit meaning assigned to rather brief and encrypted radio transmissions, the need for backup in risky areas, and, to a lesser degree, the workload generated on the MDT. Officers do not always know other officers' activities when they are working through the MDT; but they can "punch up" the officer's number to check, as can supervisors.

TRUST AND COLLEAGUES

Colleagues' trustworthiness is closely connected operationally to the work they undertake (or don't) in particular areas (insofar as they are working in their assigned patrol areas), conceptions of potential work, and work usually accomplished in such areas. In high-crime areas, officers back each other up, or "swing by" without being assigned (often leading to several cars appearing at a stop) because they distrust the area. Officers who do not do so, or who refuse calls or are out of service for a long time, give off read-ings of their trustworthiness. These readings bear on how and the extent to which they are playing their part, sharing the load, and being equal part-ners in the moral burdens of the work. This assessment is made by moni-toring radio calls, calls for backup or backups done informally, and other shared routines and points of visible intersection of officers—in the sta-tion, at meal and coffee breaks, at roll calls and shift changes.

Alternatives to the model of colleagues in full moral, trustworthy part-nerships exist. Some colleagues are less trustworthy than others. Officers vary in their lust for work, arrests, investigation, and easing or sliding by obligations (Walsh, 1986). These styles are based on how one avoids work, hides from the sergeant, or eases out a bit of personal time (Van Mannen, 1998). These, in short, describe how one engages in what the French call *la perrague* or the wig—the covering of the illegitimate with the appear-ance of legitimacy (Bogard, 1996: 111, quoting DeCerteau). Predictable untrustworthiness is routine. An officer can deviate in a trustworthy or un-trustworthy fashion. Untrustworthiness from a sergeant's point of view may not suggest untrustworthiness in the eyes of one's colleagues. The "deviance" may be acceptable to colleagues, such as lying to citizens in or-der to get them to agree to a search, or it may appear to be "normal de-viance" rather than condemned "goldbricking" or avoidance. Even ser-geants, of course, appreciate and prefer predictable to unpredictable deviance.

Unpredictable work styles lead to uncertainty and distrust and the usual police management style is to pair people to minimize overt differ-ences. In some departments, such as the Los Angeles Police Department (Rayner, 1995), partners are rotated regularly as a management technique so that they do not produce untrustworthy dyadic collusions. The same effect is produced by union contracts that mandate officers' choice of precinct or division every year or so, thus creating opportunities for hori-zontal mobility and turnover in partners. The most awkward issues arise around questions of partners. While individual male officers may trust a female partner, the male's wife may not, and gossip always abounds about partners of different gender. Ethnicity patterns partnerships in most cities I have studied. These are often informal decisions, but the ethnicity of partners tends to be consistent, while females are invariably coupled with a male. This is an indication not of their trust of each other, but of the bind-ing distrust of female partnerships. These trust matters are reflected, as Haarr (1997) found, in interactions, informal and formal, social activities and friendships. They clearly pattern stress on the job (Morash and Haarr,

1995). This discussion of trust is relevant to the new developments in police technology that move the question of trust "above" or away from the immediate here and now of the policing as seen by patrol officers: the view from the streets.

THE BASELINE OF POLICING: THE VIEW FROM THE STREETS, HERE AND NOW

Patrol work requires trust. That trust is ironic and context bound, yet necessary. The shared nature of "police work," taught, learned, and valued, rests heavily upon learning to manage trust-contingent interactions. Policing is about establishing or verifying trust in the here and now, and often quickly. Recall also the outlines of the traditional patrol officer role and the police mission in Anglo-American society. The officer on the ground bears the burden of the work. Policing has been inspectorial, randomly patrolling territories in search of untoward events that might require notification or response, and deterring and providing visible presence and reassurance. Patrol routines locate and fix officers in the institutional world of police work. More than identity or self, routines shape both the round that orders the day and long-term agendas, and they stabilize the otherwise differentiated audiences and uneven events encountered. The shared workload, audible and visible radio communications, and visible encounters with fellow officers also pin down the connection between work and the individual officer. Written records, insofar as they are shared, car logbooks, electronic and visible activities that appear on the MDT screens, oral reports and briefings at roll calls all serve to connect officers to each other as well as to reify the active presence of the other (both colleagues and citizens) as a vibrant unpredictable force. Stories told by colleagues communicate about colleagues and about others via the readings that colleagues render of others' behavior. This capacity is a minidefinition of culture—one can read off the meaning of others' behavior from the descriptions, stories, jokes, and satires displayed by one's colleagues or near-selves.

Through patrol records, logbooks, radio calls, MDT transmissions, cell phone calls, and electronic files (to a lesser degree), and face-to-face interactions among officers, the surface reality of policing is connected to the structures of sentiment that animate the work and the officers' selves. This documentary method (Mannheim, 1960; Garfinkel, 1963) is a reflexive construction of social order. Much of this connective tissue is metaphoric: nonverbal, taken for granted and truncated, almost encoded, and dramatized through stories that configure the work (Waddington, 1999; Shearing and Ericson, 1991). Both within and outside the force, the symbolic power is "inarticulate," silent and even unarticulated, known and felt rather than spoken about.

Police work is a self-sustaining mirror or means of reflection. Like all work, it can be read as based on autopoesis, or self-affirming and reproducing an enclosed world. It is not all that, as the world is penetrated and shaped by facts. The officers' activities, including arrests, stops, inquiries, surveillances, and dealing with disorders, indicate to them their work's significance, the ongoing need for their work, and sustain the visible presence of those surveilled. Surveillance and watching, even in the most cursory fashion, are thought to connect the routine grounds and activities of villains with the unpredictable yet inexorable police. Routines of police as well as citizens pattern crime (Felsen, 1994).

Police work, a craft (Chatterton, 1995), is thus a visible, empirical in the sense of being seen and heard daily, clinical, on-the-spot and ready to act, pragmatic activity that generates indicia to self, to colleagues, to sergeants, and to the public that establish, albeit in a suspect fashion, recognizable, attestable products of the otherwise somewhat opaque work of patrol. Although patrol officers value somewhat different aspects of policing—time off, comp time, overtime, holidays and vacation time, rank promotion or nichelike promotion—or they play politics, either in the union or the department or both, and thus are embedded in different games, of time and of promotion and rewards, they all recognize that the fundament of the work is patrol activities.

Granting credibility to the indicia, especially official data on performance, is another matter. The hesitancy of officers to fully believe their own statistics is well known (Meehan, 1992, 1993, 1998). According to Meehan, they are called variously "cheat sheets," "my lies," or fairy tales, yet officers recognize the need to show work—to "put some meat on the table," "keep up the stats," or "show activity." Meehan (1998: 247), for example, demonstrates a volatile tipping point between generating statistics and policing a problem. Pushed to show evidence of problems they consider trivial, such as a nonexistent gang problem, officers manipulated the stats rather than the environment. The ambivalence toward all forms of record keeping, essentially data, especially that which is used to monitor individual officers, reveals much about the capacity of the organization to gather, analyze, and use information.

Police cynicism was manifested in my fieldwork as deep ambivalence toward supervision. Patrol officers believed that "they [sergeants] are never there when you need them, and always there when you cock up and need no assistance" and "they never back you up" (as evidenced in the feelings about the felony stops discussed above). New forms of cynicism arise

in cities using video cameras to record traffic stops and activity in designated patrol cars with video cameras. Officers may not take out the tapes
when told to, may not put them in and record with them, or may turn off
the mike or turn the camera at an angle, thus rendering the control-
surveillance ineffectual.

In the several medium-sized Michigan police departments I studied
(1996–98), supervision and crime control are balanced between surveillance and recording via traditional means, confirmed by craft-based face-
to-face interactions, and video cam records used to review crises such as
fatal shootings in hostage situations, deaths in custody, or serious citizen
complaints. Thus, while the here-and-now grounding of policing remains
as a powerful constraint, the penetration of the new mediated communications signals change. Many of these changes are not manifested directly
at the "cutting edge," but in planning and policy that encourage the introduction of new modes of abstracted models of policing that lift the contours of the work up and away from the patrol officer on the street. I describe these as the new levels of abstraction that now are shaping police
work. In other words, while the job remains on the ground, increasingly
there are other modes of viewing and managing risks on the front lines.

LEVELS OF ABSTRACTION AND PATROL WORK

One can trace the passage through the police organization of a natural
event in the real world that is encountered by an officer as a result of a dispatch. The pathways are much the same now as they have been since the
advent of CAD, but new developments now on the horizon may change the
way these natural events are framed, classified, and then further analyzed
as a part of new forms of policing such as problem solving, crime analysis,
crime prevention, or "risk management."

Organizational Processing and Framing

In order to understand the new and emergent levels of abstraction that are
confronting police officers, one has to begin with the contexts in which decisions are made. I use the paradigm of framing to explicate the new uncertainties. If we use the Goffman framing perspective, the ways in which
calls are framed, this analytic tool can be used to contrast (below) with a
natural event.

As I noted above, the contexts within which decision making occurs in
policing vary (Manning and Hawkins, 1983). If they are arrayed according
to the level of abstraction involved, we see that they move up and away
from the officer on the ground.

1. Officers on the ground deal with primary information—the information of the senses, of the situation, of the here and now. They convert selectively the information to official records, and record some of the facts in those records, as do others who process the information through the PCS. They also verbally report aspects of the context from which the primary information was derived while processing the information.
2. Once delivered to investigators, internal affairs, or supervisors, the primary information is transformed into secondary information.
3. This information, passed on to top command, becomes tertiary information.

Presently, it is well understood in policing that the lamination of the realities arising from the different contexts in which decisions are made is problematic. Still, the authority to punish lies in the hands of those twice removed from the "action" on the streets, and their perspective and data differ. Modern patrol work is rooted in surveillance, and from this basic posture toward the environment, the natural events, the "to-be-transformed" raw or primary data arise.

In the framing context, all messages contain a core and a fringe of relevance. These internal features of a message are a combination of the format effect (what items are present in the form) and the salience of the items in the form for the pragmatic purpose of dealing with the job at hand. "Message" is a relative term. It is what remains when the other aspects of context are sorted out or eliminated from consideration. These include equivocality and noise.

Equivocality refers to uncertainty about source, or the trustworthiness of the message source, but in the case of mediated communications it can refer also to trust in the channel, e.g., radio, MDT, personal radio, cell phone. Police trust messages from police-based sources most, and within those, trust most of all the channels that provide them with direct, work-related data (on motor vehicles, warrants and arrest records, and driver's licenses). These have low equivocality. Equivocality increases as one moves from there out to the least trusted communicators, criminals, minority youths, and "assholes" or incorrigible members of the public.

Noise can be seen most readily as unwanted data. Noise is thus a more variable matter because it shifts as the boundary between "message" and field (other messages, subjective and objective forces such as occupational practices and traditions) changes. The field necessarily contains more material than an officer can use.

The term *frame* is used in many fields and does retain a cognitive basis toward that which is relevant to deciding or giving meaning to an event or "strip of activity," as discussed in chapter 1. Framing (Goffman, 1974: 8), or isolation of what's going on, sets out meaningful materials from the rest.

A message has internal features as well, more detailed discussion of which is not needed here (see, for example, Manning, 1980: 163–67), other than to note that modern organizations as a rule are procedure and format driven, and increasingly these shaping formats are electronic. Recall (see chapter 5) that the in-car computer has a command-demand set of menu items and a response set, selections from each of which create status, action, process, and outcome data both on-line and later. When the organization is adapting to the environment and the officer is adapting to the role and organization, and these processes are mediated by technology, framed meaning joins organizational constraint.

Here is an example of how the police frame a message and how the message is a part of organizational action.

> A police officer in a car listens to the police radio, cruising the streets during a summer storm, talking to a passenger, and looking at a car stopped beside the road. The officer at this time can be oriented to one of several channels (sight, sound [two channels], or smell), but for working patrol officers, the sound of the radio is usually foremost. The officer must sort the valued communication (if it is radio transmissions) from noise, in this case, noise on the radio call as well as the sound of the summer storm, any informal chat in the car, and the stalled car she sees at the roadside. If the police radio is the information source, she may listen to the voice of the dispatcher to determine if the dispatcher is trustworthy, a sign of equivocality (officers' trust in dispatchers is more complex in a large police department because there are many dispatchers, turnover is high, and voice recognition may not be possible), sort out the content, the elements formatted in the message (e.g., an address, a description of the problem, a general location), and then establish mentally their relevance (rank them) in taking on the possible (imagined) assignment. Such framing can change if new events arise en route, if other problems require more immediate attention, or if the call is taken by another officer. Having framed and layered these meanings, the officer may undertake further communication via MDT, personal or departmental cellular phone, or radio.

The "message" the officer frames can change over time. This is a function of the coding scheme used, or the second-level framework for observation. The concept of message is rather broad and varies with the setting, audience, and the roles of the actors involved. The message must be sorted out in a given context, but context (in this case, noise, equivocality, information and other matters in the surround, or nearby in social terms) influences how framing the message is done with respect to both form (the police message format, usually "dispatching by the numbers" or formal categories) and content. In this sense, the message is a key to what people take as real, or the social reality that they inhabit.

In this example, the radio transmission is the message and the stalled car is noise, but if the officer makes the car a priority, the visual imagery and its associations become the message, while the radio represents the noise. The "channel" through which the message is sent and received patterns both form (the elements of the formal message) and content (items and their particulars). Communicational channels differ in their meaning, although the medium is not the entire message. Often, the message is the message. Using the radio presents different contingencies for a performance than does the MDT, e.g., who is listening given the wide broadcast range of the call, voice quality and volume, the strictures and regulations limiting radio time, given bandwidth and competition for the same channel. The MDT is a computer wired in parallel for multiple users simultaneously, uses a screen and several menus to present data, and can be dedicated to a single user for a given transmission.

Once the officer arrives on a scene, similar framing unfolds and sets off routines. "Message" is a matter defined or framed, a nominal idea and social form, and may be also a concrete entity (a piece of paper, an electronic file, a disc, or a tape recording). A message, whether communicated by a group, a person, or a machine, is context dependent, as is the message's meaning. To understand a message implies understanding a context. The paragraph above describes a message (or several, depending on one's orientation to the communication) in context that takes meaning because it is a part of a work-related routine.

Once framing is done and the job completed, accounts are often required. Why did you decide as you did? If paperwork is needed, it must be written out or transmitted. Teamwork requires some coordination of written records as well. Providing an account implies an audience to whom one is accountable. Deciding and accounting may become well integrated. The resultant mix of meanings indicates enactment or interpretation (Weick, 1995). The process of control has its own attractions, independent of the kind of control, and the ends and means involved are frequently opaque to those engaged in the deciding.

What this brief analysis suggests is that from an information-processing point of view, street policing is potentially very rich in stimuli, and the quantity and quality of these stimuli vary over time. Officers with whom I have ridden in my fieldwork could drive, monitor stop signs, lights, and traffic, on-the-street events as they passed, point out sights to me (places, buildings, people), identify and respond to calls directed to them on the force radio, note the weather and road conditions, and converse with me. I could do one thing, perhaps listen or write, or daydream, while they were simultaneously doing several very competently. This elegant focusing reduces noise, responds to "normal silences," manages equivocality, frames relevant data, and imagines them as features of a decision or series of decisions. The preference for concise, closed, and finished reports, as noted in the earlier discussion of police data gathering, is produced by the inspectorial, call-driven model of policing, but also is overdetermined by the cognitive complexity that officers face. The interpersonal strategies and tactics and the routines that are learned reduce complexity to manageable level. They are, in Weick's (1995) terms, "sense-making."

In many respects, this set of pressures is not a result of the occupational culture but of cognitive complexity that must be reduced and managed. This exists whether the workload is heavy or light, because the environment of policing is rich and variegated, and very open ended. On the other hand, as many observers have noted, the wish that many officers have of keeping a low profile, avoiding or minimizing work, and keeping a tidy "patch" and a clean shift, and their wish to see the job as primarily one of keeping their streets in order on this shift, for today, roots the job in the here and now, even though variations on this modal type certainly exist. Supervisors, if they rely on second-level reports such as MDT output rather than on-the-street observation, are torn between observation and abstraction. Top command has little control or sense of the street in general, being outward oriented.

I want to make the point that the culture of the road officer in large cities has been seen as the police occupational culture, ignoring even the general patterns of service identified by Wilson (1968), the many occupations working within the police, and the segments of policing that exist.

Alterations in Level of Abstraction

We can imagine the range of abstraction available to patrol officers based on such a natural event as the one described in this hypothetical report:[1]

> The officer arrives at the address, 409 Rose Hollow, dispatched on a "man on premises" call at 4 A.M. on Monday, October 16, 2000. She speaks to the resident, searches the premises, including the garage, back and front yards, basement, and the entire interior of the house. She checks closets and enclosed spaces. While she is there, the K-9 unit appears (called as backup), and the dog is used to search the garage and grounds. A VCR, DVD player, television, and

1. This was created for the purposes of illustration, but is the kind of event I have often observed. I am the narrator here, not the officer.

speaker system are missing. The owner has no records of purchasing them, nor serial numbers. There was no evidence of breaking and the resident said he "never locks the back door." While there, the officer smells marijuana in the air, checks the MDT and finds a list of recent calls to the same address for breaking, domestic disturbance, loud party, and complaints by neighbors (seen by checking dispatches made to addresses on the same block via MDT); she has been here twice before in the last month on nuisance calls that resulted in no report. The yard is littered with car parts, a sofa, several abandoned microwave ovens, and a Winnebago RV with flat tires. Loud music is playing. A report was taken, including all the relevant formatted items—name, address, time, incident number, crime report number, and so on. The yard, the previous calls, the suspicious smells, the absent serial numbers and receipts, the previous complaints and dispatches, are not included in the report.

The officer can "see," define, and describe this event in many ways; the ways are not mutually exclusive. She may broaden her horizon to include the neighborhood, or narrow it to the reported incident or "crime." She could see this as an instance of taking a crime report; as indication of a problem of crime for which follow-up and criminal investigation are required; as a potential matter of domestic violence, disorder, or neighborhood problem or issue; as one in a series of runs she made that night; as one of a series of runs made for things of this kind; as one of several visits to this address; as a type of situation (messy, multiple issues, dubious residents); as one in a series of burglaries she has seen and investigated; as merely a break in the middle of a long boring night; or as a potential deception for insurance fraud (based on the fact that the "owner" has no proof of owning the television, DVD player, speaker system, or VCR). If it is a crime, it is something that may well be discredited by a detective or declared "unfounded" for lack of evidence of possession of the claimed items. The event may be seen as part of a neighborhood problem—noise, litter, disorganized, poor single-parent homes, animals and children running loose, and other criminal activities nearby. In short, this is a crime-dependent neighborhood. If the officer knows the house, the persons, or the neighborhood in detail, she may place this event in the context of a larger series of personal encounters. The natural event can be put into many contexts and responded to here and now in many ways, and later, once processed within the organization, in many additional ways.[2]

The described version above displays the here and now of this event

2. Malcolm Young (1991: 253–390) on the ambiguity of crime statistics is brilliant, consummate, a virtuoso performance. I cannot imagine this material being surpassed as a description of police construction of the meaning of crime for its detail, irony, and clarity of exposition.

from the patrol officers' perspective. It is important to note that the working rules of most officers would lead them to write up the event using a set of unstated premises. One should collapse the context, omitting matters that one "did not see" or "did not hear" or otherwise are viewed as outside the scope of the report to be written; produce a brief report that would not come back on you; cover the facts relevant to this report as framed (no more, no less); provide facts one imagines might be needed for further investigation by burglary detectives; write a report consistent with those written by the K-9 unit and by any other units there who write reports; not take too long (i.e., exceed the tacit time limits for the associated paperwork); and produce a report consistent with any other evidence gathered and with any radio or MDT transmissions. Furthermore, the spelling should be correct and the handwriting legible, all the boxes should be filled in, and the document should be signed and filed.

The relationships between this event, this report, and other associations such as a metonymic grouping (all my runs that night; that week; that month), or a metaphoric grouping (bad calls; burglaries; false or dubious reports; things in that neighborhood, at that house, or with those people), or a longer-term allegorical reading (the dirty work of policing) are rooted in the individual and collective experience of this officer, on duty, as a patrol officer, in this town on this shift and at this time of day, week, and month. In short, she can reproduce this as an instance of something and associate it with other instances of the same kind, whether the associations are connotative or denotative (see Manning, 1989). No other officer could do this, although their classifications doubtless would overlap as they reflect the working rules of the organization and the patrol officers' perspective. Given the perspective of the officer, the narrow definition of the event—something that allows one to handle it, close it, and return to service—will obtain unless other matters intervene. These include, among other things, a supervisor showing up, a fight occurring at the scene, repeated and abrasive lack of deference, and the availability of overtime. As Garfinkel (1967) has noted, there is always the "etc. clause"—more can be said or done in any given instance.

Clearly, tensions are present in such a process of information gathering and processing (Manning, 1997b). The clinical assessment based on trust of others and trust in one's senses may be at odds with the legalistic or quasi-legalistic requirements of "writing something up." All reports are edited and shaped (Young, 1991: 253–390). The written story varies from the actual events in their fullest explication as experienced. The parallel is the analogue between the text (what is written) and the fabula (the story that is being told) (Eco, 1979). The translated, encoded, written record of events may vary from the sense or spirit of the event as seen and responded to on the ground. Such familiar tensions have a credible history in policing, make the study of "discretion" a black hole, and explain why the common law reflects an unwillingness to state acontextually what is proper violence or restraint and why discretion remains quite wide and deep in less than visible police decisions (Klockars, 1994; Goldstein, 1960; Bittner, 1990). Abstract problem solving exercises have very little meaning for officers and are rarely undertaken, even in organizations with a community policing mission, because they require time, effort, and skills that are rarely present and not rewarded. Something (an actual concrete event, with people and their vicissitudes) officers see, touch, hear, feel, or otherwise experience and that they can lodge in their memories produces a viable social reality.

This rooting in the here and now, or concrete thinking, is in part due to class and discourse limits, in part due to the social organization of work that typically places officers in charge of a given place (a precinct, a district, an area) for a given stated and limited time period (a shift of eight or ten hours at a time) and expects them to look after it, to "clean it" and leave it tidy for the next officer. Officers are held responsible for it within a limited set of well-known parameters that do not include managing deeply embedded chronic problems of people, groups, places, or economics. The paradigm is shaped proximally by the job control values in the patrol world, not with respect to the actual events, processes, people, problems, or moral state of an area. Concrete thinking is also a function of the immediate sensate power of the here and now and the demand conditions for action that lie in the pragmatic ideology of patrol work held almost universally by officers up to and including top command.

Recall that the first few levels of abstraction described in the natural event shown above reflect the current working rules and operational bases for police work. Except for the ability to query databases directly from the MDT if it is in the car (about one-third of vehicles are now so equipped), these rules and bases are unchanged in my experience since the late 1960s, when I first began to interview officers, keep clippings, and do ride-alongs. Such events as recorded are, in short, redolent with the empirical sense data possessed to varying degrees by all officers.

Now, let us consider the levels of abstraction required to "elevate" this natural event into something else. The levels of abstraction are relative to the hypothetical baseline, or "zero-point," the sensate awareness of the officer. Consider these several, quite complex, analytic transformations of the base, or the natural event described above.

NEW LEVELS OF ABSTRACTION FOLLOWING THE INITIAL
ENCOUNTER WITH THE NATURAL EVENT

First level of abstraction. This is the police report as written. Many aspects of what is seen, heard, smelled, and noted are not included in the narrative or report proper. See above for an explication of some of the translation processes.

Second level of abstraction. Here, concrete sense data recorded in some fashion change location, channel, and form in the organization and become more abstract and decontextualized. Such abstractions include lists of the number of burglaries in a given neighborhood, precinct, city, or political area. These can be variously represented or displayed: as a series of points on a pin map or computer-produced crime map; in a table of crimes reported in UCR; or in organizational statistics. The points on the map remain icons, or representations that mimic the real thing—a burglary is indicated in the Western police department by a cartoonish figure in a black eye mask. These are "pictures" and possess a low level of abstraction. When data are processed into intelligence reports, or even into "packages" or generalizations produced by crime analysis or crime mapping, the "territory" becomes a "map" and the "map" changes. This first-level analysis can no longer be validated by individual observations made by a person or persons about others acting in an event, the sine qua non of policing. The validity depends on the assumptions of the means by which the abstraction is produced. Whereas if an officer arrests a person who has burglarized a house, the event is sharply etched in her memory. If, however, the crime analysis unit constitutes a series of ATM robberies, a set of similar rapes, a clustering of prostitutes at a park, or "youth gang" activity, such generalizations and inferences move beyond the experience of the officer. Given an address, date, and time, an officer can still derive personal location and connection to the event and its particulars, but this is collapsed in the second level of abstraction.

Third level of abstraction. This results from using the signifiers (the words) of the first and second levels to create another level (the referred-to idea)—a "crime package," an assemblage called a "hot spot," a series of processes, cooffenders, victimization patterns (repeat victims vs. others), or gang activities. These tend to be time bound, recent, a metonymic series, usually bound together by denotative meanings.

The fourth level of abstraction. In this case, signifiers in the second and third levels of abstraction, now shown in tables, graphs, printouts (of reported crimes), statistical analysis of the time sequencing of burglaries, or the percentage of repeat offenders in a given precinct, are produced.

These data collapse many incidents and aggregate and count them. Their unique features, their "fuzzy edges" and ambiguities on the ground vanish. For an officer, such tables are no longer rooted in the familiar context of a given case, or even an area for which a patrol officer feels responsible; the signs float. A new context links signifiers and signifieds. Metrification appears. Numerical logic provides a new sort of difference. This is the difference not among burglaries, but between burglaries and other crimes. Other differences are those between the event on the ground as a burglary and another crime (how are they different? how are they the same?) or among natural events that become "burglaries" (how are they different? are they ironically and counterintuitively different, yet the same?). These are best captured as tales told as a part of policing's rich oral culture.

The fifth level of abstraction. Another level of abstraction arises when raw data are not only transformed, made numerical, or encoded in some analytic fashion, but become part of a system. The expert system used in a burglary investigation is an excellent example. If the system simulates or models the phenomenon—burglaries, drug investigations, or complaints against officers—it foreshadows the future based on the past. It is not about today. Such devices and schemes, expert systems, simulations, models, games and gaming substitute abstract social space for concrete time and place phenomena (Arney, 1991; Bogard, 1996; Cicourel, 1986). Expert systems, for example, are "expressions of simplicity formulated from . . . enormous complexity" (Arney, 1991: 63).

The sixth level of abstraction. The abstractions of experts, academics, and other researchers produce distant and often very complicated pictures of police work. The sixth level is illustrated by research reported in academic journals, books, reports, papers, and presentations. These are encountered by officers primarily in training, course work in school, or continuing education seminars.

It should be emphasized that these are not mutually exclusive levels and that they come in and out of discourse and discussions in modern policing—e.g., at crime analysis sessions as in the Boston Police Department—but they sit uneasily together on the ground of the here and now, and are constantly contrasted with this primary level of abstraction.

THE PROBLEM OF HYPERREALITY IN POLICING

The kinds of analysis urged on contemporary police vary from the second to the sixth level of abstraction. The sixth level of abstraction is the product of five cumulative sets of meanings and therefore is a "hyperreality" (Eco, 1990b). Practitioners, rooted in the here and now of practice, time and place bound, have understandably great difficulty placing themselves and imagining their work in the context of general, immutable, timeless laws and principles (Arney, 1991: 52). This hoped-for capacity to imagine otherwise is changed by additional IT, but not substantially modified. The creation of a rationalistic, abstract superstructure of knowledge is generally, but not always, disconnected from practice. Practitioners see themselves in the present, dealing with a particular event, with a particular history, and carrying inside it a mystery or at very least an unpredictable future (Arney, 1991: 52). This holds true for police as much as nuclear physicists. Ambiguity is the one certainty in modern life. This escalation of abstraction is one of the major forces now transforming policing.

The now abstract connection among events, cases, and suspects is unclear. It is necessary to conceive of an imaginary connection to produce an abstraction, but is not possible given knowledge of a case to abstract its features, without a suspect, to encompass a set of cases. Detectives work generally from features of the case, or a suspect, to interviews and interrogation that lead to "TICs" (admissions of crimes other than the one for which the suspect is being investigated, to be taken into taken into consideration—hence the acronym—in sentencing) or admitted crimes. Working from abstractions, models, and predictions reverses current and familiar practice. These abstractions are in a struggle in a police department, and the penetration of rational means of crime investigation and control, computer programs, maps, simulations, expert systems, and models of the clustering of crime (of burglaries, murders, or routine crimes in an area) are used by few officers and avoided by many. They raise once again the question of trust—who is trusted?, what is trusted? Trust tends to disappear when it appears.

Among police, as in other organizations, rationality shows its face in several forms, what Espeland (1998) calls "competing rationalities." This suggests that organizations are not all of a piece, that internal struggles vary in intensity, and that case studies can capture the range of these changes. For example, in the chapters on the drama of technology I argued, using case studies of CAD and other information technologies, that the drama of technology could be understood as a process of assertion, the introduction of technology, then a series of adjustments, or countertheses, leading to a reconstitution and eventually a reintegration of technology in the organization.

Levels of abstraction exist within decision making and within the craft of patrol work, and produce struggles between competing rationalities in police organizations. Another aspect of the ladder of abstraction, seen at a low level in the CAD and MDT and the development of semi–virtual reality in-car "heads up" technology (Meehan, personal communication, 1998; Rochlin, 1997), is the movement away from the "concrete reality" or "clinical police work," empirically based sensate work, to modes of imagining that supersede and surpass everyday realities.

That which is seen or the images surrounding us can be called the actual, or what is perceived, or seen, and in a sense is the past now known to us. This is much like the concept of the "me" that arises in response to behavior that has just taken place. The images on a television screen, or on a computer monitor as I type this, are actual images, representations of action that has been, the passing present.

SOME COMPARISONS

The relevance of these abstracted models, or images, is that they change the pragmatic decisions that are taken on the ground. When at the ground level of abstraction, images, crimes that have been entered into a computerized record-keeping system and assembled and displayed on a map, actual images (crime data as dots, or records, or addresses) are being converted into virtual images (Bogard, 1996: 44–45). This once-past, now represented in virtual images, creates a new structure, a set of algorithms or possible choices, based on accumulated past knowledge. Instead of surveillance on a neighborhood, following known burglars or interviewing them, this map now allows "prediction" or simulation of risks by blocks for residents (or addresses) to "repeat victimization." This risk is a statistical artifact of the model, and would not allow prediction of the next house to be burglarized, but it would over the course of a year allow the prediction of the rate of repeat burglarization with a high degree of accuracy. Simulation in this sense "seeks to perfect existing knowledge" (Bogard, 1996: 47).

Simulation in the form of statistical modeling, the highest level of abstraction, allows one to collapse space and time. For example, the model of burglaries can be run forward for five-year periods, extending and interpolating the current rate, or with substitute parameters and values, or regressed toward the mean in previous earlier years. Space can be altered by transposing these rates onto other areas of a city, or adding or subtracting officers on patrol and saturation tactics and the like to guess at the likely costs and consequences of such crime suppression tactics.

Another meaning of simulation is reproduction of the appearance of the real in everyday life. Simulation ideally aims to reduce the illusion of its own existence so that running a simulation of gun crimes or truancy rates or the impact of pawn shops on burglaries at one level and at another is not mistaken for "crime control"; this reduction of illusion breaks down when simulation is built into surveillance in the use of video camera data from airport entrances such as in Denver, when it is used for running checks on suspicious cars and outstanding warrants, or when data from credit cards at supermarkets to track criminals' movements. Simulation is used by the Chicago Police Department to map and show the address of a call on a screen to the left of the dispatcher. She or he can also call up all the previous calls to the address, that phone number, or that block or section of blocks for a given time (usually up to a week, depending on computer memory capacity). Computer-based models are designed to assign the next available car to a call (Larson, 1972). This is in effect on-line simulation.

Consider in this context the development of two forms of surveillance that shade over into simulation because they act as deterrents regardless of whether they actually work. The first is the ever-prevalent burglar alarm system with the small sign up front indicating the home is protected by a security company. In the Hollywood Hills, one informant told me, people bought the signs and put them up or stole them from their neighbors, to use as a deterrent even though they had no burglar alarm system. The "free rider" problem is reproduced through simulation. A second simulation that is increasingly used is the video camera placed in a park, at the train, subway, or bus station, trained on the passersby. There are other cameras, of course, which are concealed. Surveillance can be simulated: an art gallery across the street from the surveillance camera shed housing police and videos watching Washington Square in New York City shows pictures of cameras pointed at the shed and the officers standing nearby. Parking police cars and walking about is a popular tactic of community policing. This simulates the act of surveillance even if no one appears to be in the car. In East Lansing, where the city hall and police station are in the same building, police at the end of a shift leave a marked car in the nearby convenience store lot for four hours until another officer drives it away. Surveillance can be feigned to induce belief in it, and then ultimately disappear as it becomes "built into" cognitive apparatus and assumed to be working. Much of the work of "security" at airports is simulation of surveillance, since the fundamental documents required—picture identification, a passport—can be easily counterfeited in any large city in the world.

TRANSPARENCY

Modern forms of regulation and control in America have been influenced in the last twenty years by laws mandating "openness" of records, "freedom of information," and "accessibility." These reflect, on the one hand,

the historic American antiauthoritarian attitude and distrust of government, its agents, and its information, and on the other, the growth of
linked information networks in which "private" or once private information, from credit to medical records, are now available electronically
(Lyon, 1994). The police, most government law enforcement agencies,
and schools have adapted to this in simple but effective fashion—by hid-
ing information, making it expensive and time-consuming for citizens to
obtain, by avoiding putting many things in writing or in accessible files, by
overwhelming the requester with useless information, and by keeping sets
of records that are only partially copied.

The notion that life, events, people, interactions, and books should be
transparent, or that one can "see through" them to "truth," is a historical
residue of Platonism, which saw the true form lying concealed inside a
cave of darkness and obscured by other forms, surface features, misleading information or even disinformation.

Transparency assumes then a true vision and a true form somewhere
beneath or behind everyday understanding, a truth that the assiduous and
undeflected person can discover by penetrating the mysteries of the cave.
This formulation elevates reasoning, ratiocination, and individualism,
denying the essentially collective and dependent nature of all social life.
The transformation of thinking and reasoning, initiated by Kant's idea
of the form as organizing the "data" or "content," further advanced by
Cassirer, Langer, and the later Rorty, presupposes that form anticipates
content.

Behind such epistemological notions lies the idea of trust, trust that
presupposes the game-furnished conditions of interactions, the stability
of others' intents as like one's own, recognition of the framing and reframing as well as metaframing are ongoing. The difficulty in postmodern
times, illustrated by the changes in policing indicated by IT, is that the locus of trust is problematic when the surface features can be so easily manipulated and alternative sources are denied or not present.

While the courts and the law serve as receptacles for resolving reality
conflicts based in property disputes, other common domains have blurred
boundaries and consequences. The mediating of policing works in both
directions, shaping policing and social control and ideas about social control and policing. The democratization of risk proceeds apace, so that individuals around the world can know earthquakes as soon as satellite-
based seismographs measuring earthquake reality, location, intensity, and
duration; anyone can call in to any talk show on radio or television and express an opinion, a problem, a solution, a hatred or fixation, and find an audience. Like all television images, flat and equal, so are these trivial every-

day expressions, and all are entitled democratically to express them. If screens are equally available to all—via the Internet, for example—and equally valid, public and private "confessions," redemption, falls from grace, forgiveness, and the like are as likely to appear on morning network television professed to some smiling face as to a priest in the privacy of a confessional. Television, like many other forms of simulation, including policing itself, is only a partially visible barrier, creating a sense of depth and insight but concealing emptiness. Its transparency, the "you are there" rule of the increasingly sentimental and celebrity-based nightly news and "reality television," misleads. If films are used as the basis for modeling controls as now seen in the last few American attacks on underdeveloped nations (Panama, Grenada, Iraq twice), then the manipulation of visual evidence stands to "prove" changes in the "real world." If authority connects itself to visual records, and imagery, as in these wars, and in some recent "trials," then truth is a difference between simulations. There is no final arbitrator or "guarantor" of truth in a system of simulation; nor in a system of images that can be crafted and created at will, like photos can be created at photo shops. It is obviously true that seeing is not believing and that little else is available in a highly mediated society.

CONCLUSION

Although the centrality of trust in social life and policing is introduced in chapter 1, the concept is again reviewed here as a situational matter of concern of everyday policing. This outline of changes in level of abstraction in policing elaborates the previous theorizing about the mediated society, reflexivity, and policing by linking the visual and the imagination to everyday life. It is clear that the transformation of policing is slow, that the edges, the knowledge held by some officers, but not applied by patrol officers, is new and different, but the practice is unaltered. It lies there and is in potential a very powerful source of change. The prevalence and potential of these models was limited to the first two levels of abstraction in the early 1970s, although the CAD system was imagined to operate automatically at a very high level via hypercube modeling.

I have argued that as police communications become more mediated, and interpretation requires higher levels of abstraction, the communicational system itself becomes a source of mistrust. The seven or eight layers of information that are possible are also confusing and interdigitated in practice and in discourse. While the rationalizing of policing has been in process for more than thirty years, it is now possible that the communicational capacities may introduce alienation. This is true because the officers deal with the here and now, a profoundly demanding reality, while their supervisors and top command deal with second- and third-hand information. As these types of formal information systems increase, social distance between the bottom and the top will increase, stretching the stratification system. Of course, abstraction at various levels lurks, and simulation and surveillance practices coexist in policing. They are complementary, not in competition. But as abstraction rules, contact with realities may be transformed (Zuboff, 1988) so that work is formatted and lifted above the sensate base that has governed policing since the early part of the nineteenth century. On the other hand, belief in the magic of technology proceeds apace with solutions to security problems vested in "smart cards," eyeball-reading devices, video cameras in stores, concealed devices to set off alarms in stores to alert security personnel of shoplifters, and other fundamentally misplaced loci of trust and trust assessment. Do we trust what we trust to assess it?

PART FIVE
REFLECTIONS

TEN

REPRISE

INTRODUCTION

This book is a collection of observations around several themes that hinge on uncertainty and trust in policing as they illuminate the changes in policing over the last thirty years. I have made much of the role of the media, of politics, of the new technologies of information, of the apparent changes associated with community policing. This chapter considers the role of increasing abstraction as it bears on the changing pattern of police work (see Manning, 2001a,b). Insofar as *abstraction* is the central driving force in the analysis of new crimes, and new forms of crime—terrorism, bioterrorism in particular, cybercrimes, and computer-based crimes—it is essential that police understand the power of abstraction. This means considering the limits of retaining the nineteenth-century model of crime and the face-to-face bases of trust that now order policing. The shorthand for these changes in technological mastery is rationalizing, setting out ends and articulating means toward them and evaluating the degree to which the goals are achieved. Since many goals and means are in conflict within the police organization, rationalizing has many faces or aspects and cannot be easily discussed in the fuzzy buzzwords of modern management or economics.

CHANGE, TRUST, AND MEDIATED SOCIAL CONTROL

In societies in which change is constant and communication increasingly mediated, social control, and its communicative base, is changing as an oc-

cupation and organization, manages contingency, and produces performances, the allusion and illusion of control and dramas of control. While
standards and norms operate, they operate situationally and are governed
more by context than by abstract standards. Local knowledge and practices come into conflict and their contradictions are often obscured in ideological claims and rhetoric. This book selectively addresses these changes
and their consequences within a dramaturgical framework. Drama arises
under conditions of contingency, when decisions are required about performances before audiences and where the nature of the risk is unclear.
Deciding becomes more salient when authority and accountability are an
aspect of the deciding. Media and technologies, each in their own way,
have expanded and elaborated the extant uncertainties, and the changing
roles and routines of officers on the ground have also been affected. There
are many ironies in these mini-tales, for the intent of innovations in the
modern age is to reduce complexity, decrease overhead and transaction
costs, speed the delivery of "products," and simultaneously improve the
quality of service and life. Obviously, these are in some tension, as well as
the source of new and laminated problem sets unanticipated by the optimistic innovators. The role of trust in the escalation of the ongoing abstraction in policing is not well explored, even as new systems of information gathering and processing are being acquired (Dunworth, 2000). The
rhetoric of community policing, problem solving, and crime analysis and
mapping hinges on the capacity of officers to connect persons, places, and
meanings to these vague solutions to unidentified problems.

The mandate of the police is shifting, and arguably mediated imagery
has a role to play. Policing is, of course, a naturally fascinating occupation;
no one need exaggerate its importance. As Gusfield (1986: 208) observes,
politics, like policing, is certainly more than theater and drama, but to say
that (about policing) is not to reduce the importance of the performative,
ritual, and expressive dimensions. Furthermore, terms like the "drama of
control" and the "performance of policing" are not intended as cynical
readings of motive or disingenuous communication. The terms "sacred"
and "profane" mark a fundamental question in ahistorical, sensate, and increasingly visual cultures—how do we know anything beyond the range of
experience and the senses? Durkheim (1961) answered this by showing that
the categories "sacred" and "profane" conferred qualities upon phenomena, gave them life, and the contrast so created was in some way fundamental cross-culturally and through time. Contrasts between the sacred
and secular are context bound and time bound. The sacredness of policing
is always relative to the grounding of the secular. In a highly material,

changing, very secularized, individualistic, and competitive society, that which is sacred may not be very much so. Management techniques, career planning, budgeting, management training, contracting, and outsourcing in policing, unheard of thirty years ago, are indications of rationalization and indeed of secularization from within. This dramaturgical view is limited in some respects, as this analysis has shown. It overstates for purposes of argument the role of the media in life, the passivity and dislocated character of the modern self, the fragility of social relations, and the irrelevancies of science and history. Perhaps the police are seen as too "conservative." It perhaps sees politics as too rarefied and insufficiently organizational and people work oriented. While communicational schemes such as dramaturgy exaggerate, they nevertheless capture subtle yet undeniable features of policing in postindustrial societies.

The working question of this book is what changes since 1970, especially in the media and technology and the role, have produced what alterations in policing practice? This question concerning change and uncertainty suggested that a dramaturgical framework was appropriate for exploring how social control, in this case policing, operates in a mass society. The theatrical metaphor, furthermore, seems to fit postindustrial societies, where play, games, and consumption compete for attention with work and where much interaction is brief, situationally guided, and with strangers. Many of the forces described here are emergent and their overall effect and power are as yet undiscovered. These trends in massification, rapid communication among strangers, often mediated, and globalization work before our eyes yet escape our understanding.

Drawing on police studies, this book addresses one aspect of the larger question of how policing fits and adapts to the global-informational society (Castells, 1996, 1997, 1998; Sheptycki, 2000) because it analyzes the tensions between performance, roles, organizations, and networks of information (Castells, 1997: 7–12). The future effects of worldwide communications networks on the political economy are yet to be understood. These change processes, viewed abstractly, and the contingencies they add to everyday policing reconstitute social control and interdigitate the known, the seen, and the invisible. The illusion of control and the promissory nature of human interactions are being reshaped by the processes outlined here. They bound and constrain, but the police maintain choice and reflection and creatively construct the problematics of their encounters.

OVERVIEW OF THE ARGUMENT

The book is organized into a preface, five parts, and two appendixes. The preface and chapter 1 introduce dramaturgy. Dramaturgy is a rhetoric or second-order observation scheme that makes sense of performances, whether they are mediated or face to face. Chapters 2 through 10 include the argument, findings, and conclusions, while the appendixes deal with methodological questions.

The first part, "Policing Contingencies" (chapters 1 and 2), makes the case for the perspective adopted and the definition of policing in Anglo-American societies. I define police as many diverse agencies that are authoritatively coordinated legitimate organizations that stand ready to apply force up to and including fatal force in specified territories to sustain political ordering. They mediate between the citizenry and the legal system. Their obligations, as Reiss writes (1971: 2), are a combination of accountability and the appearance of justice. The title of the part (as well as of the book and of chapter 1), "Policing Contingencies," is a pun because police both attempt to control contingencies and face many themselves. They communicate about contingencies and uncertainties, as well as about their own interests, politics, and plans. Yet they are constrained by obligations to be just, to appear fair, and to shape cases that make their way through the formal procedures of the legal system and other modes of formal social control (bureaucracies at the state and federal level). Chapter 2 presents a working definition of Anglo-American policing and considers several features of Anglo-American policing. These definitions and renditions of police organization identify the substantive issues shaping the police management of uncertainty or contingency. Police organizations—rational, created, and artificial systems designed both to regulate and order by using the threat of force in a given territory and to reduce uncertainty— are a social structure shaped by technology that stands between the environment, including the media, and the enacted police role. They are also fraught with managing the contradictions of a conflicted and complex society with values and practices that are in direct conflict with stated ideology, religious beliefs, and chauvinistic rhetoric. They are a mirror of as well as a shaper of society.

Part 2, "Picturing Policing" (chapters 3 and 4), sees police both as subject (an attitude seeing policing as a sympathetic phenomenon) and as object (a more distant, ironic or debunking attitude seeing policing as flawed and inconsistent) of imagery. It links the visual to social control and policing. The section includes material on the media and the visual in postindustrial society, the role of the media in shaping the mandate, aspects of reflection, and the dynamics of police reflections. In contrast to the past, where the police mandate was based on belief and some experience (varying by race, class, and gender), perhaps the police mandate and actions are shaped also by media reflections and reflections upon them. While the police are the most visible representatives of the state, and arguably the most numerous, they work backstage and are seldom directly observed in action. The performances rendered by agents of all formal agencies of control, public and private, are only partially seen, and visible to even a small part of any society. They are increasingly mediated or presented and represented to us. Our knowledge, tacit and cognitive, about any given encounter or police action is limited and we must therefore trust images and infer risks indirectly. Much of our "risk-assessment processes" are based on perceived reality, imagination, and institutional formulations of risk.

Electronic equipment and related screens act as surrogate extensions of our senses, and citizens as well as police have become both subject and object of surveillance and are screened in many ways, known and unknown, every day. It appears that screening and surveillance both are more common and have greater acceptance as other forms of informal control seem to attenuate and drift away. The visible is no longer principally embodied copresence, but includes graphics, spreadsheets, Internet visuals, television and videos (both watching us and being watched), and images that are acontextual yet powerful in their effects.

It is through the acceptance of the authority of the "realism" of the media that policing is known to many for whom otherwise it remains a collective representation. This form of knowing strips citizens of a meaningful sense of their voice, their role in politics, and their obligations to others. It does provide a powerful source of identity and pleasure and thus is linked to the circulation of symbols and identities, politics and economics. That visual representations found on television are thought to be (a special kind of) real is itself a source of power and shapes politics. The police are both subject of, and communicated about, and create and distribute visual images themselves.

Using Goffman's frame-analytic perspective, I argue in chapter 4 that "policing" as a subject or object can be framed as technical redoings, regroundings, drama, or play. My primary concern is with the first three, and with the media's "looping" of them to create confusing and confounding framings for commercial gain. These framings are seen in mass media versions of policing (external to the policing function), as well as in films and visuals used for internal policing purposes. The police are frequently able to use the media effectively to shape their own dramas, such as a perp walk, a press conference or release, or an arrest or raid and to engage in containment games with the media to enhance their status, avoid criticisms, or repair damage. Police can be subject to media explosions where their actions become part of national and international consciousness. This is described as a matter of moving from little to big theater. When an event is seized, shaped, amplified, and reframed repeatedly by the media, it becomes BIG theater. Some events move from media event to spectacle, a visual evocation of social conflict removed from direct human actions and choices among the viewers. Exploring the powerful link discussed in these chapters between the visual and meaning, or interpretation, should become part of a new perspective, or perhaps mediated dramaturgy.

Part 3, "Technologies and Information," includes three chapters. The first explores the police material technology (the vehicle) and the frontline (the officer or driver). Technology is not a thing, but a process, part of the drama of information technology. The car and the driver's equipment have changed, but the vehicle remains the frontline "office," communications center, and private space, and the space where data and intelligence are collated. Technologies both are means and have expressive and symbolic aspects because they play into the increasingly "technicized" performances that constitute a growing segment of modern occupations (Barley and Orr, 1997). The nature of police fact gathering and the creation of information, how it is gathered and processed, resists easy systematization. The many and growing networks of information in which the police are linked suggest pressures to become less a sanctioning mechanism and more a data processing center, part of a system of actuarial justice (Ericson and Haggerty, 1997). Uses and appreciation of the potential of these network of information are a source of tension, in spite of attempts by the command segment to regulate information technology. But technology also produces attempts at adjustment, reconstitution, and reintegration. IT produces counterstatements, resistance from the bottom, as well as creative responses and learning. The power of IT to transform is limited nevertheless by other factors in the organization. These include the inability even of experts to coordinate the many operative databases, secrecy and competition among forces, and the glut of available information, most of which is never referred to by patrol officers after the initial encounter. The existence of capacity, or of storage or programs, does not ensure use. Finally, the irony of increased information technology is not just that data are unavailable or the databases inaccessible; it is the ideology of patrol officers and the expectation that faster is better and their impatience that lead them to use only the simplest and most directly useful sources, such as (local) databases containing outstanding warrants, motor vehicle registrations, the stolen car list, and driving licenses. The encounter between officer, format, and machine remains the fundamental setting in which to understand the impact of information technology on policing. Thus, the patrol officers' role is constrained organizationally and by the values that shape practice, as well as by the routines developed by individual officers.

Part 4 covers police roles and change. Based on my ethnographic evidence, the attempt to introduce community policing—a crude and ill-formed technology—little alters the role of the officer in practice but produces a number of contingencies that must be faced tactically day to day by both officers and supervisors. Trust, acceptance of a matter as it appears, is fundamental to policing; in many respects, the police are trust assessors for society at large. As more elaborate information processing systems emerge in policing, such as expert system software, crime analysis, crime mapping and tabular social survey data and models, the trust assessment problem shifts its locus and meaning. It is no longer located in the here and now, "on the streets," but in more abstracted, complex, polysemic systems of meaning.

Appendix A explores methods and dramaturgical analysis; appendix B discusses my data and fieldwork.

INFERENCES: POLICING AS COMMUNICATION AND AS COMMUNICATED

What theoretical inferences can be drawn from this review? This section is organized around five areas: the impacts of the media on policing over the last thirty years; the environment in which the police find themselves; changes in the police organization; new policing technologies; and the changing police role. Policing is a form of communication: policing, perhaps universally, communicates to society, is communicated about and to, and responds in some loosely coupled sense. It must sustain compliance internally, shape and maintain a mandate within a chaotic interorganizational environment, and adapt to new developments in technology. The role itself is reshaped. Each of these sources of contingency, both within the organization and in the environment, produces the likelihood of drama and animates police work. They also affect civility, a point to which I return at the end of the chapter.

Media and Drama

Dramaturgical theory must somehow encompass both the centrality of the features of the society of the spectacle and the impact of television to explicate the interpretive problems of modern societies. To understand the dramaturgical or communicational theory of policing, one has to take into account the features of television in the society of the spectacle. The role of the spectacle in politics is yet to be appreciated in social science of mass society. It is a tentative and fascinating conceptualization of politics, the visual, and reflexivity (see Edelman, 1988; DeBord, 1990, 1993; Merelman, 1991).

As social differentiation (Black, 1980) increases, social distance can be created via media, shrinking and expanding the scope of one's indirect experiences. It plays promiscuously with sometimes cruel immediacy, inducing copycat responses to media events, constructs the world as an inexplicable series of controlled and dangerous disasters, and presents a jumble of panics, wars, disasters, famines, and vulgar spectacles as representations of the world (Ignatieff, 1999: 27). The police as an agent of government are shaped by media and visual aspects of control, using and being used by the media, being the primary subject of media news, drama, and simulations, and increasingly using information technology with digital transmission and receipt.

These mediated processes affect the mandate and occupation of policing, although the book has used the windows of information technology and community policing as ways to open general questions about dramaturgy and social control. While "governmentality" seeks to distribute or reduce identified negative risks, policing takes up image work, media relations, spin tactics, and containment and countercontainment as fixed aspects of police management. As a result of these changes, the symbolic work of policing, both expressive and instrumental, at the micro and macro levels has been interwoven with media and imagery. Abstractions edge out empirical or sensate experience as the basis for policing, and problem solving is touted as the new management tool on the ground level. Meanwhile, at the command level, expert systems for weighing suspects, forensic tests for DNA, automated records and fingerprint files, crime analysis and "intelligence-driven" policing are the latest buzzwords in North America and the UK.

Specifically, although policing is dramatic, the meaning of the drama appears to have changed as a result of television's amplification of police work. Viewing police actions may be mediated by technology and separated in time and space from the original events. The police do not perform in the context of shared emotional responses, although they may elicit feelings of awe, respect, deference, or even mystery. A substitute for emotional identification and ritual solidarity as a source of compliance is authoritatively administered violence. The police oscillate between acting as a rational legal arm of the state, legitimated by state authority, and a charismatic, mysterious, personalistic, quasi-bureaucratic form (Manning, 1997b).

Oscillation amplifies contingency and therefore power. As the effects of the widespread viewing and response to the video of the savage beating of Rodney King illustrate, democratic authority creates paradoxes. To maintain authority the police routinely use coercive force. When reproduced by electronic means, instances of police authority have a symbolically transformed ritual power not based on face-to-face interaction and thus lack context. Police violence shown in mass-circulation magazines and on television is stark and ominous: personal and immediate, as well as distant and abstract.

Perhaps it is obvious that the King beating was natural activity converted into a televised event. The reality of the event as a powerful televised reality has not been questioned. It apparently fits the reality rules that enable viewers to see a brief video as an instance of real events and become outraged and active. By seeing this video as real and embedded in the course of activities, viewers endowed televised reality with political power. The film surely had a mobilizing or rallying point function in the May 1992 Los Angeles riots. If such axial events shape views of society and of policing almost as much as do our personal experiences, knowledge of local events, newspapers, and gossip, then politics, media, and banal entertainment commingle. They shape a spectacle that is watched but not fully understood. Ironically, the media create a cynical distance from politics in order to enhance their credibility, while one consequence is reduced interest and lower political participation (Merelman, 1991).

It takes little imagination to move from the example of the King beating and other media events to consider television's potential to create constraining collective representations, for example, to stimulate or suppress social movements (Gitlin, 1980). A semiotic process creating a sign, a sign-signifier relationship, may denote or connote, but since signs are always embedded in an interpretive context, in part drawing on epistemological and ontological assumptions brought to the message by the reader (viewer, hearer), signs always carry (often invisible) ideological freight (Fiske, 1987). As Mary Catherine Bateson observes (1994: 31), "Beyond the denotations lie unexplored connotations and analogies." Put another way, culture in the form of communication is altered by being mediated, and communicational processes at second remove continuously shape culture.

Although the self is not my focus here, natural activities, once mediated, link society and the protean or saturated self. Specifying and explicating the logic of reality rules and the cognitive preconditions for viewing permit one to interpolate between viewers and codes (Fiske 1987: 5), as well as to explore the politico-ideological implications of imagery. These rules might be analogous to the rules of grammar that structure sentences. If so, developing a grammar of the mediated society should enable us to understand the transformations of activities into events and to illuminate the cognitive framework that facilitates construction of massive and continuing media spectacles such as the Gulf War(s), the Clinton impeachment, and the O. J. Simpson trials. If axial media events become the markers by which collective memories are organized, they are harbingers of the future. Collective memories are shaped by experience and repeated imagery derived from many sources (Wagner-Pacifici and Schwartz, 1991).

The context(s) of axial visual events should be examined to discern the impact of the video of the police beating of Rodney King and the riots that followed the acquittal of three of the four officers who beat him. Lying behind this axial event are the processes by which the most salient of the mass media, television, has become a dominant force in social life. It shapes our view of policing and virtually everything else. Media processes are not natural processes, as much as media employees may wish to define them as such. Politics has become media politics, but not all politics is shown or visible, and not all major events become media events subject to copycat responses or media looping and amplification.

Little dramas amplified become big dramas, often out of the control of police, and axial media events stage life as it is imagined, rendering politics a show of some kind removed from life chances, interests, and direct experience. The current linkage of politics, aesthetics, and consumption gives power to visual events. The mass media and technologically driven media realities arise as a source of information control, authority, and power, as well as the means by which these are sustained while maintaining the fiction of the presence of a democratic polity. In the society of the spectacle, key figurative evocations, like graphic moots or massified copies (Eco, l976), elevate a cultural theme that is then animated and elaborated within the context of the spectacle. These visual events obviate the absence of interpersonal communication and punctuate, or are epiphanies of experience that draw the concrete into, the objectivated reality of the society (Debord, 1983: 8). The role of the spectacle is a needed facet of a mediated dramaturgy.

The New Shape of the Environment

The nature of the environment that the police inhabit is partially of their own construction and partially rooted in the material and physical world (Manning, 1988). Policing and the environment stand in a transactional, not interactional, relation.

Demand is variable and can be controlled. Short-term impacts arise, are measured, and vanish. Planned demand—allocation to sporting events, parades, and the like—can be scheduled. Differential response and allocation can be planned. Some police departments, such as San Diego's, use the overlap between afternoon and evening shifts as a problem solving period. Unfortunately, civic life is not based on short-term dips and rises in such measures. The flexibility in scheduling now available in many kinds of work has not been adopted by police; they still require the employee to work at least three shifts around the clock or 4/10 (four ten-hour days on and three days off). The ability to set one's own hours, used by community police in Britain and in specialized units in this country, is still subject to periodic abuse.

The slightly more proximal environment, the media (now in some symbiotic relation with police given media offices and officers), and the new image-producing capacity of computers have their own agendas, based on competition for audience and short-term ahistorical practices of reporting. The media present more risks to police and are less cooperative; nevertheless, they also present more potential for image management.

The environment of policing is replete with other agencies and organizations in competition with police, another source of contingency. Analyses of local policing rarely take on the joint character of much enforcement; police may cooperate or be in competition with city services, parks and recreation, social services, mental health and hospitals, and federal and state agencies. The movement to community policing and zero-tolerance policies made use of civil law and other agencies' powers into a new and powerful tool. Thus far, other agencies have been used primarily as a negative sanctioning force to displace homeless people, destroy crack houses, evict drug dealers or unwanted tenants in public housing, and sanitize parks (Kelling and Coles, 1996). Laws, especially liability laws, are changing rapidly, putting police at risk for civil suits, federal civil rights suits, and settlements made by cities outside the control of the department. This threatening aspect of the law is perhaps more problematic than the enforcement maze presented by American criminal law.

Changes in the Organization

Now, consider changes to the traditional police organization with its features outlined in chapter 2. Current research shows little change in the structure (number of ranks, rules, and other aspects of hierarchy and specialization) or function of police agencies in spite of the rhetoric of "community policing" (Greene, 2000; Maguire, 1997).

The inspectorial police bureaucracy, focused on reacting to rare events, patrolling, and selectively investigating, now possesses a network of informing and informating technologies that rest uneasily in juxtaposition to a well-shaped organizational culture. I have deemphasized the role of the occupational culture here as a far too vague sponge concept that is used to explain far too much and therefore explains very little of organizational dynamics. The organization is loosely coupled with the environment and maintains this via ideologies and practices. In many respects, the police organization enacts its environment and symbolizes this enactment in public statements (Weick, 1995). The loose coupling between command, management, and officers, the sensitivity of command to external audiences, and the local context of police funding and support means that the flexibility of the organization as an environment scanning structure is essential. While bounded, the organization contains segments that differentially dramatize autonomy and control. Prestige accrues for different reasons in different segments—investigative work, street work, and supervision rest on different assumptions about "good police work." The segments of the culture, a response to hierarchy, isolation, and information based at the bottom, communicate more within than across, creating constant misunderstandings and a sense of arbitrary discipline. This in turn creates negative rituals of resistance against command. There is a loose coupling of segments, especially when investigative work is included. Originating as a rather loosely organized bureau, the present police are bureaucratic, i.e., rule bound and routinized; the shadow of the rules and discipline plays off the concrete here and now of the work and the ability of officers to conceal and obfuscate the basis for their decisions.

Police, since the reform movement, have emphasized their service and crime fighting capacities and their "responsiveness" in general to demand. The organization has been designed over the last fifty-plus years to respond to calls, meet demand, and come when called and has used this as the fundament of its political base as reform politics stripped policing of its patronage linkages to the larger political system. Policing, organizationally speaking, stands balanced between internal legitimacy based on compliance to command and the shared commonsense bases of the work (Manning, 1997b) on the one hand and the struggle to redefine its mandate on the other.

Technologies

The characteristic technology of modern policing, social skills, is often overlooked and attention drawn to weapons and militaristic arsenals. But new forms of police information technology are slowly emerging, city by city, town by town, metropolis by metropolis, until the larger informational network will emerge complete, linking databases across North America. Information is not data, for information must be processed to become valued and useful or to become "knowledge." Data-gathering capacity is not equivalent to assiduous and consistent use of IT. Most large police departments and federal agencies such as the FBI, DEA, and ATF are swamped with data and swim in a sea of noncomparable datasets (Ericson and Haggerty, 1997; Haggerty and Ericson, 1998).

A natural history would appear to organize responses to the introduction of information technology in policing. Any technology or means of carrying out work that extends human capacities holds the potential for sociotechnical change, anticipated or unanticipated. The process of technological regularization, seen from a dramaturgical point of view, preserves aspects of ambiguity in the paradigms revealed in the four meanings of the symbol "technology" (see the table in chapter 7). These ambiguities are organizationally exploited. One of these is that lower participants can manipulate data processing codes, create new informal categories, and circumvent classification systems. If messages are redefined using the lower participants' culture, then a bifurcated meaning of incidents results. On one level, the official, computer-maintained reality exists, and on an another, an informal or "real" meaning remains. This lamination creates organizational ambiguity: what layer of reality is referenced by a written document, video, or verbal report? This ambiguity can be used to maintain uncertainty and advantage officers. The dialectic expands and contracts the situations that contain uncertainty yet require decisions.

Not all of the dramas are major and "organizational," because some are fought out every day as call takers make sense of calls, dispatchers juggle and reorder assignments, and jobs are finessed, redefined, avoided, and carried out on the ground. Technology competes with bureaucratic rules and structures because it introduces entropy, or information that must be routinized and compressed into useful formats for record keeping (Merelman, 1998). It also segmentalizes police and civilian users within the organization, regardless of position, thus challenging the bureaucratic notion of equal skill of the holders of comparable bureaucratically defined offices. The formatting and preprocessing of data via MDTs and CAD constrains choice but creates contingency because complex situations based on conflict cannot be easily squeezed into boxes and forms.

Technology exacerbates the stratification of information within the organization. Earlier cohorts know less computing skills than later ones, and this is roughly duplicated in all ranks, although the computer-literate percentage shrinks as one moves up the rank structure. There is a sense in which the growth of the network of information shrinks the role of the individual in the craftwork of policing, thus setting identity and network in opposition (Castells, 1996: 22–23).

While officers work in a social structure and in organizations shaped by a historically derived mandate and a set of domain assumptions, they also carve out roles for themselves in and around new information technologies and organizational reforms. While all technologies produce contingencies reflected in role relations among workers, changes in the patrol officer role outlined in chapter 8 raise general issues associated with uncertainty and power in organizations. Those who create uncertainty can manipulate others in an organization subject to this unpredictability (Crozier, 1964, 1972). Those in power attempt to routinize and regularize exchanges. They attempt to cloak unequal exchanges in myth and ritual such as the idea that the command directs the forces from the top by means of a paramilitary bureaucracy, to maintain the fiction of stable organizational authority and equality. The lower segments can gain and retain power if they master techniques of reproducing uncertainty and gaining a measure of symbolic capital—the excess of deference accruing to those controlling the modes of domination (Bourdieu, 1977: 171–83).

The Patrol Officer's Role

Other changes are under way, perhaps slowly. When teamwork is questioned as in the community policing movement, the patrol officers' role must be redefined with new tactics and routines, and new relations with supervisors must be fashioned. The bases for police authority are always somewhat tenuous and rely on many sources of legitimacy in addition to the organization in which the officer is embedded, including informal social controls, beliefs, values, and practices. Policing, like any formal control system, is but a small and uneven source of sanctioning when compared to informal sources such as the family, the neighborhood, class, ethnicity, and gender. As abstraction in the form of algorithms, expert systems, tables, graphs, maps, and crime management programs gains authority in policing, role tensions increase with the practice on the ground.

The dominant practices of the patrol segment, the topic of chapter 8, sustain organizational strategies—random patrol, dispatching of calls, and investigative follow up. The fundamental communications problem of policing, managing a turbulent environment with limited resources while maintaining compliance, is heightened, it would appear, in times of reform and crisis. The adaptations and tactics of patrol officers, and their redefining of teamwork, is a force in the dialectic of organizational change. Community policing modifies the police role and introduces contingencies. CP is a social reform movement seeking to reduce social distance between the various publics served by the police, thus raising the issue of the basis for consistent performance, teamwork, and loyalty. It often combines a sparkling selection of glittering managerial reforms. Such reforms alter the patrol role, since they target some practices, raise reflections upon practice, and disequilibrate sentiments and exchange patterns sustaining formal institutional patterns for patrol officers and sergeants. It is disruptive. Yet, as chapter 8 shows, from the patrol officers' role-standpoint, community policing is yet another "presentational strategy," a means of selectively highlighting some changes in urban policing while suppressing information about others. The underlying structure, evaluation, allocation of resources, and management remain largely unchanged, but pressures to alter the role on the frontline are considerable. This means, ironically, that an occupation defined pragmatically pauses and is forced into self-reflection. Officers see it as just another variation that changes the meaning of what they are nevertheless required to do daily—manage problems on the ground in the here and now.

OBSERVATION

In previous works, I had sustained a rather distant and dubious attitude toward policing's claims and its rhetoric and questioned the argument that police worked from information using evaluation and feedback to sharpen their practices. At this time, I am more optimistic that the combination of new techniques—crime analysis, crime mapping, rational allocation of personnel using CAD, enhanced 911 and 311—and the innovations in roles that are being pressed on police will in fact alter their practice. The shift into what might be called rational crime prevention and reduced emphasis on random patrol, reactive policing, and an investigative case clearance focus is coming. But that is another story, another book perhaps, not this one.

APPENDIX A

Methods and Dramaturgy

INTRODUCTION

Dramaturgy is best suited to a selected kind of problems and does not stand alone; it requires the support of a variety of empirical materials. Dramaturgically inspired theorizing seems inevitably shaped by and based upon descriptive materials. Its emphasis is on context, reflection, and interpretation and makes the idea of "structure" fragile and its constraints subtle. Yet I wish to emphasize structure, negotiated and fluid, rather than actors' work. Dramaturgy remains ambiguous and unsettlingly calls "instructive ambiguities" (Burke, 1962: xx) to guide analysis. I want here to set out some strengths and weaknesses of the perspective when combined with ethnographic evidence.

The dramaturgical perspective implies a specific methodology, or logic of proceeding from "data" to analysis. Unfortunately, systematic works cast in this perspective provide cautionary canons and critiques of other methods, rather more than presenting a dramaturgical method (see Duncan, 1968, 1969, 1985; Burke, 1989; Perinbanayagam, 1984; Brissett and Edgley, 1990). In many respects, the classic works, which complement dramaturgy, such as Blumer (1969), are more exercises in description and prescription than in method. Several useful methodological works (Lofland and Lofland, 1991; Emerson, Fretz, and Shaw, 1995; Strauss, 1978; Strauss and Corbin, 1990; Denzin, 1992), argue the case for qualitative methods rather than for dramaturgy specifically. The most useful methodological statements are Douglas's *Investigative Social Research* (1976), Denzin's *The Research Act* (1989), Glaser and Strauss's *The Dis-*

covery of Grounded Theory (1968), and Lofland and Lofland's *Analyzing Social Settings* (1991). The recent *Handbook of Qualitative Research* edited by Norman Denzin and Yvonne Lincoln (1994) charts new and dramatic ground, urging rethinking of the principles governing qualitative methods (at least since the Chicago school outlined and exemplified them) and emphasizing the need to alter perspective to avoid the biases of the conventional canon.

"Qualitative methods," and indeed the general term "fieldwork," with its important commitment to what might be called local descriptions, understandings, and taken-for-granted knowledge and practices, is an imprecise and richly connotative term. Such methods are made sensible primarily as conceptions contrasting with the quantitatively oriented radical positivism and enduring empiricism that dominates American social science. This contrast does not clarify the meaning of "context," or the practices permitting unpacking it, and thus the comparison signaled is an empty one. The conventions of statistical technique, a means for inferring from quantitative materials (numbers) patterns or differences that bear on social life, dominate reasoning in the social sciences. Cressey, following the ideas of Znaniecki, drew a very useful distinction between statistical inference based on probabilities and analytic induction that aimed for causal statements, arguing that correlational arguments and statistical inference were means for disaggregating relationships, but were essentially inductive in character. Developments in "analytic induction" (Manning, 1982), a qualitative technique for causal analysis, have not been forthcoming since Lindesmith (1967) and Cressey's (1960) masterful synthesis.

When seeking something less grand than a methodological synthesis, perhaps etching a problematic, placing it in context, and connecting it, ideally, to structure and history, qualitative methods are superior. The orientation of fieldworkers—for it is initially an orientation, not a "framework," "theory," or "perspective"—should be sensitive to the problematics of everyday life. Without an explicit and identified problematic, description is fatefully boring. Conversely, a problematic such as "class inequalities" has little meaning outside a context.

FOCI

A "problematic," as argued in chapter 1, is but another term for a source of the dramatic and dramatic themes. The "dramatic" is that which captures attention, draws the eye, turns one toward it, causes reflection and rethinking. The dramatic is not an absolute, but emerges from context. Difference in context is dramatic in different ways in each case. Are these differences comparable? The dramatic is also often used analogically—to identify how emotions are generated by a scene, a reading, or a series of events coupled as a ceremony; how a play or book affects an audience or critics; how actions are "deviant" or selves saturated (Gergen, 1992). The dramatic can be captured complexly as in Greimas (1987), contrasting contradictions, oppositions and relations among them (Jameson, introduction to Greimas, 1987: vi–xxvii). Jameson, using Hayden White's work (1960) shows how the "dramatic" is captured by manipulating writing styles, or tropes, such as metonymy, metaphor, irony, and tragedy, and combinations and transitions among them such as tragic irony and so on. Goffman established the connection between performance and the drama by suggesting that interaction necessitates drama. Here, I have argued that drama is precipitated by encounters between strangers where past or present information is scanty or absent, yet interaction must take place.

DRAMA

The dramaturgical perspective is not suitable for framing all problems, even when the questions asked require qualitative materials. I suggest five conditions under which a dramaturgical perspective will strengthen an empirical investigation. One should have in hand the following:

- A considerable number of close-up, well-ordered, and focused observations and interviews. This is necessary because to isolate the problematic from a context, one needs both the ongoing banality of routines, the taken-for-granted grounding of everyday life, and some understanding of the "normal," as well as a detailed knowledge of the problematic. One requires a database of observation, of interviews and demarcation of the problematics, before one can play on the dramatic.
- A clear delineation of the problem to be studied. This need not be determined prior to fieldwork, but should emerge fairly soon after entering the field.
- A grasp of the range and location of the phenomena of interest. Some phenomena are better suited to dramaturgical analysis than others. For example, the secret, the unknown, the corrupt and deviant, often concealed "backstage" and not captured in official records, nor admitted in standard survey research interviews, is amenable to "dramatization."
- A clear understanding of what the (relevant) differences are and what they mean. Drama, as noted above and in chapter 1, is about

difference. In order to explain differences, one must know the context, the assumptions brought to the situation. One needs more than the journalist's "news," today's differences, but those that persist and bear on the human condition in some fashion. "High-risk narratives" (Manning, 1998) are engaging reading, but they depend, as does life, upon contrasts with less engaging events. On the other hand, some have found mushroom hunting and cooking sources of subculturally generated nuances and therefore dramatic.

• The scope of the generalization expected should be determined in analysis. Is this a case study (such as Goffman's *Asylums* [1960])?; an illustration or exemplar of some process (Goffman, 1959)?; a collocation of stories (Ewick and Silbey, 1997)?; a personal biography cast as social science (Richardson, 1997)?; a matter "typical" of groups or cultures of a kind (Barley, 1983)?

These five points presume that the qualitative work is fieldwork based, not archival in character, and that the work has a determined domain of empirical reference in which study has been undertaken. Many newer forms of ethnography, imaginative ethnography, explore bases for generalization and hold a radical notion of social fragmentation, cultural change, and integration (Rosaldo, 1989; Clifford, 1990).

STYLE AND PERSPECTIVE

The dramaturgical perspective does not sharpen a research focus easily, because in order to use metaphor, one must have a clear understanding of what is being framed, or seen as "something else." If life is a theater, how is this metaphor limited, and why? In what ways is life not theatrical? In what ways is it determined by forces that limit performance? It is important to identify how dramaturgy works or does not, and how it differs from my orientation.

Before adumbrating some aspects of method, it is valuable, I think, to show that Goffman's work is connected closely to ideas that were powerfully articulated in the years between the wars. I refer here to existentialism with its attendant phenomenology, and the literary versions of it that are seen dramatically in the writing of Hemingway, Gertrude Stein, and other naturalists, and in extreme in such writers as Robbe-Grillet, Saurrate, and Butor (see Cowley, 1994; Young, 1966). The writer is in a social place, describing minimally the surrounding conditions; the text speaks, interwoven with commentary by the author qua author; events unfold, as described, one after the other, with minimal adverbs and adjectives; and the author seeks the illusion of reality that reality in its full complexity does not give (Young, 1966: 205). In some way, they are ahistorical, conveying little from memory. The figures face contingencies—losses, slights, demurs, falls from grace, and failures of nerve. The existential world is, as Young remarks (1966: 245), about Hemingway's perspective, "a world seen through a crack in a wall by a man pinned down by gunfire, who can move outside to look only at the penalty of death he seeks but also seeks to stay." This world is quite clearly Goffman's habitat.

Through action and choice observed, imitative similarities result—routines, little encounter forms, constraints. These are the core of symbolic action. Yet the social produces tensions and paradoxes, for it is not possible to fully understand the present or to extrapolate it into future choices. The knowledge we possess is embedded and extends only minimally into the future. The requirement to act and to eschew history does not deny the constraints of time or the future; it denies only that relying on their guidance is impossible.

In the short stories of Hemingway, existential themes emerge, not via philosophic cogitation, but via the roots of experience, anxiety (generalized worry), and fear (a specific worry or concern), and their connection to what stands for nonbeing, death. There are a number of passages that illustrate this preoccupation; perhaps *Death in the Afternoon*'s final propaedeutic will resonate:

> The great thing is to last and get your work done and see and hear and learn and understand; and write when there is something that you know; and not before; and not too damned much after. Let those who want to save the world if you can get to see it clear and as a whole. Then any part you make will represent the whole if it's made truly. The thing to do is work and learn to make it. No. It is not enough of a book, but still there were a few things to be said. There were a few practical things to be said. (Hemingway, 1977: 244)

There are other themes in Hemingway: the inability to control death and disaster but the need to die bravely; the recognition of the call of death but the assertion of self against it (counter-phobic); the surface of life as constituting the contours of constraint; and the urge to press on to create the next challenge. These are presented as observed, much as in Goffman, and often without comment.

Granted that Goffman's world is a subtle version of this, it is still this. And the sense of loss and impending almost palpable terror is abiding in Goffman, especially in his classic studies of illness and ineptitude—

Stigma (1963), *Asylums* (1960), and his truly grotesque masterpiece, "The Insanity of Place" (1970). Yet, like Beckett's characters, Goffman's actor must go on in face of the meaninglessness of the moment and the haunting and bracketed fear of death. The small gestures of civility for Goffman resemble the occasional acts of humanity, love, or altruism seen in Freud's writing—punctuation of an otherwise bereft and rather stark landscape of cruelty, awkwardness, distance, and pathos.[1]

DRAMATURGY IN GOFFMAN AS A METHODOLOGICAL GUIDE

Consider Goffman's writing as an example of the evolving of dramaturgical methodology. The several phases of Goffman's work are not cumulative, marked by a continuous narrative thread, or linear development. Rather, they represent differential emphases (Manning, 1992b; Chriss, 1995) on aspects of social life based on his continuing preoccupation with explicating a kind of situation: face-to-face, human and embodied copresence, involving communication. In his work, themes of performance, drama, ritual and game, strategic (or information-based) interaction, stigma, valuation and devaluation, and cognitive framing or processing all appear. A sensitivity to the situated nature of talk informs his writing, but he does not dramatize talk to the exclusion of the nonverbal conditions sustaining it (Goffman, 1983a).

Unfortunately, "Goffmanesque analysis" is strongly associated with the early "performance-oriented" work, namely *The Presentation of Self in Everyday Life* (1959), and much less to his language-based tour de force, *Frame Analysis* (1974), his later sociolinguistic essays in *Forms of Talk* (1981), and his penultimate publication, "Felicity's Condition" (1983a). In the last nine years of his life, Goffman polished a particular writing style found even in his first publications. The features of this style are important in part because they distinguish it from most other writers. It contains a method in part created by his stylistics (Manning, 1979b). Goffman does not gather and use "data" to build up or prove an argument as much as give examples of or exemplify a tightly reasoned case or instance he has previously located in the symbolic and subtle interactional grid of face-to-face communication in Anglo-American societies. Unfortunately, his work is not cumulative either, but a string of insights that penetrate the complex-

1. There is some evidence that these are not mere coincidences. Goffman lived and worked in Paris for a time before completing his dissertation. This may be the basis for his use of quotes from Sartre in the first few pages of *The Presentation of Self in Everyday Life*. The overall tone of his work, like Hemingway's, echoes courage in the face of inevitable loss, death, and discovery.

ities of the interaction order. In that sense, Goffman's work does not cohere as a theory of modern society.[2]

Turning now to a text, the starkness of Goffman's opening statement in *The Presentation of Self in Everyday Life* is perhaps unique in the social sciences. It strips the person to an almost pathetic imitator, lost without history, cues, or knowledge of the other. It is concrete—entering a situation—and it is ahistorical, or more accurately, anytime. It sets the person aside, alone against an inexplicable existence of others. Yet it has an ominous, compelling force to it—a force leading to action, choice, doing. So, set aside the person in the situation who acts, does and does it with others, with some degree of commitment to the act. This action is possible because the person steps back, reflects, looks, and imitates others. It may not be about a person at all, but like a Robbe-Grillet snapshot, is merely a scene. The first sentence of the introduction to *The Presentation of Self in Everyday Life* reads, "When an individual enters the presence of others, they commonly seek to acquire information about him or to bring into play information about him already possessed" (Goffman, 1959: 1).

This is a hypothetical situation nowhere located, named, or characterized, containing stipulated persons with attributed actions (and by implication, attitudes), who are said to universally seek information or to bring it into play. Does this happen always, sometimes, rarely, or never?, a methodologist might ask. The proposition doubtless is attractive, elegant, and with intellectual merit. Indeed, Goffman's book and this one both assume just such a fundamental principle about the seeking and use of information. The key attribution is about the audience, those into whose presence the individual comes, and their monitoring and approbation sensed by the performer about the forthcoming performance. Information is sought and used to establish (Goffman, 1959: 1) the actors' socioeconomic status, trustworthiness, competence, and virtual identities.

Goffman in this example has framed a strip of activity as "real" in that it involves face-to-face copresence and mutual monitoring and argues that a social framework is employed to discern causation, motive, and needs.

2. Goffman's paper "The Interaction Order" (1983a), elaborated and clarified by several lucid papers by Anne Rawls (e.g., 1987), is his last attempt to explicate his view of a structural social psychology. He was deeply connected to the "primary matters" of social structure, power, and authority (Chriss, 1995; Branaman, 1996). That the interaction order is problematically and situationally shaped by other matters—rituals, social organization, and space—is to surface the brilliance of his analysis. To use a cliché, the shapes of situated interactions are not rule governed or generated by an algorithm. In short, "it depends." The links or connections, perceptions, frames, or typifications between these external, constraining, and primary matters and a situation require empirical investigation. Social life, like a linguistic act, requires structure and performance, and the two are enacted conjoined.

His writing assumes that meaning has been delineated or, as argued in *Frame Analysis* (1974), that the encounter has been framed. The aim of the exercise, in *The Presentation of Self in Everyday Life* and in his other writing, is not to accurately represent a particular global reality or to establish its existence. His concern is not the distribution of a phenomenon, or a sample of a social fragment. He locates a piece of meaningful behavior within a rather elaborate set of implicit principles. Goffman is not a representational writer, but a dramatizing writer.

From this kind of writing, one cannot draw out objective propositions or inferences that resist being bent to the time and the place, once reflected upon. This is true because the knowledge of others is thin and weak and is constituted only by the performative configuration that results, not something like "knowledge of." The actions observed can be described; they can be detailed; they can be revealed. And the results or consequences of these actions cannot be "predicted," because the general features of the experiences are not yet understood. And the knowledge remains intuitive in large part.

Given this linguistically created state of affairs, we can create some social content and work it through as an example. An individual coming into the presence of others, say an officer coming into a group of young women in a park, will be alert and, logically, is expected to engage in information seeking and exchange, whether stated or not. Should any one participant be unwilling to produce information, or distort, hide, or alter her identities, documents, or appearance, inferences can be drawn by anyone—that she has something to hide, has devious motives, is unwilling to offer the basic currency of human exchange, and could well be untrustworthy in other ways. The officer, in turn, will seek to penetrate the performance, which may include a variety of fronts and modes of concealing and revealing. This set of responses will lead to containment moves by the observer, and countercontainment moves, and so on, until the interaction is concluded.

Notice that Goffman's first move is to plunge the careful reader into a socially created world, linguistically sustained, in which action is imminent. The resultant ambiguities—Who are these people? Why are they here? What does this guy want?—and information-based games or exchanges, including perhaps ritual openings such as "Hello, how are yah?" and resultant interactional content, are a product of the described hypothecated situation. The posited situation and interactions have power for the reader because they engage the reader in seeing how a universal situation might unfold. We see it, and can imagine it, can see its contours and risks. It is an inherently contingent situation. The phrase "we see it" is important, for other than attributing to the actors a wish to seek and use information, he names no other functions, values, institutions, norms, or role expectations in making the first move or claim. Including more, such as these matters, clearly would refine the analysis, or add contingencies.

The attribution of "deeper" motives, character, "personality," or biographical continuity, matters we associate with extensive interactions in Anglo-American society, are not invoked. The consequences of commingling, the requirements to greet, to exchange particulars of life and mutual acquaintances (Goffman, 1983b), enstructures situations more than do values, norms, and personalities. And if talk arises, it too is attended to as a ritual obligation of deference to the speaker more than to the content. In this way, Goffman correctly identifies the universal autotelic, or self-structuring, aspects of much interaction between passing acquaintances or strangers.

Goffman's sociological language is thus well suited to description of modern interactions between strangers where little but basic premises are involved, and where what is seen becomes the basis for an unfolding interactional process. It is, by the same token, apt for analysis of television and images where the same conditions hold. Once framed as real, television can laminate realities, or definitions of the situation, almost endlessly. Television itself, like Goffman's sociology, requires only that we attend the performance, not believe totally in what lies behind it. Reality is already mediated (Lemert, 1997: xxxvii), dependent upon an extension of belief (or suspending disbelief), and in some sense directed to the fact that the world is fabricated, or copied, in stories told, the language we use, and the actions we perform in aid of the telling.

A NOTE ON POLICING

Let us think through a police example to illustrate this idea of copying and fabricating. Police officers learn to police by watching other officers do the job, in the academy, on the streets, often with a field training officer, but always with a partner, and listening to stories about how policing went wrong ("cautionary tales" in the drama of work, as E. C. Hughes calls them [1958]), when it went right, and by implication containing lessons about what not to do. When officers begin to police on their own, they simulate or emulate what they have seen and heard about. They may use the same ritual phrases used by other officers during their first traffic stops, and in the same order, much as a routine. In this way, they copy what they have seen and heard, but they are also copying some "reality." There are variations possible from this framing of the stop. The officer may think of it as a "game" in which flirtation or sexual innuendo is involved (Kraska and Kappeler, 1997); the officer may view it as merely a "rehearsal" for more serious stops with unruly drunks, or as a performance in "make-believe" if the young officer is being filmed for the *Cops* show. Each of these frames is keyed back in some complex and perhaps unknowable fashion to "reality," but it is only in contrast to each other than they have meaning in everyday life (Lemert, 1996: xxxix). Lemert observes (1996: xxxix) that Goffman's writing was "displaced." Lemert means that Goffman is writing about an already framed reality, one Goffman constructed from the known scraps of everyday life. Goffman wrote and perhaps lived in that world. Any kind of social reality copies something, and a reality, as Goffman writes near the end of *Frame Analysis*, takes its meaning from contrast, not from its verisimilitude to an unknowable mystery.

This means that when Goffman asks us readers to picture a magician rehearsing his tricks, a fabrication lying lodged inside a rehearsal, he has produced a framed example already. His aim in *Frame Analysis* (1974) and in his brilliant later work, *Forms of Talk* (1981), "Felicity's Condition" (1983a), and "The Interaction Order" (1983b), is to set out a logic of and for frame analysis, but he does not perform a frame analysis (Manning and Cullum-Swan, 1992). In the last two articles he was again returning to the tacit grounds of constituting the conditions for action, rather than the overt character of that which is constituted. Goffman often creates taxonomies of kinds of reality, unwinding long and imaginative lists (Goffman, 1974: chaps. 5, 7). Examples, footnotes, or newspaper clippings often animate such epistemological exploration, but these are not "data" intended to establish the existence of the category, but to explicate the contents of the stipulated category. Having done that, Goffman points to or indicates perhaps that kind of experience that resonates with many readers. In so doing, he has not established the category or its connections to other types of reality. This kind of taxonomic thinking is found in descriptive or naturalistic sciences in general. But perhaps his power comes not from the examples chosen, but from other features of his writing.

Reading Goffman beings with it an intuitive grasp, a taking in, of the thing as seen. If seen, in its variety, it can be located. If located, it can be reproduced and re-reproduced. This reproduction does not arise from rules, norms, values, or predetermined routines, but from emulation, simulation, copying, and getting along with others. This is well suited to modernity, for the flexibility of interactions in mass society is largely unhindered by the past, biographical preferences, and perhaps crushing economic constraints. Goffman's persons have no innards, only eyes and surfaces; they "play it by ear," yet they are situationally competent. Furthermore, the situations and their logic seem to hold rather better than the "personalities" we carry around. This means, strangely enough, that how the situations are constituted and reconstituted is not "personal" or normative, but emergent, collective, and sometimes even playful. It is such an argument that makes small claims that the occupational culture determines, drives, shapes, orders, sustains, and produces the interactional sequences measured in such tedious detail, the violence that flashes occasionally in the media, or the corruption so abundantly necessary. If anything, performances are little figurines, mostly out of sight, and ways that one reads off other peoples' readings.[3]

TEXTS AND POWER

I suggest that Goffman's textual power arises from eight features of his writing:

- Goffman stands in the world about which he writes. He writes from within the epistemology he asserts. "If one is here, then one feels this about X" might be a proposition from Goffman. He continues then to explore the vertiginous feelings and disorientation resulting from "breaking" that frame, or the intrusions of "negative reality" that threaten the continuity of the posited frame that the reader now shares with the author.
- Goffman strives for closure. Frame confusions are brief and intolerable, Goffman writes in *Frame Analysis* (1974), because some frame is needed for sustained interaction. Conversely, he would argue, sustained interaction indicates the presence of some shared frame or frames.
- Goffman provides an example, say of a frame, in order to demonstrate its existence in, at very least, his written social world. Thus, he suggests the attractiveness of it to interactants or its presence in our everyday lives.
- He is a storyteller; brief, pointed, sharply focused. Reading Goffman is like hearing a story—we honor it not so much because we like the content of the story, or the figures it animates, or even their utterances, but because to honor the text is, like honoring a storyteller, a requirement to understanding and gathering information. The concern of *Frame Analysis* is how frames help one to understand "what's going on here."

3. I am grateful to Anne Rawls for her patient dialogues with me on this topic, on the front porch and elsewhere.

- A "here," or a felicity condition, is always assumed by Goffman. There is always a here here or a here there in the text.
- The observer is always the reader, and "you are there" is the textual operator.
- Goffman always denotes or suggests the role of structure, never eschewing it, in his arguments.
- The writing unfolds impersonally, without reference to particular persons except in examples, and is in the third person, even when it is Goffman's voice speaking.

Let us contrast this writing and method to that used here. I assemble data from clippings and interviews, focus groups, and observation, as well as observations and interviews done by others. I try to capture the perspective of the patrol officer on the role, whether this arrives via my insights or interviews. I do not place the reader in the unfolding frame, but instead simultaneously try to describe the local situation, the surround or field within which the frame is located. The ethnographic context is both a topic and resource (Garfinkel, 1967). To a lesser extent, frame analysis organizes a portion of the materials presented here. I draw on ethnographies of police, including my own as well as those by Van Maanen, Young, Waddington, and others. Here, I explore and redefine "context" so that Goffman's terms order the events and bear on the police role and its social location. The interaction order illuminates policing as an organization and an occupation.

The grounding of policing, as I have argued, is in the moment. As Hemingway and other writers of war, conflict, and disorder have well recognized, the risks of conflict resist deep understanding and prediction; while fear and paralytic flight are destructive of self and others, action is always required. Action, of course, is often confounded with memory, and memories of past action. In this sense, Goffman's essay "Where the Action Is" (Goffman, 1967: 149–270) is a document that generalizes the obvious and somewhat exotic risks of gambling and trapeze artistry to other risks in everyday life. Continuously one is expected to act, but this may not fit the emotional requirements of the actor, bring meritorious results, nor be valued. All this cannot only be imagined. The "concrete imagination" (Warnock, 1970) is the centerpiece of policing because it mediates between the other and the officer.

Because we are, at least from time to time, public beings, subject to judgments, evaluations, and social control, we experience shame, dishonor, and valuation and in turn attribute these to others as terms, categories, labels, and interactive tactics. Police hold out these labels as working tools.

The violence and risk taking of policing is both sought and avoided; but the underlying question is always how to confront the unknown and the unseen. Like the combat soldier, the officer varies between a sense of fatalism and a sense of self-control and fate control. The grounding of the patrol officer's social world is uncertainty, and responses to it a mode of coping. But this is not determinant; this does not give rise to "values" or crude lists of tenets, or epigrams. These are surface manifestations of an underlying code that is about risk and trust. In this sense, the notion of the occupational culture is a vast, misleading reification of the complexity of reducing complexity to manageable contingencies.

This grounding arises from the working-class culture from which most officers come, and their family and relatives. It is a code of concrete particularities—persons, places, times, events, stories, narratives, and longer-running allegories of the work. It begins and ends with "once upon a time." These stories, in turn, embed the cases, the runs, the stops, the encounters, and are partially revealed in the oral culture (Meehan, 2000a). This embeddedness means that attitudinal studies of police and police culture (Worden et al., 2000) rend asunder the complex melding of subject and object that takes place. An attitude toward something cannot create the object, nor does the object create this attitude; they are meshed in a transactional network. Nor can the working grounds be reduced to some semi-Marxist rules, or a regulatory structure imposed from theorizing (Herbert, 1998). Externally imposed rules, norms, and structures cannot explain the here and now of encounters, and the encounters themselves cumulate in some tension between form and content.

ETHNOGRAPHIES AND JOURNALISTIC WORKS AND ENTERTAINMENTS

Finally, data can be derived from many sources and types of experiences. I use the terms "ethnographies," "journalistic works," and "entertainments" (a phrase borrowed from Graham Greene) to distinguish serious social science from journalism and mere pseudo–investigative work that is more accurately termed an entertainment. I do hold a loose but important distinction between "ethnography" on the one hand and "trade books," movies, biographies, and autobiographies on the other and assert the relevance of reliability and validity in judging fieldwork. Many popular books about the police, for example, are engaging and interesting and contain exciting, grand illustrative stories. They are often organized around the rare, commonsensically dramatic, violent, and stressful aspects of policing such as undercover work, shootings, and chases, bizarre crimes and criminals,

and heroic deeds. However, they are limited sociologically for several reasons. How valid are such works to making general claims about social life?
They are limited and of dubious merit because:

- They lack any systematic articulated framework, which locates the
  stories in some explanatory or logical framework. Otherwise, they
  hang in social space and take on the colorations the reader desires.
  Like the work of a bad artist, this may not produce a pleasing picture.
- They do not originate from a question that shapes the study, organizes the material, limits the scope of evidence, and makes possible
  comparison with other similar or dissimilar works.
- There is rarely a form for assembling the work so that comparisons
  can be made across works. Consider the formats of anthropological
  monographs—they begin with the geography, climate, politics,
  and history of the area and then proceed to the characteristics of
  the group(s) studied and the particular focus of the monograph.
  This enables cumulative evidence to be gathered and weighed.
- These sorts of books play with and on the dramatic, so that the
  story line and "hook" overshadow "the facts" as they might be the-
  oretically gathered by a scrupulous researcher. Ideally, a running
  argument or logic of the presentation should be developed that en-
  compasses the concrete evidence presented—the descriptions
  offered of problematic events.
- The "hook," the journalist's definition of what the story is about
  and how attention will be drawn to it (apart from the headline or
  the cover of the book), determines the shape and structure of the
  story. It guides what evidence will be gathered, who will be quoted,
  how the story will be constructed to demonstrate the worthiness of
  the initial premises, and how it will be closed (see Epstein, 1974).
  Hooks, once set, seldom are loosened.
- At worst, they do not adhere to what might be called "ethnographic principles": that people must speak for themselves; that
  persons are not conflated or created; that the person named actually spoke the words, and spoke those words as exactly as translation or the research situation allowed; that the source of the data on
  the events described is noted, whether from interviews, personal
  observation, records, hearsay, or second-hand analysis; that pseu-
  donyms are identified as such and that fictive characters are not introduced to carry the evidentiary argument; and that some reflec-

tion on the role of the interviewer, observer, fieldworker, or writer accompanies the analysis (usually as an appendix).

- Journalistic "ethnographies" often treat of rare events or detail unusual responses to events that unfold in an engaging manner. Social scientists emphasize something of the distributional argument to establish the character of their argument—How frequently does such a thing happen? Why? Where? Who is involved? In other words, the problematic and the dramatic must be seen in the context of the constraints of social life. The intersubjective reality of the organization is respected.

Using these criteria, we can conclude that such works as the writings of Mark Baker, Connie Fletcher, Harvey Rachin, E. W. Count, Charles Sasser, and Ed Nowicki are pseudoethnographies. The organization, region, politics, traditions, occupational culture, and assumptions about the appropriate and acceptable "normal" level of violence and malevolence are unspecified in the vignettes. They are gratuitously dramatic in my view, precisely because they play on unexplicated contexts and readers' naïve expectations and employ editing conventions, stylistic transgressions from "natural speech," genre requirements of commercial storytelling. They may produce social changes in police attitudes and practices as well as those of the public. With the same logic that sees today's rare events as "news," the pseudoethnographies make such rarities the central events and thus are misleading. Furthermore, even the rather sensitive and insightful renditions of "real life" key figures in the underworld and their connection to policing and writer-assisted autobiographies are not ethnographies. Nor are they failed attempts at systematic ethnography. They are poignant snapshots of a social world or worlds only partially revealed.

Useful, perhaps in connection with ethnographies and fieldwork, are such multifaceted works as Roger Graef's *Talking Blues* (1989), James McClure's *Spike Island* (1980) (on Liverpool) and *Cop World* (1984) (on San Diego), David Simon's brilliant *Homicide* (1991) (on Baltimore detectives), and the most original commentary upon detective work, and John Van Maanen's jewel, *Tales of the Field* (1988). Their value is that they provide vignettes, scenes, encounters, and case narratives, often quite typical, that can be used to illustrate identified problematics and sources of drama; but they often impose a narrative line that serves to omit contrary evidence, disconfirming materials, anomalies, and the deceptions and self-deceptions that so usefully serve to comfort us.

APPENDIX B
Data Sources and Limits

OVERVIEW

I have used several kinds of fieldwork and data in this book. These include interviews, observations, newspaper and magazine clippings, the observations and interviews of colleagues, and television viewing. I have incorporated them into the risk-uncertainty drama framework outlined in chapter 1. The ritual/drama and games themes in Goffman are illustrated in the chapter on technology, and its relations to authority, skills, supervision, and the craft of policing. The framework in chapters 1 and 4 is adopted from Pfaffenberger and Burke as well as Goffman and outlines the dynamics of the introduction of new technologies and responses thereto by the several segments within policing. I have tried in the final two chapters to summarize the findings and the inferences of this work for future research. In some sense, this book is an overview of themes and transitions in policing over thirty years, and the data are both background and foreground in this exposition.

In general, the ethnographic core of this book has been emerging for some years, and the original aim of my fieldwork, drawing on Goffman's *Presentation of Self in Everyday Life* (1959) and "The Nature of Deference and Demeanor" (1957), was to explicate the sentient basis of the police role—honor and duty—as the twinned substance of police work (see Manning, 1997b: preface). In due course, I did not focus on the public-police interactional nexus, perhaps the most consistent interest of police scholars to this day, but on the tacit bases of the work and social integration within the police subdivision I studied. From this ethnographic work,

I developed the broader critique of rational, information-driven policing in *Police Work*. I refined it in *Narcs' Game* (1980), an assessment of violent and crime-focused policing, and in *Symbolic Communication* (1988), a critique of information-oriented and ideological-administrative models of policing, and other abstractions free of data derived from observations, interviews, and records. The explosion of media effects and technology, or at least the rhapsodizing of technology, so powerful in the last few years, precipitated the focus of the present work.

CLIPPINGS AND VIEWING

The materials in chapter 3, on high politics, media, and reflection, and materials on which I reflect in chapter 4, were gathered from newspapers, other periodicals such as the *New Yorker, Newsweek,* and *Time,* and the social science literature (as cited in those chapters). I kept a clippings file from the local newspaper for three years from fall 1995 to late summer 1998 for chapter 8. I draw on my own undisciplined television viewing. I don't use the VCR to tape snippets for research and teaching, as do many of my colleagues. I code and file newspaper articles using such topics as "cybernetics," "social control and the visual," "the modern [computer-assisted] house," "computing and the self," and "policing" (with subheads on the media, selves, and technology). It has never been clear to me how Goffman organized his vast clippings file, nor have I completely understood his awesomely whimsical, often ironic, pattern of footnotes. Some of the analysis of "high politics" in Western is based on my clippings file (for 1996–98) from the local Western papers and television newscasts.

FIELDWORK, INCLUDING INTERVIEWS
AND OBSERVATIONS

Ethnographic fieldwork in several police organizations and interviews as well as published evaluation studies provide the primary data for the several chapters on technology and trust (5–7 and 9). Systematic data on police uses of technology were gathered in a large Midwestern police force in 1979–80 (see Manning, 1988: chap. 2); in London in 1973, 1979, and 1984 (Manning, 1997b); and in a large constabulary in the English midlands in 1979, 1981, and 1984 (Manning, 1988: chap. 2). Some additional, less systematic, materials were gathered at (Texas) Law Enforcement Management Institutes in 1991 (Lubbock) and 1992 (San Antonio).

The effects of technology on policing were the explicit ethnographic focus of the midlands study (Manning, 1988). However, some of the materials on the sailor phone were not gathered systematically, and the chapter is intended as a framework for further research on the introduction of new technologies. Given the limitations of the data, it is not possible to examine whether there is a natural history of technological responses in a given organization, or the conditions under which the "stages," responses, or minidramas unfold. These arguments and examples, although promising, are tentative and subject to further analysis with additional data.

My fieldwork in 1999, in Manchester and Cheshire, England, and Toronto, Canada, focused on the rationalization of policing via information technologies such as crime analysis, geocoding of crime, management by objectives, and performance indicators. It provides a backdrop to the arguments developed here. While editing this book, I was studying rationality in a Canadian department, a large constabulary in the UK, and a large Southern force. I am doing similar work now in Boston.

Changes in the officer's role occasioned by the advent of community policing have been claimed, rather than shown. Most of the critiques and commentaries focus on the "big picture"—criticizing the paucity of problem solving, lack of definitions of community, the contrasts between heroic and self-serving rhetoric and actual practice—rather than the dilemmas created by redefining the role, routines, and significant others. The theme of chapter 8, on roles and routines, is struck by Reiss in *The Police and the Public* (1971) and echoes and sharpens Goffman's ideas about the relationships between roles and routines, and the pervasiveness of teamwork in policing.

In the fall of 1995, I conducted unstructured interviews with a sample of command and supervisory officers in Western, including the chief, three captains, a former captain, a lieutenant, and two sergeants. My interest there was in command conceptions of community policing and related problems of evaluation and supervision. These interviews ranged from an hour to two. I interviewed a set of officers on the crime mapping capacity of the department in the fall of 1999. I write now in 2002 at the end of a period of transition, as noted in the epilogue to chapter 8. My focus is upon patrol officers in Western who underwent a command-led reform labeled "community policing" or "team policing." In many respects the case study revealed some of the institutional contradictions in organizational reform and the vulnerability of the chief in such a transition.

FOCUS GROUPS

The author and Jane White conducted four focus groups on CP, work conditions, and technology, with top command and three groups of sergeants and inspectors in a very large Midwestern police department in May 1994. Two focus groups (two with sergeants, two with officers) were conducted by Tim Bynum, Joe Schafer, Steve Mastrofski, and me in Western in December 1995. We discussed community policing, its strengths and weaknesses, problems of training, evaluation and supervision, and the role of technology in community policing. With Albert "Jay" Meehan, I studied the natural history of the adaptation of IT in two police departments in middle-sized Michigan cities. Both departments have advanced IT and use cellular phones widely. Two focus groups on community policing were done in summer 1998 by Jay Meehan and me in a COPS-funded study of community policing in Tanqueray.

REFERENCES

Abt Associates. 2000. Police Department Information Systems Technology Enhancement Project (ISTEP). Washington: Department of Justice, Community Policing Services Agency.

Ackroyd, Stephen, R. R. Harper, John Hughes, Dan Shapiro, and Keith Soothill. 1996. New Technology and Practical Police Work. Buckingham: Open University Press.

Alpert, Geoffrey, and Lorie Fridell. 1992. Police Vehicles and Firearms: Instruments of Deadly Force. Prospect Heights, Ill.: Waveland.

Alpert, Geoffrey, and William C. Smith. 1994. "How Reasonable Is the Reasonable Man?" Journal of Criminal Law, Criminology, and Police Science 85:481–501.

Altheide, David. 1993. "Electronic Media and State Control: The Case of Azscam." Sociological Quarterly 34:53–69.

———. 1997. Ecologies of Communication. Hawthorne, N.Y.: Aldine.

Altheide, David, and R. Sam Michalowski. 1999. "Fear in the News." Sociological Quarterly 40:475–503.

Altheide, David, and Robert Snow. 1991. Media Worlds in the Era of Postjournalism. Hawthorne, N.Y.: Aldine.

American Bar Association. 1967. Arrest. Boston: Little, Brown.

Appier, Janet. 1998. Policing Women: The Sexual Politics of Law Enforcement and the LAPD. Philadelphia: Temple University Press.

Arney, William. 1991. Experts in the Age of Systems. Albuquerque: University of New Mexico Press.

Bailey, W. G., ed. 1987. Encyclopedia of Police Science. Dallas: Garland.

Banton, Michael. 1964. The Policeman in the Community. New York: Basic Books.

Barley, Stephen. 1983. "Semiotics and the Study of Organizational and Occupational Cultures." Administrative Science Quarterly 28:393–413.

———. 1986. "Technology as an Occasion for Structuring." Administrative Science Quarterly 31:78–108.

————. 1988. "Technology, Power, and the Social Organization of Work." In Research in the Sociology of Organization, edited by S. Bardach. Greenwich, Conn.: JAI Press.

Barley, Stephen, and Julian Orr, eds. 1997. Technical Work. LIR Press: Ithaca, N.Y.

Bateson, Gregory. 1972. Steps toward an Ecology of Mind. San Francisco: Ballantine.

Bateson, Mary Catherine. 1994. Composing a Life. New York: HarperCollins.

Baudrillard, J. 1993. Selected Writings. Edited by Mark Poster. Stanford: Stanford University Press.

Bayley, David. 1975. Police in the Political Development of Europe. In The Formation of National States in Europe, edited by Charles Tilly. Princeton: Princeton University Press.

————. 1985. Patterns of Policing. New Brunswick: Rutgers University Press.

————. 1992. "Comparative Organization of the Police in English-Speaking Countries." In Modern Policing, edited by Michael Tonry and Norval Morris. Chicago: University of Chicago Press.

————. 1994. Police for the Future. New York: Oxford University Press.

Bayley, David, and Egon Bittner. 1986. "The Tactical Choices of Police Patrol Officers." Journal of Criminal Justice 14:329–48.

Bayley, David, and James Garofalo. 1989. "The Management of Violence by Police Officers." Criminology 27:1–25.

Bayley, David, and Clifford Shearing. 1999. A New Paradigm for Policing. Washington: USGPO.

Becker, Harold K., and Donna Lee Becker. 1986. Handbook of the World's Police Systems. Metuchen, N.J.: Scarecrow.

Benjamin, Walter. 1969. Illuminations. New York: Schocken.

Berman, Marshall. 1982. All That Is Solid Melts into Air. New York: Penguin.

Bittner, Egon. 1970. The Function of Police in Modern Society. Washington: NIMH.

————. 1974. "Florence Nightingale in Pursuit of Willie Sutton." In Reform of the Criminal Justice System, edited by H. Jacob. Beverly Hills, Calif.: Sage.

————. 1990. Aspects of Police Work. Boston: Northeastern University Press.

Black, Donald. 1976. The Behavior of Law. New York: Academic Press.

————. 1980. Manners and Customs of the Police. New York: Academic Press.

————. 1983. "Crime as Social Control." American Sociological Review 48:34–45.

————. 1996. "A Pure Epistemology of Law." Law and Social Inquiry 20:829–70.

Blumberg, Abraham. 1967. Criminal Justice. Chicago: Quadrangle.

Blumer, Herbert. 1969. Symbolic Interactionism. Englewood Cliffs, N.J.: Prentice-Hall.

Blumstein, A., and J. Wallman, eds. 2000. The Crime Drop in America. Cambridge: Cambridge University Press.

Bogard, William. 1996. Simulation and Surveillance. Cambridge: Cambridge University Press.

Boorstein, Daniel. 1987. The Image. New York: Athenaeum.

Bordua, David. 1967. "Law Enforcement." In The Uses of Sociology, edited by P. Lazarsfeld, W. Sewell, and H. Wilensky. New York: Basic Books.

————. 1968. "The Police." In The International Encyclopedia of Social Science. New York: Free Press.

Bordua, David, and Albert J. Reiss Jr. 1966. "Command, Control, and Charisma." American Journal of Sociology 72:68–76.

Boulding, Kenneth. 1956. The Image. Ann Arbor: University of Michigan Press.

Bourdieu, Pierre. 1977. Outline of a Theory of Practice. Cambridge: Cambridge University Press.

——. 1998. On Television. New York: New Press.

Bourdieu, Pierre, and Loïc Wacquant. 1996. An Invitation to Reflexive Sociology. Chicago: University of Chicago Press.

Branaman, Laura. 1996. "Erving Goffman's Sociology." In The Goffman Reader, edited by Charles Lemert and Laura Branaman. Boston: Blackwells.

Brandl, Steve. 1992. "Detective Work." Ph.D. diss., College of Social Science, Michigan State University.

Bratton, William, with Peter Knobler. 1998. Turnaround. New York: Random House.

Brewer, John. 1996, ed. The Police, Public Order, and the State. 2d ed. Oxford: Clarendon.

Brissett, Dennis, and C. Edgley, eds. 1990. Life as Theatre. New York: Aldine.

Brodeur, Jean Paul. 1983. "High Policing and Low Policing." Social Problems 30:507–20.

——. 1998. How to Recognize Good Policing. Thousand Oaks, Calif.: Sage.

Brown, Ben. 1995. CCTV in Town Centres: Three Case Studies. London: Police Research Group, Home Office Police Department.

Brown, Julia S., and P. Duguid. 1991. "Organizational Learning and Communities of Practice." Organizational Science 2:40–57.

Buckner, H. Taylor. 1967. "The Police: Culture of a Social Control Agency." Ph.D. diss., Department of Sociology, University of California, Berkeley.

Burke, Kenneth. 1959. Attitudes toward History. 2d ed., rev. Los Altos, Calif.: Hermes.

——. 1962. A Grammar of Motives and a Rhetoric of Motives. Cleveland: Meridian.

——. [1954] 1965. Permanence and Change. Indianapolis: Bobbs-Merrill.

——. 1989. On Symbols and Society. Edited and with an introduction by Joseph Gusfield. Chicago: University of Chicago Press.

Burns, Tom. 1977. The BBC: Public Institution and Private World. London: Tavistock.

——. 1992. Erving Goffman. London: Routledge and Kegan Paul.

Burns, Tom, and George M. Stalker. 1960. The Management of Innovation. London: Tavistock.

Cain, Maureen. 1972. Society and the Policeman's Role. London: Routledge and Kegan Paul.

——. 1979. "Trends in the Sociology of Policework." International Journal of the Sociology of Law 7:143–67.

Cannon, Lou. 1997. Official Negligence. New York: New York Times Books.

Cao, Liqun, and Steven Stack. 2000. "Confidence in the Police among Industrialized Nations." In International Criminal Justice: Issues in a Global Perspective, edited by Delbert Rounds. Boston: Allyn and Bacon.

Carte, Gene, and Elaine H. Carte. 1975. Police Reform in the United States: The Era of August Vollmer. Berkeley: University of California Press.

Castells, Manuel. 1996. The Rise of the Network Society. Oxford: Blackwells.

——. 1997. The Power of Identity. Oxford: Blackwells.

——. 1998. End of Millennium. Oxford: Blackwells.

Cathcart, Brian. 1999. The Case of Stephen Lawrence. London: Viking.

Cavender, Grey, and Louise Bond-Maupin. 1992. "Fear and Loathing on Reality TV: A Study of America's Most Wanted and Unsolved Mysteries." Sociological Inquiry 63:305–17.

Cavender, Grey, and Mark Fishman, eds. 1998. Entertaining Crime: Television Reality Programs. New York: Aldine.

Chan, Janet B. L. 1996. Changing Police Culture. Melbourne: Cambridge University Press.

———. 2000. "The Technology Game." Final report to Australian Research Council. University of New South Wales.

Chatterton, Michael. 1989. "Managing Paperwork." In Police Research, edited by Molly Wetheritt. Aldershot: Avebury.

———. 1993. "Targeting Community Beat Officers: Organizational Constraints and Resistance." Policing and Society 3:189–203.

———. 1995. "The Cultural Craft of Policing." Policing and Society 5:97–107.

Chricos, T., Kathy Padgett, and Marc Gertz. 2000. "Fear, TV News, and the Reality of Crime." Criminology 38:755–85.

Chriss, James. 1995. "Habermas, Goffman, and Communicative Action: Implications for Professional Practice." American Sociological Review 60:545–65.

Cicourel, A. 1966. Method and Measurement. New York: Free Press.

———. 1969. The Social Organization of Juvenile Justice. New York: Wiley.

———. 1986. "Expert Systems." In Cultural Systems, edited by R. Schweder. Chicago: University of Chicago Press.

Clark, A. L., and Jack Gibbs. 1965. "Social Control: A Reformulation." Social Problems 12:398–415.

Clark, John, and R. Sykes. 1974. The Police. In Handbook of Criminology, edited by D. Glaser. Chicago: Rand McNally.

Clifford, James. 1990. The Predicament of Culture. Cambridge: Harvard University Press.

Cohen, Stanley. 1980. Folk Devils and Moral Panics. New ed. London: Martin: Robertson.

———. 1983. Visions of Control. Cambridge: Polity.

Colton, Kent W., ed. 1979. Police Computer Technology. Lexington, Mass.: D. C. Heath.

Colton, Kent W., and S. Herbert. 1978. "Police Use of Advanced Development Techniques." In Police Computer Technology, edited by Kent W. Colton. Lexington, Mass.: D. C. Heath.

Combs, James, and Michael Mansfield, eds. 1976. Drama in Life. New York: Hastings House.

Cook, Philip J., and Jens Ludwig. 2000. Gun Violence: The Real Costs. New York: Oxford University Press.

Cordner, G. 1995. "Community Policing: Elements and Effects." Police Forum 3, no. 3:1–8.

Corsiaros, Marilyn. 1999. "Detective Work and High-Profile Cases." Ph.D. diss., Department of Sociology, York University.

Cowley, Malcolm [1934] 1994. Exile's Return. New York: Penguin.

Crank, John. 1998. Understanding Police Culture. Cincinnati: Anderson.

Cressey, Donald. 1960. Other People's Money. Glencoe, Ill.: Free Press.

Crozier, M. 1964. The Bureaucratic Phenomenon. Chicago: University of Chicago Press.

————. 1972. "The Relationship between Micro and Macro Sociology." Human Relations 25:239–51.

Culler, Jonathan. 1966. Structuralist Poetics. Ithaca: Cornell University Press.

Davis, Stephen. 1983. "Restoring the Semblance of Order." Symbolic Interaction 6:261–78.

Dawson, R. 1998. The Mountie: From Dime Novel to Disney. Toronto: Between the Lines.

Dayan, M., and Elihu Katz. 1993. Media Events. Cambridge: Harvard University Press.

Debord, Guy. 1990. Comments on Society of the Spectacle. London: Verso.

Debord, Guy. [1970] 1994. Society of the Spectacle. New York: Zone.

Denzin, Norman. 1986. "Postmodern Social Theory." Sociological Theory 4:194–204.

————. 1989. The Research Act. 6th ed. Englewood Cliffs, N.J.: Prentice-Hall.

————. 1992. Cultural Studies and Symbolic Interactionism. Boston: Blackwells.

Denzin, Norman, and Yvonne Lincoln, eds. 1994. Handbook of Qualitative Research. Thousand Oaks, Calif.: Sage.

Douglas, Jack. 1976. Investigative Social Research. Beverly Hills: Sage.

Duncan, Hugh Dalziell. 1968. Symbols and Society. New York: Oxford University Press.

————. 1969. Symbols in Sociological Theory. New York: Oxford University Press.

————. [1962] 1985. Communication and Social Order. New Brunswick: Transaction.

Dunham, Roger, and Geoffrey Alpert, eds. 1998. Critical Issues in Policing. 3d ed. Prospect Heights, Ill.: Waveland.

Dunworth, T. 2000. "Criminal Justice and the Information Technology Revolution." In Policies, Processes and Decisions of the Justice System, Criminal Justice: 2000. Vol. 3, edited by Julie Horney. Washington: NIJ/Office of Justice Programs.

Durkheim, Emile. [1915] 1961. The Elementary Forms of Religious Life. New York: Collier.

Dykehouse, S., and Robert Sigler. 2000. "Use of the World Wide Web, Hyperlinks, and Managing the News by Criminal Justice Agencies." Policing 23:318–38.

Eco, Umberto. 1979. The Theory of Semiotics. Bloomington: Indiana University Press.

————. 1990a. Open Text. Cambridge: Harvard University Press.

————. 1990b. Travels in Hyperreality. New York: Harcourt, Brace, and Jovanovich.

Edelman, Murray. 1967. The Symbolic Meanings of Politics. Urbana: University of Illinois Press.

————. 1988. Constructing the Political Spectacle. Chicago: University of Chicago Press.

Emerson, R., Linda Fretz, and Linda L. Shaw. 1995. Writing Ethnographic Fieldnotes. Chicago: University of Chicago Press.

Empson, William. [1930] 1973. Seven Types of Ambiguity. Harmondsworth: Penguin.

Epstein, Edward. 1974. News from Nowhere. New York: Random House.

Ericson, Richard. 1981. Reproducing Order. Toronto: Butterworths.

————. 1982. Making Crime. Toronto: University of Toronto Press.

Ericson, Richard, Patricia Baranek, and Janet B. L. Chan. 1989. Negotiating Control: A study of News Sources. Toronto: University of Toronto Press.

————. 1991. Representing Order: Crime, Law, and Justice in the News Media. Toronto: University of Toronto Press.

Ericson, Richard, and Kevin Haggerty. 1997. Policing the Risk Society. Toronto: University of Toronto Press.

Espeland, W. 1998. The Struggle for Water. Chicago: University of Chicago Press.

Ewan, Stuart. 1988. All-Consuming Images. New York: Basic Books.

Ewick, Patricia, and Susan Silbey. 1997. Legal Narratives. Chicago: University of Chicago Press.

Fagan, Jeff, and Gareth Davies. 2001. "Street Stops and Broken Windows." Fordham Urban Law Review 28:457–504.

Fallows, James. 1996. Breaking the News: How the Media Undermine Democracy. New York: Pantheon.

Feeley, Malcolm. 1970. The Process Is the Punishment. New York: Sage.

Feldman, Martha. 1989. Order without Design. Palo Alto: Stanford University Press.

Felsen, Marcus. 1994. Crime and Everyday Life. Thousand Oaks, Calif.: Pine Forge.

Fielding, N. 1988. Joining Forces. London: Tavistock.

————. 1995. Community Policing. Oxford: Clarendon.

Fine, Gary Alan. 1996. Kitchens: The Culture of Kitchen Work. Berkeley: University of California Press.

Fischer, Benedikt. 1998. "Community Policing and the State." Ph.D. diss., Department of Sociology, University of Toronto.

Fiske, John. 1987. Television Culture. London: Tavistock.

————. 1989. Reading the Popular. Boston: Unwin and Hyman.

————. 1991. Understanding Popular Culture. Minneapolis: University of Minnesota Press.

————. 1994. Media Matters. Minneapolis: University of Minnesota.

Forst, Brian, and Peter K. Manning. 1999. The Privatization of Policing: Two Views. Washington: Georgetown University Press.

Foucault, Michel. 1973. The Order of Things: An Archaeology of the Human Sciences. New York: Vintage.

Fuld, Leonard F. [1909] 1971. Police Administration. Reprinted with a new introduction by Sam Chapman. Montclair, N.J.: Patterson-Smith.

Fyfe, James. 1988. "The Police Use of Deadly Force: Research and Reform." Justice Quarterly 5:165–205.

Fyfe, James, and Jerome Skolnick. 1993. Beyond the Law. New York: Free Press.

Gabler, Neil. 1998. Life: The Movie. New York: Vintage.

Gaines, Judith. 2001. "Mr. Nice Guy." Boston Globe Magazine, January 27, 23–29.

Gans, Herbert. 1979. Deciding What's News. New York: Pantheon.

Garcia, Angela, and Penelope Parmer. 1999. "Misplaced Trust." Symbolic Interaction 22:297–324.

Garfinkel, Harold. 1963. "Conceptions of and Experiments with 'Trust' as a Condition of Stable Concerted Action." In Motivation and Social Interaction, edited by O. J. Harvey. New York: Ronald.

————. 1967. Studies in Ethnomethodology. Englewood Cliffs, N.J.: Prentice-Hall.

Gates, Daryl. 1996. Chief. New York: Bantam.

Gates, William. 1993. The Road Ahead. New York: Penguin.

Geertz, Clifford. 1970. Interpreting Cultures. New York: Basic Books.

Geller, William, and N. Morris. 1992. "Relations between Federal and Local Police." In Modern Policing, edited by Michael Tonry and Norval Morris. Chicago: University of Chicago Press.

Gergen, Kenneth. 1992. The Saturated Self. New York: Basic Books.

Giddens, Anthony. 1981. The Class Structure of Advanced Societies. London: Hutchinson.

———. 1984. The Constitution of Society. Berkeley: University of California Press.

———. 1990. The Consequences of Modernity. Stanford: Stanford University Press.

———. 1991. Modernity and Self-identity. Cambridge: Polity.

Gitlin, Todd. 1980. The Whole World Is Watching. Berkeley: University of California Press.

———. 1983. Inside Prime Time. New York: Pantheon.

Glaser, Barney, and Anselm Strauss. 1968. The Discovery of Grounded Theory. Chicago: Aldine.

Glassner, Barry. 2000. Fear. New York: Basic Books.

Goffman, Erving. 1957. "The Nature of Deference and Demeanor." American Anthropologist 58:473–502.

———. 1959. The Presentation of Self in Everyday Life. Garden City: Doubleday.

———. 1960. Asylums. Chicago: Aldine; New York: Doubleday Anchor.

———. 1963. Stigma. Englewood Cliffs, N.J.: Prentice-Hall.

———. 1967. Interaction Ritual. Chicago: Aldine.

———. 1969. Strategic Interaction. Philadelphia: University of Pennsylvania Press.

———. 1970. "The Insanity of Place." In Relations in Public. New York: Basic Books.

———. 1974. Frame Analysis. New York: Basic Books.

———. 1981. Forms of Talk. Oxford: Blackwells.

———. 1983a. "Felicity's Condition." American Journal of Sociology 89:1–53.

———. 1983b. "The Interaction Order." American Sociological Review 48:1–17.

Goldstein, Herman. 1990. Problem-Oriented Policing. New York: McGraw-Hill.

Goldstein, Joseph. 1960. "Police Discretion Not to Invoke the Criminal Process." Yale Law Review 69:543–94.

Goode, W. J. 1960. "Norm-Commitment and Conformity to Role-Status Relations." American Journal of Sociology 66:507–19.

———. 1972. "The Place of Force and Violence in Human Society." American Sociological Review 37:507–19.

Gordon, Diana. 1990. The Justice Juggernaut. New Brunswick: Rutgers University Press.

Gouldner, Alvin W. 1960a. Patterns of Industrial Bureaucracy. Glencoe, Ill.: Free Press.

———. 1960b. Wildcat Strike. Yellow Springs, Ohio: Antioch Press.

Graef, Roger. 1982. "Police." Television film shown on ITV Central.

———. 1989. Talking Blues. London: HarperCollins.

Greene, Jack. 2000. "Community Policing in America." In Policies, Processes and Decisions of the Justice System, Criminal Justice: 2000. Vol. 3, edited by Julie Horney. Washington: NIJ/Office of Justice Programs.

Greene, Jack, and Carl Klockars. 1991. "Workload." In Thinking about Police, edited by Carl Klockars and Stephen Mastrofski. 2d ed.. New York: McGraw-Hill.

Greene, Jack, and Stephen Mastrofski, eds. 1987. Community Policing. New York: Praeger.

Greenwood, Peter, Joan Petersilia, and Jan Chaikin. 1977. The Criminal Investigation Process. Lexington, Mass.: D. C. Heath.

Greimas, A. J. 1987. On Meaning. Foreword by F. Jameson. Minneapolis: University of Minnesota Press.

Gusfield, Joseph. 1981. The Culture of Public Problems. Chicago: University of Chicago Press.

———. 1986. Symbolic Crusade. 2d ed. Urbana: University of Illinois Press.

Haarr, Robin. 1997. "Patterns of Interaction in a Police Patrol Bureau." Justice Quarterly 14:53–87.

Haggerty, Kevin, and Richard Ericson. 1998. "The Militarization of Policing in the Information Age." Journal of Political and Military Sociology 27:233–55.

Haggerty, Kevin, L. Huey, and Richard Ericson. 2000. "The Revolution Will Be Televised." ASC presentation, San Francisco.

Hall, Peter. 1972. "A Symbolic Interactionist Analysis of Politics." In Perspectives in Political Sociology, edited by A. Affrat. Indianapolis: Bobbs-Merrill.

———. 1987. "Interactionism and the Study of Social Organization." Sociological Quarterly 28:35–75.

Hallett, Michael, and Dennis Powell. 1995. "Backstage with the Cops: Dramatic Reification of Police Subculture in American Crime Infotainment." American Journal of Police 14:101–29.

Harper, R. R. 1991. "The Computer Game." British Journal of Criminology 31:292–307.

Harvey, David. 1989. The Condition of Postmodernity. Oxford: Blackwells.

Hatty, Susan. 1996. "Police, Crime, and the Media." International Journal of the Sociology of Law 19:171–91.

Heidegger, Martin. 1977 [1953]. Being and Time. Albany: SUNY Press.

Heim, Michael. 1993. The Metaphysics of Virtual Reality. New York: Oxford University Press.

Hemingway, Ernest. [1932] 1977. Death in the Afternoon. London: Granada.

Herbert, Steve. 1996. Policing the City. Minneapolis: University of Minnesota Press.

———. 1998. "Police Subculture Reconsidered." Criminology 36:343–69.

Hickman, Matthew, and Brian Reaves. 2001. Local Police Departments, 1999. Washington: USGPO.

Holdaway, Simon. 1983. Inside the British Police. Oxford: Blackwells.

———. 1996. The Racialisation of British Policing. New York: St. Martin's.

Hough, Mike. 1980. "Managing with Less Technology." British Journal of Criminology 20:344–57.

Hughes, E. C. 1958. Men and Their Work. Glencoe, Ill.: Free Press.

———. 1994. On Work, Race, and the Sociological Imagination. Edited with an introduction by Lewis Coser. Chicago: University of Chicago Press.

Hunt, Darnell. 1996. Screening the Los Angeles Riots. New York: Cambridge University Press.

———. 1997. "(Re)Affirming Race: 'Reality,' Negotiation, and the Trial of the Century." Sociological Quarterly 38:399–414.

Hunt, Jennifer. 1985. "Police Accounts of Normal Force." Urban Life 13:315–42.

Hunt, Raymond G., and John M. Magenau. 1993. Power and the Police Chief. Newbury Park, Calif.: Sage.

Ignatieff, M. 1999. The Warrior's Honour. New York: Penguin.

Jacobs, David. 1996. "Civil Society and Crisis: Culture, Discourse, and the Rodney King Beating." American Journal of Sociology 101:1238–72.

James, Caryn. 2000. "Real Cops, Real Crimes." New York Times, December 5, B2–B3.

Jameson, Frederic. 1992. Postmodernism, or the Logic of Late Capitalism. Durham: Duke University Press.

Jaspers, Karl. 1953. The Origin and Goal of History. New Haven: Yale University Press.

Jay, Martin. 1973. The Dialectical Imagination. Boston: Little, Brown.

———. 1993. Downcast Eyes. Berkeley: University of California Press.

Jermeir, John, and Leonard Berkes. 1979. "Leader Behaviour in a Police Command Bureaucracy: A Closer Look at the Quasi-military Model." Administrative Science Quarterly 24:1–24.

Jermeir, John, John W. Slocum, Louis W. Fry, and J. Gaines. 1991. "Organizational Subcultures in a Soft Bureaucracy." Organization Science 2:170–94.

Johnston, Les. 1993. The Rebirth of Private Policing. London: Routledge and Kegan Paul.

Jones, Trevor, and Tim Newburn. 1998. Private Security and Public Police. Oxford: Clarendon.

Kaminski, Robert, and Eric Jefferies. 1997. "The Effect of a Violent Televised Arrest on Public Perceptions of the Police." Paper presented to ACJS, Louisville, March.

Kappeler, Victor, Richard Sluder, and Geoffrey Alpert. [1996] 1998. Forces of Deviance. Prospect Heights, Ill.: Waveland.

Kelling, George, and Catherine Coles. 1996. Fixing Broken Windows. New York: Free Press.

Kellner, D. 1990. Television and the Crisis of Democracy. Boulder, Colo.: Westview.

———. 1992. The Persian Gulf TV War. Boulder, Colo.: Westview.

Kelsen, Hans. [1945] 1961. General Theory of Law and the State. Translated by A. Wedberg. New York: Russell and Russell.

———. 1967. A Pure Theory of Law. Berkeley: University of California Press.

Kendall, Lori. 1998. "Meaning and Identity in Cyberspace." Symbolic Interaction 21:129–53.

Kidder, Tracy. 1999. "Small Town Cop." Atlantic, April, 47–64.

———. 2000. Hometown. New York: Random House.

Klapp, Orin. 1986. Overload and Boredom. Westport, Conn.: Greenwood.

Klinger, David. 1997. "Negotiating Order in Patrol Work: An Ecological Theory of Police Response to Deviance." Criminology 35:277–306.

Klockars, Carl. 1994. "A Theory of Excessive Force and Its Control." In And Justice for All, edited by William Geller and Hans Toch. Washington: PERF.

Knapp, Whitman. 1978. Report on Corruption in New York City.

Kornhauser, W. 1959. The Politics of Mass Society. Glencoe, Ill.: Free Press.

Kraska, Peter, and Victor Kappeler. 1997. "Militarizing American Police." Social Problems 44:1–18.

Kunda, Gideon. 1992. Engineering Culture. Philadelphia: Temple University Press.

Kurtz, Howard. 1998. Spincycle. New York: Free Press.

Larson, Richard. 1972. Urban Police Patrol Analysis. Cambridge: MIT Press.

——. 1989. "The New Crime Stoppers." Technology Review 10:28–31

Larson, Richard, Kent W. Colton, and G. Larson. 1976. "The Uses of Vehicle Locators in Police Work." Unpublished report, Department of Engineering, MIT.

Latour, Bruno. 1996. Aramis. Cambridge: Harvard University Press.

Latterell, B. 2000. "Police-Media Relations." Presentation to ASC, San Francisco.

Laurie, Peter. 1972. Scotland Yard. London: Penguin.

Lawrence, Regina. 2000. The Politics of Force. Berkeley: University of California Press.

LeBeuf, Marcel. 2000. "Police Technology." Working paper. Canadian Police College, Ottawa.

Lemert, Charles. 1997. "Goffman." In The Goffman Reader, edited by Charles Lemert and Laura Branaman. Boston: Blackwells.

Lemert, Charles, and Laura Branaman, eds. 1997. The Goffman Reader. Boston: Blackwells.

Lemert, Edwin. 1967. Human Deviance, Social Problems, and Social Control. Englewood Cliffs, N.J.: Prentice-Hall.

Leonard, V. A. 1980. The New Police Technology: The Impact of the Computer and Automation on Police Staff and Line Performance. Springfield, Ill.: Charles C. Thomas.

Levinson, Steve. 1981. Pragmatics. Cambridge: Cambridge University Press.

Liang, Hsi-Huey. 1970. The Berlin Police Force in the Weimar Republic. Berkeley and Los Angeles: University of California Press.

——. 1992. The Rise of the European State System from Metternich to the Second World War. New York: Cambridge University Press.

Lincoln, Bruce. 1991. Discourse and Society. New York: Oxford University Press.

Lindesmith, Alfred. [1936] 1967. The Addict and the Law. Chicago: Aldine.

Lipsky, M. 1986. Street Corner Bureaucracies. New York: Sage.

Loader, Ian. 1997. "Policing and the Social: Questions of Symbolic Power." British Journal of Sociology 48:1–18.

Lofland, Lyn, and John Lofland. 1991. 3d ed. Analyzing Social Settings. Belmont, Calif.: Wadsworth.

Luhmann, Niklas. 1998. Observations on Modernity. Stanford: Stanford University Press.

Lukes, Stephen. 1975. "Political Ritual and Social Integration." Sociology 9:289–309.

Lyon, David. 1994. The Electronic Eye. Minneapolis: University of Minnesota Press.

Lyons, William. 1999. The Politics of Community Policing. Ann Arbor: University of Michigan Press.

Maas, Peter. 1973. Serpico. New York: Bantam.

Magenau, John M., and Raymond G. Hunt. 1989. "Socio-political Networks for Police Role-Making." Human Relations 42:547–60.

Maguire, Edward. 1997. "Structural Change in Large Police Organizations." Justice Quarterly 14:547–76.

Maguire, Edward, Jeffrey Snipes, Craid Uchida, and Miriam Townsend. 1998. "Counting Cops." Policing 21:97–120.

Maines, David. 1977. "Social Organization and Social Structure in Symbolic Interactionist Thought." Annual Review of Sociology, edited by R. Turner. Palo Alto: Annual Reviews Press.

Maltz, Michael, Andrew C. Gordon, and Warren Friedman. 1991. Mapping Crime in Its Community Setting. New York: Springer-Verlag.

Mamalian, Cynthia A., Nancy G. LaVigne, and Elizabeth Groff. 2001. "Use of Computerized Crime Mapping by Law Enforcement in the United States, 1997–1998" (computer file). Ann Arbor, Mich.: Inter-university Consortium for Political and Social Research. (Abstract at http://www.icpsr.umich.edu:8080/ABSTRACTS/02878.xml?format=ICPSR.)

Mannheim, Karl. 1960. Essays in the Sociology of Knowledge. London: Routledge and Kegan Paul.

Manning, Peter K. 1979a. "Metaphors of the Field: Varieties of Organizational Discourse." Administrative Science Quarterly 24:660–71.

———. 1979b. "Reflexivity and Facticity in Criminal Justice." American Behavioral Scientist 22:697–732.

———. 1988. Symbolic Communication. Cambridge: MIT Press.

———. 1989. Semiotics and Fieldwork. Thousand Oaks, Calif.: Sage.

———. 1992a. "Information Technology and the Police." In Modern Policing, edited by Michael Tonry and Norval Morris. Chicago: University of Chicago Press.

———. 1992b. "Technological Dramas and the Police." Criminology 30:327–45.

———. 1996a. "Dramaturgy, Politics, and the Axial Media Event." Sociological Quarterly 37:101–18.

———. 1996b. "Policing and Reflection." Police Forum 6, no. 4: 1–5.

———. 1997a. "Media Loops." In Media, Culture, and Crime, edited by Frankie Bailey and Donna Hale. Belmont, Calif.: Wadsworth.

———. [1977] 1997b. Police Work. 2d ed. Prospect Heights, Ill.: Waveland.

———. 1998. "High-Risk Narratives." Qualitative Sociology 22, no. 4: 417–97.

———. 2000. "Virtual Justice, Violence, and Ethics" (review of Lou Cannon's Official Negligence). Journal of Criminal Justice Ethics 19:44–54.

———. 2001a. "Technology's Ways." Crime and Justice 1:83–103.

———. 2001b. "Theorizing Policing: The Drama and Myth of Crime Control in the NYPD." Theoretical Criminology 5:315–44.

———. 2002a. "Authority, Loyalty, and Community Policing." In Crime and Social Organization (festschrift for Albert J. Reiss Jr.), edited by David Weisburd and Erin Waring. New Brunswick: Transaction.

———. [1980] 2002b. Narcs' Game. 2d ed. Prospect Heights, Ill.: Waveland.

Manning, Peter K., and Betsy Cullum-Swan. 1992. "Semiotics and Framing." Semiotica 92 3/4: 239–57.

Manning, Peter K., and Keith Hawkins. 1983. "Police Decision-Making." In Police Research: Now Where?, edited by Mollie Wetheritt. Aldershot: Gower.

Manning, Peter K., and Jennifer Hunt. 1991. "The Social Context of Police Lying." Symbolic Interaction 14:51–70.

Manning, Phillip. 1992. Erving Goffman and Modern Sociology. Stanford: Stanford University Press.

Marcuse, Herbert. [1964] 1991. One-Dimensional Man. New ed. with introduction by D. Kellner. Boston: Beacon.

Martin, Susan. 2001. "Women Officers on the Move." In Critical Issues in Policing, edited by Roger Dunham and Geoffrey Alpert. Prospect Heights, Ill.: Waveland.

Martin, Susan, and Nancy Jurik. 1996. Doing Justice, Doing Gender. Thousand Oaks, Calif.: Sage.

Marx, Gary. 1989. Undercover. Berkeley: University of California Press.

Marx, Leo. [1964] 2000. The Machine in the Garden. New York: Oxford University Press.

Mastrofski, Stephen. 1983. "Police Knowledge of the Patrol Beat." In The Police Working Environment, edited by Richard Bennett. Beverley Hills, Calif.: Sage.

———. 1998. "Community Policing and Police Organization Structure." In How to Recognize Good Policing, edited by Jean Paul Brodeur. Thousand Oaks, Calif.: Sage.

Mastrofski, Stephen, M. Reisig, and J. McCloskey. 2002. "Police Disrespect toward the Public: An Encounter-Based Analysis. Criminology 40:519–52.

Mastrofski, Stephen, and R. Richard Ritti. 2000. "Making Sense of Community Policing." Police Practice and Research.

Mastrofski, Stephen, R. Richard Ritti, and Jeffrey B. Snipes. 1994. "Expectancy Theory and Police Productivity in DUI Enforcement." Law and Society Review 28:101–36.

Mastrofski, Stephen, Jeffrey Snipes, and Roger Parks. 2000. "The Helping Hand of the law." Criminology 38:307–42.

Mastrofski, Stephen, Robert E. Worden, and Jeffrey Snipes. 1995. "Law Enforcement in the time of Community Policing." Criminology 33:539–63.

Mawby, Rob. 1996. "Making Sense of Media Representations of British Policing." Paper presented to conference, International Perspectives on Crime, Justice, and Public Order, Dublin.

———. 1999. "Visibility, Transparency and Police-Media Relations." Policing and Society 9:263–86.

———. 2002. Policing Images: Policing, Communication, and Legitimacy. Cullompton, Devon: Willan.

McClure, James. 1980. Spike Island. London: Macmillan.

———. 1984. Cop World. New York: Pantheon.

McGibben, Bill. 1993. The Age of Missing Information. New York: Plume.

McNamara, John. 1967. "Uncertainties in Police Work: The Relevance of Police Recruits' Backgrounds and Training." In The Police, edited by David Bordua. New York: Wiley.

McRae, James, and James McDavid. 1988. "Computer-Based Technology in Police Work." Journal of Criminal Justice 16:47–60.

Mead, George H. 1934. Mind, Self, and Society. Chicago: University of Chicago Press.

Meehan, Albert J. 1992. "I Don't Prevent Crimes, I Prevent Calls." Symbolic Interaction 15:455–80.

———. 1993. "Internal Police Records and the Control of Juveniles." British Journal of Criminology 33:504–24.

———. 1994. "Information Technology, Patrol Work, and Recordkeeping Practices." Presented to the Midwest Sociological Society, March, Chicago.

———. 1998. "The Impact of Mobile Data Terminal (MDT) Information Technology on Communication and Recordkeeping in Police Work." Qualitative Sociology 21:225–54.

———. 2000a. "The Organizational Career of Gang Statistics: The Politics of Policing Gangs." Sociological Quarterly 41:337–70.

———. 2000b. "The Transformation of the Oral Tradition of the Police through the

Introduction of Information Technology." Sociology of Crime, Law, and Deviance 2:107–32.

Meehan, Albert J., and Michael Ponder. 2002a. "How Roadway Composition Matters in Analyzing Police Data on Racial Profiling." Police Quarterly 5:306–33.

———. 2002b. "Race and Place: The Ecology of Racial Profiling African American Drivers." Justice Quarterly 19:399–430.

Merelman, Richard. 1969. "The Dramaturgy of Politics." Sociological Quarterly 10:216–41.

———. 1984. Making Something of Ourselves. Berkeley: University of California Press.

———. 1991. Partial Visions: Culture and Politics in Britain, Canada, and the United States. Madison: University of Wisconsin Press.

———. 1998. "On Legitimalaise in the United States." Sociological Quarterly 39:351–68.

Meyrowitz, Joseph. 1985. No Sense of Place. New York: Oxford University Press.

———. 1992. "Redefining the Situation." In Beyond Goffman, edited by Stephen Riggins. Berlin: Mouton de Gruyter.

Miller, Jerome. 1998. Search and Destroy. New York: Cambridge University Press.

Miller, Mark. 1988. Boxed In. Evanston: Northwestern University Press.

Mills, C. Wright. 1956. White Collar. New York: Oxford University Press.

Mitroff, Ivan, and Warren Bennis. 1993. The Unreality Industry. New York: Oxford University Press.

Monkonnen, Eric. 1981. The Police in Urban America, 1830–1920. Cambridge: Cambridge University Press.

———. 1992. "History of Urban Police." In Modern Policing, edited by Michael Tonry and Norval Morris. Chicago: University of Chicago Press.

Moore, Mark H. 1997. Creating Public Value. Cambridge: Harvard University Press.

Morash, Merry, and Robin Haarr. 1995. "Gender, Workplace Problems, and Stress in Policing." Justice Quarterly 12:113–40.

Nadel, S. F. 1953. Self Control and Social Control. Social Forces 31:265–73.

National Institute of Justice. 1993. "Toward the Paperless Police Department: The Use of Laptop Computers." Research in Brief, September, 1–8.

Nesbary, Dale. 1994. Politics and Discretion: The Acquisition of Technology in Municipal Police Agencies." Paper presented to the Michigan Sociological Society.

———. 1998. "Handling Calls for Service: Organizational Production of Crime Rates." Policing 21, no. 4:576–99.

———. 1999. Criminal Justice Resources on the World Wide Web. Boston: Allyn and Bacon.

Newburn, Tim, and A. Hayman. 2002. Policing, Surveillance, and Social Control. Devon: Willan.

Nogala, Detlef. 1995. "The Future Role of Technology in Policing." In Comparisons in Policing: An International Perspective, edited by J. P. Brodeur. Aldershot: Avebury.

Norris, Clive, Jade Moran, and Gary Armstrong. 1998. Surveillance, Closed Circuit Television, and Social Control. Brookfield, Vt.: Ashgate.

Nunn, Samuel. 1993. "Computers in the Cop Car." Evaluation Review 17, no. 2:182–203.

Orlikowski, Wanda, and J. Baroudi. 1991. "Studying Information Technology in Organizations: Research Approaches and Assumptions." Information Systems Research 2, no. 1:1–28.

Ortega y Gasset, José. 1932. The Revolt of the Masses. New York: Norton.

Packer, Herbert. 1968. The Criminal Sanction. Palo Alto: Stanford University Press.

Parks, Roger, Stephen Mastrofski, C. DeJong, and M. Kevin Gray. 1999. "How the Police Spend Their Time in the Community." Justice Quarterly 16:483–518.

Pays, T. S., E. Boyanowsky, and D. Dutton. 1984. "Mobile Data Terminals and Their Implications for Policing." Journal of Social Issues 40:113–27.

Perinbanayagam, R. 1984. Signifying Acts. Hawthorne, N.Y.: Aldine.

Perlmutter, David. 2000. Policing the Media. Thousand Oaks, Calif.: Sage.

Pfaffenberger, Bryan. 1992. "Technological Dramas." Science, Technology, and Social Values 7:10–35.

Peirce, C. S. 1936–57. Collected Works (vols. 1–6, 1936; vols. 7–8, 1957). Cambridge: Harvard University Press.

Pilant, Lois. 1999. "Going Mobile." NIJ Journal. January, 11–16.

Porter, Theodore. 1995. Trust in Numbers. Princeton: Princeton University Press.

Poster, Mark. 1990. The Mode of Information. Stanford: Stanford University Press.

Preiss, Jack, and Howard Ehrlich. 1967. An Examination of Role Theory. Lincoln: University of Nebraska Press.

Press, Andrea. 1991. Women Watching Television. Philadelphia: University of Pennsylvania Press.

Purdy, Jedediah. 2000. For Common Things. New York: Vintage.

Radelet, Michael, Hugo Bedau, and C. E. Putnam. 1992. In Spite of Innocence. Boston: Northeastern University Press.

Rafter, N. Hahn, ed. 2000. Encyclopedia of Women and Crime. Phoenix: Oryx.

Rappaport, Roy. 1971. "Ritual, Sanctity, and Cybernetics." American Anthropologist 73:59–76.

Rawls, Anne. 1983. "The Interaction Order Sui Generis: Goffman's Contribution to Social Theory." Sociological Theory 5:136–49.

Rayner, Richard. 1995. "Wanted: A Kinder, Gentler Cop." New York Times Magazine, 22 January, 26–50.

Reaves, Brian, and Andrew Goldberg. 1996. LEMAS Data. Washington: Bureau of Justice Statistics, Department of Justice.

Reiner, Robert. 1992. The Politics of the Police. 2d ed. Brighton: Wheatsheaf.

———. 1997. "Media Made Criminality: The Representation of Crime in the Mass Medial." In The Oxford Handbook of Criminology, edited by M. Maguire, Rod Morgan, and R. Reiner. 2d ed. Oxford: Oxford University Press.

———. 1999. "Coloured Judgments" (review of B. Cathcart's The Case of Stephen Lawrence). (London) Times Literary Supplement, August 13, 35.

Reiss, Albert J., Jr. 1971. The Police and the Public. New Haven: Yale University Press.

———. 1974. "Discretionary Justice." In The Handbook of Criminology, edited by D. Glaser. Chicago: Rand-McNally.

———. 1992a. "Police Organization in the Twentieth Century." In Modern Policing, edited by Michael Tonry and Norval Morris. Chicago: University of Chicago Press.

———. 1992b. "A Theory of Police Organizations." Paper delivered to the American Society of Criminology, Phoenix, November.

Reiss, Albert J., Jr., and David Bordua. 1967. "Organization and Environment." In Police: Six Sociological Essays, edited by David Bordua. New York: Wiley.

Reuss-Ianni, Elizabeth. 1983. Two Cultures of Policing. New Brunswick: Transaction.

Reynolds, Larry. 1993. Interactionism: Exposition and Critique. 3d ed. Dix Hills, N.J.: General Hall.

Richardson, Laurel. 1997. Fields of Play. Philadelphia: Temple University Press.

Roberg, R., J. Crank, and Jack Kuykendall. 2000. Police and Society. Los Angeles. Roxbury.

Rochlin, Eugene. 1997. Trapped in the Net. Princeton: Princeton University Press.

Rosaldo, Renato. 1989. Culture and Truth. Boston: Beacon.

Rose, D. R., and Todd Clear. 1998. "Incarceration and Social Capital and Crime." Criminology 36:441–80.

Rosenbaum, Dennis, ed. 1996. The Challenge of Community Policing. Thousand Oaks, Calif.: Sage.

Rossmo, D. Kim. 2000. Geographic Profiling. Boca Raton: Fla.: CRC.

Rubinstein, Jonathan. 1973. City Police. New York: Farrar, Straus, and Giroux.

Sackman, Sonja. 1991. Cultural Knowledge in Organizations. Thousand Oaks, Calif.: Sage.

Samora, Julian. 1979. Gunpowder Justice. Notre Dame: University of Notre Dame Press.

Sampson, Robert, J. Morenoff, and F. Earls. 1999. "Beyond Social Capital." American Sociological Review 64:633–60.

Sampson, Robert, and S. Raudenbush. 1999. "Systematic Social Observation of Public Spaces." American Journal of Sociology 105:603–51.

Sampson, Robert, S. Raudenbush, and F. Earls. 1997. "Neighborhoods and Violent Crime." Science 227:918–24.

Scheingold, Stuart. 1984. The Politics of Law and Order. New York: Longmans.

———. 1991. The Politics of Street Crime. Philadelphia: Temple University Press.

Schiller, Lawrence. 1999. Perfect Murder, Perfect Town. New York: HarperCollins.

Schlesinger, P., and T. Humber. 1994. Reporting Crime. Oxford: Clarendon.

Schwartz, H. 1996. The Culture of the Copy. Cambridge: MIT Press.

Scott, R., G. Brock, and S. Crawford. 2000. "Agency Networking and the Use of the Internet and Intranets in the Field of Law Enforcement." Police Forum 10, no. 4:1–6.

Sellen, Abigail, and R. R. Harper. 2002. The Myth of the Paperless Office. Cambridge: MIT Press.

Shapland, Joanna, and Jon Vagg. 1988. Policing by the Public. London: Routledge.

Shearing, Clifford. 1992. Private Policing. In Modern Policing, edited by Michael Tonry and Norval Morris. Chicago: University of Chicago Press.

Shearing, Clifford, and Richard Ericson. 1991. "Culture as Figurative Action." British Journal of Sociology 42:481–506.

Shearing, Clifford, and Philip Stenning. 1985. "The Police." The Canadian Encyclopaedia. Toronto: Encyclopaedia Press.

Sheptycki, James, ed. 2000. Issues in Transnational Policing. London: RKP.

Sherman, Lawrence W. 1990. "Police Crackdowns." In Crime and Justice, vol. 12, edited by Michael Tonry and Norval Morris. Chicago: University of Chicago Press.

————. 1992. "Attacking Crime." In Crime and Justice, vol. 15, edited by Michael Tonry and Norval Morris. Chicago: University of Chicago Press.

Siegel, Larry. 2000. Criminology. Belmont, Calif.: Wadsworth.

Silverman, Eli. 1999. The NYPD Battles Crime. Boston: Northeastern University Press.

Simon, David. 1991. Homicide. Boston: Little, Brown.

Simon, David, and Jack Burns. 1997. The Corner. New York: Broadway Books.

Skogan, Wesley. 1990. The Police and the Public in England and Wales. London: HMSO.

————. 1991. Disorder and Decline. Berkeley: University of California Press.

Skogan, Wesley, and G. Antunes. 1979. "Information, Apprehension, and Deterrence." Journal of Criminal Justice 7:7–42.

Skogan, Wesley, and Susan Hartnett. 1997. Community Policing, Chicago Style. New York: Oxford University Press.

Skogan, Wesley, and Arthur Lurigio. 1998. "Community Policing in Chicago: Bringing Officers on Board." Police Quarterly 1:1–26.

Skolnick, Jerome. 1966. Justice without Trial. New York: Wiley.

Sorkin, X. "Irony." 1987. In Watching Television, edited by Todd Gitlin. New York: Pantheon.

Soulliere, Nicole. 2000. "Police Technology." Working paper, Canadian Police College, Ottawa.

Sparks, Richard. 1992. Television and the Drama of Crime. Buckinghamshire: Open University Press.

Sparrow, Malcolm. 1993. Information Policing and the Development of Policing. NIJ Perspectives on Policing, report no. 16. Washington: U.S. Department of Justice.

Sparrow, Malcolm, Mark H. Moore, and David B. Kennedy. 1990. Beyond 911: A New Era for Policing. New York: Basic Books.

Spelman, William, and Bill Brown. 1981. Calling the Police about Serious Crime. Washington: Police Foundation.

Standards and Goals Commission. 1974. Standards and Goals for the Criminal Justice System. Washington: Department of Justice.

Staples, William. 1997. The Culture of Surveillance. New York: St. Martin's.

Stark, Rodney. 1970. Police Riots. Belmont, Calif.: Wadsworth.

Stead, John. 1977. Pioneers in Policing. Montclair, N.J.: Patterson-Smith.

Strauss, Anselm. 1978. Negotiations. San Francisco: Josey-Bass.

Strauss, Anselem, and Juliet Corbin. 1990. The Basics of Qualitative Research. Thousand Oaks, Calif.: Sage.

Stroshine, Meghan. 2001. "Police Supervision." Ph.D. diss., College of Social Science, Michigan State University.

Suchman, Lucy . 1987. Plans and Situated Action: The Problem of Human-Machine Interaction. Cambridge: Cambridge University Press.

Sudnow, David. 1965. "Normal Crimes." Social Problems 12:255–76.

Surette, Raymond. [1992] 1998. Crime, Media, and Criminal Justice. 2d ed. Belmont, Calif.: Brooks/Cole.

Taylor, Laurie, and Bob Mullan. 1986. Uninvited Guests. London: Chatto and Windus.

Thomas, Robert J. 1994. What Machines Can't Do. Berkeley: University of California Press.

Thompson, James. 1963. Organizations. New York: McGraw-Hill.

Tien, James, and Kent W. Colton. 1979. "Police Command Control and Communications." In What Works?, edited by James Tien and Kent W. Colton. Washington: Law Enforcement Assistance Administration.

Tobias, J. J. 1972. Origins of the Police. Journal of Contemporary History.

Toobin, Jeffery. 1996. The Run of His Life. New York: Simon and Schuster.

Tuohy, A. P., and M. J. Wrennall. 1995. "Seeing Themselves as Others See Them": Scottish Police Officers' Misperceptions of Public Opinion." Journal of Community and Applied Psychology 5:311–26.

Toronto Metropolitan Police. 1997. Annual Report of Toronto Metropolitan Police. Toronto: Toronto Metropolitan Police.

Trojanowicz, Robert, and Bonnie Buqueroux. 1994. Community Policing. Cincinnati: Anderson.

Tuchman, Gaye. 1978. Making the News. New York: Free Press.

Turkle, Sherry. 1984. The Second Self. New York: Simon and Schuster.

———. 1995. Life on the Screen. New York: Simon and Schuster.

Turner, Ralph. 1976. "The Real Self." American Journal of Sociology 81:989–1016.

———. 1978. "The Role and the Person." American Journal of Sociology 84:1–23.

———. 1990. "Role Change." In Annual Reviews of Sociology. Palo Alto: Annual Reviews Press.

Turner, Victor. 1969. The Ritual Process. Chicago: Aldine.

Van Maanen, John. 1973. "Observations on the Making of a Policeman." Human Organization 32, winter: 407–18.

———. 1974. "Working the Street." In The Potential for Reform in Criminal Justice, edited by H. Jacob. Beverley Hills, Calif.: Sage.

———. 1983. "The Boss." In Control in the Police Organization, edited by M. Punch. Cambridge: MIT Press.

———. 1984. "Making Rank." Journal of Contemporary Ethnography 13:155–76.

———. 1988. Tales of the Field. Chicago: University of Chicago Press.

———. 1998. "Identity Work: Notes on the personal identity of police officers." Unpublished paper, Department of Organizational Studies, MIT.

Van Maanen, John, and Joanne Yates, eds. 2001. Information Technology and Organizational Transformation. Thousand Oaks, Calif.: Sage.

Vester, Helmut. 1989. "Erving Goffman's Sociology as a Semiotics of Postmodern Culture." Semiotica 76 3/4:191–203.

Waddington, P. A. J. 1999. Police (Canteen) Sub-culture. British Journal of Criminology 39:287–309.

Waegel, William. 1981. "Case Routinization in Investigative Police Work." Social Problems 28:263–75.

Wagner-Pacifici, Robin. 1986. The Moro Morality Play. Chicago: University of Chicago Press.

———. 1994. Discourse and Destruction. Chicago: University of Chicago Press.

Wagner-Pacifici, Robin, and Barry Schwartz. 1991. "The Vietnam Veterans Memorial: Commemorating a Difficult Past." American Journal of Sociology 97:376–420.

Wakeman, Frederic. 1995. Policing Shanghai. Berkeley: University of California.
————. 1996. The Shanghai Badlands. Berkeley: University of California.
Walker, Samuel. 1994. A Critical History of Police Reform. Lexington: Lexington.
Walker, Samuel, C. Spohn, and M. DeLone. 1996. The Color of Justice. Belmont, Calif.: Wadsworth.
Walsh, William. 1986. "Patrol Officer Arrest Rates." Justice Quarterly 4:271–90.
Warner, Barbara, and Glen Pierce. 1993. "Reexamining Social Disorganization Theory Using Calls to the Police as a Measure of Crime." Criminology 31:493–517.
Warnock, Mary. 1970. Existentialism. Oxford: Oxford University Press.
Weber, Max. 1966. Max Weber on the Sociology of Law. Edited by Max Rheinstein, translated by Max Rheinstein and Edward Shils. New York: Simon and Schuster.
Weick, Karl. 1979. The Social Psychology of Organizing. 2d ed. Reading, Mass.: Addison Wesley.
————. 1988. "Technology as Equivoque." In Technology and Organization, edited by Paul Goodman and Lee Sproull. San Francisco: Josey-Bass.
————. 1995. Sensemaking in Organizations. Thousand Oaks, Calif.: Sage.
Weisburd, David, Stephen Mastrofski, and Cynthia Lum. 2001. "A Survey on the Uses of Compstat." Unpublished paper, Institute of Criminology, University of Maryland.
Weisheit, Ralph A., David N. Falcone, and Edward Wells. 1999. Crime and Policing in Rural and Small Town America. Prospect Heights, Ill.: Waveland.
Westley, William. [1950] 1970. Violence and the Police. Cambridge: MIT Press.
Whalen, J., and D. Zimmerman. 1998. "Observations on the Display and Management of Emotions in Naturally Occurring Activities: The Case of Hysteria in Calls to 911." Social Psychology Quarterly 50:172–85.
Whalen, J., D. Zimmerman, and M. Whalen. 1988. "When Words Fail." Social Problems 35:335–62.
Whalen, M., and Donald Zimmerman. 1987. "Sequential and Institutional Context in Calls for Help."
White, Hayden. 1960. Tropisms. Baltimore: Johns Hopkins University Press.
Wiley, Norbert. 1992. The Semiotic Self. Chicago: University of Chicago Press.
Wilkins, Leslie. 1965. Social Deviance. London: Tavistock.
Williams, Raymond. [1974] 1992. Television: Technology and Cultural Form. With an introduction by Lynn Spigel. [Middletown, Conn.]: Wesleyan University Press; Hanover, N.H.: University Press of New England.
Wilson, J. Q. 1968. Varieties of Police Behavior. Cambridge: Harvard University Press.
Wilson, J. Q., and Barbara Boland. 1978. "The Effect of Policing on Crime." Law and Society Review 12:367–90.
Wilson, O. W. 1942. Police Records: Their Installation and Use. Chicago: Public Administration Service.
Wilson, William. 2000. "America's Finest Cops." Parade Magazine, November 5, 1–3.
Wilson, William J. 1987. The Truly Disadvantaged. Chicago: University of Chicago Press.
Woods, Gerald. 1973. "The Police and the Progressives." Ph.D. diss., Department of History, University of California, Los Angeles.
Young, Jenny. 1999. "Interactions in Police Chat Rooms on the Internet." Term paper, Department of Sociology, York University, Toronto.
Young, Jenny, and Amanda Rigby. 1999. Report on the Use of Information Technol-

ogy in Two Police Departments. Unpublished report, Department of Sociology, York University, Toronto.

Young, Malcolm. 1991. An Inside Job. Oxford: Clarendon.

——. 1995. In the Sticks. Oxford: Clarendon.

Young, Phillip. 1966. Hemingway: A Reconsideration. New York: Harcourt.

Young, T. R. 1990. The Drama of Social Life. New Brunswick, N.J.: Transaction.

Zimmerman, Donald. 1992a. "Achieving Context: Openings in Emergency Calls." In Text in Context, edited by G. R. Watson and R. M. Seiler. Newbury Park, Calif.: Sage.

——. 1992b. "The Interactive Organization of Calls for Emergency Assistance." In Talk at Work, edited by Paul Drew and John Heritage. Cambridge: Cambridge University Press.

Zuboff, Shoshana. 1988. In the Age of the Smart Machine. New York: Basic Books.

INDEX